# Keaton's Silent Shorts

## Beyond the Laughter

Gabriella Oldham

Southern Illinois University Press
Carbondale and Edwardsville

Copyright © 1996 by the Board of Trustees, Southern Illinois University
All rights reserved
Printed in the United States of America
Edited by Ruth Kissell
Design and production by New Leaf Studio

99   98   97   96      4   3   2   1

Library of Congress Cataloging-in-Publication Data

Oldham, Gabriella.
  Keaton's silent shorts : beyond the laughter / Gabriella Oldham.
    p.   cm.
  Includes bibliographical references and index.
  1. Keaton, Buster, 1895–1966—Criticism and interpretation.
I. Title.
PN2287.K4048   1996
791.43′028′092—dc20                                        95-13970
ISBN 0-8093-1951-9                                          CIP
ISBN 0-8093-1952-7 (pbk.)

The illustrations used in this book are from the collection of the author and are reproductions of film and publicity stills originally copyrighted by Metro Pictures. The author gratefully acknowledges the Academy of Motion Picture Arts and Sciences (Los Angeles) and the Museum of Modern Art/Film Stills Archive (New York) for their assistance in providing the duplicates of the stills from which the illustrations were reproduced.

*Frontispiece: Cops* (March 1922). Courtesy of the Academy of Motion Picture Arts and Sciences.

The paper used in this publication meets the minimum requirements of American National Standard for Information Sciences—Permanence of Paper for Printed Library Materials, ANSI Z39.48-1984. ∞

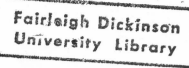

To my Italian grandmother,
whose favorite actor was Boo-stair Kay-ah-tohn.


To my Italian mother,
whose strength and beauty come from the storms of Life.
Boo-stair would be proud.


*Tutto arriva a chi sa aspettare.*

# Contents

# Illustrations

# Chapter 1

## *Introduction*

Courtesy of the Museum of Modern Art/Film Stills Archive

It started with *King Kong*. That film marked my first visit to a New York revival house and the end of watching classic films on television. It was also the moment I picked up a flyer in the lobby advertising a silent film comedy series at the Elgin Theater.

I recognized the name of the star comedian but couldn't quite place the "stone face." That face drew me to the entire Elgin program and into a world of film I barely knew. On that fateful day, King Kong introduced me to Buster Keaton, and this latter giant of the screen has overwhelmed me ever since.

This book is both a tribute to the brilliance of the nineteen independent short comedies of Buster Keaton and a lengthy response to those who ask, "Why do you like him?" My admiration for Buster Keaton was so instantaneous that I never considered the why's. I hope to answer that question and do justice to the subtly forceful and visually ingenious comedy of Buster Keaton.

In 1949, film critic and Pulitzer Prize-winning novelist James Agee, in his essay entitled "Comedy's Greatest Era," lamented the "lost negatives" of the short Keaton films. He felt that "for plain hard laughter" they even surpassed Keaton's longer work.[1] Since their rediscovery and re-release over the following three decades through the work of Raymond Rohauer, many of Keaton's short films have been acknowledged by critics for their sophisticated visual comedy and filmmaking. However, a full critical study of the nineteen independent short silent comedies from 1920 to 1923, with Keaton as director, writer, and star, is overdue. Keaton's less successful shorts (*My Wife's Relations*, *The Haunted House*, *The Electric House*) are usually mentioned in passing or dismissed in favor of such favorites as *One Week*, *Cops*, and *The Boat*. In addition, the short comedies as a whole have been regarded as a springboard for discourses on Keaton's ten feature-length masterpieces.

Keaton's silent film comedy developed from his impressive physical agility, his inventive manipulation of the camera, his eye for intriguing composition, and his instinct for "getting laughs." These talents pervade the nineteen short comedies and lay solid groundwork for Keaton's features. His favorite themes, plots, gags, characters, cinematic techniques, and relationships (Buster-Machine, Buster-Woman, Buster-Self, Buster-World) are rooted in the shorts and grow, evolve, transform. By focusing on each short film, we can see Keaton's style and artistry fuse. We can also enjoy each short as a condensation of the dynamic qualities Keaton worked more fully and leisurely in his features.

As we consider the short films for their strengths and weaknesses, for their interwoven threads, we see the genesis of Buster the persona and

Keaton the film director. Divorced from their full-length offspring, these short films hit us with the rich essence of the Buster Keaton character in his world. He gives us a comedy that is visually beautiful, robustly funny, and strangely unsettling.

Vaudeville audiences were captivated by the serendipitous stage appearance of a nine-month-old boy crawling to his father during a monologue.[2] Joe Keaton knew success when he saw it; two years later he introduced his son, Joseph Francis "Buster" Keaton, into the family act "The Three Keatons," along with mother Myra. Reputedly one of the roughest in the business, the act toured the United States and England on major vaudeville circuits. In a usual routine, Buster disturbed his father's performance, and Joe highkicked Buster into the backdrop, orchestra and/or audience, who enthusiastically shouted for more.

After twenty-one years in vaudeville, Buster Keaton needed to move on. He was offered a solo role in the Shubert Brothers' *Passing Shows of 1917*. As he walked the streets of New York City pondering a routine, Keaton met a vaudeville colleague who urged him to visit the Talmadge movie studios on East 48th Street. A new slapstick comedy short filming there was *The Butcher Boy*, starring the popular babyface comedian and director Roscoe "Fatty" Arbuckle. Keaton was intrigued with the camera, and Arbuckle willingly introduced him to it. Destiny had walked in with Keaton that day: the former vaudevillian joined Arbuckle in a small but outstanding role in *The Butcher Boy*, his screen debut and the start of a lifelong career. The two-reeler was favorably reviewed in the trade paper *Moving Picture World*, with a special mention for the newcomer: "Buster Keaton does some excellent comedy falls."[3] Keaton stayed with Arbuckle, became his assistant director on fifteen short films from 1917 to 1920, and remained his friend throughout the rape-murder trial that shattered Arbuckle's career in 1921.

When Keaton entered comedy film in 1917, Arbuckle was a top comedian, rival to Charlie Chaplin. Within three years, Arbuckle moved into feature comedies, and Keaton graduated to independent stardom in what would be nineteen silent two-reelers, produced by Joseph M. Schenck at the Buster Keaton Studio in Los Angeles. While working on his first short, *One Week* (1920), Keaton also starred as a "poor little rich boy" in the Metro Productions feature *The Saphead*, a film adaptation of a contemporary Broadway play called *The Lamb* with Douglas Fairbanks

Sr. Through the shorts, however, the Buster character quickly took shape. From his debut with Arbuckle, Buster was identified by a porkpie hat, pale deadpan expression, daring physical agility, and underplayed moral resilience in outrageous situations. Eventually, Keaton directed, wrote, and starred in ten independently produced features between 1923 and 1928. Through these, his position as a king of silent screen comedy, in the company of Charlie Chaplin, Harold Lloyd, and Harry Langdon, was assured.

Ironically, Keaton's brilliance as a master clown was only acknowledged in Agee's article more than two decades after his last independent silent feature. His pictures had garnered mixed reviews, including *The General* (1927), now considered his most exquisite film and rated in a 1977 American Film Institute poll as one of the fifty best American films of all time.[4] Yet at its release, the *New York Times* called it "by no means as good as Mr. Keaton's previous efforts"; the *Herald Tribune*, "long and tedious—the least funny thing Buster Keaton has ever done."[5] A relatively positive review in the *Brooklyn Daily Eagle* offered an insightful view of the more intellectual aspect of Keaton's comedy: a "financial *faux pas*, perhaps" but "a comedy for the exclusive enjoyment of the matured senses."[6] On the other hand, the *Daily Mirror* advised Keaton to "pull yourself together."[7] Meanwhile, fan magazines of the 1920s dug for details of Keaton's pastimes, marriage, divorce, and "philosophy" of comedy—"What makes the public laugh."[8] For all of Hollywood's ferreting, Keaton remained intensely private: a sphinx who posed questions yet answered them with a knowing silence.

Keaton was more at home with the serious business of comedy than with the frivolous glitter of Hollywood. He extended a slapstick stereotype into an introspective character teetering on a plank over a sea of emotions. He strayed into the gentle terrain of Chaplin's tramp figure but bailed out before his comedy became too sentimental. His daredevil acts paralleled Harold Lloyd's feats, but his reactions to physical challenges were incomparably reflective. He mirrored the innocence of Harry Langdon but never regressed to a helpless babe. Keaton also championed the camera as a vital component of comedy. With the camera, he moved the audience into what he saw as the best perspective. For someone who loved inventions as Keaton did, the camera was the perfect toy.

In 1928, Joseph M. Schenck, Keaton's producer, financial adviser, and brother-in-law, urged him to join Metro-Goldwyn-Mayer. Although uncertain, he agreed, even over the warnings of Chaplin and Lloyd to remain independent. As the silent era faded, Keaton starred in two MGM features, *The Cameraman* (1928) and *Spite Marriage* (1929), which evoked the genius of his independent work. But as they entered the talking 1930s, Keaton and MGM proved incompatible. MGM mass-produced stars and films within strict schedules and budgets. Keaton craved a familial cast and crew with informal budgets and shooting schedules, even improvising a baseball game if the mood hit him. A liberal producer like Schenck was not to be found at MGM.

At this time as well, Keaton's marriage with Natalie Talmadge (sister of screen stars Norma and Constance) was disintegrating. His wrecked home life and loss of creative freedom led Keaton into alcoholism. While most of the ten MGM films he starred or costarred in between 1929 and 1933 were popular at the box office, Keaton's unique talents were squandered by poor scripts and increased drinking. One critic, Pare Lorentz, commented on Keaton's first "talkie," *Free and Easy* (1930): "He is no longer the enigmatic personality, the persevering, misunderstood stranger with a knack for falling on his ear. He is a hoofer, and there are thousands who can do his tricks just as well. . . . Keaton would have been worth twice as much as a comedian if, in a day of talking pictures, he had remained silent."[9]

In addition to an unfortunate second marriage, Keaton's contract was terminated by MGM in 1933. Considered unemployable by the major studios, Keaton could only find jobs in unchallenging projects at small film companies such as Educational, for which he made sixteen shorts between 1933 and 1937. After a year in a psychiatric clinic, old friends at MGM eased Keaton into work as a behind-the-scenes, usually uncredited, gag-writer for comedies starring Clark Gable, the Marx Brothers, and Red Skelton. Although acknowledged in a 1944 *Colliers* article as "Hollywood's No. 1 Gagman" and "Pie-Pitching Champion of the World," the only tribute to Keaton's silent film career was capsulized in a vague reference: "He made a series of comedies that are still remembered." Such articles kept Keaton's name in print but implied that he was a Hollywood has-been.[10] Even though he worked, Keaton was becoming certain of his own obscurity, for in 1937 he was told that "a failure in the cooling system of the vaults where the negatives of all his silent films had been stored had resulted in their total destruction." As Dardis writes, "Except for the films that he had personally retained for his own collection, Buster believed for the next decade that most of his best work had perished."[11]

Then the miracle. The magical device that Keaton sometimes used in his silent comedies, the "deus ex machina" solving the hero's problems, descended into Keaton's troubled life. James Agee's article in 1949 reawakened readers to the legacy of the silent movies. Agee recaptured the madness and methods that produced the great laugh-films from 1912 to 1930, naming many forgotten clowns and designating four "most eminent masters" or "kings" of comedy.[12] In discussing Keaton, Agee ranked his face "with Lincoln's as an early American archetype . . . haunting, handsome, almost beautiful, yet . . . irreducibly funny."[13] In describing Keaton's comedy, Agee used vivid phrases to capture its essence: "disturbing tension and grandeur to the foolishness"; "a freezing whisper not of pathos but of melancholia"; "a fine still and sometimes dreamlike beauty."[14] By 1949, Keaton was struggling to reassert himself in his work; Agee noted that "he gallantly and correctly refuses to regard himself as 'retired.'"[15] Unfortunately, Agee wrote without reviewing all of Keaton's films, particularly his shorts, but his reexamination of Keaton's genius boosted his image in the public eye.

Keaton by now had settled into a new life. Having overcome alcoholism and finding a secure third marriage with Eleanor Norris, Keaton made cameo appearances in *Sunset Boulevard* (1950) and *Limelight* (1952), where with Chaplin he gave an uproarious performance that echoed his best silent routines. Paramount attempted to rekindle public enthusiasm with a bio-pic, *The Buster Keaton Story* (1957), starring Donald O'Connor, for which Keaton was hired as technical director. The effort was a disappointing shadow of Keaton's life and work.

In 1954, Keaton approached Raymond Rohauer, distributor and archivist of "lost" films, at his Society of Cinema Arts theater in Los Angeles. As Rohauer recalled:

[Keaton] said he had a number of prints of his films and knew they had to be destroyed, since the nitrate film was badly decomposed. He knew they had some value, but was equally concerned because they were taking up space in his garage! . . .

The following day, I went to Keaton's house. There were original prints of . . . *Sherlock Jr.*, *Go West*, *Steamboat Bill Jr.*, *College*, and some of his best two-reel shorts, such as *The Boat* and *The Playhouse* . . . and true enough, nitrate prints in a deplorable state. Keaton, living in obviously reduced circumstances, seemed defeated. The films seemed almost an embarrassing reminder of his former eminence. I couldn't help feeling that under his mask of diffidence was a desire for recognition, not of himself, but of the intrinsic merit of his films.[16]

Rohauer transferred the films to safety stock, unraveled Keaton's ownership rights to the films, and reinstated the Buster Keaton Corporation. Over the next three decades, The Rohauer Collection became the sole legal representative of the Keaton films, and until his death in 1987, Rohauer tirelessly pieced together the "lost films" from myriad private collections and vaults around the world. Keaton himself gradually opened up more to interviewers, this time not notorious fan magazine reporters but scholars studying his films. In April 1960, Keaton was presented with a special Oscar from the American Academy of Motion Picture Arts and Sciences for "having made pictures that will play as long as pictures are shown."[17] The renewed interest prodded Keaton to coauthor with Charles Samuels his autobiography *My Wonderful World of Slapstick*. Like his film biography, however, this was a lukewarm narrative of Keaton's life. Even now, it seemed, Keaton found it difficult to talk; his remained the joyous world of silence and vision.

Rohauer arranged for Keaton's magnificent return to the public in a 1965 tour of Germany with *The General*, promoting the event with Keaton on board a locomotive similar to the Civil War engine of the film. Keaton's personal appearance at the Venice Film Festival that same year resulted in an emotional twenty-minute ovation.[18] To critics John Gillett and James Blue, Keaton seemed to be "warming up" to the task of being a star again.[19] Keaton had voiced his hope that he would return to Venice; but in February 1966 he died while playing bridge, a passionate pastime. Shortly before his death, Keaton shared a poignant insight into his new-found fame with Lotte Eisner after the Venice tribute, a view that reflected the comic paradox that his film persona often endured: "Sure it's great," he said, "but it's all thirty years too late."[20]

Throughout the 1970s and 1980s, Keaton's resurgence and devoted following inspired biographies, dissertations, critical analyses, a three-part documentary film, film festivals in Europe, America, and Asia, and even postage stamps. When a nearly exhaustive (at the time) program of ten features and twenty-one short films (including Arbuckle-Keaton shorts) opened at the Elgin Theater in New York in 1970, with many films seen for the first time since the 1920s, Andrew Sarris proclaimed the showing "the most important cultural [event] of this or any other

**7**

season in this century."[21] In 1992, Film Forum in New York City exhibited an unprecedented festival, "The Most of Buster Keaton," with over eighty films, television shows, commercials, and rarely seen short sound films. Once again, in 1995, to celebrate the one hundredth anniversary of Keaton's birthday, Film Forum held another retrospective of Keaton's career; the program contained a commentary that Buster would have applauded: "Born during a cyclone (or so a family legend goes) 100 years ago, Joseph "Buster" Keaton (1895–1966) began convulsing audiences at the age of three and, nearly thirty years after his death, he's still dropping 'em in the aisles from Minneapolis to Marrakesh. Sure the Hirschfeld postage stamp was nice, but there's only one tribute that counts: laughing your keister off at the finest works of one of the world's greatest film artists."[22]

Keaton sometimes worried about the seriousness with which his films were being analyzed. His priority was laughter; he was baffled when deep significance was attributed to a pratfall or stare. Yet for all the analysis, the common denominator is *still* laughter. Stanley Kauffmann's critique of the Elgin festival acknowledged the impact of Keaton's work, which should have reassured the comedian that his priority had not been undermined by heady dialogue: "[Keaton] couldn't believe . . . that his pictures mattered any more. If only he could hear the audiences at the Elgin."[23]

Laughter was Keaton's principle, although he would not crack a smile on-screen and gave the impression of being unable to do so (offscreen he smiled frequently). The image of Buster smiling broadly in *Coney Island* (Arbuckle-Keaton, 1917) initially shocks a Keaton aficionado, until one realizes that it is the "great stone face" early in his career. We become fascinated by the depth of the Keaton hero in the independent short films: that he laughs deeply, without sound or smile, and allows us to laugh unreservedly in the process. In this, Keaton was a master, controlling his face so we can lose control of ours.

For Keaton, comedy was serious business. He once remarked (ironically, given his battle with alcoholism): "Making a 'funny' picture is like assembling a watch; you have to be 'sober' or it won't tick."[24] His analogy is perfect, for timing is crucial to the successful delivery of a visual or verbal gag. The pulse connecting the gag to the punch (and ultimately to the laughter) permeates every successful comedy routine. A comedian activates the pulse through certain comic structures that are mastered to perfection, until every gag builds to a crescendo of visual and/or verbal comedy. Every facet of plot and character strives for unity of the whole. The end result is seamless and interwoven. With any thread frazzled or missing, the comedy fails. The doomed comedy becomes tragedy—principally for the comedian's career.

In the skilled hands of a silent comedy film director, the comic pulse beats primarily through visual *structures* that affect our reason to laugh as well as create artistic images.[25] In the structure of *repetition*, the comic image snowballs, layering itself with its own mirror image or with "variations on a theme." For example, in the classic slapstick pie-throwing routine, comic tension mounts as the frenzied custard attacks repeat through two characters to a roomful of characters. Another structure, *symmetry*, creates sheer visual delight; in Keaton's silent films, his symmetrical handling of objects, characters, and actions triggers our "sight-gag nerve" as he paints an image beautiful in its form. A third structure, *equation* or *transformation*, allows one object to equal or become another completely different object, while the context in which this equation/transformation exists allows us to accept the absurdity. We are startled to laughter as our placid anticipation is disturbed and our world is set comfortably awry. With these and other structures in place, the comedian romps his way through them effortlessly, an unobtrusive laughmaker. The hero's display of his best or worst traits, and his interactions with the best or worst traits of others, creates the comic *plot*. The hero's attitude and reactions to dealing with events of the plot create the comic *persona*.

Keaton's persona, Buster, has his own particular, sometimes peculiar, reactions to conflicts with his nemeses—Bully, Love Rival, Fate, Machine, or Self. Buster often cherishes dreams to escape conflicts. Keaton as filmmaker, and in charge of Buster's destiny, establishes the dream device to condone a fantasy in the "real world" and to permit our *suspension of disbelief*, our willingness to believe the impossible or fantastic. We may think that we see reality, until the ending explains that the odd occurrences are but a dream; the dream has been the only reality. We are shocked into laughter; or if we are as romantic as Buster is, we feel bittersweet disillusion. A dream tag-ending can also be a feeble, unconvincing escape for a filmmaker who is trapped in a corner searching for a solution. Sometimes Buster is so helpless in his surreal escapades that we hope we *are* seeing a dream. But Keaton's dream films are not always successful, for the dream device dilutes our confidence that a wide-awake Buster will triumph in the end. This is not as much a failure of the comedy as it is of the hero who derives his power from the power of the dream. Keaton's greatest short films are those compact gems of pacing and striking images, with a fully awake hero who inhabits an "other-world" floating somewhere in our world of concrete edges.

The life-battered comic hero teeters on a precariously thin threshold between comedy and tragedy. But physics demands that no two objects can occupy the same place at the same time; thus, these neighbors knock each other about for the same footing. The narrow threshold is never more obvious than when we realize the human paradox that tears accompany both sorrow and joy. Keaton almost revels in the notion that we should laugh-till-we-cry. Using another metaphor, Keaton tightens the coil of emotions until it pops with the pulse that is perfectly timed, with the image that repeats, aligns, or transforms. The resolution that releases the coil may restore our comfortable view of the world, in which case we experience the "pop" as comedy. Dark humor, however, leaves the complications disturbed and unresolved; in this bleak subgenre, the coil has not quite popped but rattles loose in our psyche. Then again, the coil may tighten and pop from a tension like that of Chaplin and Langdon, who highlighted the pathos of their personas.

More than any comedian of his day, Keaton challenged our emotional and intellectual resilience. Though he may not have admitted it, his artistic deliberation in developing a routine or composing the frame served the deeper visions of his inner mind. His comedy is no longer surface but multilayered and multidimensional. His world is not just funny but funny/sad, absurd/real, dream/concrete, delightful/dreadful, romantic/bittersweet—at the same time. Keaton lives most often within the duality, always ready to whip us away from emotional vulnerability and remind us to laugh. Only in the trailing afterimages, once the film has ended, do we see how emotional Buster has been behind his stone face. The deeper, darker, complex visions linger to characterize Keaton's persona and philosophy.

These nineteen short comedies are the mirrors of the themes and traits that are Buster Keaton, in and beyond the laughter. Unencumbered by the history and period costumes of such features as *The General*, *Steamboat Bill Jr.*, *Our Hospitality*, and *The Three Ages*, the two-reel stories revolve exclusively around the figure in the porkpie hat. Any variations in costume or location, in short films as *The Blacksmith* or *The Frozen North*, still contain his trademarks. In the features, Keaton extends and layers the narrative as a backdrop for his character. All the "Buster elements" are in the heroes of the features, of course; whatever the name of the character, he is always Buster. Even in Keaton's sound work (1930–66), the Buster persona surfaces. The character endures throughout Keaton's career because it was so vigorously nurtured in the short comedies. These nineteen films were opportunities for Keaton to experiment with camera, plot, gags, pacing, composition, dreams, secondary characters, themes, and moods. He eagerly anticipated working in features to expand the techniques he had learned. But the heart of Buster's comedy would never be as concentrated and undisturbed by story, history, costumes, or characters as in the nineteen independent short films. Buster is larger than life in these snapshots of a boy who grows up to be (to our surprise) much like one of us.

## Chapter 2

# One Week

(September 1920)

Courtesy of the Academy of Motion Picture Arts and Sciences

In his first independent two-reel film, Keaton produced a comedy with a layer-by-layer accumulation of visual gags within a simple and familiar plot. Buster and his bride, played with blushing enthusiasm by Sybil Seeley, build a home together—literally—and cope with obstacles that threaten their bliss. The first title sets the mood: THE WEDDING BELLS HAVE SUCH A SWEET TONE BUT SUCH A

# One Week

SOUR ECHO, followed by a close-up of pealing bells. We join Buster and Sybil marching from the church as husband and wife under a shower of rice and old shoes. Buster is quickly presented as one who makes the most of a situation, for among the shoes, he finds a pair that fits him and tucks them under his arm. His sharp eye and adaptability will prove his salvation in the week to come.

We have entered into Buster and Sybil's one week by the deliberate use of a strictly filmic, now outdated and clichéd, device: the iris, which opens and closes on a calendar page announcing the first day of the week, TODAY IS MONDAY 9. For the remaining six days, we will return to this symbol of passing time. The iris will open whenever Keaton decides that Buster has suffered enough for one day, and we will stare at a calendar page. Suddenly, a hand will reach in from the right to remove the page, signaling that a new day has clattered onto the newlyweds. This device becomes a convenient signpost, dividing the film into chapters or chronological pauses that refresh. The hand never changes or falters in its duty of marking time; it is an anchor to steady us. We might at first think it is Buster's hand, but its disembodied appearance seems more to be the miraculous hand of Fate calmly serving time. The hand provokes both relief and irritation: relief that a bad day has ended, irritation that another will follow. Thus, the first theme in Buster's life has been introduced via the most mechanical of film devices; through the camera's eye, the hand of Fate churns time, and Buster with it. In upcoming films, this hand will become an ironic symbol, invisible yet present. But in *One Week*, the hand is a concrete visual gag that induces humor by repetition, one of the structures of comedy.

As the first "chapter" of *One Week* proceeds (that is, once the first day has been visually announced), the wedding is established, Buster's utilitarian personality is introduced, and we meet Buster's rival, HANDY HANK—THE FELLOW SHE TURNED DOWN (in one close-up, we know why). Pinch-faced, snarling Hank is chauffeur; as the couple climb into the backseat, Hank thrusts a note at Buster, which we read in close-up:

> DEAR NEPHEW,
>    AS A WEDDING PRESENT, I AM GIVING YOU
>    A HOUSE AND LOT NO. 99 APPLE STREET.
>        WISH YOU JOY,
>        UNCLE MIKE

Within two minutes, we have met the three pivotal characters who will interact during the two reels with a major prop, the "wedding present." This is a situation ripe for comedy, although we might not yet know how or why. However, Keaton's tangential tailgate sign on the car, GOOD LUCK—YOU'LL NEED IT, is a premonition.

On route to Lot No. 99, Buster and Sybil engage in loving behavior that never comes to fruition. Thus, we are introduced to one trademark of Keaton's approach to emotion in comedy, the touchstone for comparing Keaton with Agee's other "kings" of comedy. In the relative intimacy of a medium three-shot with Hank in the driver's seat, Buster kisses Sybil. Each time they try for more, Hank grins at them. Expressions of love are thwarted and Buster seeks to escape, only to find himself in a worse predicament. Another car rolls alongside, as revealed in the next long shot that plants us at the rear of the parallel cars. Sybil transfers over, but Buster never makes it. He stands, back to us, bisecting the frame, a human wishbone flailing his arms, one foot on the running board of the bridal car and the other on the running board of the second car.

Keaton composes this frame with visual symmetry as the two cars balance the space. He uses our position behind the cars to provide the denouement of this gag: a motorcycle zooms from the foreground, dynamically as if from our midst, plucking Buster onto its handlebars. Keaton then shifts our perspective to follow Buster a few yards before he topples off. Buster spots Hank—as we do in a cutaway—joining Sybil in the second vehicle. Buster persuades the cyclist to rush him to Sybil. Recalling his practical nature, Buster hops off behind a traffic cop, kicking him to the ground and snatching his hat and stick at the same time. Buster dons the temporary guise of authority, a force that Keaton will continue to parody in future short films, particularly *Cops* (1922). He stops the car, helps Sybil out, and places the stick in the hand of Hank who is arguing with the cyclist just as the cop revives. To tie up the first comic sequence with perfect circularity, Buster and Sybil rejoin their wedding car, which is rolling toward us down an empty street; he gracefully steers it around the corner while standing on the running board.

Buster and Sybil enter frame-left into a vacant lot and puzzle at a small sign reading 99. We are diverted by a man suddenly appearing on the open back of a truck, jutting unobtrusively into frame-right. He slides a large crate onto the ground and announces, "HERE'S YOUR HOUSE!" Buster verifies the sign, as do we in close-up, HOME     PORTABLE HOUSE CO. Buster's hand enters the close-up—a callback to the first hand—and pulls

off an envelope marked DIRECTIONS. A long shot reestablishes the bewildered couple reading the fine print, which then we see:

PORTABLE HOUSE COMPANY

DIRECTIONS:

TO GIVE THIS HOUSE A SNAPPY APPEARANCE, PUT IT UP

ACCORDING TO THE NUMBERS ON THE BOXES.

We return to find Sybil pull a hammer from the car as Buster opens the
crate of their giant Tinkertoy house. The scene fades and Day One ends.

Obvious from this sequence is Keaton's ability to make a simple prop
the nucleus of a routine. Keaton's talent for "milking" a prop was honed
in vaudeville. He often said he could do everything with a broomstick
but sweep: drop it through stage knotholes, use it as a swatter, tripper,
baseball bat, hatrack, drumstick.[1] A simple prop was rich in potential
when teamed with Keaton's imagination. We scarcely begin Day One
when the prop potentials become clear. As the days pass, each prop becomes both familiar and novel in its handling. One prop is Buster's trusty
hammer, surfacing at crucial moments. We wonder what Buster was
thinking when he packed a hammer in with his honeymoon baggage.

The hammer is an important ingredient in the major routine of Day
Two. Once "the hand" silently pronounces the new day, we find Buster
at the top of a wall. Sybil lifts a plank that Buster lays on the wall,
extending one end over the ground. In medium shot, so there is no question of what he is doing, Buster teeters over the edge as he saws the plank
down to size. He nails the plank to the top of the wall, thinking he is
now secure. Keaton has moved us to an ironic vantage point: we are one
up on the hero who is unaware that he sits over the ground, although he
has placed himself there. Cut to straight woman Sybil frying eggs on an
impromptu stove; she utters the preparatory line, "BREAKFAST IS READY."
Cut again to Buster's precarious position for the inevitable conclusion of
the routine; he speaks his fate: "I'LL BE RIGHT DOWN." In the ensuing long-
shot pause that lengthens the humor of the inevitable, we patiently wait
for Buster to complete sawing, crash to the ground, and fulfill our expectation. Sybil rushes in to kiss him, and we switch positions again to
witness a grumbling Handy Hank at the side gleefully repainting the box
numbers—3 to 8 and 1 to 4. This time the "hand" of Fate works through
him (after all, he is "Handy" Hank) to deliver the catastrophic comedy
that has been foreshadowed from the start.

**15**

We are now treated to a wall variation that is not as predictable as the prior one. Buster is sitting atop a two-story-high wall, with Sybil perched in the first-floor window frame. She tosses the hammer to Buster, who catches it without a glance. In one shot, the top of the wall slants toward the ground and pivots in a half-revolution; Buster is transported to the ground and Sybil up to where he had been hammering. He walks forward; we cut to a medium close-up to ascertain that he is baffled. In the next long shot, the wall falls on Buster, who stands precisely where the window (the only opening in the wall) slips neatly over him. He turns, hands on hips, to look at Sybil. Day Two ends in a closing iris.

Keaton's physical dexterity in the Arbuckle films and vaudeville certainly reinforced the name "Buster" ("Uncle" Harry Houdini christened him so when he picked the toddler up from a tumble downstairs and remarked to Joe and Myra, "That's some buster your baby took!").[2] We can again see his extraordinary precision and strength in *One Week*. Keaton thrived on confrontations between his body and objects. Each stunt was to be perfect, without substitution or camera magic. One of Keaton's writers, Clyde Bruckman, said, "This guy's honesty was impressive. He wouldn't fool his audience. None of the easy camera tricks cutting an action into several parts with a new camera angle for each, then splicing it all together."[3] The wall-fall of Day Two had a trial run in an Arbuckle-Keaton short *Backstage* (1919);[4] it was perfected in his feature *Steamboat Bill Jr.* (1928). Here, during a cyclone, the Keaton character is "unaware" that a two-story building front will fall on him and stands precisely under the window opening. Keaton described the clearance of the window as "exactly three inches over my head and past each shoulder. And the front of the building—I'm not kidding—weighed two tons. It had to be built heavy and rigid in order not to bend or twist in the wind [from powerful gale machines]." It was said Keaton's crew looked away as the wall fell.[5]

When the hand removes Tuesday's calendar page to herald Day Three, Keaton's opening shot is an effective visual gag. The iris paces the timing as a small circle opens at the bottom of the frame to reveal Buster, back to us and hands on hips, studying something uncertainly. After a pause, the iris fully opens; the completed house looms before him, a masterpiece of architectural miscalculation. Its lines and corners cut the frame like a crazy maze, with windows askew and roof overlapping the wrong ends of the house. Buster is dwarfed by the reality of his efforts, having trusted the box numbers and marveling that something has still gone wrong. We have been privy to the "hand of Fate" by seeing Hank's misdeed in a cutaway. We could be unfeelingly amused by Buster's misfortunes, except that he is not one to remain naive or manipulated. Our amusement is tinged with mercy; we root for his resourceful character and yearn to warn him of the giants that rear their horrible, crooked heads.

Still, the die is cast, not only because Fate has the "upper hand" but because seeing the contrast between Buster and Nemesis has permanently carved an important facet into his persona. The house dominates Buster until he becomes as small as a figure seen through the wrong end of a telescope. In fact, if we personified the objects that confront Buster, we might allow each personification its own telescope through which it sees Buster as a speck to toss about. Through upward stares, rounded shoulders, and other significant poses, Buster regards his Nemesis with the strength of a miniature tank in which lies a vulnerable core. Keaton places us, his objective audience, eye-level to both perspectives in the battle between Buster and Goliath.

Day Three perpetuates this theme of contrasts. A second iris opens to reveal a giant of a mustachioed man (played robustly by Joe Roberts, who remained with Keaton until his death in 1924 and often was Buster's "heavy"), carrying an upright piano on his shoulder. When Buster approaches to accept the order, Joe hands him the piano and flattens him to the ground with it. Buster paddles vainly with his arms to slide out from under. Joe hands him the receipt book, lifts the piano while Buster signs, and drops it again on him. Buster paddles furiously; Joe irritably lifts the instrument and hoists Buster up by his shirt. With a glare from Joe, Buster hops and runs out of the frame.

The piano is a curious prop, for it creates the illusion of both heavyweight (on Buster) and featherweight (on Joe). As with the house, the piano reinforces a Keaton trademark in amusing, tantalizing illusion: Buster appears as a small figure when pitted against his opposite. Joe has been made even more gigantic by merging with the piano, and the two forces leave Buster as helpless as a turtle on its shell. Even when Buster stands, he is only as high as Joe's massive shoulder, further enlarged by the height of the piano. Keaton creates an intrinsically funny image for his hero through physical contrast, undisturbed by cuts or camera movement. The image is formed only by the visual elements meeting within the frame. Opposites usually attract, as proved by Laurel and Hardy, Dumont and Marx, Burns and Allen, Abbott and Costello, Martin and Lewis. The pairings are as much complements as collisions.

Sybil begins the second movement of the piano routine by tying a rope around the piano. Buster hammers at a rectangular section of the wall, which he removes and through which he enters, pulling the other end of the rope. Once again, the solidity of the wall is shattered by a twist in perception: now you *don't* see it, now you *do*. The fragmented-wall motif has already pervaded the day even prior to Joe's arrival. Much like the man on the truck in Day One, who unexpectedly breaks into the frame, our perception is teased with transformations that amuse us by their unsettling nature. Buster now examines a curiosity: a door on the second floor opens out to nowhere but down, and the kitchen sink on the first floor is on the outside wall. The misplaced door is momentarily left unused as a prop; instead, Buster taps the sink with his hammer, ponders, tosses the hammer into the sink, and pushes on the wall. It turns inward and he steps into the house with the sink. Logically, if the wall can pivot to allow the sink to be *inside* the kitchen, why is it outside in the first place? Buster silently refers to his mental blueprint and considers the pivot, while we are kept in the dark until he activates it. In so doing, he transforms the surreal/absurd into the norm, the outdoor plumbing into the ideal kitchen. Just as quickly, however, the surreal/absurd returns, for fixed in our mind is the anticipation that what we are seeing will *not* be believing. We begin to doubt that any wall is solid. When Buster removes the rectangular panel as entrance for the piano, we feel that wall-breaking is an almost commonplace occurrence. We are now accustomed to fragmenting the solid, chipping the certain. We find the repetition to be an odd consolation: at least the unpredictable is predictable. Buster is as much the creator of the unpredictable as he is its unsuspecting hostage.

In the living room, Buster shinnies up a pole to pass the rope through the chandelier. Handy Hank enters the hall with a bucket and mounts the staircase. Upstairs, he sits and scribbles in a chair placed purposely in the middle of the floor. Downstairs, Buster tugs on the rope to haul the piano in; with each tug, the chandelier drops, pulling a remarkably pliable ceiling with it. We switch perspectives to see the effect upstairs: the second floor is becoming quicksand. Alternating long shots, we see Buster pull and Hank sink; Buster yanks the rope again and, in an upward glance, notices the ceiling closing in and releases the rope. In rapid sequence, we cut to Hank who flies to the top of his frame when the ceiling snaps back, then cut to a close-up of the roof through which his head breaks. Buster looks out the window and exits. In exterior long shot, the victorious house dwarfs Hank's tiny screaming head in the roof and helpless Buster staring up from below. But once more, a transformation of the parts: Buster removes the front porch railing, leans it against the house, and climbs up the ladder it has become. Buster's utilitarian nature triumphs over adversity—temporarily.

Once on the roof, we witness action born out of desperation: Buster uses a crowbar to pry out Hank's head. Hank is a sight gag, even more so now framed by shingles. Our double perspective of him—a tiny shouting head in long shot or, conversely, a large shouting head in close-up—adds to the humor, particularly when Buster eyes him with perplexed rigidity. The crowbar bends to a 45-degree angle. Buster casts it aside in disgust, knocking Hank into the house with it. Buster scurries down the ladder to find Sybil below, wagging an admonishing finger at him in an iris, a subjective view from Buster's overhead perspective. We switch to the objective view as Buster argues, swinging the ladder from the house until it free-stands perpendicular to the ground. Buster shifts to the other side to pull it back. Sybil kisses him, then shoves him three times as they quarrel into the living room, ending the exterior action. Sybil's demonstrations of affection and impatience seem so fragmentary as to be intrusive and detract from Buster's reactions, but Keaton is giving her "equal time." Keaton is more fascinated with the dynamic possibilities between Buster and inanimate objects. Once the piano swings into the room, Buster dances with it before it smashes to the floor. Sybil rushes in with a wifely smile of encouragement and sheet music, which Buster sets exasperatedly on the collapsed keyboard. In concluding this "chapter," an iris encloses the ironic song title: THE END OF A PERFECT DAY.

The action on the roof has been embedded in the piano routine, and it is both intrinsic to the routine (it is a result of what occurs with the piano) as well as a sequence unto itself. The piano routine, in fact, has a circular development: the business with the instrument begins and ends the sequence, and whatever happens in between is due to the piano's miserable presence. Thus, Buster's interactions with Joe, Hank, and Sybil continually echo the piano's existence. The piano routine is like a pair of bookends to the stack of gags that lies between; it creates structural symmetry within Day Three. Instead of being a prop that launches a string of comedy acts, each one leaving the other behind, the day becomes a careful circular assembly of stunts, interactions, and props.

Day Four again recalls old props and introduces new ones to provide extended gags. As the hand comes and goes, Buster surveys the living room before laying down his jacket and nailing down the carpet. We are next purposely diverted by Sybil in the kitchen who splatters milk on her face; the point of this insert, however, is not immediately apparent. We return to Buster who admires his work, only to discover that he has nailed his jacket under the carpet. When he cuts out a square from the carpet to retrieve the jacket, his utilitarian nature converts the useless scrap into a new object with a nearby paint bucket. In a medium shot, we see Buster's arm at work—the hand motif again—as he writes WELCOME on the piece, then turns it right side up. Why would Buster deliberately paint WELCOME upside down, knowing he must turn the word around to be comprehensible? His disembodied arm in this shot becomes the only human link exerting control in a helter-skelter world. Only he can create confusion and comprehension at the same time with a twist of his wrist.

As Buster next focuses on setting the chimney in place, Sybil has gone upstairs to bathe away the milk. Through intercutting between Buster's exterior actions and Sybil's bath indoors, we suddenly realize how very carefully we have been diverted into a series of gags that are layering this day from its dawning. Sybil's milk-drenching has been a sight gag that functions in a triple role. Through her accident, we had momentarily forgotten (or not noticed) that Buster laid the jacket on the very spot he covered with the rug; thus, we are briefly as baffled as he is when we see the lump. Sybil's moment also provides a respite from Buster's vain cavorting with the rug and gives him time to begin a vain cavorting with the chimney. Thirdly, her mishap justifies her bath, which contributes a visual gem that again illustrates Keaton's treatment of audience and emotion. When Sybil's soapbar sails to the floor, she leans over to retrieve it but eyes the camera shyly. A helpful hand partially covers the lens as Sybil seizes the soap with a grateful smile.

Not yet in *One Week* has the presence of the camera, and the event of watching a film, been so directly admitted as through the hand covering the lens. We have already been made aware of "film" through the filmic device of the iris, or through Sybil's glance at the camera (us). But the hand that appears here is not the one marking time; nor is it Buster's hand turning nonsense into sense (we know his hands are literally occupied with the chimney). This third hand becomes the driving force behind our experience as an audience. In satirizing the moral code—or lack thereof—in movies of his time, Keaton obscures our view while making it perfectly clear what we are *not* seeing. The gag is a startling insert, yet it fits neatly into the hand-at-work motif, manipulating, controlling,

**20**

holding us and Buster in its palm. We know that as a film audience, however close we move to the characters via the camera, there is always a barrier between us and them.[6]

The barrier extends to Keaton's granite countenance. Not even a grimace distorts his face in the most grueling experience. Agee had noted Keaton to be the sole comedian to exclude sentimentality and exalt physical comedy, in contrast to Chaplin whose very being was enough to "shrivel the heart."[7] But Keaton's stone face seems to be his defense of the vulnerability behind it. As his audience, we have already been confronted by Buster's back instead of his face at crucial moments. Yet his nonverbal, even nonfacial, expressions are clearly ones of perplexity because the objects of his regard are usually conundrums: Through these bits of apparent non-communication, we vividly understand what pictures roll through his mind. Keaton's straight back is like his straight face, which is vital to his goal of laughter. It is the shield against Buster's storms of Life, a significant metaphor for *One Week*.

On the roof Buster is silhouetted against the sky with the chimney around his chest. He slips and plunges through the chimney hole into the tub. Sybil scolds him from behind a dressing curtain as he runs out the door; finally, the misplaced door of Day Three is activated. We cut outside to Buster's bewildered step into space. According to his autobiography, Keaton filled a deep wide hole in the ground beneath this door with straw and replaced the sod on top. "The lawn looked solid, but collapsed like paper when I fell on it." Keaton's arms had swollen (the first of many injuries to come), but olive oil and horse liniment helped.[8]

The hand returns to update: TODAY IS FRIDAY 13. It is THE HOUSEWARMING. Each day has been leading to this climax, not only through the gradual construction of the house but through the delivery of gags. Daily routines have been growing more complex and layered. The first gags with motorcycle and cars led into gags around one object (a wall); then into a routine with a circular development united by a piano; and, finally, into two distinct routines (carpet and milk-splatter) that connect and recall an earlier prop (door-to-nowhere). The housewarming now merges all elements under one roof, including a large number of new characters in the house, so that the entire frame fills with frenzy.

Handy Hank is among the guests. Before long, a chase between the rivals ensues so that Buster can rid himself and us of this pest through the very prop he activated the day before. Buster opens the misplaced door through which Hank runs—literally—across the air and into a fence. With his human nemesis gone, Buster's greatest challenge awaits: his battle against Machine and Nature. As Buster escorts three guests on a house tour, he suddenly ponders the rain now pouring through the ceiling. Characteristically nonplussed, Buster sets hands behind back, then reaches offscreen for a convenient umbrella. He becomes a sight gag as he marches through the kitchen with his open umbrella and heads out the door.

The "quiet before the storm" is graphically depicted in one medium long shot. As Buster's quiet mannerisms are juxtaposed with the teasing actions of the house behind him, tension mounts. The comic pulse quickens each time Buster ponders, then turns to find the house has shifted behind him. Repetition and symmetry are worked into the subtle moves of Buster and house: Buster thinks, the house shifts left; he faces front, the house shifts right. All tension snaps as the house shoves forward before his eyes. In an extreme long shot, the house spins like a giant mad weathervane. Buster grabs onto the corner and travels with the house in four revolutions. We cut once to a medium long shot of Buster helplessly transported. Inside, the camera in the static center of the spinning house follows Sybil and guests tumbling over each other. As in any high-tension sequence, editing is vital to the timing. Keaton crosscuts to pace the action and build tension; long shots of total frenzy alternate with medium shots of Buster's frenzy. The crosscutting pulsates: it broadens to all the guests and narrows to Buster; it cuts to interiors, then to exteriors. Keaton also uses repetition to intensify the "chase scene": Buster chasing after the door as he races over porch and rail. In a variation on this routine, when finally inside the house, Buster rattles around with the guests, then flies back *out* the door, emphasizing his vain struggle. Soon the helter-skelter nature of the storm reverses itself, as those indoors are propelled outdoors: Sybil soars out, followed by the guests. In a pantomime of futility, Buster jumps up to stop the house, falls, rises, falls, sits, and simply shrugs. The guests leave with an innocently ironic comment: "I'VE HAD A LOVELY AFTERNOON ON YOUR MERRY-GO-ROUND. IT'LL BE BETTER WHEN YOU PUT IN YOUR HOBBY HORSES." In a final blow, Buster finds a horseshoe. He hugs Sybil as they regard their revolving domicile and wait. The iris closes.

With the storm, Buster rises to his full potential, physically and mentally. The scene is reminiscent of a story Keaton often related from his childhood: when he was almost three years old, in one day he entangled his index finger in a wringer (the first joint was amputated), shortly thereafter gashed his head with a stone he flung at a peach tree, and then was sucked out his window by a sudden cyclone and landed four streets away.[9] Though Keaton had scars from these "accidents," one speculates on their accuracy because of plots like that of *One Week*. Knowing his fantastic childhood, it becomes difficult to distinguish between Buster the hero surmounting obstacles, and Keaton the director striving for filmic reality because these obstacles were real to him.

The last two anticlimactic days of the week are the shortest, and fittingly so, as the greatest tension has been released. Keaton serves up a short array of gags that deal specifically with both the house and Buster in a battle of wits against Fate. The hand returns: TODAY IS SATURDAY 14. —AND AFTER THE STORM—we need read no more. An iris opens to encircle Buster and Sybil who, asleep, are still clutching each other as on the previous day. The iris pauses, teasing us again as it did when Buster regarded his house on Day Three; now it widens slowly to reveal the house, even more of a disaster. The couple slowly turn, then after a pregnant pause, collapse against each other. Sybil cries: "NOW LOOK AT THE DARNED THING!" Buster rationalizes: "I GUESS IT'S NOT USED TO THE CLIMATE." A man enters from the left with the Lot 99 sign, turns it to read 66, and explains: "YOU'RE ON THE WRONG LOT. YOURS IS ACROSS THE RAILROAD TRACKS." The couple begin to plan the move; the iris closes.

In such a short day, there is a startling number of titles creating a verbal tension, now that the visual tension has reached its zenith. For once, Buster reflects aloud; his practical response does not consider his taunting Fate but rather expresses sympathy for his house. Silenced by the news that his efforts are misplaced again, he responds with determination to finish the job. He uses barrels as wheels for the house, while Sybil uselessly but well-meaningfully pumps the house with a tiny jack, certifying her principal role once more as frequent sight gag. Keaton has also perpetuated the "revolving" theme of the film: the revolving wall, the revolving kitchen-sink panel, the revolving mat that reads "ƎWOƆ⅂ƎⱲ/WELCOME," the revolving house; now the revolving sign that has transformed 99 into 66 and once more spins Buster's world.

TODAY IS SUNDAY 15. And on the last day, the house has been roped to the car and Buster commands the hauling. Into a starkly empty long shot rolls the car from the right, towing the house on barrel-wheels. In an ironically composed shot, Sybil pushes the house with her head bowed yet does not see the train tracks at her feet as we can from our objective stance. Keaton adds another rich sight gag as the car pulls away from the house. Buster hammers nails through the backseat into the wall. He returns to the driver's seat, gazing into the empty left half of the frame. Pause, and wheels, floorboard, and engine ride off, leaving Buster still seated and attached to the wall. In one specially composed visual commentary, Keaton again makes Buster the butt of mechanical machinations.

We suddenly cut to a smoke-spewing, whistle-blowing locomotive rounding the bend into the foreground. Buster and Sybil freeze, then pull each other in opposite directions. In a long shot of the inevitable crash, Buster and Sybil huddle to the side. Traversing the planes of the frame, the train hurtles toward the house in middleground. Suddenly the camera pans the train at the moment it follows unseen tracks *behind* the house. The camera pans slowly back to the couple; we cut to them as they revel in their unexpected fortune. With a sudden cut to a long shot (a cut to shock us), a second train roars in from the right (symmetrical balance) and *through* the house. We cut to the couple as they walk off resignedly. Buster sticks a FOR SALE sign before the splintered heap, then in an afterthought, attaches an envelope—DIRECTIONS—to the sign. Buster and Sybil walk on, again, holding hands. Iris closes. THE END.

As the storm was the editing climax of the film, the crash is the emotional climax and defines Buster Keaton's spirit for the rest of his career. When Buster and Sybil abandon their wrecked house, the gesture echoes the pathos of Chaplin's final walk into the sunset. However, Buster has endured physical and emotional battles that would destroy any more sentimental soul. He has tossed minor hindrances aside with disdain, but the bigger the opposition, the greater the fight. The chimney and piano merited prolonged battles. During the week, Buster becomes energized for his biggest confrontation. Here, Buster the hero and Keaton the filmmaker excel in their roles. Keaton speaks with smooth irony in the careful language of film during the last sequence, where we become as disillusioned by the passing train as the couple are. Keaton has only shown us one set of tracks and knows our expectation, since we sense disaster before the victims do. We think the highest level of humor for this gag is our being one up, for we automatically associate *that* train with *those* tracks coming from *that* direction. Yet Keaton's previous consistent play with space and symmetry nudges our security, and against our better judgment, we cannot trust that this will be the only conclusion to the gag. We are thinking too predictably, and Keaton will not allow us to do so. Thus, we laugh cautiously, anticipating another resolution under Keaton's control. He gives us full view through his camera, distancing us by the scope of the overall picture. By that distancing, ironically, we become involved in the emotional action, and especially in the character who continually holds us back while beckoning us to look deeply within.

Once the house is in pieces again, bringing the week full circle, the film has no further opportunity for gag development. The hero and his mate must move elsewhere. We tiptoe on the threshold that separates comedy and tragedy. We filter through black and white images into pointillism of varying intensities of gray. The intensities derive from Keaton's simple reflection: "I never realized that I was doing anything but trying to make people laugh when I threw my custard pies and took my pratfalls."[10] His innocent words are strangely superficial now, since the images are too strong and deep. Where words fail, Keaton in his films speaks more eloquently.

## Chapter 3

# Convict 13

### (October 1920)

Courtesy of the Museum of Modern Art/Film Stills Archive

Only a fragment of *Convict 13* from a European archive had been available until the 1970s when Raymond Rohauer pieced together the missing sequences of Buster Keaton's first dream short. Without the restoration, *Convict 13* was a relentless display of mildly comic physical violence in a prison setting. The missing dream-frame gave the film a new atmosphere and perspective. An airy golf course is now juxtaposed to the stark prison, and to his persona Keaton adds a childlike quality that is both imperiled and preserved by his dream.

The opening title establishes a subtle freedom theme: GOLF—NOT THE ONLY THING THAT MAKES A FELLOW LONG FOR FRESH AIR. Buster steps from a car on a golf course where Sybil Seeley readies to play. Buster and a black caddy watch as she sinks a hole in one. The title implies she will be Buster's love interest, but meanwhile part of the wooing ritual is to flaunt his prowess. He limbers up and hits his ball, which rolls past the hole. Already, the invisible hand of Fate from *One Week* seems eager to misdirect a sure shot and push Buster's "je ne sais quoi" into oblivion.

Sybil's exuberance over her obviously lucky play contrasts sharply with Buster's cocksure stance, and his lofty pose is the cue for Fate to start the battle of the ball. His physical reactions intensify the humor that derives from the mockery of his "unseen" opponent. Without Buster's reactions, the mockery would be most unkind; but his unemotional responses allow us to enjoy the misfortune rather than feel any sad twinge. Buster places the ball on the tee and, with a few kneebends, prepares to swing, but the invisible hand knocks the ball off. Buster holds the ball in place with his slapshoe toe as he swings into a bone-crunching full-twist pratfall. Spectators who earlier cheered for Sybil now laugh at Buster. Undaunted, he swings with a double-spin-flip to the ground. His body forms a pyramid as he rises and he searches with his caddy for the ball, which, in a cutaway, rolls into a stream. Buster crawls along a log onto a handy raftlike object on the water and rows toward the ball using the iron as oar. In an intriguing medium shot, Buster is visually "fragmented" as his slapshoes stand on the raft, but the rest of him reflects in the water *under* the raft. His rearranged body frames the center space, into which a fish suddenly leaps, devours the ball, and disappears. We return to Buster full-body as he dives in and emerges with the fish. We cut closer as he sits on the raft, squeezes the fish, and discards it. He stands into the next long shot, dives, pauses, and surfaces. Buster repeats this methodical peering-squeezing-diving routine twice more until the ball pops out of the right fish. Before tossing it back, Buster spanks the fish. Then he delicately "molds" the water into an imaginary tee, sets the ball on it, mouths "Fore!" and swings with a splash. The ball rolls into the next long shot where it stops so-near-yet-so-far from the hole. Buster rows on with his club-oar. Before the raft exits the frame, we see an aftergag: he uses the club as a rudder.

Buster's idiosyncracies are forming a permanent vocabulary. His slightest gestures are major reactions, as well as artistic embellishments on ordinary actions. After all, Buster does not merely stand to his feet after falling but feels compelled to create a triangular "modern-dance" pose to do so; it becomes a natural bodily expression. Keaton's visually stimulating and amusing movements, however slight, divert our attention from all else in the frame. For example, in a long shot of Buster and caddy against the landscape, our focus is riveted to the only movement in center foreground of the frame: Buster's slapshoe toe gently resting on the ball. This motion was paralleled earlier by an equally quiet one in which Fate knocks the ball off in the lower half of the frame as Buster is frozen in mid-swing. Silent subtlety, however, yields to the "noise" of Buster's spins and pratfalls. Similarly, through movement, Keaton contrasts Sybil's haphazard swings with Buster's controlled ones. Her amateurish approach and lucky accuracy are as unwittingly laugh-provoking as a pompous man with an April Fool's joke on his back. Naturally, the comedy resulting from this contrast intensifies for Buster, not for Sybil; she has merely propelled it, "warmed" us up for the main act.

Another important trait in Buster's nonverbal communication is evident in this sequence: his childlikeness. Even as the groom in *One Week*, a self-imposed role of adult responsibility, Buster is childlike—rarely childish. He skips along the threshold of adulthood like a child hobbles on the edge of a sidewalk, one foot on the pavement and the other on the road. In his dual nature of adult/child, he is mature/naive. When needing to be firm, he never resorts to tantrums and assumes a stern adult role. As the adult, he is angry and parentally spanks the fish, believing it will recognize its transgression; his demeanor, however, closely resembles that of a child who spanks a mischievous doll.

Buster has already demonstrated his talent for transforming objects in *One Week*. Now in just one sequence, he has transformed driftwood into a raft, a golf club into an oar/rudder/walking cane, and more surrealistically, water into a tee. He fervently believes the last metamorphosis is possible, and we allow Buster his fantasy because we too have come to believe it. Within a realistic setting, Buster has convincingly reversed Fate's twists into minor victories by changing one layer (a fish devours a golf ball) into multilayers (if Buster squeezes the right fish, he gets his golf ball back and communicates with the miscreant). He gives new interpretations to a literal, mundane world and designs a unique context for the possible-impossible. Of course, these small transformations are teasers for the crucial metamorphosis of the next sequence.

Cut to the prison. A con in striped uniform sneaks around a prison wall, which angles toward us for depth. We crosscut between Buster's golfing and the prison. A guard pulls the ALARM WHISTLE; in visual response, a whistle shrieks with steam. The proximity of prison to golf course is immediately clear as Buster and caddy look up at the "sound." The caddy drops to the ground for lunch and Buster returns to play. The deliberate spaciousness in this long shot prepares for the next gag: a dog races in, seizes the ball, and speeds out, followed by Buster.

Keaton sets up visually tantalizing compositions with unique audience positions as the prison-escape plotline develops. Looking toward a dirt incline cutting across the top half of the frame, ten armed guards race from the bushes. Juxtaposed to this chaos, Buster remains oblivious as he prepares to swing. He mouths "Fore!" as three sour-faced ladies on the green glare at him; although these spectators seem trivial, they will soon play into Buster's chaotic situation. Buster swings; the ball bounces off a house jutting (unobtrusively, until now, like the truck in *One Week*) into frame-right, and knocks Buster unconscious. The next development merges prison with golf course: the escaped con switches clothes with the sleeping Buster. Guards emerge from trees; in addition to marking official progress, this shot also lapses time, for we return to find the con leaving in Buster's suit and our unconscious hero in stripes. Next, two guards confer before trees and head front. This shot again lapses time, for in the next long shot, Buster awakens. He swings, this time accompanied by a title card reading "FORE!" The three terrified biddies flee into the background. Their reaction will become sensible when the dream structure is revealed at the end. For the present, however, we and Buster wonder at their abrupt change of heart.

By being positioned between guards, the escapee is visually trapped but, ironically, not caught. He quickly directs them to Buster. Through their subjective view, we see Buster's striped back, even more vulnerable against the dwarfing landscape. The guards pull abreast of Buster who only belatedly discovers his dilemma through a casual movement: as he swings the club overhead, he spies the arm patch reading "13" and touches his uniform for the first time. The biggest clue to his transformation—a striped uniform—has completely eluded Buster; only the small detail of "13" enlightens him. Thus, Buster will tend to stare at the entire forest of a problem without seeing it, until he smacks into one tiny tree. Just as the "13" detail had to be brought directly up to his eyes, Keaton inserts a stunning extreme close-up for us: piercing official eyes and a hatband labeled GUARD. The shot fills our vision just as the problem fills Buster's hypersensitive mind. In a long shot of the trio, Buster bounces nervously on his heels as he prepares to swing, even repositioning a guard to make space. For the first time, Buster perfectly fires the ball (and Fate actually allows him). As the guards eye the ball, Buster strolls down an unobstructed aisle of vision between the guards, who belatedly notice and resume pursuit.

Once again, a transformation for comedy: Buster = con, with the unluckiest number, in a change beyond his control. Fear has finally transformed Buster's chaotic swings into a successful shot; he cannot enjoy the triumph, though, for Fate has gleefully provided a greater quandary than a temperamental golf ball. The tone of the film changes as well. We have already been startled by a "fragmented" Buster on the raft: his real legs above his reflected upper-body foreshadow a topsy-turvy view of reality. Now fragments of guards appear in stunning close-ups. Ironically, Keaton once commented on his dislike of close-ups: "When I do use cuts I still won't go right into a closeup, I'll just go in maybe to a full figure, but that's about as close as I'll come. Closeups are too jarring on the screen and this type of cut can stop an audience from laughing."[1] Given this opinion, Keaton's close-up inserts are probably experiments in visual punch lines that intensify our focus on those elements affecting Buster; they stun us into laughter as Buster is stunned into shock. With these two shots, we become trapped with Buster in the illusion of prison, even before he has entered its physical confines.

Imprisonment is also suggested by the choreography in the next shots. A fluid cut joins Buster strolling from one shot into the next shot of a road, golf club tucked under his arm and guards pacing alongside him. Suddenly other guards break left and right into this shot behind the first two. Like an advancing army, more enter from left, two from right, one right, left, right, left, left, right. Buster in the center only notices the last few guards. We cut once to a medium shot for his wide-eyed observations, with the surreal fragmentation of guards' stomping feet behind him. The next long shot captures the whole formation: three lines of guards stripe Buster's background, with the verticals perpendicular to his uniform's horizontal stripes; shadows also spread bars to the left. The group enters middleground when, like one body with Buster as head, they about-face and march to the background, then about-face toward us and back again as one ensemble sight gag. Buster breaks the pattern by fleeing toward us. In one extreme long shot, Buster appears tiny and vulnerable; despite his helplessness, however, he begins to *stroll* toward us. As he does, a trucking shot equalizes the distance between us and the guards who pour into three rows once more. Keaton cuts into the next shot, anticipating Buster's entrance, to tease us with what seems to be the fortuitous arrival of a car to ensure his escape.

As we switch to the car interior, Buster relaxes beside a cigar-chomping passenger. Already influenced by the previous extreme close-up, we are once more alerted to Buster's predicament (before *he* even realizes it) when a second extreme close-up of penetrating eyes and a hatband reading WARDEN fills the frame. In a replay of *One Week*'s car exchange, Buster emerges from the car and switches to a passing vehicle. Guards stumble left to right in a profile view of the road as Buster's car passes right to left, creating visual-gag nonsense and play with symmetry. Keaton continually choreographs the frame's space, which is purposely devoid of detail to accommodate the moving elements. He uses the guards to shatter the bottom frame as they rush in to confront the car. The number of heads increases laterally from three to ten as the guards stalk the car, which remains in the distance. The human barricade acquires height and length yet never obscures Buster's middleground action of abandoning the car and fleeing into the trees uphill. Mid-flight, Buster picks a daisy. The title clarifies Buster's primary concern even in his life-or-death situation: SHE LOVES ME, SHE LOVES ME NOT, SHE LOVES ME. With a sigh, Buster discards the bare stem and resumes his flight.

Only the child in an adult world would express himself so innocently, as Buster now does, reminding us of Sybil, his love interest. He also trusts that the police are bumbling and unthreatening so that he may pause to daydream of romance. The child's playfulness blends with adult caution in this methodical choreography of a "chase scene," leagues from Sennett's Keystone Kops where laughter derived from exaggeration. Here, laughter escalates as the elements within the frame increase and multiply in controlled movements. In *One Week*, we witnessed the "see/don't see" phenomenon in Keaton's composition: train tracks are "there" and "not there." Here, we see an unobtrusive house suddenly become prominent to fling a ball at Buster's head; "no car" suddenly becomes "a car" that shatters the marching formation. The choreography is an ironic parade symbolizing a lockstep prison life. Buster's trepidation requires slow, cautiously advancing steps, aiming to make the opposition march to *his* beat. These confrontations are soundless, for Buster's nerves tingle with silent intuitions. And clearly, just as movement within the frame is choreographed for symmetry and formation, so has the total film been choreographed. Because of its plan, we as omniscient audience feel we can jump ahead of Buster, and Keaton lets us believe we know more than our hero. Ironically, that preknowledge is also controlled by Keaton to fool us, as the conclusion of the film will soon reveal.

The next gag does not advance the plot but rather expands the prison symbolism. Buster pushes a painter in white overalls onto a newly painted dark bench. The striped-back/solid-front halves of the overalls distracts the guards and hints at Buster's dual nature, but the gag is a weak interruption in the coherent whole, for Buster stops his flight to watch the action. Once he resumes his flight, he locks himself behind a barred gate, relishing the apparent security, only to be deluded when he turns. An arched doorway frames a moving diorama of prison life. Buster hands the gate key to a waiting guard, an ironic gesture no doubt conditioned by his hopeless golfing. Buster knows his actions will be thwarted, so why not help frustration on its inevitable journey? Such "psychology" allows Buster to accept his destiny; thus, when he enters the prison, he even wipes his feet on an imaginary welcome mat. Once more, through purely visual devices, Keaton creates both internal and external representations of prison life. Buster is visually trapped in a close shot *and* physically backed up against a brick wall. Into this shot walks Buster's breath of fresh air, Sybil. Her intellectual acuity is once again in doubt because of her comment: "HOW SWEET! HAVE YOU DONE THIS JUST TO BE NEAR ME?" An onlooker (the Warden) turns the two-shot into a three-shot. Sybil's innocent title "ALLOW ME TO INTRODUCE MY FATHER" tightens the symbolic clutch around Buster. He is physically and visually sandwiched between the two people vital to his situation. Accommodating his miserable fate, Buster offers a handshake to the Warden before setting his hands on hips, a mannerism that snarls his prospects. The "13" patch and the Warden's fingers appear in close-up, a cue that again zeroes in on damning details. The Warden confirms Buster's inevitable destiny: "YOU'RE GOING TO BE HUNG TODAY!" and leads him off.

The gallows dominates the next sequence to dwarf Buster and those who serve it. The ineptitude of the prison officials is easily mocked by their own actions and speech, and as a result, Buster increasingly doubts their capacity to execute their duties—or merely to execute. Warden:

# Convict 13

"THIS IS THE BIRD WE'RE SUPPOSED TO HANG TODAY." The hangman shakes hands and feels his neck, prompting Buster's mocking inquiry: "ARE YOU SURE YOU KNOW HOW TO WORK THIS THING?" When the hangman leaves, we see clearly how the crossbeams of the scaffold form an appropriate maze above Buster. The impact of his destiny stuns Buster and, stiff as a plank, he falls forward and staggers out, with a last look at the gallows. Keaton leads us to a brief non-Buster scene to show Sybil, in a stroke of rare genius, finding an elastic rope that she will substitute for the gallows rope. When we encounter Buster again, he has moved on to shoving a wheelbarrow, another weak scene interrupting (postponing?) his fate. Despite his inevitable and unjust demise, however, Buster forgets all but the memory of the daisy. If he must die against his will, he will not die with unfulfilled love. He scoops Sybil up in the wheelbarrow—making the most of an "unmilked" prop—to profess his love with melodramatic gestures before he is carted off by guards again.

Gallows humor is played to its most literal. The hanging sequence is steeped in nonverbal communication, subtle gestures, and bitter ironic images that mock Buster's potentially tragic situation. The hangman shakes Buster's hand as the victim positions himself expectantly near the noose. Hangman: "DON'T WORRY. IT'LL WORK FINE WITH YOU." Buster asks how the machine operates; his expression is a collage of emotions: he nods, pauses, looks resigned, bewildered, disappointed, blank. Sentries glide dreamily along the wall top across middleground as Buster and hangman occupy foreground.

Adding to the macabre tone, we cut to convicts on bleachers cheering for Buster's hanging. His courage lashes out as he rejects a blindfold, straps his arms across his chest, and shakes a vehement NO. The hangman uses the blindfold to polish a medal on his jacket: in iris, it reads CHAMPION HEAVY WEIGHT HANGMAN 1916–17–20. The interplay between Buster and hangman continues the sardonic attack that Keaton is launching at official ceremony, and it extends into its spectators, as Buster's callous fellow cons eagerly call on a snack vendor. The rope itself becomes a sight gag as the hangman tightens the noose around Buster's head, the knot sitting jauntily on his hat. Like a mannequin manipulated by the irritable hangman, Buster fully accepts his fate and throws a kiss to the crowd. Although unclear in the existing film, Buster may know of Sybil's rope switcheroo (perhaps he even gave her the idea—so much for her ingenuity) and may have wheeled her over to the gallows for that reason. Thus, he is more than willing to play along with the "ceremony" since he knows how it will turn out. The comic humiliation and outrage he feels because of the spectators and officials could well be offset by his secret knowledge that he has reversed his unkind fate—at least for the time being.

Editorially and figuratively, the film snaps Buster's doom in half with a quick cut to a shot of the control ropes, followed by a quick cut to Buster bouncing through the gallows floor. The spectators boo (again, a hostile crowd as on the golf course). Buster confidently salutes the hangman, drops through the gallows holding onto the noose, and lands on his feet. He walks into freedom, but the visual frame (trap) of the crossbeams suggests another illusion: indeed, two guards appear to escort him away. Keaton mocks the travesty of justice; the very cons who applauded Buster's dilemma will shortly fill his shoes, for the vendor announces: "EASY, BOYS, WE'LL HANG TWO TOMORROW ON ACCOUNT OF THIS."

Buster is demoted to the rock pile. Again, the sequence is rich in nonverbal behavior, small gestures, and childlike curiosity about work. Buster knocks his hammer against a pebble and collects the chips. A guard angrily demonstrates the proper way. Buster readies the hammer but stops to add another pebble to his pile, then robustly swings the hammer overhead into the guard's face. After two more whacks at the rock, Buster discovers the unconscious guard. What seemed like a deliberate move to dispense with the guard was in fact coincidence. The benevolent child in Buster is concerned about performing a task and satisfying his curiosity. But the unconscious guard stirs an afterthought in Buster's adult psyche; he uses the transformation potential lying at his feet and switches clothes with the guard.

A LITTLE DARLING. The unexpected title cuts to a small iris in which appears the head of an ornery con (Joe Roberts) puffing leisurely on a cigarette. As the iris opens, the full beast is revealed as a sight gag, leaning upon his sledgehammer with one foot poised on a rock pile. After dispensing with one guard, the con begins his odd massacre of violence and playfulness: he swings one guard three times, propels him toward the wall, then strangles him. Eliminating guards as quickly as they lunge at him, king con symmetrically balances the frame by throwing bodies from left to right until they are piled as high as his knees. The Warden looks anxiously from his window. Who will protect Buster from this new threat? Though he has reversed his identity by chance, Buster is really not able to reverse Fate itself. His world is filled with persistent opponents, no matter which side of the law he visits. The con is merely a colleague (employee) of Buster's eternal nemesis, Fate.

Buster has dressed the unconscious guard in the striped uniform, even placing the hammer in his hand as a final touch. We cut to the other side of the door before he enters, thus learning of his proximity to the ornery con. Buster's assurance, demonstrated by straightening his tie and dusting off his uniform, disintegrates when he encounters the con. The two-shot depicts how Buster is again physically and psychologically trapped; his awkward verbal reaction is "NICE WEATHER WE'RE HAVING." He proffers an amiable handshake and receives the sledgehammer. Just as he dwarfed Buster as the piano deliverer in *One Week*, again Joe Roberts diminishes Buster. The duo shows an ease of interactions / reactions, which makes Buster Keaton and Joe Roberts a successful comedy team in silent film— not of Laurel and Hardy fame, perhaps, but with a comfortable collaboration that would grow over the next seventeen short films and one feature until Roberts's death in 1924.

Once Buster realizes the danger from his new identity label GUARD, he and the con participate in gags that switch between each other's respective power positions. For example, Buster who has opted to stand in a corner rather than walk to the con is visually obliterated by the hulk before him, as well as by a slight pan of the camera that fills the frame with the con's back. In another example, Buster watches the con fire a guard across the yard, then tally the hit by chalking an X the size of a brick in the wall. Like his effort to beat the guards at their own game by luring them into parade formation, Buster massages the con's ego by applauding. He distracts him in order to highkick him through the arched doorway, lock the gate, and throw away the key. Buster now taunts, "IF YOU WANT TO KNOW WHO'S BOSS HERE, JUST ASK!" and points to the word GUARD, an emblem of his dread only shortly before. The sequence becomes a seesaw of power plays: once Buster holds the upper hand, the con overcomes him until Buster can create another distraction, reducing himself to the level of his opponent in order to reclaim the upper hand. When Buster is too certain of himself and fumbles, his opponent scores. This is checks-and-balances, keeping Buster strapped to Fate's treadmill.

When so countered, Buster's most endearing childlike traits surface, as in the conclusion of this sequence when the con bends the bars apart and steps behind Buster who lights a cigarette. Buster again backs into the corner when he sees the bars, his fear-filled eyes stretching to their farthest corners. In a graphic translation of terror, the left side of his jacket begins thumping outward. Only a child in an adult body would dare to express so plainly and simply one's fears (pumping heart), anger (spanking fish), curiosity (pulverizing the rock pile), and love (picking daisy). Buster presses his pounding ticker; he checks his pulse and presses his wild heart twice more. However, the resourceful adult Buster falls on his hands, jump-kicks the con, and flees. The elastic rope gag begins a second phase, bringing the routine full circle. Buster lures the con up the gallows, nooses his foot, speeds to the "control room," and sends the con bouncing upside down. This sequence is cut with the same rapid editing of the earlier hanging sequence. After Buster is presented with an ASSISTANT WARDEN's hat before Sybil, we return to the con who is seated and gnawing through the rope.

Other characters are infused with some of Buster's traits, although we never stay long with these "satellites"; they affect us as sight gags, visual punch lines, patches in a comic quilt. They build on one external defining characteristic. Just as Handy Hank was restricted to his peculiar "charisma," the hefty hangman is a callous show-off and the ornery con is a beast. On the other hand, by contrast, Buster resonates many solutions to problems and many emotions that span a lifetime. His pale face is a translucent mirror reflecting the moment at hand; perhaps even reflecting the mind of The Opponent, who eventually exposes its inner workings, to which Buster responds with his creative duality.

Buster's rich behavior playing against stock characters helps to create a lighthearted atmosphere that keeps the prison brutalities from overwhelming us. Violence spreads from the ornery con to the entire prison, as in the next sequence that begins with a moving diorama of the prison yard seen through the arched doorway. The ornery con whispers to another con, "RIOT AT 3 O'CLOCK." He passes on the message while the ornery con bursts into the Warden's office where Buster and Sybil chat. He leans one hand on the desk—in a vise—while smothering Sybil with his savoir faire. Buster spins the vise closed; the con howls but then picks up the vise and slams it into the Warden. Buster tips his hat in light of this defeat and leaves. With the open door, Keaton opens the frame's depth, for straight ahead of us are another door and a wall, the route Buster travels when the con socks him in the face. He is transported in Buster-esque fashion, with double-flips to the back wall. The con stalks out with Sybil on his shoulder and tosses Buster aside.

The "storm" of this film, as was the climax of *One Week*, is about to begin. Around a table stand three guards at leisure and a lanky con (Joe Keaton, Buster's father), who asks for the time. In irised close-up, to dispel any doubts, it is three o'clock. The con in reply kicks one guard with a foot to the head and swings his leg back to kick another guard. This was Keaton's first independent film tribute to his father's vaudeville specialty, Irish highkicking, which Keaton knew only too well.

Again looking through the arched doorway, a "proscenium" behind which the prison tableaux play out, a riot is framed as the ornery con signals revolt with Sybil ashoulder. The riot intensifies by its concentrated focus through the doorway. A guard standing middleground center serves as a visual anchor to the scene; once the cons lynch him, the anchor is gone and the prison sinks like the Titanic. The prison is fragmented with rebellion; fittingly, fragmented shots dominate the sequence. Looking to the wall top, sentries silhouetted against the sky shoot down at cons who throw rocks and hammers at them. A long shot records the rock-ball game until we cut abruptly to the wall top bisecting the frame into light and dark horizontal bands. Suddenly the heads of five guards poke over the wall, creating a sight gag of simultaneity. Just as rapidly they disappear in a volley of rocks. As sentries and cons play into the final inning, Buster takes a nap on a dismantled punching bag in the sportsroom.

We look up from low angle to one guard on the wall stark against the sky, who shoots offscreen. We see the effect in subjective long shot as a con flips full-body to the ground. Another con races in to retrieve his fallen gun and shoots upward at us. Here, crosscutting works as a wordless question-answer or cause-effect device. Keaton responds to the firing by cutting to a guard who stiffens and drops off the wall. The effect is more dramatic and sobering through its subjective approach than if we viewed the firing in a long shot. To offset this with levity, one con approaches, salutes, and confers with the ornery ringleader who directs the riot while holding Sybil. A con shoots an offscreen guard, and in the next long-shot response, the guard falls with a flip and double dying-kick. Buster slowly awakens to the anarchy. Recalling the elastic-theme of the film, his deus ex machina, Buster studies the elastic string on a punching bag and hurries toward us with it.

Buster next runs along the background wall top, leaps down to the preestablished table, and transforms his punching bag into a lethal bolo that he swings over the top of his head, extending it further out until it strikes the lanky con and everyone after him. The editing mirrors the frenzy of the attack and directs us to the pivotal actions of each shot, either moving in close range to stricken cons or widening to broad movement. In one amusing routine, Keaton uses the height and depth of the prison yard to build gags that also advance the situation (Buster's battle and cons' escape). Three cons stand on each other's shoulders against the wall, as a fourth stands on the brink of liberty. Buster whacks the bottom man out, tumbling the next two; he lengthens the elastic and flings the fourth con over the wall. In this one scene, both depth (through the bolo's circular flight) and height (through the convict column) cross and fill the frame.

The punching bag deflates on the ornery con's bayonet. The con pulls the elastic until it stretches the length of the frame. The bolo ricochets on Buster, who soars into a wall where he immediately retrieves a ball and chain. The con retreats to a barred doorway where, in a profile perspective, the swinging ball whizzes into his shot. Physical movement and editing increase the tension of the sequence as we are concentrated in one set with the dynamism of human and filmic movement. Buster swings wildly on the table; the elastic wraps around the con's body. In this lengthy bolo sequence, the shots are many and quick enough to see the main action—the "cause" (Buster's swing), and the secondary action—the "effect" (elastic wrapping around con). We usually remain in one location but cut to different sections of it: table, corner, gateway. We always return to Buster, the "sun" in this solar system. Buster stands proudly over the tied-up con, leaning on a sledgehammer that extends from the table. It flips up and beans him on the head. Sybil bends over his unconscious form. Dissolve to the golf course, where Sybil "melts" into the identical stooped position over Buster, an image of technical precision that also reveals that most of the film has been a dream. Buster awakens. Sybil leads him off left. THE END.

So much unconsciousness is rendered in the final sequences of *Convict 13* that every knockout seems to be a reverberation of Buster's original freak stunning. The number of violent assaults, no less than forty, is staggering for a comedy short.[2] Keaton often keeps bodies in view not only so that Buster can balance the sight with comic business (heart-thumping, for example) but also to recall the prison—a "reality" that is comically ironic when we learn of the dream.[3] Keaton inserts humorous business to lighten the violent sequences and to distance us from empathizing with the victims. As jarring as it is, Keaton's fragmentation motif conveys both humor and a dreamlike tone to the film. Buster himself is torn by Fate, figuratively divided into sharp black and white stripes with his pieces tossed to hungry cons. The prison sequence creates unrest, even with the salvation of Sybil's rope-switching. But Keaton has allowed Buster to be saved; thus, comedy requires some ultimate personal salvation even after defeat (*One Week* proved as much).

The whole of *Convict 13* presents a fascinating portrait of Buster's fragmented state and a far more optimistic one than the prison sequence would imply. In truth, Buster has never left the free and beautiful golf course. While Buster indeed heard the whistle signaling escape, the convict in reality never came near him. Buster devised his own dream of clothes-switching, imprisonment, hanging, salvation, rank promotion, battles, victory, romance. Knowing of the dream, we add a deeper level to Keaton's fragmented images: dreams present abstractions, bizarre and restless visions. From the golf course to the last prison sequence, Keaton constructs a dreamlike state through the images, causing us to wonder at how "real" Buster's situation as Convict 13 is. We doubt, for instance, the reality of swinging an iron ball on an elastic rope. The dream-frame, then, is the most crucial element of all: we can laugh at Buster's dilemma, for all of it is possible since none of it is "real."

Until Buster awakens, we accept only the dream's contents as reality. We succumb to the somberness of the prison. Still the dream feels obvious (we know Buster is unconscious; should we abandon the possibility of a dream because we *see* him wake up?). It is also subtle (we do abandon the possibility because, until the film's final dissolve, Keaton has not used any "dream-sequence clues" such as a superimposition or even a spinning camera for a fall into unconsciousness). The dream revelation is more a relief than a surprise, for we must admit that Keaton never deceived us: there is a golf course, there is a prison, and he has merely provided a concrete environment in which to enact his illusion. Yet all the while, his images have planted clues of a dreaminess in the prison and a subliminal anticipation of the unknown.

Keaton's dream device is also loaded with implications about Buster's state of mind, another facet of his personality that moves the character light-years away from the slapstick clowns of early film comedy, who did not have much of a mind nor a particular state of it. Buster confesses to a fair amount of paranoia: not only does he dream he is victimized by the convict but he in fact becomes the convict and target of a manhunt.

He dreams of a horrible persecution where no one knows his face, only a number and uniform. The guards must know the real con's face, yet they pursue Buster because they recognize his striped back while playing golf (nor do they have much logic—typical of Keaton's officials—for they assume that a striped escapee would stop to golf in open country). Even the three biddies do not recognize Buster; they were scowling at him in his street clothes only *minutes* before they fled from him in his stripes. An astute viewer might suspect the first indication of a dream in the works, for how can the biddies react so differently to the same person minutes apart? However, by not witnessing a tangible dream-frame, we see this as a reality in the form of comic symmetry: the horrified reactions of the women are balanced with Buster's satisfied nod that they will finally leave him in peace, whatever the reason.

Enter yet another curious facet of Buster's prism personality: he is unaware of his paranoia, and hence of his victimization, while he also creates it. The dream confesses to Buster's haunted psyche. Once we recognize the dream device, we observe how much is displayed of Buster's child/adult behavior and of Keaton's view of his persona. Since the dream fills over half the short, its filmic components are as vital as its psychological ones to create a three-dimensional portrait of Buster. Numerous shots in the prison compel us to see Buster as a victim trapped by mechanical and/or human powers. Buster is often dwarfed in his placement to the ornery con, the road, or the gallows; he is sandwiched between opposing forces (Sybil and Warden, Warden and hangman); he is with his back to a wall and in a tight shot to boot. In addition, as much as Buster is the mastermind of his dream, he also presents (like a filmmaker) a complete picture of every skirmish in the prison, even those in which he plays no part. We glimpse not only what affects Buster directly but *indirectly* through other con/guard confrontations. We have whole routines between the ornery con and guards long before Buster meets the con. Perhaps Buster's dream is so fragmented yet all-encompassing of the terrors in his mind that he presents them in elaborate sequence to warn us of what he will soon meet. Then again, perhaps Buster enjoys dreaming up a great film story, with ordered details and suspenseful continuity. Thus, Buster = Keaton as much as Buster = Buster.

To build on the first possibility—that of dreaming all possible terrors, Buster concocts fastidious pictures of what lurks in the recesses of his subconscious (in other words, Life). Guards approach Buster from behind; he cannot possibly know they are searching for him, yet fatalism reigns and he will include it in dream form. His belief in Fate was evidenced earlier in his waking state when he loses his golf ball (which was never meant to be a hole in one) or when he is knocked out. Therefore, we readily accept Buster's first "waking" as real, for his willing reactions toward his fate are so natural.

Because this is a dream, Buster reverses his hanging fate by allowing Sybil to find the elastic while he is staggering about offscreen. He conjures up a series of winning strategies to overthrow first the guards (parade formation, car escape), then the cons (sundry kicks and jumps, bolo). His most crucial move is also the one that reverses his mistaken-identity nightmare: he switches clothes with a guard, as the real Convict 13 did with him. Buster's sense of honor pervades his dream as does his paranoia, for he seeks justice in the often unjust hands of Fate. He does not choose to remain in stripes. Out of Buster's subconscious, thanks to the liberating power of the dream, comes the primal urge to survive on the side of the law.[4]

Despite the prowling shadows of his unawareness, Buster dreams himself the hero with his love beside him. He even provides the perfect exit from his dream after his victory over the con. Rather than abruptly wake, Buster dreams of another knock on the head, bringing us full circle to the episode that began his jailhouse blues. As he shakes his head free of incredible visions, driving the horrors back to his subconscious, Buster recognizes the freedom of dreams to indulge in miracles. The greatest impossibility—the elastic rope—cannot be true, yet it succeeds in dreams. As tribute to Keaton's directorial perfectionism, the gag ironically worked within the reality of shooting the film. Although the gag is part of the "dream sequence," Keaton actually performed such a daring illusion in order for it to appear dreamlike and impossible. The elements comprising *Convict 13*—film, reality, dream, Buster, Keaton—are soldered together; they are separate yet collective forces that boggle our ability to distinguish one from the other.

The dream film liberates Buster's personality and Keaton's direction to express their fantasies. Yet the dream cannot exist in and of itself. It is only a part of life adding comic interpretation to a serious mistaken identity. The only resolution *must* be awaking. Buster finds that he has "in reality" been nowhere, yet in his subconscious, he has seen and done the impossible. By contrast, being awake is too tame. Keaton has set his subconscious performance in a prison, for how like a prison are the hidden recesses of the mind. The ravages of the dream are scattered in a blink. On the return trip from such visions, Buster is reinvigorated, relieved, and self-confident, and once again far from prison. While the world is still hostile and dangerous, it seems not as inescapable.

## Chapter 4

# The Scarecrow

(December 1920)

Courtesy of the Academy of Motion Picture Arts and Sciences

One reviewer of *The Scarecrow* announced that "without parallel
. . . is the phenomenal rise of Buster Keaton. In many parts of the
country exhibitions make Keaton the whole show for a week, playing the Keaton feature [*The Saphead*] along with a Keaton comic
two-reeler."[1] *The Scarecrow* reveals yet another facet of Buster's

persona set in a fantastical playground of inventions that Keaton must have relished. Together, Buster and Joe Roberts spin out transformations in a pastoral setting that spoofs melodrama as much as it rejoices in romance.

Pastoral poetry is harpooned with the opening title and expository shot: SLOWLY AND MAJESTICALLY THE SUN STEALS GRADUALLY OVER THE HILL-TOPS. A white box house nestled amid trees behind a picket fence fades into view in an extreme long shot; clouds laze in the sky. The bright orb of the sun "steals" indeed—in fast-motion from behind the house and straight up the sky, hitting high noon in two seconds.

ALL THE ROOMS IN THIS HOUSE ARE IN ONE ROOM. The curious paradox (all rooms = one room) of the second title of the film establishes the tone for the wondrous transformations/equations of the next sequence, once an establishing shot and incidental business introduce our heroes. After a closer cut to the house, we cut to the "multiroom" where Buster moans at the foot of his bed, a handkerchief knotted around his head like rabbit ears. His roommate (Joe Roberts), considering a tie to wear, opts to wrap his shoelace under his ample collarboard (Transformation 1: shoelace = tie). Joe's hand reaches into a medium close-up to turn the mirror; on the reverse is a photograph of Sybil Seeley (Transformation 2: mirror = picture frame). We crosscut for actions/reactions: Joe kisses the picture, Buster stares, Joe gushes, Buster clasps the picture to his chest. The two boys in one shot instantly portray their rivalry. Joe towers over Buster who announces in sublime convolution: "I DON'T CARE HOW SHE VOTES—I'M GOING TO MARRY HER." Despite the friction, Joe comforts his buddy over his tooth. Transformation 3: Joe = dentist. He extends a string between Buster's tooth and the doorknob. Buster's responses to the extraction are eloquently nonverbal, particularly during a "conversation" between Joe outside the house and Buster within. Joe bellows: "ARE YOU READY?" Buster shakes his head. A door slam extracts Buster's tooth, which he tucks into his vest pocket. Thus, Transformation (4) of a Transformation (3): *door* = dentist.

Unexpected changes continue to layer the sequence. From under a chest, Buster pulls a tray of buns to slide into it (Transformation 5: chest = oven). He lifts the top of the chest to uncover a turntable (Transformation 6: chest/oven = victrola). He hangs a record on a wall hook (Transformation 7: wall = record-cabinet) and lifts the turntable to reveal a burner (Transformation 8: chest/oven/Victrola = stove). With Buster's order to "SET THE TABLE," transformations increase in rapid orchestration.

**44**

# The Scarecrow

Joe unfastens a rope on the wall to lower four bowls and shakers, each balanced by weights, from the ceiling (Transformation 9: ceiling = cupboard). He unhinges a side lock on a bookcase to open an icebox door (Transformation 10). Filling a tiny checkered wagon on the table with fruit and butter, he calls out Transformation 11 as a verbal simile: "HURRY UP! MY STOMACH IS AS EMPTY AS A SALOON." Buster pours coffee by pulling a long spout from the side of the pot over the cup—like a railroad engine watering spout (Transformation 12), then piles buns into the wagon "train." In a lengthy long shot, we witness a symbolic Transformation 13: simple meal = aerial/surface choreography. As part of the ballet, Buster does not even sit in simple fashion but swings his leg over the back of the chair. Joe symmetrically balances the opposite end of the frame by sitting across from Buster. Each following activity perpetuates the visual balance within the frame, either through pulling ropes and objects or through the boys' interactions. They tug the chuck wagon the length of the table or crisscross shakers and bowls through the air to each other. Buster hurls a tomato that Joe catches on his fork and stuffs into his mouth. Buster opens the top of the icebox with one rope while manipulating a milk bottle on the other. The boys wipe their mouths on a "communal" napkin hanging front center of the table. After the meal, they rearrange the dishes and carry the table top to the middle of the room. Once the choreography is complete, Keaton introduces more transformations. Buster steps down on a trapdoor (Transformation 14: solid floor = trapdoor) to dump in the leftovers. We cut to the basement as food pours into a trough surrounded by four hungry pigs (Transformation 15: pigs = garbage disposal).

Buster and Joe attach the table top—a still life of plates and utensils— to the window corners. With a hose from a sink that was hidden under a rolltop desk (Transformation 16), Buster sprays the dishes. Joe raises the shakers and lowers a fringed lamp, while Buster revolves a table trapdoor to unearth a bucket of flowers (Transformation 17). Joe lifts the bathtub toward the wall; exterior, water pours through a slat into a hole in the ground. Inside, Joe lifts a board on the tub to create a striped sofa (Transformation 18). Outside, a duck family flops into the water (Transformation 19: bathwater = duck pond). Buster pushes his bed to the wall; it becomes an upright piano (Transformation 20). Buster and Joe lift the board to the wall; the reverse is a sampler (Transformation 21), reading WHAT IS HOME WITHOUT A MOTHER. After a reflective pause, Buster snatches his porkpie as Joe takes his jacket and hat from the door (Transformation

22: door = hatrack) and closes the door behind them. In an exterior long shot, the boys stroll from the house through a picket fence that Buster parts, slanting half right and left (Transformation 23: picket fence = scissor gate). Sybil steps through a sculpted hedge; the boys, with backs to us, run for her, trip each other, and fly clenched fists (Transformation 24: buddies = rivals).

The "dual-purpose" theme of the film is hardly exhausted once the mechanical transformations turn into a personal transformation. The most important transformation, which will also define the title of the film, is yet to occur. In the meantime, we are barraged with the equations of a mechanical, almost mathematically designed house. This theme of transformation/equation is solidly based in this film, having grown from its roots in Keaton's first two shorts where objects, when least expected, turned into what they were not originally. In this first major sequence, however, both Buster and Joe have created and *control* the alternatives. Transformations weave in and out of time and space, to the boys' matter-of-fact approval. The house is tame, an extension of every whim, not a devious mechanical monster as in *One Week*.

In what seems an abrupt shift in content and tone, we move from the mechanical setting to the great outdoors, from the unemotional to the ripely romantic. Sybil's farmer-father (Joe Keaton), a tall stick of a man with beard and straw hat, hears a ruckus while hoeing. Once he enters the feud, the boys split, leaving Sybil to demonstrate rare backbone in her character. Pop sternly directs her home, but she snaps her fingers in his face and marches through the hedge. With his best vaudeville highkick, Pop aims his foot too high at her rear end and lands on his.

STUNG BY HER FATHER'S TREATMENT SHE PLANNED TO RUIN HIS RURAL STOMACH—SO SHE BAKED HIM A CREAM PIE. Sybil sets her confection on the window ledge and joins Ma reading a magazine on the porch. In irised close-up, we glimpse the ad that catches Sybil's eye: pictures of ballerinas bordering the name MLLE. DANCEABITSKI. Sybil strikes a pose and tiptoes off the porch. This spawns a routine with Joe and Sybil, a pas de deux with the hay bales as backdrop. This odd diversion further develops the pastoral comedy setting that Keaton inaugurated from the beginning, parodying romping nymphs and pseudo-Pans in a forest primeval. Likewise, the impulses that seize Sybil and Joe to twirl down on the farm substantiate their exaggerated cardboard characters. Played against our dimensional hero, this routine will highlight Buster's subtlety by visually juxtaposing him with his buddy. After the brief insert of Luke the Dog

# The Scarecrow

(who is more interested in the pie than the performance), the two separate actions of Joe/Sybil and Buster merge into a third sequence to resolve the film's underlying rivalry. Keaton had similarly joined two unrelated events in *Convict 13* (on the golf course, in the prison) to create a pivot on which the film turned toward resolution.

On its own, however, the choreography between Sybil and Joe represents above all the continual contrasts between the "satellites" and Buster, their "sun." Their silly movements become a blank slate on which Buster writes his reactions. Here, Sybil's prancing is as amateurish to ballet as her golf swings of *Convict 13* are to the U.S. Golf Open. Her partner's girth and coy gestures mock the romantic ideal. Buster's entrance into this tableau clinches Keaton's ridicule of his pet peeve, melodrama. As he enters, he freezes and collapses against the bales, clutching his heart; after a well-timed pause, he flings his arm across his eyes. Buster has commented melodramatically on the cloying scenario enacted by these two unintentional buffoons. Buster is Keaton's spokesman venting his delicious lampoon. His purposeful anguish continues as Sybil uncoils herself from Joe's embrace. Buster turns away and, with a flourish of one arm pointing toward his lonely route, he sulks out.

This has not been Buster's usual vocabulary of reactions. To gesticulate so grandly at romantic disappointment is contrary to the subtle persona of the last two films and clearly signals a deliberate effort to mock. Melodrama was a genre that blended the opposing forces of tragedy and comedy through grand theatrics, remarkable plots, and stereotyped one-dimensional characters.[2] Reviewing his stage career, it is easy to trace Keaton's aversion to melodrama. He delighted in burlesquing tear-jerker melodramas that played on the same bill with his family act. In his biography of Keaton, Blesh writes: "Joe and Buster Keaton helped to kill melodrama. . . . Melodrama acts got down on their knees and begged not to be booked on the same bill with the Three Keatons." Keaton's unhappy experience when he was age eleven, replacing an ailing juvenile of the Fenburg Stock Company in the part of Little Lord Fauntleroy, impacted his attitude toward melodrama. In Keaton's words:

> That infernal part . . . was the longest speaking part in the theatre next to Hamlet. Seventy-five pages . . . and no action.
> About Wednesday matinee I just got too tired. Onstage she was saying, "Here he comes now, as if his little heart would break"— my cue—and I warble "Dearest!" and trip over the center door

fancy and do a face slide onto the stage.

"An accident," I tell Fenberg.

"Oh?" he says.

That night I misjudged a fall onstage and knocked the Tiffany lamp off the center table.

"*Still* an accident?" [Fenburg] asks, with murder in his voice.[3]

Melodrama worked well in silent film, for it thrived on the unspoken. Dialogue via intertitles was florid, but a trademark of melodrama (and considering dualities, perhaps its greatest drawback) was emoting. D. W. Griffith's first four-reeler *Judith of Bethulia* (1913), *Orphans of the Storm* (1922), *Birth of a Nation* (1915; based on Thomas Dixon's novel and a 1906 Broadway melodrama, *The Clansman*), Bible and fantasy epics, and Westerns all included melodramatic episodes.[4] Melodrama was nurtured by the tempo and morality of the era and became outdated as audiences grew more sophisticated and less tolerant. The Roaring Twenties were speeding too quickly past the heavy steps of melodrama. Coincidentally, Keaton joined the stock hero, heroine, and villain as the kindly comic William in the 1940 RKO film of a melodrama *The Villain Still Pursued Her*, based on the 1844 play *The Drunkard; Or the Fallen Saved*.[5] In the play, a standard "delirium tremens" melodrama, the "sturdy Yankee comic of the piece" flings open the door and saves Mary, the faithful wife of the drunk (soon-to-be-reformed) hero Edward, from the villain Cribbs. "[H]e hurls the viper to the floor, denounces him as 'the most contemptible of earth-born creatures,' and thrusts him out the door ['noise of falling downstairs']."[6]

Keaton's spoof of melodrama in *The Scarecrow* is brief but clear. He plays with the visual postures that characterize melodrama at emotionally intense moments. Buster becomes the "suffering hero" and Joe the villain, albeit without real hiss-worthiness about him. Buster's reactions are exaggerated and soon spent. His character abandons his moribund theatrics to return to the filmic reality of transformations. The newest one is thrust upon Buster by Fate, wreaking havoc on his peaceable existence.

When Buster drags himself from the balletic tableau, he encounters Luke the Dog at the empty pie plate, muzzle bathed in cream. The previous seemingly extraneous insert of the dog and pie now launches a confrontation that speaks of Keaton's love for his persona "in conflict with"—here, a conflict derived from the transformation theme of the first reel. Buster calls out "MAD DOG!" In two quick long shots, Luke races around one corner as Buster disappears behind another. Joe and Sybil are aghast; chivalry notwithstanding, Joe makes a hasty solo flight.

A chase scene between man and beast ensues, again a carefully orchestrated ballet atop a four-walled, roofless brick structure with window and door openings; bricks over windows are missing, with planks bridging the gaps. This startling structure figuratively hangs, like limbo, between the well-controlled house and the liberating elysian farmland. Now that Buster is embroiled in Transformation 25 (hungry Luke = mad dog), his tranquility is shattered by his obsessive habit of finding dualities in his surroundings. With a transformation occurring "behind his back" (Luke = mad dog), Buster must participate in a race driven by Fate and his active imagination. His lifestyle of equations has distorted his perception. Accustomed to A = B, Buster automatically thinks Cream = Rabies, forgetting in panic that A and B can also be separate and unequal. Saturated with equations, we too are swayed, easily forgetting the pie cream as Buster flees from a "rabid" dog.

Another duet begins on the "stage" of the eerie brick structure, a dance of stamina and wits. Buster and Luke repeat two rounds of leaping through the right and left front windows. Keaton includes chase scenes that balance the frame as much as they balance the actions, again creating symmetry and humor from the playful manipulation of space. As Buster runs right, Luke zips left from the same doorway. Momentary relief vanishes when Buster thinks he has escaped, only to spot Luke streaking through another opening. In a moment, we are teased into pretending Buster is reprieved and the routine ended; but we sense that it has only just begun, for the chase has not reached a visual or rhythmic climax that satisfies our expectations of comedy. Part of those expectations is fulfilled by Keaton's symmetrical answering shots that capture the essence of the encounters. For example, in medium long shot, Luke looms in the doorway. We cut to Buster sliding through a hole in his hiding place. In the next shot, he crawls out of the hole and plants his feet on rocks on either side; Luke leaps through the hole; Buster crawls back inside; outwitted, Luke follows him. Buster climbs a ladder against a wall, as does Luke.

Curiously, Keaton has begun to intercut a sequence with Joe that, at first, seems to interrupt the chase with unrelated business; but it will be necessary to merge his adventure with Buster's chase, as well as to resurrect the "love interest." Nearly each exchange between Luke and Buster is now punctuated with a shot of Joe approaching, entering, or emerging from a drugstore with medical supplies. By the time his task is complete, these inserts have paced Buster's run, serving as figurative "steps" to the top of the brick structure for the tensest laps of the race. Buster and Luke sprint relentlessly along the walls and leap over the windows. The interruption of Joe placing iodine, dogbite, arnica, and gauze cotton on a curb returns us to yet another expended lap around the roof. These two tactical geniuses, Buster and Luke, run several times in opposite directions along foreground and background walls, hurtling plankless windows, backtracking over the same routes as each approaches the other. Once, Buster sits on the wall and lights a cigarette, waving off Luke who has stopped at a gap, but then leaps over. Melodramatically, Buster tosses the cigarette, throws a kiss, and rolls off backwards into the next shot, which completes his fall to the ground. Positioned within the structure, we see Luke bullet into the foreground, kicking up dust after Buster who, framed by the door, grows small with the distance.

In this race, Keaton quickened the tempo even more by using brief shots of action-reaction that match human and canine wits.[7] Joe's progress at the drugstore marked laps and changed the players' positions each time. The duration of the race was thus emphasized so that we imagined its continuation even while seeing Joe onscreen. Whenever we returned to the race, its pace heightened both by emotional and physical (to the roof top) degrees. A peak by nature implies ascent and descent simultaneously; and so once the race reached the roof, it began to spiral down to the ground, completing a visual highway of routes, corners, and temporary havens.

In a variation on "the chase," Keaton returns us to his magical cottage, balancing the shell of the brick structure with the gadget-filled dwelling. Buster and Luke tumble separately into a window, with each fall bridged by editing between exterior and interior. Then, as we remain stationary in the "multiroom," Luke and Buster tumble through the windows again, as if channeling the energy into the room instead of splitting it between exterior and interior. With each leap out the window, Buster also manipulates one of the preestablished transformations. Leap 1: he knocks down the back of the sofa; leap 2, he uncovers the tub; leap 3, he hops into the tub, pulls it to the wall, and disappears. Outside, he drops into the pond. Inside, Luke slides into the porcine dining room.

Whether furnished or bare, obviously each building has failed to be Buster's haven; his resilience alone propels him unscathed through the race. Removing a plank, hiding in a corner, or escaping through his bathtub/sofa—these actions are only tools by which Buster secures his own refuge. Lest we forget, Joe waves to Buster offscreen, oblivious to the onrushing truck that rockets him into another shot (the driver is Al St. John, Arbuckle's comedian nephew). As the truck passes, Joe begins to bandage his knee.

In the first three short films, there is a discernible softening of the madcap frenzy that was a trademark of slapstick comedy. Keaton surely draws from this heritage for some gags, but his persona is not intended for pure slapstick. He did not believe Arbuckle's early advice about simplistic gags: "They're all twelve-year-olds. That's the mental age of your audience."[8] Arbuckle may have learned this from his experience, but Keaton's nature desired a more cerebral audience. He intuited ways to evoke fascinated amusement through more than slaphappy exertion. For example, Keaton lengthens a single gag narratively by complicated story twists, as well as filmically by crosscutting between actions and providing several audience perspectives of the action.

As we move into the last half of the film, another machine lurks in the fields: the hay-thresher. From the foreground of a long shot, Buster runs toward it with Luke after him and vanishes into another long shot of haystacks. As the hay rolls onto a chute, Buster's legs and head jut out. We cut to a long funnel, stark against the sky, spitting out hay, shirt, trousers, and finally Buster in his underwear, who lands in a haystack. "FRIENDS?" Buster asks of Luke, and they shake. Joe meanwhile hobbles off on crutches as Sybil dances on (a title explains: SHE BELONGED TO THE DANCERS' UNION AND COULDN'T STOP UNTIL THE WHISTLE BLEW). Buster in his BVDs strolls past Sybil who faints into Pop's arms. Buster runs toward the prominent figure in the center of the field—a scarecrow.

The subsequent action of Pop's banging into Joe during the chase has lapsed time, for when we return to the cornfield, Buster is gone. However, after a pause, the scarecrow comes to life (Transformation 26). In straw hat, dark suit, white gloves, and straw cuffs, Buster cautiously dismounts until Pop enters to scout the area. Buster demonstrates his ability to assume the character of his disguise by dangling his arms over the crossbeam and knocking his knees together. Pop scans the field and drinks from a bottle of booze in the scarecrow's back pocket; when he leaves, an amazed Buster also takes a swig. Pop's suspicion was not even related to Buster as scarecrow; the hidden liquor bottle presents the familiar irony of so-near-yet-so-far and insures Buster's identity/transformation for the next sequence, which revolves around his disguise.

Joe, now positioned before the scarecrow, openly gesticulates his love for Sybil. She is shocked when the scarecrow spins from the post, kisses her on the lips, and resumes his stance; she runs breathlessly from the shot as Joe obliviously dries his eyes. Again, Buster's subtlety is made outstanding by the contrast in personalities.[9] Through Joe, we see how well Buster belongs in the silence of his medium. Surely, he howls over his tooth, and his slapshoes scrape the ground as he runs. But silent film nourishes Buster's subtlety, small physique, noiseless existence. On the contrary, Joe's very being bellows; the loudest sounds and largest moves accompany his interpretation. For instance, Joe digs into eating and stuffs his mouth with a whole tomato, while Buster is etiquette-conscious. Joe falls with a resounding thud, while Buster adds distinctive postscripts to each featherweight tumble. Joe exaggerates his love expressions, while Buster less demonstrably but no less passionately confesses them with closed eyes, a touch, and a sigh (unless he is purposely mocking). In any two-shot, Joe's obviousness becomes blinding, while Buster's soft-spoken manners rivet our attention. From the outset, when Sybil's photo was revealed, Buster and Joe point to each other's essence by contrast. In that one shot, we also glimpse Buster's duality. His anger with Joe flares realistically but is tempered by humor. He is dominated by, in conflict with, up against, *but* in control. He responds furiously and placidly with the same regulated intensity. In disguise, however, there is only one mode of behavior: Buster whips into action, knowing the exhilaration of freed emotion in a passionate kiss.

After Sybil's hasty exit, Buster's position on the post allows him to kick Pop and Joe. But his uninhibited revenge, also due to the disguise, backfires when the post falls; nevertheless, he whips into the scarecrow posture *without* the post. The depth of the frame and the field is maximized for visual comedy as Buster thrashes toward us and drops out of sight into the middle of the frame, with Pop and Joe thereafter crossing sideways. In the next long shot, Pop and Joe pounce on a scarecrow—a real one. We cut back to the empty field; Buster cracks its stillness by lunging at us from its midst. We cut to a stream. In an odd gesture reminiscent of the fantasy "tee" in *Convict 13*, Buster tests the water with his slapshoe toe and shivers. He strips off his gloves and walks on hands into the stream as the camera pans with him to the other shore. In the field are constant collisions between Pop and Joe, again punctuating Buster's offscreen progress, for when we return to him, he has reached the opposite shore and runs right out of his slapshoe. This is enough of a distraction for Pop and Joe to spot Buster and begin their own splashy, entangled fording of the stream. This, in turn, creates a respite for Buster to retie his shoe just as Sybil walks in and sees him in a bended-knee position. She smiles adoringly, "THIS IS SO SUDDEN" (Transformation 27: tying shoe = marriage proposal). Unlike Joe, who thrust himself on his knee to request her hand, Buster accidentally falls into the position, and unintentionally materializes the outcome he has longed to achieve. He flies to his feet, looks deeply into her face, and proposes. With a slight lift of his brow and eyes opening as from a faint, he notices the waterlogged pursuers and leads Sybil out.

With the gentler emotions, Buster seems even more noiseless than usual. Love is bewildering, the result and/or beginning of a struggle; it is uncertainty *and* necessity. Keaton's titles that describe this strange phenomenon of life are often bitingly funny when it culminates in marriage (Wedding Bells = Sour Echo, from *One Week*). But in confronting love's duality, Keaton transforms its essence—the magic of romance—into a delicate scene. Here, sunlight caresses Sybil's hair; bushes create a filigree of light and shade. The fortuitous transformation of the bended-knee pose (mundane task of tying a shoe = culmination of one's heart's desire) cancels slapstick and melodrama. In this frozen moment, spoofing falls by the wayside as Keaton yields to the poetry of romance.

Sentiment, however, is reluctantly disturbed since Keaton's overarching objective of comedy must continue. Buster and Sybil approach a Harness Shop, the start of the last major sequence and the setting for more transformations to close the circle of this theme. As Sybil races off on a dark steed, Buster slaps a white horse. It does not move; it is a wooden horse (Transformation 28). At a loading ramp, Buster leaps for Sybil's horse who darts off without him. Pop and Joe enter, announcing to the Harness Shopowner, "HE'S RUNNING AWAY TO GET MARRIED WITH YOUR HORSE." This grammatical twist is one more example of the film's rich "dialogue" and an inkling of the more complex punnery of later films.[10]

The tension of this chase increases as the pursuers follow in a convertible and Buster "borrows" a motorcycle. The chase intensifies by the accumulating variety of vehicles, the brevity of shots, and the multiple directions of movement. The excitement also mounts through the "audible silence" suggested by seeing the vehicles chase one after the other. The pounding hooves give way to the chug of the automobile that rips into the roar of the motorcycle. Our adrenalin races with the sounds we imagine hearing through the carefully edited visuals.

At a road crossing, a minister on a curb is swept up into the motorcycle sidecar as Buster rounds the corner. In a three-shot, Buster notes the clerical collar and looks gratefully up to heaven. He speaks, and the minister stands between Buster and Sybil, pulling a book from his pocket and instructing the couple to join hands as they ride. Crosscutting to the pursuers punctuates the passage of the wedding ceremony, now abbreviated to only key words. "WHERE'S THE RING?" Buster unscrews a nut from the cycle and screws it on Sybil's ring finger (Transformation 29). Cut to two cars running in opposite directions perpendicular to the onrushing convertible. Cut to the conclusion of the ceremony: "—THEN I PRONOUNCE YOU—" They do not notice, as we do in the next long shot, that they are careening toward a stream and are pitched overboard. The dripping minister adds: "—MAN AND WIFE." The intervening visual has acted as the rhythmic pulse connecting the titles.[11] The minister raises his arms over the couple as they hug, cheek to cheek. An iris pauses in closing: Buster spits out a stream of water. The iris closes. THE END.

Once one of the great transformations of anyone's life—marriage—occurs, the "sour echo" begins. We are reminded of a publicity shot of Keaton with a ball and chain around his ankle as his wife Natalie stands beside him armed with a rolling pin. This portrait is poignantly ironic in the aftermath of Keaton's bitter divorce. Early in his blissful marriage, however, Keaton does not hesitate (at least in film) to lacerate the "happy occasion" in visions of a rough life ahead (the 1922 short *My Wife's Relations* is a particularly relentless blow to the institution of marriage). In *The Scarecrow*, the ceremony occurs by chance, is protested by others, becomes a bumpy ride through an unelegant setting with a comical ring, and is capped by Buster's final ungroomly gesture (an editorial?) of spitting out water. The marriage ceremony is transformed into a series of gags, just as melodramatic poses were earlier reduced to visual punch lines. With a desire to satirize, any universal gesture or ritual can be flattened into cardboard. Some rituals are certainly worthy of Keaton's unbridled spoofing.

For Keaton, however, the deeply serious emotions, not the rituals that surround them, deserve subtlety, not satire. These tender or emotionally intense moments register awe and speechlessness. Thus, Buster greets them with small and careful gestures: he simply stares at the wooden horse hampering his escape or the thresher imperiling his life; he clasps his hands after futilely diving off the ramp to join his beloved; he lifts his eyes to heaven at the appearance of the minister making his dream come true. We also recall Buster's hands-on-hips and shrug when his precious house spun in *One Week* or his silent staring at the splinters that used to be his home. In a way, these reactions also reflect the ease and self-composure with which Buster hopes to master his life, just as he mastered his mechanical house. Once more, this is the duality of Buster, the boy and the man. He enjoys his games and his toys, but in his maturity, he understands the necessity of control in order to play well. He can easily be master of strings and trapdoors, but how much more control must Buster exert when meeting the invisible devices of his eternal nemesis, Fate? Without self-control, Fate will kidnap, transform, and demolish his freedom, sweeping him into its jaws. In this film, that dreadful destiny is literal when the thresher swallows him up whole.

The optimism of *The Scarecrow*, however, lies in the fact that the mechanical element here is principally good for Buster. Although the impersonal farm equipment strips him almost bare, his own inventions serve him well. Even when Buster seems to lose control in the field, the disasters become stepping-stones to his goal: mad dog = lost clothes = chase = scarecrow = loose shoe = proposal = marriage. Buster weds Sybil and transforms his life through a forceful "baptism by water" (which, ironically, can be either a cleansing *or* a drowning, however deep one plunges). Transformations can swerve two ways; in the back of Buster's mind, marriage = menace, and so he must ever brace himself.

Still, Keaton named this film *The Scarecrow*, its focus. It is the disguise Buster willingly accepts. Through it, Buster encounters the one fragile experience with no duality: romance. Because it is the title, we acknowledge the scarecrow as the central image of the film. We wait patiently for its appearance; when introduced late in the film, it stands tall and isolated in the cornfield. The scarecrow signifies *only* our hero and his ingenuity. Like melodrama, which is a pitiful shadow of emotion, the scarecrow is only a straw and rag mockery of a person. Buster animates the stick figure with his flesh, blood, and spirit; in so doing, he freely embraces his romance while protected in a perfect disguise. Skirmishes with Fate, machine, animal, and human become insignificant; dualities in home, field, and future are trivial. The sunlight of romance warms a promise of the heart. For Buster, there is no equal.

## Chapter 5

# Neighbors

## (January 1921)

Courtesy of the Academy of Motion Picture Arts and Sciences

*Neighbors* sets Buster's poetry of romance within an optimistic Romeo and Juliet tale. The original name of this short was *Mailbox*, which also evokes a twentieth-century Pyramis and Thisbe wearing porkpie and gingham, passing notes through a barrier to love.[1] This love story, however, leads to marriage, which creates antagonisms of the most acrobatic sort. Keaton's barbs at marriage, women, and, this time, blacks probe the theme of duality that will pervade subsequent films with growing subtlety.

The opening title sighs: THE FLOWER OF LOVE COULD FIND NO MORE RO-MANTIC SPOT IN WHICH TO BLOSSOM THAN IN THIS POET'S DREAM GARDEN. The opening iris reveals the Dream Garden: a tenement yard divided by a tall plank fence. Buster and The Girl (Virginia Fox, later married to Darryl Zanuck, head of Twentieth Century-Fox) appear small in this establishing shot as they lean wistfully on each side of the large fence—even though the door stands wide open, an ironic barrier. As we cut to a medium shot of Buster, a note suddenly pokes through a shoulder-high knothole. I LOVE YOU, the message reads in close-up. After mutual shy peeking, Buster appends his passion to the note: I LOVE YOU 2. As the romance plays out, the parents are introduced: Ma and Pa K (Joe Keaton) and Mr. and Mrs. Joe (Joe Roberts). Each couple interferes with the suspicious correspondence and drives their respective offspring home.

This and the following sequence are fraught with the image of the barrier, which creates comedy from the clashes between humans and objects. The sequences also imply the powerful emotional barriers that can exist in families. While this is the stuff of tragedy, passing through this fence approaches comedy, since the family rivalry is humorously exaggerated. The fence tangibly represents the obstruction created by the feuding parents, although for the lovers, the barrier is symbolically invisible. Its physicality gradually disappears with each of their efforts to surmount the fence. Through persistence (certainly not through the door), Buster and The Girl bound over physical and mental fences. While this bodes well for "true love," reality is a merciless test. Buster as Keeper of the Dream Garden revives long-lost chivalry; however, Keaton as Keeper of the Film pokes fun at Buster's pursuits. The barrier is as real as the dreams that counter it. Unfortunately, the battle of reality versus dream is often weighted toward the more concrete opponent, simply because it is easier to see and feel. Under such battery, dreams can collapse and disappear. Buster's dreams of love and marriage will be continually assaulted by the weapons of argument, distrust, and confusion—all of which the parental role models epitomize with grand agility.

Once Ma K and Joe stand on opposite sides of the fence, Pa K and Mrs. Joe enter in respective symmetrical balance. Pa K is aghast at his wife scrutinizing the knothole; Joe passes the note back. Thinking his wife is the recipient, he hotly returns the note just as Mrs. Joe swipes it and staggers at its import. The love note wrings the worst from each party through suspicion of infidelity and lifelong lack of affection. Buster and The Girl rise above these hostilities—literally, for she calls to Buster from a third-floor window. He passes unnoticed through the fence door to her building, where he jacknifes himself smoothly up to and into her window. We cut to the darkened hallway as Buster croons to The Girl before Joe suddenly lunges at him. The family feud has not been restricted to the yards; when true love threatens, the parents obviously keep a strict lookout even if they are in the midst of argument. In three shots, we follow Buster's daring escape: (1) as he travels across the laundry line into the third-floor window of his building; (2) interior shot, as he careens down the banister out the second-floor window; (3) exterior shot again, as he travels the laundry line into the opposite window and Joe. Buster is like a Knight in Shining Armor who has traveled far through treacherous lands to save the Damsel in the Tower; he also knows the Four-Headed Dragon (parents) lurks not far from him. Perhaps for Buster, part of what makes his Quest of Woman so precious is that the journey is fraught with danger. Buster endures the first of such dangers as Joe clothespins the Poet by his slapshoe toes to the laundry line and tugs him over to Pa K who is industriously beating a carpet.

This routine shows Keaton's impressive use of a set as an integral part of his routine.[2] Ground-level props (fence, knothole) develop the plot and establish theme and complications. The complications expand upward emotionally and physically—emotionally *because of* the physical upward action that the routine follows. The action opens to the upper floors of the tenement buildings, which in fact become props themselves. This setting is home for a phenomenon that Walter Kerr has dubbed "The Keaton Curve," illustrated by Buster's circuitous route to escape Fate, only to return innocently and promptly to it.[3] Buster retreats from Joe and returns to him on the laundry line; although it was a natural reaction, Buster really should never have tried leaving! This escape/no-escape dilemma, the fateful "curve," will makes its rounds in future sequences as well. The curve implies motion, the image of a boomerang. The curve creates a powerful illusion paralleling Keaton's own evolving outlook on life, as glimpsed in his first three short films. As lovely as a circle is, symbol of unity and wholeness, it is frustratingly endless. The "vicious cycle" fastens Buster to its unending track.

The curve functions in the next major sequence, offering as well a timely and significant issue in social and film history. Buster has now traded places with the rug. Propelled by the whack from Pa K's rug beater, Buster completes a full revolution around the line, attached only by his shoes. Pa K unclips Buster who drops into a barrel of water. As Pa K lifts the bottomless barrel, Buster's head sinks into the mud. Buster's vocabulary of leg movements is not slapstick gesticulation but a rhythmic, repetitive language: cycling; slow jerks; knee-folding; a final V pose with wiggling toes, like vibrating dots at the end of exclamation points. Pa K calls out, "ARE YOU COMFORTABLE?" The legs shake a reply. Pa K twists Buster's legs as if trying a safe combination. Joe announces: "I KNOW A BETTER WAY THAN THAT TO BREAK HIS NECK." Pa retorts with a jot of paternal devotion: "HE'S MY SON AND I'LL BREAK HIS NECK ANY WAY I PLEASE." After a half-twist, Pa K unplugs Buster. In a startling close-up, Buster raises his wide-eyed, mud-blackened head. Buster now converts the fence into an implement of warfare; with a broom, he whacks a dark hat, much like Joe's bowler, bobbing over the barricade. We cut to Joe's yard to find the owner of the hat is a cop. In another startling close-up, we see Buster's shocked black face all the darker against the bright sky, looking down at the "enemy." At the side, Buster cleans his face on laundry and looks on as the cop arrests a passing black man, dressed similarly to Buster. Distracted by four boys shooting craps, the arresting cop mistakenly carts off another officer as the black man runs into a doorway. This blackening routine spawns a subroutine involving another means of disguise, paint. Ma K discovers the dirty laundry and blames the painter above her. She calls her son, sneaking behind a sheet, to reprimand the painter who drops a full bucket on Buster's head in reply, in fulfillment of the curve. Once again, Buster's face is blackened; seeing this suspicious color again, the returning cop leads him away. The following diversionary gag of Buster smacking into a lamppost is slapstick relief before the next disturbing illusion.

As the two men are panned along a lengthy street, Buster vigorously mops one side of his face with a handkerchief. In a cutaway, the black man throws a kiss to Buster from over a fence, yet another barrier that now represents both separation and protection. The cop rings on a station phone while a mind-boggling transformation occurs around the corner. A close-up shows Buster's face bisected, half wiped white, the other half still black. He turns his head toward the offscreen cop, exposing the white side, then turns front and feels his face, as if touching the illusion. When the cop looks up, Buster spins to reveal the white side of his face, then turns to become black again. The cop recoils, allowing Buster to run out of the frame. The cop passes a telephone pole from which Buster descends. Before another cop, he stirs up a riotous leg dance, adding behavioral madness to his facial lunacy.

Once more, Keaton demonstrates the ineptitude of his authority figures. Outside yet another fence painted GRANDSTAND 50¢, Buster peers into a knothole, seen through a slatted masking device; cutaway to a ball game and title, "BABE RUTH IS AT BAT!" The cop is flattened by a homerun ball. A third cop leads Buster past a fruit stand where he pilfers a banana. As the cop slips on the peel, Buster jumps unseen into a laundry basket wheeled in by a heavy black woman. As she meets her family, a sheet rises eerily in the basket. The terrified family flee down an alley in awkward acceleration. Buster removes the sheet and the remaining paint from his face.

Keaton derived these "darky jokes" (and others to surface in future shorts and features, particularly *College* [1927]) from a form of racism that film critic Andrew Sarris has called "but one symptom of the most uninhibited American film art since D. W. Griffith's."[4] In the late 1800s, gifted black performers on the stage had to adapt their mannerisms to the preset mold of the shuffling, slow-witted, dialect-drawling Negro. The minstrel show, which will constitute a major and technically superb sequence in the short *The Playhouse* (1921), was in fact a burlesque of Negro life in the South. White entertainers applied burnt cork to blacken their faces, except for exaggerated outlines around mouths and eyes. Indignities in comedy and drama since the inception of story films included white actors in blackface, with blacks in subordinate roles.[5] A 1909 Edison comedy *Drawing the Color Line* and a 1913 Pathe comedy *Mixed Colors* based their humor on the premise that whites who turn "black" with paint immediately lose their public standing or become suspect in the eyes of authority. According to Daniel Leah, one reviewer for the trade publication *Moving Picture World* claimed "[*Drawing the Color Line*] shows graphically how merely putting a little black on a man's face changes status . . . [the] subject is one that never fails to arouse much merriment." A 1913 reviewer noted how "there have been more jokes perpetuated on the colored race than on any others."[6]

The tortured route of blacks in films is clear in *Neighbors*, where Keaton's familiarity with racism in vaudeville, minstrel shows, and on screen licensed him to center an otherwise innocuous routine on race (already hinted at in *Convict 13* with the black caddy). Stereotyping in *Neighbors* first occurs with Buster's accidentally mud-blackened, wide-eyed face, with each feature carefully covered. The color is further darkened by its stark presence against the light sky. The joke is meant to be purely visual as Buster's face is presented in a series of close-ups. The forced nature of the gag is apparent because the face is not streaked with mud but is evenly painted, and then, by "coincidence," we meet a black passerby for contrast. The cop suspects the black man because he has seen one black face over the fence and, to him, all black faces look alike. Once the mistaken identity due to mixed colors is introduced, the routine expands to include stereotype slurs with the "mammy," the naive fear of the supernatural, and the quivering, gaping, comically accelerated flight of the family.

Unlike his deliberate impersonation of a wide-eyed shuffling Negro in *College* to guarantee himself a waiter's job, Buster here presents an accidental mix-up in a tenement setting inhabited by blacks and whites. Both groups are linked by their impoverished condition, but a barrier still exists between them. The powerful fence that bisects the opening shot, initially a barrier to love, now seems an obstacle between all groups. A fence separates Buster from the ball game; the black man peers over his side of the protecting-yet-separating fence. Working against an invisible barrier, the black woman who helps the white cop is brusquely pushed aside. Nevertheless, as in *Convict 13*, the consequences of mistaken identity are ultimately suffered by Buster alone, whether black, white, or black-and-white.

Keaton uses blacks as a springboard for his complex gags, much as he uses his good-natured, dim-witted females or his fumbling men-in-blue as warm-ups to his jokes. "Becoming black" allows Keaton to create a brief, almost hallucinatory effect that perpetuates the barrier motif of *Neighbors*. The gag of his bisected face is propelled in three consecutive shots: (1) medium shot, Buster wipes half-face while around the corner; (2) close-up of the evenly bisected face as he hatches his plan; and (3) long shot, Buster spins to expose black and white sides. By dividing his face, Buster has considered his options: remaining black would incarcerate him; returning to white would tempt the Fate-curve to blacken him again; being *both* insures distraction for escape. The ultimate issue for Keaton is illusion and control. But for today's audience, the human issue persists because of the mockery of race. It haunts the ingenious gag while it hypnotizes. The illusion is tainted with the realization that humor is derived from the shock of crossing color lines in public.

When Buster returns to his familiar self and milieu, he is reintroduced to us in scientific terms, unlike his earlier romantic description: THAT AF-

TERNOON THE YOUNG INVENTOR TRIES HIS PATENT FLY-SWATTER. Buster's invention is a plank nailed to the top frame of the fence door that balances into a potential seesaw; he demonstrates by pushing the door, causing the plank to swat his back. Buster raps a snoozing Joe on the forehead with a hammer. Joe: "COME IN!" Buster flings a trash can lid over the fence, compelling Joe to pursue and be swatted through the door. Buster perches on the fence behind a dress on the line. A fourth mistaken identity occurs (after those of spouses = rivals, Buster = carpet, Buster = black): now Pa K = swatter, when Joe finds him with the rug beater. In long shot to record simultaneous action in both yards, Buster nervously spots a cop below the plank. Joe's reentry into his yard activates the plank to hit both the cop and Pa K. Shots of the swinging plank and a growing crowd of cops are intercut with long shots and cutaways of Buster's innocent peeks. A cop and Joe finally discover Buster on the fence. Buster leaps onto the swatter, one end launching Pa K into an incredible arc over the fence.

Buster's apparent escape into Joe's building proves to be an illusion when the cop sees the shadow of a telephone pole by the fence looming on the ground. The cop directs his billy club along the shadow that becomes the pole itself; the camera tilts up to find Buster seated at the top of the pole, swinging his legs. The earlier suggestion of Buster escaping up a telephone pole is finally actualized in a gag executed through camera movement (tilt), shadows, and angles. Through this, Keaton accomplishes a triple objective: he maintains the ascending movement of the billy club along the shadow; he creates a sight gag of Buster on the pole; he "illusions/disillusions" us, for Buster is not indoors, as we thought, but above everyone. After catching a rock thrown by the cop, Buster fastens his clip-on tie to the cable. In a wider shot, Buster glides down the slope and out behind Joe's building. He strolls into a waiting paddy wagon already holding both sets of parents. His entry is revealed by a camera pan that balances the previous tilting. As much as we are fooled, the pan creates more of a surprise for Buster since, once again, his freedom through ingenuity is thwarted by the curve.

The dormant war, broiling in the confines of a paddy wagon, explodes in a more ironic setting, as the title indicates: THEY ARE GOING TO HAVE PEACE EVEN IF THEY HAVE TO GO TO COURT AND FIGHT FOR IT. The prenuptials and wedding are presented with a large number of rapid-fire, biting, argumentative titles. Buster speaks to the fidgety Judge: "HER FATHER'S ABUSED HER LONG ENOUGH—NOW I WANT TO MARRY HER AND TAKE HER HOME TO MY FATHER." The Judge orders the fathers: "SIGN THIS BOND TO KEEP THE PEACE."

# Neighbors

Joe does so, with a fling of ink into Pa K's eye. Buster and The Girl, sandwiched between the parents, announce: "WE'RE GOING TO GET MARRIED." The Judge quells the ensuing discord, the parents part reluctantly, Sybil flings a kiss to the Judge who drops behind his desk, and the happy couple run toward us in a closing iris.

Keaton's titles skewer the institution of marriage: AFTER GOING TO COURT TO END THEIR TROUBLES, THEY HAVE A WEDDING TO START MORE. A close view of the gift table (with a sign WEDDING PRESENTS—HANDS OFF!) reveals coffee cups, clock, rolling pin, tie, funnel, horseshoe, flowers, and the book HOW TO BOX BY JIM CORBETT. We realize that the civil conversation of four relatives is ensured by the bats, brick, and crowbar they hold behind their backs. An iris pauses on the bride in a frilly veil, then opens to shatter the romantic image by revealing her throne to be a garbage can. Momentary diversion with an irrelevant timely reference further debases the solemn occasion. Joe points to a sling on Pa K's arm: "WHAT HAPPENED TO YOU?" Pa: "I BOUGHT A FORD."

The wistful sigh of The Girl awaiting her special moment could echo the sigh that Keaton's heroines might have felt playing opposite such a powerful force. Clearly seen from Sybil Seeley's early offerings, the female lead is hardly necessary, but becomes so for Buster when playing opposite him. In *Neighbors*, The Girl is the giant sponge absorbing affection, parental scolding, and daring rescues. When Buster dominates, she becomes the sounding board for any response he needs to make.

> It did not worry Keaton that his leading ladies were inconsequential:
>
> "The cast for our two-reelers was always small. There were usually but three principals—the villain, myself, and the girl, and she was never important. She was there so the villain and I would have something to fight about.
>
> "The leading lady had to be fairly good-looking and it helped some if she had a little acting ability. As far as I was concerned I didn't insist that she have a sense of humor. There was always the danger that such a girl would laugh at a gag in the middle of a scene, which meant ruining it and having to remake it."[7]

Keaton needed a "durable leading lady. . . . To Buster a thing of beauty was not a joy forever if it folded under a beating. . . . Sybil Sealey [*sic*] . . . proved a little fragile. Then he found Virginia Fox [who] was a beauty who could give mileage."[8] Years later, Keaton added in an interview with Penelope Gilliatt that he "needed romantic heroines; big girls with remote expressions and plummy thighs. . . . it was nice if they weren't too stupid."[9]

Such a heroine would ensure a more loving marriage for Buster than the matriarchs of *Neighbors*, who make the husbands even more sour than they already are. Ma and Pa K, and Joe and Mrs. Joe, have long abandoned affection for each other as well as for their neighbors; attempts to feel any warmth bring out their worst. At the end of the note-exchange sequence, calm has hesitantly fallen and the parties retreat to their corners. The word "marriage" triggers high anxiety to anyone already ensnared, not only because they will be legally forced to endure in-laws but because the horrible tradition is being perpetuated. Those giving wedding presents also sense doom: if the horseshoe cannot bring luck, the how-to-box book and rolling pin can provide self-defense. Pugilistic terms spring up in Keaton's titles referring to union: THEY ARE GOING TO HAVE PEACE EVEN IF THEY HAVE TO GO TO COURT AND FIGHT FOR IT; AFTER GOING TO COURT TO END THEIR TROUBLES, THEY HAVE A WEDDING . . . ; "HER FATHER'S ABUSED HER LONG ENOUGH—NOW I WANT TO MARRY HER . . . " Keaton questioned marriage in *One Week*, and the trend persists. A curious fan magazine item presented Keaton's "personal" views on marriage at the time of his own wedding with Natalie Talmadge. Along with the picture of his ball and chain and her rolling pin, the article "Before and After Taking" by "Mr. Natalie Talmadge" lists ironies that eventually culminated in the harsh reality of divorce for Keaton:

*Before*:      June 14, 1920
I am single and proud of it.
Many a grand love affair is
  spoiled by marriage.
The sound of wedding bells
  always makes me sad.
A friend of mine who runs a
  funeral parlor in Hollywood
  told me he thinks married
  men make the best pallbearers.
I think he's right.
And I am going to stay single.

*After*:      June 15, 1921
Marriage is ethereal.
Why, after you're married you
  never have to worry about
  making up your mind. Such
  things are done for you.
That coffee! Those hot cakes!
  Biscuits! You can take those
  exclamation points any way
  you like.
I wouldn't be single for
  anything in the world.[10]

# Neighbors

The Girl's pose on the garbage can is an extension of her home in a tenement, but it also further devalues her "happiest hour" pictorially. The Girl, however pea-brained, is still a product of her physical and emotional home. Her metal perch turns out to be a comfortable image for her, a comic image for the film, and a satirical afterimage for us. Buster has proven, however, that he can love a woman "2" much and will succumb to the formality of marriage. As Knight Errant, this is, after all, the goal of his Quest—or has it only been a windmill?

Buster's kin help him dress for the wedding as Mrs. Joe announces to Ma K: "GET THE GROOM, THE BRIDE'S OUT IN THE ALLEY." Buster brushes his trousers, which are twice his waist size (even with preparation, nothing about this occasion fits well). In irised close-up, the back suspenders pop their buttons as Buster stretches them, and as he trips down the stairs, he fastens his pants to his shirt with a tie clip. In the parlor, he announces: "IN GIVING UP SINGLE LIFE, I FEEL I'M LOSING SOMETHING—" The pants appropriately fall. We cut away to The Girl who jumps off her garbage can and marches across the yard.

The ensuing wedding becomes an orchestrated comedy routine triggered by the Judge's question, "WHERE'S THE RING?" Buster's search through his pockets for the ring alternates with rapid-fire groping for his falling trousers. As Buster hands over the ring, he slips out the Judge's belt. The Judge notices his own fallen pants and retrieves the belt from Buster, whose pants drop again. The pants routine, precisely executed in long shot, becomes a curveball from the gods: each retrieval leads to an inevitable fall. Human intervention from Pa K: he hands Buster a padlock to secure his pants to his jacket. Odd that a padlock should surface at a wedding, much like the hammer on a honeymoon; however, the wedding takes place in a tenement where padlocks mean security, and of course, it is an appropriate device to lock the "ball and chain." These catastrophes fuel the next blast that mercifully halts the ceremony. Joe seizes the ring, which is identified as "STRAIGHT FROM WOOLWORTH'S." A close-up of Joe's hand dissolves to the words ACME 5 AND 10¢ titled over a still life of crockery, then back to Joe's hand squeezing the ring into a little stick. The wedding is terminated and the children separated anew.

To answer his damsel's cry again from the third-floor window ("FATHER'S WATCHING. COME GET ME."), Buster and two friends each step out of their three respective windows to form a human totem pole. Cut to view the whole yard from the foreground, where we remain for this half of the gag. The trio speeds to The Girl's building and separates into three matching windows, then speeds back to Buster's building, reforming the pole for two missions: to fetch a trunk, and then for Buster to drape The Girl over his shoulder. For a variation within this repetitive gag, Buster waves the totem pole back inside the building as Joe or Pa K step into the yard; with a well-timed pause, the pole reforms and dashes around the building. We cut ahead to a three-level scaffold; without breaking speed, each man separates to race along his respective platform and reunite on each other's shoulders. The totem pole is gradually leveled by two obstacles it meets in its run, until the pole and the focus narrow to the only object of interest, Buster and The Girl. First, they run into a laundry line where the middle man folds over the rope; Buster and The Girl drop smoothly onto the low man's shoulders. Next, the bottom man plummets into a sidewalk opening; Buster seamlessly races on with The Girl on his back. Finally, Buster slides her down a chute; cut to interior, they land in a cellar next to the Judge shoveling coal into his furnace. At Buster's request, the Judge concludes the ceremony and resumes shoveling as the couple rock in each other's arms. Iris closes. THE END.

The continual downward movement of the film actually started with the pants-dropping during the marriage ceremony, followed by the totem pole falling from three men to one man and the descent into the cellar. This is in contrast to the rather "uplifting" movement of the first half of the film, in which Buster rises (three floors) to save his romantic interest. Obviously, marriage in Buster's family can only descend into a union that wreaks havoc even on the best of its volunteers. Buster has sought to escape the "in-laws" and their barriers throughout the film. Significantly, the ultimate escape—the marriage ceremony—occurs in the setting it deserves: underground, below the barrier, intimate, away from prying eyes, but nonetheless uncomfortable. Buster's robust chivalry, balanced by his quiet expressions of affection, help to make romance endure, as it did in *The Scarecrow*. The Girl is childlike and vulnerable enough to encourage his manly strength, and Buster croons and protectively rocks her like the child she is. This may well be enough to prompt the illusion of a lifelong marriage.

The knothole has been the powerful link to their innocence from the start. In a more cynical moment, however, confronted with the prospect of a bleak marriage, Buster reflects that a knothole is better used for a view of a ball game. His bachelor speech ("IN GIVING UP SINGLE LIFE, I FEEL I'M LOSING SOMETHING—") is not only the perfect cue for the chaotic pants routine but a potent commentary on the impending marriage. Marriage is a main event (like a boxing match), full of frenzied movement, whereas romance is an idyllic passage that creeps up shyly and tenderly and lingers in the heart. Marriage is a sudden catalyst that transforms and deprives. Ironically, the valiant characteristics that make the male and female so attractive to each other in the passage of romance reverse and distort themselves after marriage. The woman turns into a nag, losing her vulnerability and gaining the upper hand; her Knight has performed his duty to save her from one Dragon-family and she is free to begin her own. When Buster is a married man in future shorts, particularly *My Wife's Relations*, the romance is noticeably missing; if he has the nerve to be the head of the house, his wife is the neck turning the head at her pleasure (in a rather machinelike fashion to boot). His shining armor has somehow been traded for tarnished chain mail when he was not looking. In *Neighbors*, Buster indubitably senses this impending doom, if only because he has lived with a loveless couple in the form of Ma and Pa K. He reveals this foreboding even in the midst of his daring finale rescue through a significant nonverbal gesture. He carries The Girl to safety by slinging her over his shoulder; it is a heroic way to carry her, but it is also like dealing with a sack of potatoes.

The Girl—any girl—may well be both Buster's illusion and disillusion. On the heels of *The Scarecrow*, which revolved around the concrete duality of objects and people, *Neighbors* consists of a more intangible duality. Illusion reaches its surrealistic peak when duality appears on Buster's face, echoing not only the barrier within the Dream Garden but the invisible barriers within race, sex, environment, upbringing, and attitude. Keaton naturally skims the surface of these issues for the comic and filmic effects on Buster's rivals: thus, the black/white illusion for the cop; the swatting/invisible-opponent illusion for Joe. At times, we are as disillusioned as the characters themselves: we and the cop think that Buster is gone when he has only just skittled up a pole; or we think that he has entered a building when he is up another pole. Although Buster seems most in control when he is alone, that too is an illusion because of the inevitable curveballs of Fate. The only ball that briefly worked to his advantage was Babe Ruth's. The curveball invites frustration, but Buster does not dwell on it, allowing us instead to laugh and concoct the illusion of victory.

Because we find that marriage is the core of *Neighbors*, and not romance, which we expected from the first title, we reluctantly become set to have our illusions shattered repeatedly. And the string of illusions continues, from when the sheltering iris reveals the irony of the Dream Garden right through the illusion of probable disaster for Buster and The Girl. We suspect the wedding will take place, if only as an expectation of the comic plot, but our first disillusions anticipate more. Illusion/disillusion interweave; when one seems victorious, the opposite replaces it soon thereafter. Just as the wedding ring is reduced to a worthless stick, our illusion of the institution it symbolizes dissolves into coal. Still, the lovebirds persist by clinging to their illusion of a brighter future and let us do the same.

The curve works once more for Buster when it returns him to the Judge. He deserves this favor for he has worked hard to preserve the Dream Garden through his one and only personal barrier: his stone-faced ingenuity. He safeguards his inner core behind this masklike barrier when it is challenged by Reality and Fate. With romance goading him on, Buster creates illusions (the swatter, black/white face) and controls them even as they slip away. When curveballs are fired, Buster throws them back. Dexterously, he maintains the greatest illusion of all: the Dream Garden. It exists within Buster, and it seems no one else in his world cares but him.

## Chapter 6

# The Haunted House

### (February 1921)

Courtesy of the Academy of Motion Picture Arts and Sciences

*The Haunted House* has been considered one of Keaton's least-successful shorts. Of the nineteen short films, this one most resembles two distinct one-reelers joined by thin threads. Yet within its separate halves, and despite its flaws, cinematic and comedic development is complex. Characters are choreographed in a blend of slapstick and sophistication. The wordplay of the titles is at its cleverest. Reminiscent of the gags in *One Week*, some routines of *The Haunted House* follow visual peak-and-decline curves. Editing attains a new dimension in Keaton's experiment with illusion and time. In this setting of mystery, Keaton manifests phantasms of depth within a flat world.

WALL STREET    THE PALATIAL PARKING PLACE OF THE BULL AND THE BEAR— MOSTLY THE BULL. The deliberate dart, a Keaton trademark, has now veered from marriage to high finance. He satirizes an honored symbol of the financial world with a sarcastically mundane interpretation. NEW YORK IS NOT THE ONLY TOWN THAT HAS ITS MASTER MIND OF FINANCE.[1] Keaton now moves from a wide sphere (New York) into an increasingly narrow one to reach his focus (Buster, of course) like sliding from the broad edge of a funnel into its stem. The macrocosm is reduced to an unnamed town, home of the "master mind" who next appears in a literal "parking place" to refer back to the opening analogy. An iris opens on Buster with hat, cane, and boutonniere, who steps from a chauffeur-driven car and slips off the running board. He approaches the 1st National Bank (a door notice reads OPEN FROM 9 A.M. UNTIL 3 P.M.). With a bottle opener, Buster pops off a cylinder cap, exposing the keyhole on which he uses a real key. We recognize clearly that Keaton's poison dart is both verbal and visual: Buster's executive step from the car and his unique bank-opening deflates our preconceived image of a high financier. Red-taped access and layers of security are satirized by un-"capping" the keyhole. Burrowing deeper into his symbolic funnel, Keaton presents a third minimizing: Buster is really a bank teller, for inside he clambers through the teller's window over the counter. We know from Keaton's sarcasm that Buster's milieu will continue to contradict itself. By the vault door with the BURGLAR PROOF TIME LOCK, Buster attaches his cane upside down to the wall and hangs his hat on the hook. This absurd cane, attached by no apparent means, is the first effort to animate the static bank and extend the "haunted house" atmosphere that will dominate the second reel.

The scene fades to an irised long shot of a dapper Joe and a shorter man passing through a draped doorway by a high staircase. THE BANK CASHIER AND HIS BAND OF COUNTERFEITERS HAVE A STRONG REASON FOR MAKING PEOPLE BELIEVE THIS HOUSE IS HAUNTED. The shot of the two men dissolves to an earlier occasion. For the first time, Keaton employs a significant number of dissolves in a brief sequence to suggest flashback. Time lapse is also depicted by the reversed positions of Joe and his accomplice, standing before a half-moon wall gadget with a lever between the words

UP and DOWN. Joe explains, "I'LL SHOW YOU WHAT WOULD HAPPEN IF THE POLICE CAME." In a long shot, nine cops tumble down a staircase that has collapsed after Joe pulls the DOWN lever in a cutaway shot. A dissolve returns us to the present time, followed by an exterior of the three-story "haunted" mansion. To shorten distance and exaggerate the enormity of the house (which is crucial to later action), we dissolve for the last time to Joe passing through the gate, fingering his mustache with villainy.

Back at 1st National, a pretty customer hands Buster a check. In a two-shot profile of the girl with a full view of our hero, Buster regretfully indicates the clock that in close-up reads 8:01. "THE TIME CLOCK DOESN'T OPEN TILL NINE O'CLOCK," he adds. She leans persuasively closer and he suddenly decides to head for the vault. In long shot, Buster teeters on a stool to open the clock cover; in close-up, he reaches *through* the glass-less cover and sets the hands to 9:00. Once again, Keaton plays with the fantastic potential of the static bank, intruding into its flatness to provide depth where none seemingly exists—leading us to believe that the cover is glass, then fooling us. Abruptly, the vault door flies open, knocking Buster over. He then emerges from the vault with a pile of dollar bills, which he flips at his ear; after a pause, he nods—another mockery of "efficient" banking.

Returning to the two-shot, Buster hands his lovely customer a pen. Close-up of her signature: DOROTHY CASSILL   MAIN 234. In two-shot, Buster stamps the check, nodding as she leaves the frame before pulling out his "little black book." We have always been visually routed to his reaction even though the girl occupies half of the two-shot. She is a directional arrow to Buster, who is further emphasized by the window frame. When the girl leaves, we linger on Buster's gesture of noting future "transactions" by jotting down her name and number. Whenever the two-shot is exhausted for attention, Keaton cuts to gags developing on another level—for example, long shot, Buster at the vault; close-up, clock; long shot, Buster knocked over, then "counting" money. We return to Buster directly framed by the window and indirectly by the girl. To explain the black book, we cut to her signature, clarifying Buster's gesture and providing another break from a static shot.[2]

Wall Street is further reduced to Tiny Town in Keaton's next blatant, minimizing title: ALTHOUGH IT'S A SMALL BANK IT HAS A PRESIDENT AND ALTHOUGH HE IS A SMALL MAN HE HAS A DAUGHTER. This nuance-laden title challenges our belief that a small bank could have a president (much less

Buster as high financier); in the next breath, we wonder at how "a small man" could even have a daughter. The "small" president, however, is not short on observation. Joe bursts into the office, bowing to the president's daughter (Virginia Fox) who leaves in a huff and approaches Buster who gazes intently at her. Meanwhile, the president scrutinizes a bill: "I WONDER WHO PUT COUNTERFEIT MONEY IN THE BANK—I'LL ASK THE POLICE." Joe filches the money and exits.

Four men line up at Buster's window as he accepts a note from the first man. Buster dabs his fingers on a sponge and hands money to the first two customers. Through different shots, the editing "funnels" our concentration from four men and Buster, to two men and Buster, to Buster alone. He next unintentionally dabs a glue pot, beginning the prolonged business of discarding bills that stick to his hands. His familiar physical vocabulary enhances his otherwise slapstick moves: he plucks off a bill and stares at it; he applies his slapshoe to free his hands of the currency, then picks at his papered sole. Buster's dilemma spreads from hands to feet, and laterally outward to the money drawer, then to the four men as the sticky money passes down the line. The opening shot of this sequence returns full circle with a frenetic dance: the four men wave their money-plastered hands in choreographed synchrony. The last shot of this sequence places us in the "stem" of the funnel with an aftergag: Buster runs his fingers through his hair and his hand sticks to his head.

Once the gag peaks with the cast's gymnastics, it pauses, but inertia never sets in. Instead, the routine is renewed when Joe summons a janitor to clean up. The janitor sits to gather the sticky money; after a cutaway in which Buster snips off a lock of hair to free his hand, we return to find the janitor is stuck to the floor. Buster enters with a kettle of hot water and knocks out the janitor to pour the water under him. As the janitor eventually stumbles out of the frame, we think the routine is concluded when, in fact, the sticky money is spreading more deeply into the bank via a female and a male (Eddie Cline, Keaton's codirector) customer. The janitor bows to her, adhering himself to Cline's suit in the process. We interrupt for Buster's personal aside to bring the hot-water gag full circle: he stiffens himself with a mallet blow before applying water on his hand, then snaps his fingers in his own face to revive. Buster then snips apart the men's pants with shears; the woman faints at seeing Cline's underwear. Even though each gag (hot water, pants snipping) resolves its own scene (with small peak-and-decline curves necessary to telling a good "story"), the whole glued-money routine, with its many embedded gags, is still not over. Buster's sticky situation must somehow tie in with the counterfeiters waiting in the wings.

As Joe and four cronies plot outside the bank, Buster thrusts his sticky hands into his pockets. Next, to emphasize Buster's reactions, a robber's hand suddenly points a gun at him through the window, serving as another directional arrow. Trying to "stick-'em-up," Buster flies onto his back since now he is fastened securely to his pockets. Buster yanks his arms up, pulling out the insides of his pockets and staring at these thumbless "mittens." His harmless habit of stuffing hands in pockets has now finally trapped him in an hour of need. Like the "adhesive cane" fastened to the wall, the bank's static setting now contains the "adhesiveness of an image so flat everything in it must become stuck together," according to Kerr.[3] The glued-money routine has basically manipulated space and time, which of course was Buster's objective when he controlled time through the glass-less clock. Kerr calls the glued-money a "regulation gag"; such slapstick nonsense was a staple in most comedies, with dough, tape, flypaper, molasses, or glue as the medium.[4] The sequence may have been inspired by *The Butcher Boy* (1917), in which Buster drops a coin into a molasses tin and Arbuckle applies boiling water on him, following with a flour fight. Into these "regulation gags," however, Keaton inserts his own ingenuity. The glued-money travels through space into all directions. Flat money becomes crumpled balls filling the set; lateral movements become diagonal dances of panic. Pacing is equally controlled through the editing: the number of shots increases as we cut between Buster and the four men while the mess accumulates. Thanks to Buster, the flat environment is well rounded.

Winding up the sticky-money routine, three robbers try bagging the wadded money. We see Buster through the teller's window pulling off his mittens with his teeth. He notices the guns on the ledge, takes the left gun with his right hand and the right gun with his left, and fires one. In a series of cuts, Buster steps through his window as the president enters and Joe shows him the fake money with feigned concern. As in *Convict 13*, Buster's innocence turns against him with a curveball, and the sticky finger of Fate points to him as guilty. Although innocent, his escape (his impulse to survive) reinforces his assumed guilt. But the entrapment suggested by the prolonged glue routine is renewed, as the vault door closes on his jacket tail and traps him again. Ruefully observing that it is 3:00 P.M. (and the door will not open until 9:00 A.M.), Buster resigns to hang by his jacket at a 45-degree angle to the door. On some level, he must feel this is retribution, deserved because of his pretense at high finance and his failure at work. Besides, he cannot reach the glass-less clock to move time forward. Iris closes.

The glue routine has developed the main theme, which is tinged with Keaton's sarcasm: that Buster is fastened, glued, framed, trapped in the home of The Bull. Keaton has molded this subconscious understanding from the very start of the film. We first learn tangentially of the bank's hours in a notice at the entrance; the sign is obvious, yet subliminal in the landscape and never intrudes on Buster's actions. The vault door is next introduced with a burglarproof time lock, background information absorbed into our visual storehouse. Keaton also strengthens the vault gag with Buster's announcement to Miss Cassill that the vault does not open until nine. Buster manipulates physical time to impress a pretty customer, simultaneously suggesting the solution to his entrapment. Thus, the vault gag has been carefully layered from the beginning of the film, although its main business does not conclude until nearly halfway through the film. In addition, Buster's entrapment continually echoes the sarcasm of the opening titles: the "master mind" now is a victim of high finance, so encumbered by the logical-illogic of his environment that he cannot think of escaping by simply removing his jacket.

We fall abruptly into the second half of the short with what seems a remotely related event. THAT NIGHT THE DAREDEVIL OPERA COMPANY WAS EXECUTING "FAUST"—AND HE DESERVED IT. After an opening iris, Diva, Faust, and Devil are introduced in the throes of their silent arias. Alternating long shots and close-ups of falling scenery, tumbles offstage, panicked emoting, and cabbage attacks by the audience, we follow the troupe out the stage door. We revisit our hero at the bank to witness his liberation. The bank's verbal "sense-nonsense" is summarized again in a title recalling the convoluted reasoning of *The Scarecrow*: AFTER SEARCHING EVERYWHERE ELSE THE POLICE FOUND HIM WHERE HE WAS. The sheriff, two deputies, and Joe cluster around Buster now asleep at the same 45-degree angle at which we left him. Joe turns the clock to 9:00 (he knows the time trick too), the door swings open, and Buster falls forward. Given such a "small" bank, it makes perfect nonsense that the police can only find their man the *next* morning. The punch line is intensified by the repeated image of Buster at 45 degrees. This verbal-visual gag recalls the opening commentary, that runaround is "mostly the bull" in even the simplest official matter. In the confusion, Buster handcuffs the deputy to the sheriff, crawls under their legs, and slides across a desk out the window. His exit from this confinement can only be propulsion, a desperate break from the routinized, delusional existence of his bank.

Keaton merges all the characters in the next transitional sequence by crosscutting between chasers and chasees. The mayhem thickens with shots, figures, and planes rapidly traversed. Faust, Diva, and Devil race on a road from foreground left to background right; Buster runs diagonally as well and straight into the camera before jumping over the gate. Buster's pursuers scatter because "THAT HOUSE IS HAUNTED." We have already been prepared by Joe for the "haunting"; although we have not seen the Faust troupe enter the house, we know they will become part of the "hauntings." Buster also becomes part of this inevitability by running the identical path taken by the troupe.

A white tablecloth glows as eerily as the sheeted figure that passes before Buster, who himself disappears into the dark background. Keaton contrasts light and dark in a setting ripe for atmospheric "artwork." The staircase, previously introduced, now meets its match in Buster as he dashes up the steps and slides down the sudden incline manipulated by an unseen hand. The steps re-form as Buster slowly turns to stare at them; he is now aware of their devious mechanical "mind," and what he must confront in order to survive. The staircase becomes a Keaton "machine," a popular nemesis for Buster. Although not strictly a mechanical invention, as the thresher was in *The Scarecrow*, the staircase still represents the hazards that any useful inanimate and "subservient" device offers our hero. The machine is usually meant to be controlled by a wise human hand. However, Keaton's fascination comes in letting the machine control itself, go mad, run amuck after Buster. The staircase is supposedly operated by the "ghosts" offscreen; but because we are seldom reminded of them during the interactions between Buster and stairs, we tend to forget the hand on the lever. Indeed, the staircase—La Machine—takes on its own life and seeks to outsmart Buster in sundry ways; it becomes the quintessential foe, equal to any human counterpart.

Because of the house, the bank has now all but disappeared. This contributes to weakening the film, for it is as if the energy of the first reel has expired, giving way to another source of energy. Neither location is "milked" to its utmost potential for the continuity of the whole film. The bank setting is weakly recalled only by the sporadic appearance of the characters that we met in the first reel. For example, the president's daughter arrives to see Joe heading into the cellar, while three gang members inform him that "THE LITTLE FELLOW FROM THE BANK IS UPSTAIRS." The girl drops through a trapdoor into Joe's arms. The following sequences focus on Buster's run-ins with the counterfeiter-ghosts and the opera troupe, and present sight gags with machine-gun rapidity. A candle sprouts a firework; a midget-owl spreads its wings at Buster who trips over a chair into the next room (the next shot) where a gangly bearded ghost-man awaits him. Like the vault door, the ghost-man holds Buster by his jacket tail as he runs for what seems an eternity—a cut to a long shot reveals that Buster is running on a spinning disk. We are also periodically reminded of Faust and Diva, but Keaton obviously prefers the extensive gags of Buster interacting with spooks.

Buster's next sequence recalls the dimensionality created by the sticky-money routine. Just as the paper money clumped into numerous piles across the frame, one sheeted figure multiplies into many. They crisscross through doors along a hallway; one even circles Buster who stops momentarily to direct the traffic. He returns to the staircase, the opponent with the greatest presence in the film. Buster toes the first step as if preparing to dive, sits to descend one step at a time, then stands only to have the flight collapse under him. Dwarfed by the flight, he clasps his hands in disbelief when the steps reappear before his eyes.

Buster's childlike reaction to these puzzles is enhanced again as he banters with Faust, Devil, and ghosts in a combination of slapstick and subtlety. He meekly tests their existence (as when he kicks Devil in an automatic nervous response) but mostly stares in childlike wonder and curiosity. Keaton inserts a surprising number of subjective close-ups, alternating each observer's point of view. These close-ups, however, are a major flaw and lead to mechanical editing, predictable action-reaction, spoonfed detail—in short, shots devoid of creative techniques using audience imagination. The earlier dissolves of time and distance with Joe implied the spaciousness of the house, which contrasted with the confining bank. Yet now the high number of shots recording each "bump-in-the-night" chops up the space rather than luxuriates in it. The brief hall traffic jam shows Keaton's ability to fill space creatively. This routine makes us yearn for more of Keaton's carefully plotted ramblings. The preestablished size of the house and cast of unusual characters warrants such attention. Later in *The High Sign* (1921), Keaton will finally make full use of a house's space in a unique cinematic device.

Because the first reel in the bank was so dense with witty titles and choreography, the purposeful flatness of that environment became a key ingredient. On the contrary, the haunted house is flat and comes across as such. Sight gags burst out of the flatness rather than work with it for comedy, as the action in the bank did. This different treatment of flatness becomes another flaw of the film when contrasted with the ingenious treatment of the bank. Keaton rattles around the spacious house, relying more on slapstick with Halloween silhouettes. But his mature film voice whispers in a few strong examples. For one, when Buster holds up Devil's empty cape, he stomps on some evicted bugs. Behind the cape, a ghost suddenly appears, causing Buster to flip-twist to the floor. He recuperates in a chair whose arms animate to choke his waist. Buster watches two "skeletons" carry a trousered leg, hatted head, other body parts, and a bucket of glue (a reminder of the bank); they construct a whole man who, through the magic of editing, awakens to life with a jump cut. He shakes hands with Buster who trips and, with a cut, falls into the hallway. As long as Keaton develops his playful manner with the subject of illusions (manipulation of time and space), his comedy transcends slapstick. At such times, the comic characters work *with* the space rather than merely parade through space, as if Keaton makes space itself a living character interacting with others.

Keaton continues to use close-ups as breathers and stresses during the chases; for example, CU of the bearded ghost laughing at Buster in his endless "run"; CU Buster, CU Devil, peering at each other before moving. Close-ups may be Buster's way of ascertaining reality—is he haunted or not? Is it all an *illusion*? Keaton lets both us and Buster scrutinize everything with a magnified view. Similar cutting occurred in the opera sequence, but for a different end. Hit with a cabbage, Devil reels backward in one shot, tumbles into a medium shot, and completes the fall in a long shot. Near and far are joined smoothly, and we travel with the character through the fiasco. Devil destroys the flat backdrop by toppling it; even the audience shatters the proscenium and pours onto the stage. By following each of these moves through many detailed shots, we become a part of the action as well. The opera house itself is a significant transitional setting between the confining bank and the spacious house; its stage holds illusions of both flatness and depth (as *The Playhouse* will soon show). The opera audience, and we the film audience, break through all these illusions through the fluid construction of this sequence. In *Neighbors*, Keaton also effected this by placing his camera at different angles to create perspective or layering. Unfortunately, even though as audience we have creatively traveled through time and space, the second half of *The Haunted House* shifts gears to its detriment. Keaton lets the stereotypes roam an empty box rather than merge into their environment. Except for a few visual gems, in the second reel Keaton hits-and-misses as much as his characters do in the dark.

Buster and company continue to interact in lax choreography, like mannequins tumbling in a vacuum. A tall man in one room proffers Buster a handshake and then his head; in another room, Diva punches a skeleton figure. Buster arms himself with an ewer, which crashes to the floor while the handle remains in his hand. Devil's cape ignites from the fireplace, and he jumps out the window and spooks Buster's bank pursuers. In one rich gag, Keaton plays with space when Buster drops onto one end of a long sofa; on the other end, an immobile bundle slowly unfolds into a ghost. The element of surprise, for Buster as well as for us, derives from how the useless area springs to life. The whole sofa is shown, although it seems unnecessary since Buster only occupies one end of it. But this composition is vital because the bundle uncurls and fills the deliberate emptiness, working with it. This gag joins the other visual punch lines that Keaton developed in the apparently flat bank setting.

However, Buster's tour de force among all his disjointed encounters is his meeting with Machine. Keaton's favorite theme resonated throughout *One Week* and *The Scarecrow*, and with the swatter of *Neighbors* and the gallows of *Convict 13*. Buster and staircase join wits to transcend slapstick and create depth in the frame. For example, Buster hurtles himself up the flight, several steps at a time, before they vanish. After a few more ups-and-downs, he learns the secret of the hauntings: two unsheeted ghosts now eating and talking. His newfound confidence, at both uncovering the ghosts and entering the "mind" of the staircase, is nonetheless vulnerable to unseen forces: when he hops onto the third step to walk the rest, the stairs collapse again. Even though Buster knows who is "at work," he addresses the stairs rather than the stair-operators. The only freedom from control is total victory *over* the enemy, and the first order of business is getting over the staircase. When Buster finally wins that battle and prepares to hit the sheeted ghost with a vase, he adds a unique touch to wreaking vengeance. Rather than swing the vase, he throws it into the air and positions the ghost's head for it. Buster's gesture, bordering on the logical-illogic, is capped by his courtesy in helping the ghost to the floor before removing the sheet. His childlike innocence overcomes the desperate adult; sweet victory is his and he can afford to be kind.

The staircase is obviously the strongest thread uniting the halves of the film. It has appeared in both reels and defined the "haunting" of the house so necessary to the counterfeiters' plan, even though the counterfeiting is more an incidental complication than a developed plotline. The mysterious staircase is indeed the source of the hauntings. As Joe demonstrated at the start, the police were not frightened off by the ghosts but by tumbling down the disappearing stairs. Keaton needed to establish the staircase early on; given his love of inventions, it becomes a most mature and intelligent nemesis for Buster. After all, the ghosts have predictable roles in a "haunted" house; they too serve the staircase. It is the core to which all intruders adhere and only the strong know how to surmount it. Keaton once more lets two powerful suns (Buster and Nemesis) meet and collide, while their satellites (not always successfully) ramble in outer space. Buster's energy triggers the stairs to their own decisions, apart from those that an unseen hand chooses. This odd background of rising and falling steps turns into a giant winking eye, enjoying a shared joke.

The bank president, sheriff, and aide fall through the trapdoor and land among the ghosts, Joe, and the girl. A new and short ghost, unmistakably Buster, enters last and fires a gun—in a way, a reversal of his earlier firing at the bank that led to his pursuit. However authoritative this shot is meant to be, it backfires in typical curveball fashion. Joe hits Buster with his handcuffs on his way out with the sheriff. Buster falls, knocking over a heater; the girl cradles his head. The slapstick nature of this reel has clashed with the subdued and satirical routines of the first reel. Keaton's attempts to minimize the slapstick are overshadowed by the restless characters and by overcutting from room to room, interior to exterior, long to close shots. The characters' aimless wanderings stress their superficiality; there are no strong ties between characters. Even the regular Keaton players lack interest and exposure. Joe hires an army instead of personally hindering Buster; he seems to be a bystander rather than a participant, neither a sight gag (as the piano deliverer in *One Week*) nor a more extended character (as in *Convict 13*, *The Scarecrow*, and *Neighbors*). The girl, the usual pretty face, has a brief and puzzling role; her Nancy Drew inquisitiveness is too radically sensible for a Keaton heroine. Assuming that Buster will be promoted at the bank and win the president's daughter for his daring roundup of the counterfeiters, we wonder if it really matters to him. A handshake with the president's daughter does not a love story make, especially as Buster was equally smitten with his customer.

Although all the characters reunite for the finale (a curtain call, in a way), the "ending" is an illusion. Buster's knocking over the heater seems a prelude to a true resolution of the film, and we sense it is connected to an ulterior motive. It leads us into a "coda" that becomes the real ending. And it is pure Keaton, a capsule film in itself. It draws on all we have seen in the first four short films and translates our visions into images symbolizing Keaton's dream world.

Here, as in *Convict 13*, a dream is the only permissible setting for the impossible. The scene of Buster lying unconscious from Joe's blow dissolves to a long shot of two sheeted angel-tots bending over his body, which is now clad in white robe and tights. The tots lead him to a long white staircase that he ascends rapidly. Keaton twice cuts from the top of the flight (top of the frame) directly to a shot of the next section of the flight (connecting top to bottom) in order to simulate an enormous height. Buster tips his hat to two angels strumming harps in the clouds and, later in the next long shot, two trumpeters. At the top of this frame, Buster tips his hat to a dubious St. Peter and whips out a calling card. Shaking his long bearded head, St. Peter pulls a lever and the stairs collapse. Buster slides down along the staircase—a fluid fall that, shot by shot, again creates the illusion of one long slide. Without break in continuity, Buster slides into a hole dug by the angel-tots. In the netherworld, Devil reads by a coal pile and a winding slide as Buster zooms down. Devil slides his hand over a tote board—

KEATON
BULLETIN

KEATON OUT  ▭

—to reveal IN, a symmetry of opposites like the UP and DOWN of the staircase lever. A hooded demon jabs Buster with a flaming pitchfork as he chats with Devil. The scene dissolves as Buster yelps awake and begins stomping out his smoking sheet. The president's daughter rests her head against his and pats his cheek. Fade out. THE END.

In this brief dream sequence, more unearthly entities are added to the already full gallery of stock characters, masquerades of the good and bad that Buster met in his waking hours. Surrealism extends from heaven to hell along the familiar collapsible staircase. The helpful angel-tots who guided him to Heaven industriously dig his entry into Hades, in the best duality of the film. Buster dreams himself falling at the whim of higher powers, although he hardly merits fire and brimstone. The paranoia of *Convict 13*'s dream resounds as Buster assumes guilt for an unknown offense (even though he just heroically uncovered the criminals), and he willingly accepts his destiny. The dream perpetuates the weirdness of Buster's real life, the hero helpless in his fate.

This sequence either surprises us with its new sight gags (calling card, white tights, Hell's tote board) or recalls earlier sight gags (staircase, sheeted ghost, bearded ghost now as St. Peter). In Keaton's thematic evolution, the macabre sequence is distressing for, in the dream, Someone Else scores a victory on the tote board. Buster's subconscious depicts himself as the most hopeless of victims in the vainest of circumstances, condemned to an eternity of frustration. Thus resigned, Buster attempts to converse with his horned landlord. Even then, a demon prods Buster to attention; it is, in fact, Reality (the heater) prodding Buster from fantasy back into itself. Thus, in the blink of a sleepy eye, eternity (symbolized by either heaven or hell) is vanquished. Once again, it is earth time, which in Buster's world can be controlled by simply moving the hands of an ordinary clock.

The netherworld alone, or the bank alone, would have provided a fine setting in which Buster struggles with Fate until his ingenuity frees him from a flat and dead world. Summoned to the haunted house, however, Buster seems lost in its cavern. His sporadic efforts to penetrate this environment are restricted by ineffective characters and limited use of space. His presence does motivate the actions of others (ghosts, bank customers) to spread out into new spaces. But because the structure of the film is weak, its settings feebly joined, and its focus diffused, Buster is continually threatened by the very flatness he should conquer. His greatest dimension is his all-too-brief dream. Meant here only as a tag-ending, the dream instead points out the greatest flaw of *The Haunted House*: that Buster has to thrive in a dreamworld in order to express his unique persona. Given the real world of *The Haunted House*, with its prop characters and restless chases, Buster is better left in his wild imaginings.

## Chapter 7

# Hard Luck

(March 1921)

Courtesy of the Academy of Motion Picture Arts and Sciences

For the first time in more than sixty-five years since its release in 1921, *Hard Luck* was screened at the Biograph Theatre in New York City. Before his death, Raymond Rohauer had located the fragments of this "lost" film in European vaults and, with David Gill and Kevin Brownlow of Thames Television in London, reconstructed all but the final few minutes of this two-reeler. The last gag, missing except for stills from the film, was dubbed in a 1959 *Coronet* article as "The Biggest Laugh in Movie History."[1] Keaton called the comedy "the biggest one I ever made,"[2] and because of the last gag, "audiences used to go out of the theater howling."[3] With such a response, no wonder *Hard Luck* was reported to be Keaton's favorite short.[4]

*Hard Luck* provides a unique, previously unrevealed, facet in the Buster persona, which might have especially endeared this film to Keaton. The opening titles establish Buster's bizarre solution to his not-so-bizarre dilemmas: FIRED FROM HIS JOB, JILTED BY HIS GIRL, DOWN ON HIS LUCK, . . . ONLY ONE THING LEFT TO DO. The titles themselves instantly suggest the solution: Buster's suicide. The curveballs of Fate have finally driven the lad over the brink. We wonder where his resilience has gone. But we remember Buster's destiny: that however he chooses to respond to a predicament, the end result will often be the opposite of his desire. Committing suicide will probably be so frustrating that Buster will decide to end it all and *live*. The beginning of the film chronicles Buster's futile attempts to yield to his miserable fate.

Buster's first effort is foiled when he lies in front of a trolley car, curled up like a baby; the trolley stops inches from him. Next, LOWERING A SAFE—A FITTING END. Seeing two men hoist a safe to an upper floor, Buster cuts the rope but misses the safe by inches and incenses the two men in the process. Buster tries hanging himself from a tree in a zoo and creates an extended routine in which Keaton plays with space and symmetry. As Buster becomes increasingly frustrated, his gags become more intricate in variation and composition, enhancing the sight-gag potential of his actions. Buster not only falls off the branch but pulls himself up to it by the noose from which he hopes to hang. The branch drops when Buster drops, splitting the frame horizontally and vertically. Buster fails in his mission and attracts the guards' attention. When they chase him, Buster suddenly flees to save himself; suicide is momentarily abandoned when outside forces deprive him of his free choice to end it all. Buster blends in with the life-sized statues of a soldier's monument as the guards pass. (A similar gag, with a slightly different motive, resurfaces in *The Goat* [1921], when Buster merges with a sculpture to evade his pursuers.)

Buster's energy to kill himself is waning now that his energy to survive is recharged. He walks a fine line between succumbing to life's imposed "tragedies" and resisting the forces that create those tragedies; he is really caught betwixt the devil and the deep blue sea. Curiously, Buster's next suicide attempt is an allusion to this dichotomy as well as a strong sight gag. NIGHT FALLS—HE WANTS TO DO THE SAME. Under the cloak of darkness, Buster leaps before two onrushing headlights, prepared to be run over. The two headlights separate as they are the *single* headlights of two motorcycles that pass Buster on either side. Foiled again, Buster ponders another option and, en route, fleetingly considers a manicure. Keaton speaks tongue-in-cheek, of course, as he juxtaposes this peripheral distraction with his hero's quest for suicide. Buster is contemplating both death's solace and life's little pleasures—and he opts for the latter. Buster will shortly give up on suicide altogether and, in fact, adopt a nearly sardonic, self-serving philosophy based on the film's "hard luck" theme. (Keaton presents pessimistic views of his persona's struggles in life in the 1922 shorts *Cops* and *Daydreams*. Yet because these films begin optimistically and end with Buster's failures, *Cops* and *Daydreams* are truly tragic comedies; in *Hard Luck*, however, despair is reversed to an insatiable desire to live "in spite of.")

Buster's turning point in this film occurs in a scene that figuratively illustrates the thin ironic line separating tragedy and comedy. This intangible barrier is as narrow as the physical boundary that seems to keep Buster from his demise. We are introduced to a waiter who snatches a pick-me-up from a bottle of booze disguised as poison; this is confirmed by the title, A CRAFTY WAITER CONCEALS HIS WHISKY. He is at a window so that the action is neatly framed, and we are placed to see clearly the waiter's trick. But Buster can only see the bottle through the window (to him, poison is now the remedy); he remains outside the frame and thus in a position to be misled by Fate. The window becomes the line separating Buster from the truth. In order to drown his problems in liquid death, Buster breaks through the reality-deception line by entering the room and figuratively crosses the tragedy-comedy line. Keaton creates visual irony by placing Buster where the waiter was, for he essentially has replaced the waiter but lacks his knowledge.

Buster's desperate gulps of the brew quickly dissolve into lip-smacking enjoyment. Inebriated, and happy enough to live, he saunters into a scientific meeting led by an intellectual announcing: "GENTLEMEN, IN OUR ZOO WE HAVE EVERY KIND OF ANIMAL EXCEPT THE ARMADILLO." He adds, in a separate title: "WE NEED SOMEONE ADVENTUROUS TO CAPTURE SUCH A RARE ANIMAL. IF I COULD ONLY FIND SUCH A MAN, MY REWARD WOULD BE GENEROUS." Keaton sets up an absurd situation, made more ridiculous by the kind of animal that the zoo seeks. The very word *armadillo* creates a verbal gag that offsets the pompous meeting. In addition, this small rare creature with heavy-duty armor matches Buster's image as a small and vulnerable being with chain-mail skin protecting him from the outside world. Keaton has already linked Buster's suicide attempts to a zoo setting so that the seemingly irrelevant environment is merging slowly into his actions, just as it did in *Neighbors*. Thus, Buster trying to kill himself on zoo grounds (another absurd situation) leads him to a new vitality, echoing the transformation/equation theme of *The Scarecrow*: suicide = life. The next question from the scientist adds a final layer to the nearly complete hanging routine, for he asks: "ARE YOU ATTACHED TO A SCIENTIFIC ORGANIZATION?" Thinking of his earlier failure, Buster can reply with complete honesty, "I WAS ATTACHED TO A BRANCH OF THE ZOO."

A SCIENTIFIC EXPEDITION is announced. Gags are constructed so that any peripheral event really becomes Keaton's plan to make the bed in which Buster will lie. Keaton asks us to store in our memory the action of Buster's dropping ammunition into the campfire as he prepares to fish, forcing us to delay our anticipation of the inevitable explosion. By setting up this structure, Keaton is introducing a more important theme and the pyrotechnics will become its punctuation. Hunting an armadillo via a fishing trip is oddly roundabout, but this diversionary wildlife adventure is Keaton's recipe for a thematic layer cake using the next titles: BIG FISH EAT LITTLE FISH. WHAT'S HARD LUCK FOR THEM MAY BE GOOD LUCK FOR HIM. The luck theme is reintroduced with a twist in Buster's (Keaton's) philosophy: though he was "down on his luck" at the beginning, the tide has now turned and he can benefit from the hard luck of others. The hard luck analogy is enacted through Buster's nonverbal fishing routine. Buster first uses a small fish for bait and catches a medium-sized fish; in between catches, he tries to roll and smoke a cigarette. His leisurely pose to smoke is interrupted by his catches; once again, Fate taunts him for outsmarting his hard luck. Buster's frustrated cigarette-rolling perhaps indicates his wish to control "who eats whom," while (unknown to him) he is at the mercy of the biggest fish of all, Fate. Thus, every time Buster rolls his cigarette, he is interrupted by the next catch and lured into a falsely secure belief that he can get more. Three times he pulls in a satisfactory fish but tosses it back as bait for a larger catch. He forgets that, after a while, there is a limit to the size of the fish he can catch in the vicinity, and he overestimates his ability to control the powerful struggle of a bigger fish. Buster suddenly is too cocksure of himself, the opposite of his former life-weary self. Fate is not only willing to resume the taunting curveball-

game but perhaps wants to return Buster to his humbler condition. We recall that whenever Buster started to smoke casually on the roofless structure in *The Scarecrow* during his man–dog race, he was also interrupted
by the threatening canine. (A more pronounced arrogance will consume
Buster in *The High Sign*, a curious film that was Keaton's first short, but
his seventh release. The film was shelved because he was dissatisfied with
it, but he released it reluctantly when an accident left him unable to work
on a new production.) In typical slapstick, Buster reels in the largest fish
and is yanked headlong into the water, losing both supper and smoke
because of his greediness. As an aftergag, Buster approaches the campfire
and is assaulted by the exploding ammunition, a final (and literal) blast
to his ego. Buster has been the smallest fish of all, figuratively fried over
a fire by Fate, who has been waiting for him with "baited" breath.

This sequence ends and Buster must move on. He enters the swimming pool area of a fashionable country club, where he witnesses what
must seem to him a miraculous occurrence: a man is walking on water.
With a fresh new outlook on life and flaunting an adventurous spirit to
capture the elusive armadillo, Buster desires to do the same. Mixed in
with his self-glory (only slightly wilted by Fate's caprices) is Buster's
childlike superman fantasy that he too can walk on water. Buster has been
adopting a peculiar number of personalities in a brief time span, rang-
ing from despairing victim to daring explorer. Even though he nearly
drowned before when fishing, he finds the water fantasy alluring, especially in the footsteps of another mortal. His fantasy blinds him to reality,
which we see in a cutaway of the man wading out on stilts that elevated
him to the pool's surface so that the stilts were not visible. Buster futilely
walks on the pool and must pull himself out of a second drenching. He
assumes yet another personality, so to speak, when he watches a wet dog
shaking itself dry. Buster emulates, soon drying his suit completely.

With adventure and control as two sides of Buster's life triangle, what
else could be the pivotal third side but love? In each of Keaton's silent
films, love plays a role, even if it is an unhappy one. Love is both an
urgent necessity and ripe comic fodder. At THE COUNTRY CLUB—RENDEZ-
VOUS FOR A FOX HUNT, Buster finds A NEW LOVE. Every experience so far in
Buster's renewed life has had nothing to do with the armadillo hunt that
triggered his objective to live. Buster is easily distracted by other amuse-
ments like fishing and water-walking; now that he has a chance to find
love, he is even more distracted. The Girl (Virginia Fox) is on the hunt,
and with her invitation, "WHY DON'T YOU JOIN OUR HUNT?" Buster is rarin'

to go. He forgets the armadillo as quarry and substitutes a fox, but the *real* prize of this hunt is Woman. Because he appears to bounce from one adventure to another, we see how Keaton lets Buster travel in a linear path through this comedy, in a structurally primitive lineup rather than an interwoven circle of gags and routines (as in *One Week*). When Buster exhausts the possibilities of a comedy situation here (as with fishing), it is over, pure and simple. Buster has also wrapped up his suicide, the zoo, and alas, the poor armadillo. He becomes a devil-may-care type who has flirted with death and now fears nothing. He has turned his own hard luck into survival of the fittest, without realizing that he is only alive because of Fate's having toyed with his suicide attempts. Thus, Buster's life here is as much a chain of events as are the gags that create the "chain" of the film. Keaton's choice to string gags along instead of developing them through extended routines fits his character's raison d'être. Keaton, however, risks creating a film so linear that it is disjointed. The film does not even have the pervasive equation quality of *The Scarecrow*, where seemingly unconnected events led directly to Buster's goal of marriage. Each event in *Hard Luck* is a separate adventure in the carefree lifestyle of an evolving child-man.

There is an inherent beauty in the growth-development, ebb-flow, climax-denouement of a film like *One Week* and *The Scarecrow*, where routines are stepping-stones in the film. The present links with the past and future to compose a solid whole. A problem with *The Haunted House* was that each half of the film functioned as a separate entity and split the whole. *Hard Luck* simply strings along, like its hero, with each new adventure. Nevertheless, this comic structure has its own beauty also, as the comedy derives from the unpredictable. Each gag is strong and successful in and of itself, while its unpredictability leads to laughter. Its execution (growth, development, climax, denouement, the overall rhythm) carries the audience forward with it. Thematically, we cannot return to the start of this film, for to do so would be to return to despair, which Buster has abandoned. In a way, Keaton has set us in a canoe to ride the rapids or glide the stillness, but he advises us to enjoy the landscape as we pass for we cannot row backward.

Like a carefree guide on an expedition, Buster romps through his adventures, the next of which is the foxhunt. Buster plays with the sight gag of an unusually elastic stirrup on a horse that he wishes to mount in order to ride off with his love. He gets on the horse, drops his porkpie, slides down the elastic stirrup (like a mini-elevator, and reminiscent of his hanging attempt earlier), slides back up with the elastic, and slides down the leg of the horse. This prop is absurd, but it accentuates Buster's childlike quality to communicate with (indeed, become) his equally innocent companions. As he became a "dog" to shake himself dry, so Buster communicates now with the horse: as Buster ponders while standing cross-legged, the horse suddenly crosses its front legs in exactly the same pose. In his biography, Dardis described Keaton's having "a strange affinity with animals of all sorts, an eerie ability to get along amazingly well with them. At the zoo, lions and tigers would take one look at Buster's unsmiling face and come to him immediately. Birds would settle on his head and shoulders in complete trust. He often seemed to communicate far more easily with animals than with people. . . . He made people uneasy with his long silences."[5]

Except for his ultimate "love affair" with Brown Eyes the cow in the 1925 feature *Go West*, *Hard Luck* is the richest example of Buster's interplay with animals. The next animal-colleagues help perpetuate the big fish/little fish theme. A fox trails behind Buster who paces ahead on the horse, hunting for it with great concentration. The irony is verbally captured in Buster's innocent thought, "WHAT'S HAPPENED TO THE HUNT?" This pursued-turned-pursuer theme (fox versus man) will become its mirror reflection, pursuer-turned-pursued (Buster versus Fate) in *Cops*. The fox acts as innocently as Buster; rather than fleeing this dim-witted hunter, it follows him—much like Buster often sets himself up for capture at the very moment of escape. The focus draws from the fox back to the horse. MORE THAN ONE WAY TO GET ACROSS, the title alerts us. Buster fords a stream on the horse; in a variation of water-walking, Buster skims along the surface, using his rifle like an oar when the horse lowers itself below the water. Buster next runs across a small bridge as the horse walks beneath it, catches up with the horse on the other side, and mounts it again. Twice more this gag is repeated (the magical "three times" comic structure adequately milks a gag with the right rhythm and length). Unknown to Buster, the horse veers off as he crosses the planks, only to be replaced by a steer that has been hiding underneath and steps out precisely as Buster mounts. The repeated action with the horse has dulled him to the unexpected; we learn of the switch seconds before Buster learns of it and again enjoy the theme "Buster outwitted." The steer throws Buster who moves on to another adventure.

The last animal character to interact with Buster is first an offscreen presence. Buster nooses what he thinks is the fox hiding in a bush that extends out of the frame. He ties the other end of the rope around himself and pulls out his catch, never looking back to see that it is a bear. Once Buster notices it, his superficial confidence is shattered; he struggles to unknot himself from his self-made bind. He propels himself through an open window of the lodge, somersaults, and lands sitting on the floor—precisely in time to receive a cup of tea from a serving waiter. As an aftergag, he sips nonchalantly, then jolts at the bear rug next to him. Buster has literally tumbled into his next adventure, about to meet an animal of the human condition. This grizzly chap (Joe Roberts) is introduced by the title LIZARD LIPS LUKE, ALSO OUT HUNTING. Clearly from previous films, the human is one animal Buster does not communicate with too successfully.

Lizard and his gang impose themselves on the gentle guests inside the lodge, including the girl ("SOME CHANCE, LET'S GO, BOYS!"). Buster's ingenuity is sparked to erect a contraption to fish the gun out of Lizard's holster. Lizard tosses Buster out by the seat of his pants like a suitcase and assaults the girl, who in close-up melodramatically shows her fear with her fingers at her mouth, then promptly falls behind the chair. We note that the lessons Buster learned through hard luck are now being applied to survival strategies. Not only did he try his fishing on Lizard's gun (to small avail) but he now drops ammunition into a potbelly stove and waits for the "punctuation" explosion on the enemy. To do this secretly, Buster assumes a disguise: he places his clip-on necktie under his nose as a mustache. Buster innocently believes that everyone will be fooled and that he is in fact not calling more attention to himself by hanging his tie under his nose. Lizard and gang fortunately do not notice, thus fueling Buster's innocent bravado. He next barricades the door with chairs and pillows. Knowing that he must thwart his foes with anything at his disposal, Buster creates a sight gag that thrives on his innocence: he may want to hurt his attackers, but he will give them a place to recuperate. We remember his gentlemanly act of assisting the vase-stricken ghost in *The Haunted House*. Buster and the girl flee, Lizard makes a melodramatic exit (Keaton again spoofing his pet peeve), and Buster's earlier punishment at the campfire is reversed when the stove spews ammunition on Lizard's gang.

And so Buster has attained his manhood through a baptism by ordeal, through his adventures on the tramping-ground of the great red-blooded American male. He is more than ready to stake his claim, not of the armadillo but of Woman. In a romantic moment, Buster proclaims to the girl, "NOW NO ONE CAN STAND IN THE WAY OF OUR GETTING MARRIED." He speaks like a man who has tamed the wild and swept Woman off her feet. She hesitantly agrees, "NO ONE . . ." and adds in a separately paced title (for the punch to her hesitation), "EXCEPT MY HUSBAND OVER THERE." The weasely old man who owns her heart could shatter the dreams of anyone except the stalwart creature Buster has become. He finds a four-leaf clover, which he hands over to the girl: "YOU NEED THIS MORE THAN ME." Buster's spirit is intact at last; what would have sent him despondently racing toward a high-speed locomotive now drives him to abandon a time-honored symbol of fortune and refresh himself instead. He announces without a blink, "I'M GOING TO MAKE THE HIGH DIVE." He is confident and wishes to transcend all—animals, humans, problems—in order to pursue self-gratification, even though his quest for love remains unfulfilled. He has learned much on his adventures—ironically, not enough. Buster now wants to high-dive into the pool on which he thought he could walk shortly before. Since experience has not convinced him that water is for swimming and not walking, we hold our breath for the inevitable gag that will hit Buster as soon as he hits the water. Somewhere in his beleaguered subconscious, could Buster still be entertaining suicide while he pretends that everything is fine?

Buster dives and disappears into the pool. Spectators gather to look down in shock and remark, "HE IS SO FAR AWAY YOU CAN HARDLY SEE HIM." Something is clearly amiss, and we suspect that we will soon receive a stunning comic punch after this purposefully tense pause. The preparatory title: "YEARS LATER." From a crater in the dried-out pool emerges Buster in Oriental garb, accompanied by a Chinese wife and two small children. His adventure has breathed life into the hyperbole of someone's falling through a hole as if straight to China. Buster's man-of-steel nature has permitted him to go there and return, with a family in tow. THE END.

This gag, "the biggest laugh in movie history," lets us see a new Buster returning from his greatest journey. All of his adventures have not differed much from the hair-raising, strenuous stunts of Keaton's earlier films (nor will they diminish in films to come). But for the first time, we regard these adventures as a school of "hard knocks" for the character that Buster was at the outset. He progresses from his lowest grade, a student undisciplined and out of control (actually under another's control), to graduation day, becoming a grown-up who has "tested the waters" and turns a nadir into a summit. Interestingly, Keaton criticized the kind of gag that the final scene presented, even though he valued its effect on an audience: "That sort of gag I would never use in a full-length picture—because it could not happen in real life, it was an impossible gag. If we had done what we were trying to do in a feature the audience would go along with us, believing in the characters they were watching. So in pulling an impossible gag on them in a feature we were saying, 'April fool!' or 'Sucker!' to them for believing in our story."[6]

Keaton distinguished between a gag rich in and of itself for a quick punch (such gags are the essence of the shorts) and gags that evolved a truth-telling narrative for feature films. He illustrated with a scene from his most financially successful feature, *The Navigator* (1927): Beached near an island of cannibals, Keaton goes underwater in a diver's suit to dislodge the liner and save himself and the girl, the only two passengers on the ship. He employed a number of vivid gags—dueling one swordfish with another, setting up a sawhorse labeled "MEN AT WORK," washing his hands underwater in a bucket of water, and using a lobster as wire-snippers. Keaton's favorite gag involved twelve hundred rubber fish hanging on thin wires from a revolving apparatus to suggest a school of fish swimming by. Buster stops his work on the ship to pin a starfish on his chest, halts the school of fish so that a bigger fish can cross, and waves the school on its way. The audience laughed at trailers for *The Navigator* showing this gag, but Keaton learned in previews of the complete film that the audience did not find it as amusing. In his words:

> It took us a long time to figure out why that wonderful gag laid an egg. . . . It is always an interesting problem to me when an audience rejects any such sure-fire laugh-getter. I wonder whether it is because the customers were too concerned in figuring out the mechanics of the gag. . . . We showed it again in the trailer, and everybody once more liked it. That gave me an answer. . . . The other gags were accepted by audiences who saw the whole picture, because they did not interfere with my job of saving the girl. But when I directed the submarine traffic I was interrupting the rescue to do something else that couldn't help us out of the jam. . . . I threw the gag out.[7]

It seems as if Keaton took to heart that his audiences were older than "twelve years" and could identify the right time and place for the absurd. Our tolerance runs lower for features, for we expect greater cohesion and dimension in plot and character, and greater emotional involvement. *Hard*

# Hard Luck

*Luck* probably won Keaton's heart because he recognized the time and place of the film. Here, he carves absurd, nearly surreal images of a hero exploring a wide, unknown terrain. Each adventure is as absurd as life itself when seen from a "hard luck" perspective. We accept Buster's absurdities as real because of how Keaton constructs this "reality" from the outset. Buster's string of events forms the shape of the Adventurer in all of us. If Buster can leap from one end of the spectrum (despair) to the other (victory), and travel every-which-way in between, how much more so can we tame our ordinary existence? And the more extraordinary the existence, the richer the possibilities of turning hard luck into great fortune. To seek an armadillo may be, indeed, to become one.

## Chapter 8

# The High Sign

### (April 1921)

Courtesy of the Academy of Motion Picture Arts and Sciences

Keaton shelved *The High Sign* after production in the first two months of 1920 and premiered with *One Week*. Because it is chronologically Keaton's seventh released film, we might tend to consider it as the next "rung in his ladder." We must remember, though, that it was in fact Keaton's *first* independent venture. As such, we see first impressions of the Buster persona and of the filmmaker that Keaton would become. As the seventh release, however, we have the hindsight advantage of comparing *The High Sign* with his more refined comedy. We can thus understand Keaton's reluctance in releasing *The High Sign* when greater achievements were flowing through his head.

OUR HERO CAME FROM <u>NOWHERE</u>—HE WASNT GOING <u>ANYWHERE</u> AND GOT KICKED OFF <u>SOMEWHERE</u>. Speeding locomotive wheels dominate the opening frame, focusing on Buster who soars in horizontally and lands on the ground. Keaton's concern with visual space is immediately obvious from Buster's dynamic entrance. The moving train becomes a canvas, its enormity canceling the frame until it passes and the landscape reaches out into the background. The opening title's underlined words of ambiguity suggest a survival of the fittest by questionable scruples. Buster's behavior will soon suggest reasons for his placelessness. Once the train passes, Buster surveys a small town with an amusement park and strolls out of the frame. Next, he plucks a newspaper from a carousel rider; as he opens the paper, it unfurls section by section into a sheet filling (again canceling) the frame. He falls under its enormity; when his head tears through, he spies an ad:

---

HELP WANTED - MALE
WANTED - Boy in shooting gallery. Must be expert shot to attract crowd. Ask for TINY TIM, 233 Spring Street.

---

Buster folds the paper; the carousel rider hands him a coin for it, thinking him a newsboy. Further on, Buster lifts a cop's gun from its holster, substitutes a banana from a fruit stand, then casually leaves.

Upon meeting Buster, we are struck by a cocky, and what Robinson calls "positively larcenous," character.[1] His introduction includes stealing a newspaper, banana, and gun, followed by impersonation. Buster's interest in the advertised job implies opportunism rather than skill or experience (comedy often arises from contradiction; therefore, Buster's claim to be a sharpshooter suggests his ineptitude). Fate punishes Buster; the newspaper is a momentary, albeit ridiculous, nemesis. Yet Buster turns tables with "larceny" and outwits Fate: he tears the paper and pockets a profit from the reader (in fact, his "victim"). The foiler-foiled theme will persist in other films, as Keaton has already so vividly introduced it in his first production.

The amusement park fully rises into view as Buster crosses a sandy expanse by a boardwalk. We are again struck by Keaton's visual concerns as a first-time director. A lanky kid (Al St. John) tosses a bottle that Buster catches in the palm of his hand; he sets it up with two more bottles for target practice, which occurs in the foreground while other gags break into middleground. As Buster paces to the foreground and turns his back to the camera, we focus on his arm, the only moving element in the scene. With his back to us, Buster and the motionless kid eliminate distractions to the one action that punctuates each shooting gag: his taut arm over-stretching to fire the gun. His arm aligns with the center bottle, but when he fires, the right bottle breaks; he fires center, but the left bottle breaks. Buster fires at the kid mocking him, but the center bottle breaks. Buster fires at a fourth bottle but hits the kid's rear end. In fast-motion, the agonized kid races over the boardwalk and leaps into the next frame before the building of DR PULLEM    DENTIST. The boardwalk is a background anchor, fixing our eye on the distance, which the kid penetrates as he runs. This depth-breaking principle worked (or, this being Keaton's debut, *was to work*) in *Neighbors* when the view expands "beyond the frame" as Buster slides along the laundry line and "offscreen" around the banister; and in *The Haunted House* when Buster reaches into the clock or directs the ghost traffic. Buster fires one last time between two bottles to cross Fate and end the routine; in response, a duck falls on his head. Exhausting all possible directions for misfires in this setting, Buster drops the gun and races up the slope.

When we move to an interior, we find the dimensionality that had eluded the second reel of *The Haunted House*. A sign beneath an American flag outside the shooting gallery invites:

| | |
|---|---|
| 2 shots | 5¢ |
| 5 shots | 10¢ |
| 15 shots | 15¢ |

Try your skill

Buster enters the frame, pauses, and smacks his hand on a counter lined with rifles. From behind the counter rises Tiny Tim, two heads taller than Buster who falls to the floor as though physically struck; Buster then leans over to check Tiny's foundations. Tiny examines Buster for the job; Buster models with a hand on waist and the other jauntily over his head. Tiny trades places with Buster: "WHEN I COME BACK I WANT TO HEAR THE BELL RING EVERY TIME YOU SHOOT." Buster hangs his porkpie beside his jacket on the wall; the hat slides down to an invisible hook, resembling the adhesive cane gag in *The Haunted House*. Echoing the earlier misfires, Buster fires at a duncehead in a target display; a cross whirls instead. He retaliates at Fate: pulling a handy slingshot from his vest, he knocks off the head and sets the weapon on the counter with a satisfied pat.

Keaton's repetition of gags to balance sequences, particularly the misguided missiles, is also a clue to his decision to shelve the film. He stalled its release and, while on vacation before starting *The Saphead*, screened *The High Sign* for Arbuckle who was filming at the same site:

> "It's great! It's great!" Arbuckle kept saying, between belly laughs, all through the projection.
>
> That confirmed it. Buster knew for certain just where he stood. It would make money, sure. What he wanted was something else. Something new. . . . Buster had just been questioning the appropriateness of a gag [in an Arbuckle film]. "It doesn't seem to fit your story," he had said.
>
> "Story?" Arbuckle's voice had risen like a siren on the word . . .
>
> Now, as Arbuckle laughed with that particular guffaw of his that signaled . . . "good old slapstick" . . . Buster knew that this film must be destroyed.
>
> Back in Hollywood, he said to [Lou] Anger, "Throw this lemon away."
>
> "[But] it cost twelve thousand dollars."
>
> "It's not good at any price. It's my fault, not yours."[2]

Keaton was compelled to release *The High Sign* after an accident during the filming of *The Electric House* (1921—this version of *The Electric House* was destroyed, reshot, and released in 1922; see Chapter 8). But Keaton's reaction during the preview points to the problems within the story. Gags stand isolated as miniature novelties; like a decorated tree, they hang on the outer branches, arranged toward the tip where sits the most lavish ornament: a curious depiction of simultaneous action at the climax of the film. Each gag, however, dangles far from the trunk (the story) of the tree. In Keaton's successful films, gags are intrinsic to story or character, whether they follow a circular or linear development. Our sour note in this "lemon" is that, although the gags appropriately rise from the setting, they are played out mainly for sight-gag effect by a character who lacks inner depth. The gags are funny and well executed, but they begin to feel like heavy ornaments hanging on weak branches.

In the basement, Tiny raps three times on a door marked THE BLINKING BUZZARDS and emblazoned with a wild-eyed bird; the eye slips up into a peephole. Tiny responds with the "high sign": hands crossed before mouth, thumbs at each nostril, fingers straight. The door opens to THE BRUTAL BUNGALOW OF THE BLINKING BUZZARDS, A BOLD BAD BUNCH OF BLOOD-THIRSTY BANDITS WHO WOULD BREAK INTO A BANK, BLOW A BATTLESHIP TO BITS OR BEAT UP A BLUE EYED BABY BLONDE. Seven Buzzards play Ping-Pong and read the paper while Tiny begins to pace. Like the set in *Neighbors* creating a tenement ambience, this interior is especially atmospheric in its design. None of Keaton's rooms have had ceilings; yet the Buzzards' lair is a rib cage of a cell, with planks meeting ceiling and floor at sharp angles and stretching into the background. The "shortness" of the basement increases Tiny's altitude. The set is rough, contrasting in realism with the comically absurd roster of alliterative Buzzard crimes.[3]

Faced with a challenge beyond his experience, Buster must invent success. A ball of string, a three-sided crate, and a dog munching a beef leg are his guarantee until Fate intervenes. Meanwhile, we crosscut to Tiny holding a photo of a dour-looking man, the back of which reads:

AUGUST NICKELNURSER

WARNED 3 TIMES

MUST DIE

SEP. 1ST

Tiny points to the wall calendar: TODAY IS WEDNESDAY 1 SEPTEMBER. In visual response, we meet AUGUST NICKELNURSER, THE TOWN MISER. AS TIGHT AS A FOURTEEN COLLAR ON A SIXTEEN NECK. He is a blatant human pun in the following handwritten death-threat:

AUGUST NICKELNURSER

DEAR AUGUST:

THREE TIMES WE HAVE

DEMANDED $10,000 OR YOUR LIFE.

# The High Sign

As August paces in the parlor, his daughter descends the stairs. She advises, "FATHER, YOU NEED A BODY GUARD," and reassuringly leads him out. Two distinct parties—Buzzards and Nickelnursers—have been introduced before they interact with Buster, who will become their referee. Once more, Keaton's cast are satellites and stereotypes (cowardly cops, pinch-faced miser, pretty love interest, country rube, grotesque thugs, and, soon, slaphappy drunk). But the brutal bungalow has more depth in its layered construction than all these characters combined.

The excursion into the basement provides a time lapse during which our desperate hero has created a contraption to fortify his shallow talent as sharpshooter. His invention consists of the beef leg hanging in the crate and a bell nailed to the outside wall of the gallery, beside which the dog sits leashed to the clanger. Buster demonstrates it as his success (ironically, it will also be his undoing): As he tugs the string from inside, the dog lunges for the lowered meat and rings the bell—instant marksmanship. Downstairs, Tiny and Buzzards high-sign in what will become a motif of synchronized repetition. Once Tiny bursts into the gallery to assess Buster's skill, we intercut at the precise moments of gunfire to match interior and exterior actions. Buster's behavior recalls his cocksure first appearance. He lifts his brow, amazed at his "accuracy," then flips the gun with a carefree arm and swaggers to Tiny's clapping. Though the camera is fairly passive in recording the action, we still have a sense of the gallery's breadth because of its angle to the action. We seldom see Buster from over the counter as his customers would. In most cases, we see him on his side of the counter, looking toward the offscreen target wall. Thus, we feel the width and length of the gallery. Keaton's choice of a plain setting accentuates Buster's artillery routines so that he stands out of, rather than merges with, the setting. This choice also recalls the carefully composed boardwalk, with over-the-shoulder views, balanced planes of depth, and Buster's arm signaling the comic business. Carried away with himself, Buster performs military maneuvers. He kneels with an arm crooked around the rifle and shields his eyes to look at the targets, like a big-game hunter spotting prey. He fires and falls on the pedal, clanging the bell.

# The High Sign

Buster's ill-timed mishap does not alert Tiny to any contrivance; rather, he heads downstairs with an idea, not noticing that August and daughter have joined the spectators. Buster shoots while looking in a mirror; confused, he fires into the mirror yet steps on the plank. Again, the sight gags are funny and Buster's maneuvers are a pleasure; yet the gags undermine the "reality" of the plot. We are expected to accept that Buster's "bull's-eye misses" are enough to inspire both Tiny and August to hire him. We are entertained but not enthralled or sympathetic with this persona, as his attitude is deceptive, larcenous, and ambiguous. We almost root for Fate to score a victory over Buster, which indeed happens as his gun tricks draw thin. At zero hour, Fate sends a cat to tempt the dog to bell-ringing frenzy. The silent close-up of the clanging bell seems ear-shattering to us. Realizing that he is losing control, Buster fumbles to reload different guns and shoot, even with closed eyes, feebly invoking his old arrogant self. When the dog finally breaks loose, Buster is leery about the silence, waiting for yet another clang. August and daughter approach while Buster rewards himself with a cigar of triumph. August speaks: "MY LIFE'S IN DANGER AND I WANT YOU TO BE MY BODY GUARD." In three-shot, Buster shakes his head no; the girl pleads in her irised close-up; in two-shot with her, Buster nods in agreement. Once again, he is easily swayed to an opposite decision by a pretty face, as he was by the bank customer in *The Haunted House*. The miser hands Buster his calling card, AUGUST NICKELNURSER    10 MAIN STREET, before the deal is sealed with his handshake and her smile.

We soon see hints of Buster's talent to outwit human minds, which he cannot do as easily with more "intelligent" mechanical "minds." In leaving the gallery, Buster baffles Tiny by slipping through the door and closing it. Tiny opens the door and stands with hands on hips, staring at Buster in the identical pose within the door frame. The effect is of watching someone peer into a full-length mirror at a smaller reflection. Both Tiny's position and the door frame direct us to Buster. Depth, symmetry, proportion, sight gag, and paradox meld in one composition.

At the basement door, Buster apprehensively leans his head forward at the opening peephole as his legs back away. In the room, Buster becomes the smallest figure, visually pitted against and surrounded by the goons. He must swear his allegiance on an outrageous prop, a skull that suddenly nabs his fingers in the process. Tiny: "DO YOU KNOW THE NATURE OF AN OATH?" Buster: "YES. I PLAY GOLF." As the thugs high-sign, Buster half-high-signs, thumbing his nose; he hurriedly adds the other wing

**99**

under Tiny's fierce glare. "WHO DO YOU WANT ME TO KILL?" Buster inquires. When he sees August's picture, he falls like a plank. In an aside, he studies August's calling card, following a title that reveals Buster's thoughts on his dilemma: GUARDING A MAN FROM DANGER AND KILLING HIM AT THE SAME TIME IS SOME JOB. He staggers limply as Tiny leads him out by the hand; then with ho-hum melodrama, Buster hangs his head and clutches his chest with one hand as he dashes upstairs. Keaton sets us immediately in the gallery to watch the closed door open; Buster walks in, hunched over with the weight of his missions. Tiny and thug burst through, propelling him over the counter. Buster punchily high-signs and tips over; then shaking his head, he stands, ready for business as usual.

For the first time, Buster has had to choose between right and wrong, between protecting and killing. For him, the choice is not clear-cut, as the bleakly comic title of "SOME JOB" suggests. Buster almost willingly accepts both commissions for the sake of moving on to the next adventure; his ambivalence is clear from the start. Flying from a train that rejects him, our hero is a nowhere person with no patent ambitions. Despite his apparently destitute situation, Buster's expressions are remarkably haughty, such as his aloof gaze before swiping the newspaper, his disdain for the rube, his hammy display of arms, and his half-wing retort. His melodrama also rings phony. In *The Scarecrow*, it was an object of ridicule. Here, however, melodrama does not contrast romance with hokiness; it is Buster's genuine response to his plight. Melodrama is momentarily curtailed when Buster is propelled over the counter (perhaps as Fate's reprimand). When he flutters to the floor with a punch-drunk high sign, Buster seems more the little-man-against-the-world. But we are troubled that Buster resumes his shooting as if his paradox no longer exists. He has resolved his dilemma of being between sides by joining *both*. His oath was spoken with trepidation rather than with a desire to outwit the gang. And it almost seems that had August no beautiful daughter, September 1 may well have been his last.[4]

A second major problem, due to the story, further explains Keaton's reluctance about the film. More and more, Buster is seen as less than admirable, particularly in his complacent acceptance of the jobs to kill and protect simultaneously. Moreover, his complications are interrupted by irrelevant self-imposed gags. The unity of the whole story is continually shattered. Along with the biting skull, more incidental gags tax our suspension of disbelief. Buster draws a backward J on the gallery wall and hangs his hat on the hook of the letter; he removes a pipe from a duncehead, which he smokes without lighting. The pipe breaks off in Buster's teeth when a drunken customer misfires, almost as if Buster has become a target. The drunk congratulates himself with a cigar that suddenly sputters fireworks and drives him away. As Buster accidentally pinches his finger in a countertop crack, he hammers the smoldering cigar into it like a nail. Buster hands a rifle to a dapper gent, who aims it at him instead and steals the cash drawer. Next, a hunter switches the rifle for his own double-barreled shotgun, as Buster slips the coin into his sock. Knocked to the floor with the blast, Buster studies the bullet-ridden target range and piles up fifteen cigar boxes. He grabs his jacket and hat and scrambles over the counter. Fade out.

Were it not for this last catastrophic gunshot, the sequence might have gone on indefinitely, accumulating gags without resolving the life-saving issue. We remember that Keaton eliminated his favorite gag from *The Navigator* because it interfered with resolving the major conflict. Perhaps Keaton was too much of a novice filmmaker at this point to fully understand this structural concept, even though he must have sensed the problem because he chose to shelve *The High Sign*. We forget the Buzzards and Nickelnursers and note Buster's indifference, which Fate tries to control. When he strides boastfully, Fate introduces the cat (although Buster still benefits since his invention is never discovered). The invention is an incomplete routine, unlike Keaton's usual full circles. Matching crime for crime, Fate inflicts a robbery on Buster, but he reciprocates by "socking" the next cash intake, like pocketing the newspaper money. The next gag in particular troubled Keaton; he spoke of its negative impact on preview audiences. Fade-in as a cop whips out his gun at Tiny—it is the banana; the incomplete banana/gun-switch gag from the beginning is finally concluded. Tiny ominously bites the banana; the cop flees. Tiny drops the peel and hides as Buster enters. Without breaking stride, Buster sidesteps the peel, high-signs at the camera, and exits left. Mystified, Tiny walks back around the building.

> When the audience saw me approaching they expected me to slip on [the peel]. But I didn't, and then passed right before the camera. I tried to get my laugh by using the Mafia's secret sign, thumbs held crossed under the nose with the hands spread out on both sides of the face. But this was like thumbing my nose at the audience, and saying, "Fooled you that time, didn't I?"
> In the end I decided that I had made the mistake of outsmarting

the audience a little too much. But instead of cutting this scene out I added a shot. In this, after passing the camera and giving the sign, I slipped on a second banana peel somebody had dropped. That worked fine.[5]

This second slipping is not in the version viewed and may be lost or remembered by Keaton as a scene he wanted to include. This extra shot substantiates Keaton's desire to give the audience the last laugh and curb Buster's arrogance. While the hero misses one peel, the curve supplies a second. Another time, Keaton elaborated:

> They don't like it when a comic is smarter than the audience. . . . We're making some screwball picture about Black Hand or something in which there's a high sign. . . . Everybody knows that I'm going to slip on the banana peel—only I don't. I walk right over the peel and give the high sign to the camera. Okay, so we preview the picture. The scene doesn't get a titter. Not a titter and nobody can figure out why. Finally I get the idea and we go back and shoot the scene over again. We do it exactly the same, only this time, after I walk over the banana peel and into the camera, giving the high sign, the camera follows me and I slip on another banana peel that I haven't seen and down I go. Yaks. The audience wants his comic to be human, not clever.[6]

Even without benefit of the "previewed" version, Keaton's concern is clear. The high sign spoofs secret societies, who spend much of their time devising symbolic business for members. This spoof appears in such scenes as when Tiny leaves but jumps back to high-sign, without which apparently no job would be complete. Recognizing its absurdity, Buster half-high-signs during the group response; Tiny glowers at the subtle sarcasm, at which point Buster completes the sign. Because Keaton establishes the sign as one of contempt, directing it at the audience shows disdain for them as well. He meant to twist our anticipation of the expected (slipping on peel) and shock us into laughter. To Keaton's disappointment, the preview audience was only shocked.

Buster's ambiguity is further illustrated in his encounter with the nervous cop. In five shots, we alternately face Buster and the cop as each faces the other offscreen, then stops, runs forward and backward. Buster pauses to reverse his jacket and collar and punch up his porkpie, posing as a minister who bobs prayerfully past the cop. Buster's charade is puzzling: Is he trying to engage the cop's attention, or avoid it by working out guilt over his misdeeds? Buster divulges the secret of the Buzzards by high-signing to the cop at a fruit wagon. To Buster's dismay, the vendor (a fellow Buzzard) beans the cop with a blackjack, then high-signs. Buster reluctantly strolls off. Fade out. Buster is ultimately surrounded by Buzzards, creating an ironic hopelessness for someone who is already so hopelessly misplaced. The irony is humorous, but his resignedly strolling away adds a disturbing facet to his persona. Buster's development in later films will show a valiant side to his personality that will not permit him to walk away from quandaries. Here, Buster will resolve his dilemma in the last sequences, not by choice or desire to right an injustice, but by circumstance. He has fallen into this major moral conflict as randomly as he was ejected from the train, and he treats both aimlessness and duty in an equally listless manner.

The next setting, the Nicklenurser residence, is a sort of deus ex machina. It contains mechanical devices that Buster knows nothing about, but when he learns of them, he adapts to them immediately (almost too conveniently) to thwart the Buzzards and save himself and his charge. August remarks to his daughter, "NOW I'VE GOT A SECRET GETAWAY IN EVERY ROOM." A carpenter demonstrates an elastic carpet. Meanwhile, Buster in a rare cigarette-smoking pose flicks ashes on a butler's tray before handing him a calling card—a gesture meant to be comical, but which is quickly grouped with the previous arrogant gestures. Buster follows August through more devices (a wall panel and a floor trapdoor) to a yet unknown route. In another revelation as contrived as that of the disguised fruit vendor, the butler pulls off his mustache and beckons: "DO YOUR DUTY, BROTHER BUZZARD." Buster lunges to yank the trapdoor cord, but the butler steps away in time to miss the opening. We cut to the butler phoning Tiny at headquarters: "THIS GUY IS AS YELLOW AS A BOX CAR FULL OF LEMONS." Buster's ambivalent gestures appear as cowardice to the Buzzards rather than as a threat to them. The Buzzard butler quietly pours poison into a teacup as the girl entertains Buster with a ukulele. After sipping, Buster looks down at the cup; in a subjective close-up, and superimposed on the dark liquid, is the kicking end of a donkey. The clever illusion to a spiked drink seems misplaced in a film with overall uneventful camera work; however, we are reminded of Keaton's fascination with the camera to create visual punch lines.

The climactic indoor "chase" begins with a ruse, fitting in with the unsavory behavior Buster has presented from the start. Having at last chosen to protect August, Buster explains to him, "WE'LL FOOL THEM— WHEN I SHOOT, YOU FALL." Watching from outdoors, Tiny and gang think Buster is on their side until they see their tête-à-tête and are roused to fury. Once more, Keaton develops the "survival of the fittest" theme. When the gang enters, Buster makes an acrobatic escape through the devices already revealed—and some we have not seen. We are perplexed at Buster's over-smartness. We have witnessed his getaways, never breaking continuity long enough for *him* to learn of traps "behind our back." Yet suddenly he shows us more than we know: he flies through a wall panel into a side room, out the window, and up a trellis into an upstairs bedroom. Buzzards and Buster fumble; he leaps on the bed, which slides left through the wall; with a cut, the slide continues into the adjoining bedroom, pushing a second bed and shoving a thug out the window; his fall is completed in a cutaway dive to the ground. The choreography is compelling for an indoor chase, but, subconsciously, we wonder how Buster learned about these escape routes. If he is discovering them by chance, Fate is being extremely kind to him; yet his masterful swings through the rooms make us wonder about some offscreen "conference" with August. If so, Buster has excluded us as his comrades. Then again, his character has lacked our sympathy all along. He is too smart, too casual for such a "vagabond"; he is really high-signing at us again, much to our chagrin.

For the chase, Keaton constructed a set that eliminates the need for crosscutting. "Editing" occurs before our eyes, within the same shot, within the same frame, without a mechanical arrangement of shots. In an earlier sequence, Keaton used crosscutting between the gunfires and the dropping-dogbone and between Buster and cop to alternate subjective reactions. Here, Keaton attains the effect of crosscutting *without* it, using the house as a giant prop that fills the screen with simultaneous action. The newspaper had filled the screen at the beginning; now the house fills the screen room by room. As movement and tension intensify, the momentum is not interrupted by crosscutting between rooms; rather, actions in all rooms eliminate the house front and erupt concurrently.

Initially, we watch a two-room column where parallel actions are meticulously synched. Buster steps to the center of the bedroom as a Buzzard enters the parlor directly below. From the door, Tiny fires at Buster, who drops through the carpet and lands on the thug. We cut to the activities of one room again as Buster backs into the wall panel and a Buzzard enters the window. Buster climbs on the desk and dives into a *paper* mirror. Like the wall hook in the shooting gallery, the mirror is another illusion for us, but apparently not for the unusually omniscient Buster. The thug purposely moves a desk chair, creating an obvious space through which Buster tumbles through doors under the desk to kick the thug into the mirror. The energetic interplay between thugs and Buster begins to feel like a friendly collaboration as they execute amazing gags rather than oppose each other in a chase.

The mirror also echoes the illusion/deception theme with which Keaton teases his audience; likewise, he used the Buzzard skull, smoking pipe, and painted hook. These tricks cannot be explained without referring to their physical construction and shattering the cinematic experience with their absurdity. As in *One Week*, Keaton affirms the film-watching experience with the lens-as-barrier, just as Buster's deadpan barricades his innermost being. These gags are surreal, transported from a land inhabited by magicians, dreamers, and actors (all three = Keaton). Yet in *The High Sign*, these surreal gags are meant to exist in the "real" world of criminals and misers. One reality cancels the other; the result is a blank canvas dotted with impossible gags that we try to set into a very real context. Since the amusement park and Nickelnurser "fun-house" settings are too underplayed for a surreal context, we are not prepared for such a distorted reality. Too many detours into the impossible have corroded our suspension of disbelief.

The chase intensifies between real (Buster) and unreal (story), but it is weakened by the gags in the house. Buster begins a precision hide-and-seek as a thug pushes on the panel he hides behind; when the panel revolves, Buster is swallowed from sight until the panel revolves again and the thug reappears. On the third revolution of hide-and-seek, Buster causes the thug to reappear at the instant the butler fires—at the thug. When another Buzzard pokes his head in the door, Buster shuts it, trapping the head in the narrow groove between door and wall—another impossibility overstretching the comedy. When the butler enters, Buster springs out the window and arcs from the house on a drainpipe that bends in half, splitting the frame as it carries him to the ground. His feet point like spearheads into the window; his poses are like instantaneous replies to rapid-fire questions. Keaton feeds our visual appetite with geometric order in chaos. Buster's flight into the window once more opens the frame with parallel actions in the two-room column: he tumbles into one room as the butler upstairs is conked by the returning drainpipe.

The wildest portion of the chase begins, creating the climax of the film, the top ornament of this comedy-tree. Keaton finally presents a cross section of all four rooms: the left bedroom above the parlor, the right bedroom above the secret side room. By pushing vertical wall panels and climbing through horizontal trapdoors, the four rooms are rapidly traversed by Buster, Tiny, and Buzzard. The house splits the frame by doubling: from one room ▢, to a two-room column ⊟, to a four-room cross section ⊞. Every hiding place is relentlessly used; energy pours from each room in the climax of this chase sequence.

Keaton was to split the frame with more subtle sophistication in his last feature, *The Navigator* (1927). There he splits the frame by three natural dividers: the ship's deck, the waterline, and a ladder between the two. The search sequence between Rollo Treadway (Keaton) and the girl spans the three levels. *Steamboat Bill Jr.* (1927) also similarly employs three decks of the steamboat.[7] More often, however, particularly in future shorts, Keaton plays with less complex frame-splitting devices and settles for the "frame within a frame."[8] The feature *Sherlock Jr.* (1924) provides a now-classic example: as Buster, a movie projectionist, falls asleep at his job, his dream spirit literally leaves the booth, walks down the aisle of the theater, and steps into the movie that is framed by the rectangle of the screen as well as by the stage and orchestra. Keaton draws the camera past the "frame" to enter Buster's dream, which has become entangled with the story of the projected movie. Buster has literally penetrated the flat dimension of film *within* the flat dimension of film.

In a quick denouement to wind up the exhausting chase, Buster escorts August and the girl to safety, but Tiny reappears with a gun. Buster steps out but bursts in from the grandfather clock and opens the trapdoor on which Tiny stands. Buster hugs the girl. In a final medium shot, he eyes the trapdoor over her shoulder. Pause; he high-signs. THE END.

Keaton's technical mastery allows him not only to penetrate the flatness of his milieu but to roll energetically around in it. Buster's entrances through desk, window, and clock are surprises. When revealed so rapidly, these hiding places startle and amuse us; only afterward do we reflect that Buster has been superior to his audience. When Keaton the filmmaker is omniscient (as in the train collision–illusion of *One Week*), we are entertained. In that case, we are one with Buster the character, equally perplexed. But when the character we identify with is smarter than we are, our concern for his predicament diminishes. Keaton sensed that fooling his audience was perhaps the greatest weakness of *The High Sign*. As we trace the development of his character in films made after but released before *The High Sign*, we see how Keaton softened the slapstick and mellowed Buster's personality with humility: his eyes glint with less haughtiness. He might still be a nowhere-man, but he is better for it. *The High Sign* as a first film effort presents only an outline of Buster, into which Keaton would plant his values once he weeded out the unattractive traits of his "sharpshooter."

If *The High Sign* had been released first, its weaknesses would have promised future strengths. As the seventh released short, *The High Sign* appears as a fork in the road of Keaton's filmmaking, marking a turn toward more subtle, visually stimulating stories with Buster the "Everyman." Keaton had chosen correctly by shelving *The High Sign* to begin "serious" work with *One Week*. Fortunately, however, he finally released *The High Sign*; it provides us with the map of where he began and where he was heading.

## Chapter 9

# The Goat

## (May 1921)

Courtesy of the Museum of Modern Art/Film Stills Archive

*T*he *Goat* is the "most densely textured" of Keaton's short films thus far, weaving strands from *Hard Luck, Convict 13, The Scarecrow,* and *One Week*.[1] Keaton converts the amusing concept of duality from *The Scarecrow* into a poignant look at life equaling truth/untruth, fairness/unfairness, certainty/uncertainty. *The Goat* is layered with these paradoxes. Buster is an innocent, a sap, a goat walking toward the clutch of Fate, then breaking into an endless run from it. Thus, *The Goat* has been called "one long chase from beginning to end" and typifies Buster Keaton in his most honest little-fellow's struggle with the world yet.[2]

A sardonic duality is introduced by the opening title followed by its visual response: ALONG MILLIONAIRES' ROW. A small iris opens on a sign, CITY BREAD STATION   FREE BREAD, widening to a medium shot of Buster at a window. His back is to us; the roundness of his porkpie contrasts with the rectangular window and bricks in a three-dimensional depiction of the clash/confrontation theme pervading the film.

Keaton uses surprising visual perspectives to summarize Buster's situation and contrast his desperation with that of the hungry men nearby. Buster receives a loaf of bread through the window, but a nearby man snatches it and jerks his thumb to the offscreen end of the breadline. Hunger makes men desperate, for Buster has pushed himself ahead of the others although, curiously, no one protests until he leaves with his loaf. We have witnessed a dual reality: Buster at the head should be at the rear. This episode occurs in an ironic landscape, which Keaton will continue to fill with ironic visual gags.

At a slight diagonal angle to the action, we watch Buster shuffle past fifteen men before MAX CLOTHING STORE. The next major routine at the haberdashery discloses more irony. Cutting closer to ascertain Buster's crucial position, we learn that two of the five men directly before him are Max's mannequins. Buster's repositioning had momentarily diverted us from spotting the dummies among the humans. As the men filter out, though, we realize the mix-up from our frontal view, while Buster behind them cannot see. An extreme long shot of the breadline, horizontally masked at top and bottom, exaggerates the void between Buster left and the diminishing breadline right. The time Buster impatiently spends interacting with the two dummies is marked with typical gestures: hands on hips; casually sitting, then standing at the thought of moving forward; feigning innocence when he jabs a dummy with a pin; naiveté when painfully testing the pin on himself after he receives no reaction.

This scene probes the concept of a filmed reality, and film versus reality. With masking, the illusion of greater distance enhances the ironic humor more than would an unmasked extreme long shot. Masking measures the literal and figurative distance preventing Buster from receiving the bread; it is also a sight gag through a strictly filmic technique. Additionally, Keaton's juxtaposition of shots enhances the gags more than just through their composition. Structurally, the breadline gag "sandwiches" the dummy gag by starting and ending the sequence. Max's store window also frames the tableau of Buster and mannequins, emphasizing the dummy gag within the sequence and reminding us that he is being creatively duped by Fate, who is using Max as its unwitting handyman. Ironically, Buster fails to observe the mannequins, while we outside his reality can observe them clearly. Thus, Buster is "trapped" inside the window frame while being outside the store.

Once Max carts the dummies in, Buster realizes his error and rushes to bridge the distance, again in a masked shot. Length is thus artificially extended, an optical illusion of distance. In a three-quarter view, the bread man closes the window just as Buster reaches him. The window boxes Buster in with its frame, stressing his aloneness and rejection. "Outsider," a trait of *The High Sign* character, has already been implied here by Buster's round porkpie clashing with the straight lines of "the rest of the world." Buster conveys pained frustration at the CLOSED sign as he shoves his hands in his pockets, pauses, raps on the window, pauses, and walks off right. The reality of hunger, the irony of so-near-yet-so-far, is poignantly revealed through his simple gestures. The emotion in his slight expressions is not melodramatic. Keaton allows Buster a gritty but underplayed melancholy over life's ironies, well established by the film's first two conflicting titles.

The next routine contains another irony in the description of Buster's latest nemesis. DEAD SHOT DAN, A HIGHLY INTELLIGENT AND KINDLY FACED MURDERER IS ABOUT TO BE PHOTOGRAPHED FOR THE ROGUE'S GALLERY. (Dan is played by Mal St. Clair, with whom Keaton shared directing credit on this film, as he would again on *The Blacksmith* [1922].) We cut to medium long shot to focus on Buster's timely shuffle past the barred window of the room. He is again an outsider, framed (in every sense of the word) by another window. Buster holds on to the bars, curiously looking about as Dan triggers the camera on him; cut to profile medium shot of Dan covering the lens with his hat. In return long shot, Buster walks away. After Dan switches off the lights, his escape occurs in an interplay of light and dark through illumination from the window. A head silhouetted against the window bobs about and disappears; hazy light from an opened door shines on a guard before a second head sneaks past the window; the guard closes the door, flits past the window, turns on the light, and runs toward us. Keaton toys with the frame's starkest elements. By condensing

# The Goat

the unknown to light and dark elements, Keaton proves it unnecessary to see all the action. Our imagination supplies the details of the escape by watching shadows. Keaton also plays with the symbolic light/dark of Buster's circumstances, for, in the clash of these opposites, his identity is indeed about to be extinguished by another.

We cut to exterior to see Buster moping along from the left, as if the world is too heavy for him. He kicks aside a horseshoe; another man throws it over his shoulder for luck and shortly thereafter discovers a fat wallet. Buster walks from long shot to stare over the man's shoulder in medium shot. Even this simple matching of shots, moving a character from A to B, places us where we need to be. Buster's face is "framed" by the man's shoulder; his counting the money, then turning to glare at Buster, serve as directional arrows toward our forlorn hero. We watch Buster's dumbfounded stares at the man, at us, and offscreen, before cutting to his sudden dash and slide into a long shot, where he finds the horseshoe, kisses it lavishly, and tosses it—into a traffic cop. Intercutting between their reactions leads to the inevitable chase, which directs Buster first to a cigar store to catch his breath. As in *Hard Luck*, a casual smoke makes him superficially secure. He strikes a match on a cigar-store Indian, which suddenly brandishes a tomahawk. This absurdity drives Buster away—into a cop.

Typical of Buster in a desperate hour, he befriends the very force he tries to escape. Of another cop he inquires, presumably as a diversionary tactic: "WHERE'S THE BEST POST OFFICE IN TOWN?" Then he uses the distraction to push two cops into each other. Buster accumulates cops during the chase like rolling flypaper. Being a head shorter than the cop, Buster visually suggests a potentially overpowering confrontation. His size is also an effective sight gag because of the inherently funny dynamism of an energetic little bundle meeting a giant, like tumbleweed ramming Mount Rushmore. The resulting state of the "collider" determines whether the outcome is tragic or comic. This large/small, tragic/comic dichotomy, present ever since Buster met Hank and Joe in *One Week* (and Arbuckle before that), will have a vital twist in *The Goat*, since Buster will soon collide with himself and become his own nemesis.

Keaton continues placing us at angles to our hero by how he positions the camera. In so doing, Keaton creates a dynamism otherwise restrained in a straight, head-on perspective; he made much use of the angled perspective in *Neighbors*. Keaton carries us *into* the frame, dimensioning the flatness. As a director can skew the visual angle to suggest something amiss (a technique that most often works subliminally), Keaton at times shoots off the front for similar commentary. This perspective becomes an editorial on Buster's condition seen through the "omni-optic" camera. In one angled view, a traffic cop leaves his post, exposing Buster behind him, obliviously directing the cars and turning with open arms to the chasing cops. Buster distracts them with a shout (again, Keaton Kops are stupid). In childlike relief at outwitting them, Buster romps on a lawn (similarly, he pulled petals during the life-death chase in *Convict 13*); ironically, he is also leaving clear tracks for the cops. Thus, the angled view is really Keaton's wry comment that nothing Buster does is going to guarantee his success, for life in general is skewed.

Now Keaton conversely uses a head-on perspective to suggest depth. We are as surprised as the cops are when a parked car pulls forward to reveal Buster lying face down underneath; he grabs on to the spare tire as the car roars off. Buster slides into the next shot before a fourth cop who is also swept into the chase. Playing again with the space of the frame, a miniscule Buster grows in size as he races from background to train tracks lying horizontally in foreground. Buster steps over the tracks, inviting the three cops to fight with him. He can be so confident, for suddenly a train roars in left across middleground and separates them. For audiences accustomed to layered sound tracks and quick cuts in today's films, such a brief shot recalls the magic of silent film. Although we see the rails, we are not aware of an onrushing train (like the train in *One Week*). The silence of the shot almost hinders our comprehension of the situation, even though the ingredients are assembled before us. Our comic surprise is heightened because we never—cannot—hear the train. Images hang in a soundless vacuum, like wind chimes moving to someone who cannot hear. Sound films capture that same sensory play when they turn off the sounds of life and free the imagination to listen to silence.

After the next gag (Buster luring cops into a moving van), the chase stops to welcome the love interest. A pedestrian trips over a dog walked by The Girl (Virginia Fox) and argues with her. Buster intercedes and accidentally knocks out the man. He notices the man does not stir, then spots a cop in the distance; he flees, meeting up with the cops from the van. The curve of Fate strikes again, declaring open season on Buster. As Buster staggers through this film's life-disappointments, he wears a look of increasing gullibility so that even though he flees his destiny, his conscience becomes the embodiment of a "goat," Fate's scapegoat. Accustomed to curveballs now, Buster automatically responds to each new situation with the willingness of a drugged victim on a sacrificial altar. Back in *Convict 13*, Buster accepted the role of prisoner because he recognized that Cop/Authority/Nemesis presumed him guilty from the start. Although he is a Good Samaritan here, he becomes the opposite— a Criminal, again instantly and unquestioningly. Keaton's transformation/equation theme is thus replayed: Buster Innocent = Buster Criminal, secured to this destiny by the previous identity transformation: Buster = Dan. In the snap of a finger (or the wink of a shutter), Buster becomes another.

Keaton also equates Dan's fateful shooting of Buster with a larger reality: that of Keaton shooting our hero with a film camera. Via Keaton's filmic fantasy, the symbolic curve is now translated into the literal curve of more train tracks. A train stands center, curving into the background and offscreen. Buster hops on the caboose in foreground and waves goodbye. The last cars turn off into the background, leaving Buster's caboose behind; he and we have again been optically "illusioned" by the unexpected. Cut to interior of the moving train: Buster races down a crowded aisle, smashing foreground for background, as passengers crane to look and direct our eyes toward him by their movement. Buster unhooks his car from the one now containing the cops. We ride with Buster on the roof, although his back faces us. Fields of depth spread apart as the car with cops glides into the distance. Iris closes; fade in. From afar, a dot of a smoke-spewing train speeds toward us. As it grows larger, Buster becomes discernible, sitting statuesque on the cowcatcher—legs propped up, hands clasped, head tilted, porkpie cocked above eyes staring hard at the camera. This image "answers" the earlier one where Buster turned his back to us; he now responds head on. The train brakes abruptly; we and Buster scrutinize each other for a pithy pause. Cutting to a long shot, the camera pans to show that no cars are linked to this engine. Buster lights a cigarette on the engine (his films seem to be a quest for a puff), then tiptoes away from the dumbfounded engineer.

This cowcatcher insert once again demonstrates Buster's perennial habit of lingering while trying to escape. This image is also a bit of a puzzle, like the helpful hand in *One Week* blocking Sybil in her tub. We are boldly reminded of a unique film device that reestablishes our role as impartial spectators.[3] This objectivity is vital to be one up on Buster, for Keaton often allows us to see what Buster cannot; he thus affirms his belief in an intelligent audience. Neither cowcatcher nor helpful-hand advance the story, although the latter was more of a sight gag in its risqué nature. Both gags appear without warning, yet they are subtly connected to earlier "reasons": Sybil needs a bath, Buster needs to escape. Although Fate released his caboose and left him stranded, Buster retaliates by eliminating all but the engine (even the engineer, an authority figure, is oblivious). Buster's determination to lose the train is curious. Since we were with him on the roof, we know he lost the cops when the first car glided away. But his fear runs deep: until he is *totally* alone, Buster will not believe he is free of cops and therefore free of the guilt that creeps into his gullible conscience. Only at that point can he win. His actions summarize his equation philosophy: last = first, first = last, and little man = victor, despite the curve.

Apart from its thematic repercussion, the cowcatcher is a depth-creating device. In an earlier sequence, Buster had been a distant speck running into the foreground before the train laterally split him from the cops. The perspective now switches, and Buster becomes master of his crisis via the mechanical while also smashing background, middleground, foreground. The train fills (cancels) the frame, shifting emphasis instantly from machine to man within the frame.[4] Buster deserves to be at the head of the train (he missed out as head of the breadline) for reversing his "hard luck." Keaton supports Buster's reversal of fortune with a frontal view so that for once we are not one up; we do not see the missing train because of Buster's head-on arrival. Thus, the aftergag is a shock for us, even though we expect *something* because of Keaton's deliberate pause of anticipation. Buster's blank yet penetrating stare is open to readings. Perhaps its intensity is another audience-mocker as in *The High Sign*, yet more polite than a nose-thumbing; behind Buster's unblinking face, Keaton implies that he has fooled us. On the other hand, Buster might be so exhausted that he can only sit motionlessly and stare at us for a little compassion.

We carry Buster's haunting close-up into the next crucial episode, in which he resumes his persona of humble, Fate-weary, little man. The business of the photograph had been interrupted by chases, in order to reinforce Buster's destiny of being pursued. It now resumes with the title THE NEWS OF DEAD SHOT DAN'S ESCAPE HAD ALREADY REACHED ANOTHER TOWN. Buster approaches three citizens perusing a newspaper who are startled at seeing him. In close-up, the headline screams DEAD SHOT DAN ESCAPES above the photo of a pale, intelligent, kindly faced man in a porkpie behind bars. The close-up shot has excluded Buster but includes us along with the citizens, as though we are in a clique privy to important information that Buster should not learn. We again see what Buster does not, as with Max's dummies. Not understanding the real cause of the uproar, Buster looks at himself in a drugstore mirror. In medium long shot, a group of men meet before a billboard, their bulk blotting out all but the key words ESCAPED and WANTED FOR MURDER   REWARD $5000 DEAD OR ALIVE   NOTIFY CHIEF OF POLICE. Buster sighs his way into the group. Pause. All disperse in terror, leaving Buster dwarfed by his billboard photograph. As we cut closer, Buster becomes visually surrounded by the photo and words. The camera pans slightly when Buster leans over to read the giant letters, as if sympathizing with him.

Now the film reveals its greatest conflict, its strongest paradox, its most unequivocal equation: Buster = The Goat. The equation has been visually presented and enlarged by degrees: first, close-up of the newspaper; second, billboard words poking through the crowd; third, the whole billboard filling the frame. The billboard has been approached in steps, just as Buster learns of it in steps, to parallel the mounting tension of his plunge into notoriety. Fate withholds its largest announcement till the end, to trumpet it straight in Buster's face. His first real knowledge of his doom is also the biggest and most daunting. The climactic revelation of the billboard is like the cyclone of *One Week*, the apex of tension and chaos. Our steady emotional buildup has grown gradually along with the physical size of the photograph, until Buster is dominated, surrounded, overwhelmed, absorbed by its enormity.[5]

Buster's dilemma now transcends the physical. He has become his own worst conflict/paradox/equation. The face behind the bars is the reverse of Buster's open mask in the cowcatcher scene; there is no question of his perplexity and our sympathy for him. In earlier films, Buster elected to be another (scarecrow, prison warden, ghost) to further his ambitions or security. Here, he is the toy of higher powers, just as he was in the dream of *The Haunted House*. But this is not a dream, and the opening realistic landscape has eliminated all chance of one. In the greater scheme of things, we must remember that Fate has decreed Dan to fit Buster's description (and vice versa) so that the conflict centers on Buster's face once his innocent actions lead him straight into his own trap. The comedy becomes poignant, since the citizens truly believe that such a gentle face can mask a criminal soul—and ironically, since Dan has *Buster's* gentle face also, it does! (Additionally, Keaton never overlooks a chance to jab Authority, for again the cops fail to notice, much less get, "their man." Case in point: they recognized Convict 13 only through his striped uniform.) This duality of interchangeable faces contrasts sharply with *The High Sign* in which Buster could never have been a Buzzard, for his subtle face clashed with their grotesque masks.

Once introduced, the photograph dominates the film whether it appears on-screen or not; it is permanently in our minds, especially because Keaton has so inexorably filled the frame with it. Buster is trapped yet abandoned by the citizens; Keaton again plays with depth as the citizens cross grounds in symmetrical "chaos." Because we are the only objective spectators, Keaton controls our perspective of depth and camera angle in order to witness the citizens' terror and Buster's perplexity. When Buster takes a moment to reflect, we too fade to a flashback-memory of him with the unconscious pedestrian. As the memory passes, Buster droops melodramatically (Keaton reminds us not to feel *too* sorry). We cut suddenly to two plasterers behind the billboard who argue: "DON'T TELL ME HOW TO MIX MORTAR!" and one pushes the other into the trough. We cut to Buster as a whitened plasterer enters a side door through the billboard. Again misinformed, Buster is terrified by the "ghost" of the man he thinks he "killed." He runs off into a rotund man (Joe Roberts), naturally the Chief, and begins an "escape dance" of confronting and avoiding moves. Buster has fulfilled the predestined role of "murderer," through the Wanted sign, without actually killing anyone, and he believes it. After all, Fate set up the photo session long before the pedestrian run-in; Fate just stirred the ingredients together for a preordained recipe.

In a variation on the citizens' response to Buster, a woman at the billboard runs off when she sees him and drops her fur stole, giving Buster a new prop. He desperately holds the stole to his face as a beard, then pins the stole under the billboard nose. Buster reenacts his childlikeness, thinking that the 3-D disguise will separate him from his image, as much as his mustache-tie "shielded" his identity from Lizard's gang in *Hard Luck*. Buster's wishful thinking fails as the mustache sags under the Chief's scrutiny. Because of the chaos over the photo, Keaton interweaves a variety of gags and creates thematic layers. Some business initially seems tangential and slows the action around the more directly related gags. For example, Buster rushes past an armed thug (possibly Dan) in a doorway; this shadowy character is then dropped while our hero toys with the fur stole. After that fails, Buster and the Chief pass the same thug in their chase; he thrusts a gun under Buster's arm and fires at the Chief, then deposits the gun in Buster's hand and flees. Such a minimal character, at first an interruption, impacts on the theme of "Buster the Goat." The thug does not advance the plot as much as fortify Buster's character and state of mind and stresses both external and internal chases in this short.

Throughout all of his films, Buster of course participates in physical chases over land, as most other silent film comedians did. But his unique contribution is his endurance during the *symbolic* chase—with Fate. This "invisible" chase will rival, if not totally obliterate, the physical chase in upcoming films. Wherever Buster turns now, he is The Goat and cannot run far enough to escape that identity. From the start, Buster was "framed": the breadline window boxed him into an intense hunger; Max's store window hemmed him into never sating his appetite; his window curiosity wrested away his identity in the split second that he peered into a room. His innocence has been framed, cornered, trapped. His outcome is shaky but ironically still open to change. The billboard has practically burst Buster out of the tight confines of the frame, if only by its enormity. And like his train ride carrying him forward on the cowcatcher to fill the frame, the billboard fills the frame with a largeness that reinterprets Buster's predicament. The cowcatcher face can now be interpreted as wary and smart, no longer innocent. Buster must set aside his innocence and act shrewd enough to alter his future. These two faces of Buster, on the cowcatcher and on the billboard, become like the two faces of Janus—one of worldly wisdom, the other of innate naiveté. The billboard has loudly proclaimed Buster as ultimate Goat; it has also been Fate's last chance to mock his helplessness. Now Buster will choose to wear either face as he sees fit; he is able, so to speak, to flip to both sides of his own plug nickel.

Buster's desperation at being framed leads him into another sight gag as an escape: sitting *in* the spare tire at the rear of a parked car. In a variation of the train routine with Buster in the last car, the automobile roars into the background, leaving him behind in what really is a three-dimensional tire ad on an iron stand. His flight now propels him into a RECEIVING HOSPITAL, where he crawls under a bedsheet in a darkened room as the intern tells the pursuing Chief, "HUSH! YOU'LL DISTURB THE PATIENT!" and then to the nurse, "THE DOCTOR'S COMING AT ONCE TO OPERATE." The intern illuminates Buster's situation, both by his words and by controlling the amount of light from the door into the room. At the same time, Keaton works his light/dark effects with the opening door, as he did for Dan's escape. Buster, again pathetically misinformed, believes that the

carpenter come to fix the window shade is the surgeon with his "tools"—
saw, drill, hammer. Supremely paranoid by now, Buster assumes he is the
patient and jumps out the window. Keaton cuts to exterior not only to
record Buster's sprawl on the pavement but to reenact the curve, which
was the whole purpose of the hospital sequence. At that moment, two
ambulance attendants cart Buster back inside on a stretcher. What tran-
spires behind hospital doors is not shown, nor is it necessary to see; perhaps a nurse "discharges" the "patient" or Buster flees at the thought of
"surgery." The ending to the routine is Buster's tumbling exit downstairs
to land beside the Chief and, of course, resume the chase. The diversion
at the hospital reemphasizes Buster's fateful irony.

As ever, Keaton inserts charismatic "foot"-notes—footwork that
Buster instinctively uses during his adventures. Each twist and turn of
his body prevents monotonous repetition. Keaton's detailed movements
from any A to any B also fully exhibited his own athletic prowess and
kept his hero challenged. We next visit a park where footwork plus
Keaton's direction of the visual space between Buster and the Chief create
a symmetrical ballet of who-sees-whom-first. From this "stepping-
stone" gag, we move into a routine that has become a classic of Keaton
filmmaking and a touchstone for Keaton lampoons.

Buster joins a group of tophatted-and-tailed men who listen to a
bereted artist standing beside a large sheeted object. "GENTLEMEN, I HAVE
JUST FINISHED THE CLAY MODEL OF MY MASTERPIECE." Buster applauds also to
appear unobtrusive; however, the Chief spots him and Buster leaves from
our view. As the artist yanks the unveiling cord, the spectators point in
awe at the sculpture—now remodeled by Buster sitting marble-like on a
clay horse, MAN O'WAR. He sits facing left as does the nag but stares right,
hand shielding eyes from the sun as he searches for a distant haven. The
artist collapses with melodrama as the horse's legs buckle under Buster's
weight. As the Chief nears, Buster and horse topple over. Buster speeds
into another scene and crawls under a real horse and wagon loaded with
rocks. The Chief crawls after him, but Buster scrambles out, releases the
rocks, and drives off. In an afterthought, Buster returns to listen to the
pile, adds rocks, and walks off satisfied in a closing iris.

This routine, containing the unforgettable Busterian pose (nearly a
trademark) of scouting the horizon, is as intriguing in its "hidden agenda"
as the cowcatcher scene. Under the unveiling sheet is a peculiar place to
hide, since Buster must have surmised that a great cultural work was soon
to be shared with the world. Yet desperation blocks common sense. On

the other hand, Buster is in control for, upon exposure, he "becomes" the sculpture in a posture that befits the valiant Man O'War.[6] It shocks the artist but fools the Chief, which is the purpose. The Chief only realizes the camouflage when the statue sags; the inevitable "curveball" made the statue *only* a model—of clay, not metal—so that Buster is outwitted at his own game. Some critics suggest Keaton is lampooning fake art created by a pompous, stereotypical artist and lauded by stuffed shirts, a fraud with "feet of clay" buckling under scrutiny and betraying its audience.[7] But Buster's predicament transcends art (he has literally mounted it); his Man O'War enters a ceaseless war with Fate. He "rides" his steed into battle and retrieves the invisible fallen flag when the horse drops; these spontaneous actions rise from a precarious opportunity that he turns to his advantage, and from which he regains control just as he did by crawling under the parked car. Using one's wits faster than one's pursuers are apt to do (should they have any wits) is vital; it is also the total personification of Buster. He surpasses all fakery around him, for he is the "real thing," genuine to a fault. While Buster's character grows in emotional complexity, the fakers around him become more cardboard by contrast. The police, the artist, and the empty artwork all remain caricatures for lampooning.

Naturally, the film's main catalyst—the photo—dominates the last portion of the film primarily in spirit. It has been burned into our psyche so it need not appear in "person" to remind us of its presence; we simply know that without it, there would be no film and no "goat." The amazing quality of the photograph is that it zeroes in on Buster's stark face while prolonging the physical conflict Keaton presented from the start: the soft features of his pale face against cold straight bars. He stares into a world where he does not belong while standing in another world where he does not fit. He is a well-rounded person/persona grasping at clay figures and sharp edges. We begin the last portion of the film peering over Buster's sloping shoulder that partially frames the infamous newspaper photo he is holding. The chases have forced Buster to confront, grapple with, and control his dilemma. He has come to literally hold the solution in his hand and employ it to his advantage, especially as now the chase has turned into not only a running *from* (Fate) but a running *toward* (Love), Buster's most treasured dream.

Reenter The Girl with the Pekinese, witness to the "murder," trotting in to Buster's warm greeting as he steps from behind a taxi. She is not petrified of him even though she saw his "crime," for she probably saw the "murdered man" walk away from the scene after Buster fled in guilt. But for Buster, her willingness to remain with him is a welcome novelty in this town of fear. She represents true love: whether or not she has seen the Wanted sign, she obviously overlooks Buster's dire deed and accepts him. Gaining her attention and the promise of love, Buster has new confidence to reverse his destiny by literally clutching Fate's tool in his own hand. The taxi driver argues with Buster who, with a threatening wave of the newspaper, sends him off on his fearful way. Buster's upper hand is never more evident than when he uses the photo to dispense with the pesky driver. While earlier he was troubled by the frightened citizens, he now instigates the flight of someone interrupting his personal progress. With a rare show of disgust, Buster casts the paper down and follows his lady. Buster now reacts with deliberate vehemence to the catastrophe into which he was hurled. Riding Man O'War has armed him for the battle game in which he now has the winning hand.

The next setting, The Girl's lobby, is both natural and simple, including the ingredients essential for the concluding gags: (1) desk attendant providing stupefied reactions (acting as a surrogate audience caught up in "reality" but unable to laugh as we can); (2) staircase at side; and (3) elevator with windowed doors and a half-moon floor counter with arrow indicator. Through this brief exposition, we absorb the "lay of the land" and file away these details, particularly how the arrow zips from "1" to "7" as the elevator speeds past the floors. When Buster enters The Girl's apartment, he immediately sits for dinner and plays with the dog. Although we do not yet know if and how the lives of The Girl and the Chief are intertwined, we suspect this elaborate introduction is helping to complicate Buster's existence. Enter the Chief with a bashed bowler, a vestige of his encounter with the rock pile. He sits at the head of the table opposite Buster. Neither The Girl nor her mother introduces Buster, and the four jump into saying grace and eating. This odd breach of etiquette is lost in our mounting anticipation that the enemies will momentarily recognize each other. It is also as if conviviality does not exist in a senseless, ironic world; its inhabitants must simply plunge into the animosity that drives Buster's flights.

The confrontation is punctuated by shots of "nonverbal dialogue": the Chief's eyes narrow into furious slits and Buster sinks in his seat. The Chief throws back his chair and spins the "cyclone" of the inevitable chase. Each step in this nonverbal conversation (Chief locks door, twists key, Buster blinks) is a meeting of minds. The final springboard into the eye of the storm is one dynamic shot that Keaton has not yet used in his films. The Chief stalks toward us (Buster) until he becomes a menacing close-up with each step. Such dynamism recaptures what audiences must have experienced at the first silent "flickers" of powerful locomotives or crashing waves on a beach—a sense of shocked helplessness as if they were about to drown. In a long shot of the room, Buster leaps onto the table and the Chief's shoulders, then out through the transom.

Keaton takes us outside the apartment to play with the set as fully as he did with the tenement in *Neighbors*, and surely more than he did with the rambling space of *The Haunted House*. Buster closes himself in behind the windowed door—what we believe is the elevator—and his head appropriately lowers past the glass in descent. The Chief races down the stairs to catch up with him. After a pause, Buster pushes open the door and crawls out—it is a phone booth. Keaton has executed yet another transformation/equation to play with our senses. Because we have not yet visited this floor and remember the *lobby's* components instead, Keaton inserts this novel gag to startle us by the similarity of doors that we (like the Chief) think is the elevator. We have already marveled at the high-speed counter; in his frustration with the elevator holding at "1," Buster pulls the arrow to "7," with the elevator responding instantly. His forceful, confident control now spills over into manipulating the environment, which is absurdly malleable (like the clock in *The Haunted House*). Buster returns to the lobby as does the Chief; Buster returns to "4" (according to the counter) and the Chief lumbers up the stairs. We need not join them; we skip floors by cutting. The editing is intelligent, not spoonfed, calling upon our powers to observe and connect.

In case we had forgotten it in the flurry of all the chases, we return to the photo, a reminder of how it still impacts on Buster's reputation, causing all his troubles. Buster runs into an apartment to find the tenant cleaning a gun while eying the infamous newspaper propped against a lamp. The photo is shown in an interesting perspective that draws our eye directly to it: the newspaper faces us, not the tenant, and the lamp shines on the photo. Buster's hasty entrance at the left directs our eye past the tenant straight to the photo, even though it is one of the smallest items in the room. Once again, the illumination is both of trouble and clarity.

The "magical" elevator clearly represents the control our hapless goat now wields. Buster falls through an open door down the elevator shaft and into the basement. Instead of pain, his expression registers fascination with a new idea. The chase now becomes vertical, reaching upward under Buster's self-propulsion, instead of horizontally penetrating the grounds of the frame. The vertical is divided into planes, altitudes, even Buster's state of mind. SEVEN FLOORS HIGHER, the title announces, summarizing the action of a chase up and down flights to suggest the height we never actually see. Buster reenacts his earlier "elevator" plunge to fool the Chief; now he lures him past the open door into the shaft. Buster phones The Girl to "MEET ME ON THE SEVENTH FLOOR," not seeing the Chief ascend *on top of* the elevator. Buster with chagrin again "descends" in the phone booth window. Because this gag is repeated not long after its first performance, it derives its punch from the repetition itself. The first time fooled the Chief (and us); the second time reinforces the joke with a twist since the Chief (and we) are supposedly "one up." As a twist, however, Buster slips out between the Chief's legs so that we again lose our superior position over Buster.

We cut next to selected floors to keep up with Buster, The Girl, and the Chief who is finally trapped. Buster nails the floor counter arrow at "2" to brake the elevator; the result is verified in a cutaway of the Chief wedged in the space at the top of the second-floor door. Buster mans his "control" panel, steering the arrow past *all* the numbers to hang limply to the floor. We cut abruptly to exterior for the visually bizarre image of the elevator tearing through the roof, tipping on its wobbly pole and spilling out the Chief. In a tag-ending, Buster and The Girl skip out of the lobby toward us, dodge debris from above, and head for HOLLYWOOD FURNITURE CO: YOU FURNISH THE GIRL, WE FURNISH THE HOME. Buster pauses, slings The Girl over his shoulder, and enters. Iris closes. THE END.

The chase has ended in a Salvador Dali-esque vision. The bulky symbol of Authority is punished and removed in a warped image as fantastic as Buster's return from China in *Hard Luck*. Buster launches the elevator through the roof like a surrealistic rocket (reminiscent of Méliès's *A Trip to the Moon* [1902], in which a rocket lands in the eye of Man in the Moon).[8] Buster's chase is faithful to Keaton's vision of pursued-pursuer. Unfortunately, because of this, the film also degrades into the slapstick of the impossible. It transcends the ironic landscape by rising into odd visions of wishful thinking, as if Buster can only elude his persecutors in "outer space" instead of on grounds of reality. We remember Buster's rise-and-fall in *The Haunted House* dream, which, within that framework, allowed us to accept its unreality. Here, the dreamlike runaway elevator (already remarkable for its manipulable counter) creates a nightmarish illusion of meting out justice. It is a what–if–this–were–possibility that a paranoid mind conjures and science fiction or slapstick portray.

The literal chase is fraught with the action-reactions of Buster and Man, Machine, and/or Nature. These ultimately signify the symbolic Chase. Man, Machine, Nature are the handiwork, tool, manifestation, and representation of Fate. Their play with Buster's consciousness during the literal chase becomes a haunting game with his subconscious during the symbolic Chase. In *The Goat*, Fate = Buster (through the photograph) so that his self-confrontation is the most devious trick played on him thus far. We too join in the symbolic Chase, alternating one up and one down on Buster through Keaton's manipulation of the perspectives we see at any given time. In the long run (pun intended), Keaton is the Master Fate, juggling Buster and us with him. Keaton does sympathize with his lonely warrior; although he dubs him with supreme Goathood, he also bestows on him the Excalibur (arrow counter) to fight his dragon.

Like a magnet, Buster draws the illogical to himself and reasons it out, fights it off, soars above it. Although the bizarre slapstick weakens, almost mocks, the "realism" of the first reel, the ending does sustain the theme of the whole film. Logically, what would Buster do or be without the illogical? It is his reason for running—to find its opposite: Home, Girl, Furnishings, the oasis he seeks with hand to forehead. The feeling is contagious to those (few) who love Buster: The Girl forfeits father, mother, and Pekinese for the comfortable life of a potato sack (à la *Neighbors*). Buster licenses himself to attack the Chief and destroy art to save his innocent hide. Hunger truly makes men desperate, and Buster hungers for the good life. There is no other recourse for a Goat than to retaliate with the most powerful physical forces at his disposal: trains, cars, elevator, his body—the very forces that Fate also loves to use. Buster penetrates time and space to do so: commandeering the train horizontally, the elevator vertically, and his body both ways. The film can only end with the Chief's removal and the hero avenged of an unfair life on a mundane plateau.

The absurd resolution of Buster's conflicts, however, gives us little hope that someone so palatable to Fate will ever be left alone. Keaton's fantastic ending is a desperate wish (deus ex elevator) to open up the tight corner into which Buster has run. We suspect that in the future, Buster will still be "Wanted." A Nemesis will shadow his every step. And there will always be Cops. Logically, Fate will need to devise another outcome for its favorite Goat, but one within the reality of a square-edged world with a cruel curve. The outcome of that chase lies further up the road.

## Chapter 10

# The Playhouse

### (January 1922)

Courtesy of the Academy of Motion Picture Arts and Sciences

Hamlet once mused, "The play's the thing." Enter Keaton punctually on the cue "perchance to dream" with a quick run and pratfall, to conjure a daydream of extraordinary visions. In *The Playhouse*, all the world is indeed a stage—yet for all the stage, still a film. Keaton rolls his memories of vaudeville straight through the proscenium and frame for some of the most vivid illusions in silent cinema.

# The Playhouse

The darkness of the screen lifts like a stage curtain, in a curious wipe form, to present Buster reading a poster, OPERA HOUSE  TO-NIGHT TWENTY FIVE OF THE WORLD'S GREATEST MINSTREL STARS. Instantly, we enter the world of the *theater* by the opening, strictly *filmic*, optical "curtain." Buster plays a dual role: ticket-buying Audience Member *and* Actor (since he is in fact "behind the curtain"). This illusion is reinforced as Buster pays with money from a tiny wallet that unfolds to the floor like a long accordion. We have been duly warned: what seems one will be another, yet they are the same. Buster enters the playhouse.

An irised medium shot tunnels our vision to dispel any doubt on what we are about to see. It is also like a filmic "spotlight" on the Conductor who now steps into the orchestra pit; he bears an uncanny "resemblance" to Buster. Unfamiliar with this strange new world, we momentarily wonder how the Conductor can look exactly like the Audience Member. Is it Keaton's logical-illogic that the Conductor of the show has to pay to get in? Or has Buster come to see his musician twin brother? Conductor readies us for a greater shock when he taps his baton, blasts into a downbeat, and cues us to the "Strings" by looking offscreen. In long shot, Bass, Cello, and Violin perform vivace; they are all Busters. In medium shot, Conductor cues us to the other side: Clarinet, Trombone, and Drums are all played by Buster. In medium shot, the Conductor scratches his back a tempo with the baton, almost like a wry comment.

Once we are introduced to the orchestral participants in this illusion and become accustomed to the multiplicity, we realize this is not a trick of double exposure or superimposing one Keaton over another. Each musician plays his instrument in his own "cubicle" of the frame through multiple exposure. The pièce de résistance of this technique is yet to occur in *The Playhouse*, but to whet our appetite, Keaton introduces it early in the film. Keaton and his cameraman Elgin Lessley divided the picture frame into separate parts, or cubicles, for each Buster in the shot by masking off fractions of the lens, blocking those cubicles that should not be exposed. Once a role was performed, the film was rewound, the shutter reset, and the lens remasked for the next performance in the adjacent cubicle. Up to three musicians are accommodated in one shot so that the trio appears to perform simultaneously. "Keaton didn't originate [multiple exposure]. It had been used for years to show an actor in two roles at once. But it was a difficult technique. It was hard to join the halves of the picture without a tell-tale line down the middle. It was also hard to get the separate actions to synchronize—like looking up at the exact moment that your alter ego, in the earlier exposure, said something to you."[1]

Unlike multiple exposure, double exposure results from filming over another image within a full frame so that two images (say, of the same person) can literally occupy the same place at the same time. As a result, double exposure creates the kind of dreamy transparency vital to Keaton's feature *Sherlock Jr.* in which Buster the projectionist rises from his sleeping body to enter his own dream. The ghostly offspring represents a self "dissolved" into an ethereal form. Metamorphosis into a ghost or dream alter ego is generally introduced by a transparent self rising from a solid body and sometimes returns to that form when the story ends. More often, the transparent image quickly "solidifies" and does not retain its ghostly appearance once the character begins its adventures. Besides the technical difficulty of maintaining a transparent entity for the film's duration, superimposition can also be a disservice to actor and audience. The superimposed actor is not seen in a natural physique but in a perpetual "dissolved" condition; "in-the-flesh" is usually far easier to act, film, and watch. Keaton avoids signaling a dream through superimposition just to tease his audience. In *Convict 13* and *The Haunted House*, dreams were not announced; we believed we were awake and were startled by the transition revealing the dream. In contrast, *Sherlock Jr.* introduces a superimposed dream early in the film to frame Buster's adventures; the fantasy is clear and becomes an acceptable sophisticated reality.

In *The Playhouse*, Keaton wishes us to believe that the orchestra is real because the idea of multiple Busters is sophisticated humor. But we wonder what device is being used since Busters are an incredible possibility. Is this a dream? Whose and for what end? The images suggest an unconfirmed dream-frame. Logically, since each musician requires the straight-faced treatment only Buster can give, why shouldn't he be each musician? The performers play with mock intensity, a pseudoself-seriousness that hides each Buster-Musician's emotions while highlighting Buster-Persona's depthful deadpan. With furrowed brow, puffed cheek, or stares at upside-down sheet music, the musicians show how serious they are. Each one, however, reminds us of Buster who lies beneath the (melo)drama of performing. Buster is his innocent self assuming the role of Musician in a magical scenario. As in *The Scarecrow* where all rooms = one room, here all Busters = one Buster, conveying a spectrum of subtle expressions to parody the blatant ones.

To derive greater humor from the sight gag of multiple Busters, each musician plays with peculiar mannerisms. By intercutting between performers in individual medium shots, we focus on each personality, each odd musical technique. Buster-Clarinet pulls the reed out of his mouth, sticks it in his nose, and gnaws on the mouthpiece. Buster-Trombone oils his slide that zips out, plays in spurts as if he has hiccups, and tries to fit a second slide onto the first. Buster-Bass "bows" with a hollow saw and plucks staccato. Buster-Cello chalks his bow like a pool shark, attacks the strings, and stabs his sheet music with the bow. Buster-Drums taps merrily on an upside-down cymbal, fires a revolver, and raps on the snare. Buster-Conductor brushes off the sheet music and swats a fly.

For his musicians, Keaton may have been inspired by mother Myra, who before she was eleven "could play the bull fiddle, the piano, and the cornet. Later on she became the first woman stage performer in the United States to play a saxophone" (though Keaton adds that she "preferred playing auction pinochle").[2] Keaton becomes his own one-man band, more versatile than his Ma. His familiarity with a vaudeville orchestra, into which he often flew with his father's propulsion, certainly helped him concoct this madcap ensemble. The typical orchestra varied "in size from one piece, a piano (and sometimes a banjo), to seven or eight pieces. A seven-piece orchestra usually consisted of violin, cornet, piano, clarinet, trombone, string bass and drums. . . . The orchestras in the best theaters were extraordinarily good. . . . Your typical variety-hall musician could play from a vast repertoire of clogs, reels, hornpipes, sand jigs, and walk-arounds, and could fake a song in any given key. All of them had to be good readers and improvisers."[3]

Sheet music cascades to the floor, crescendo, fine, offscreen ovation. Conductor acknowledges the unseen audience (playhouse audience and us). He gives a cue, and we enter the backstage world where a stagehand (Buster) yanks on curtain ropes. We are in Keaton's hands—out front, backstage, in a barrage of Busters. We hop about the theater through cutting, finding Buster in a gallery of crazy-mirrors that makes us doubt what we see. The roles change but the same face breaks through, an anchor in a swirl of images.

The playhouse becomes a fun house and we are at the apex of a collapsible slide, suspended before the plunge. Keaton has lifted us there by his sequence of energetic Busters. Our anticipation now rises along with the curtain that Buster-Stagehand lifts as we cut to the stage. Under a pumpkin-shaped proscenium with a central encircled "K" stands a minstrel troupe, as announced on the lobby card at the start of the film. Interlocutor stands flanked by four minstrels on each side. This tour de force of multiple exposure caps our expectation (our careen down the slide): all nine gents = Buster! Wearing dark suits, white gloves, and blackface, and standing against a black background, the minstrels jiggle their arms to a snappy tune before the traditional repartee begins. Interlocutor: "GENTLEMEN! BE SEATED!" Corny jokes are hurled between Interlocutor and the end men, Bones and Sambo, in separately paced title cards: "MR. BROWN, I UNDERSTAND YOU HAD A CYCLONE IN YOUR TOWN." "YES SIR! THE WIND BLEW SO HARD, IT BLEW A SILVER DOLLAR INTO FOUR QUARTERS." "THAT'S NOTHING! THE WIND BLEW SO HARD, IT BLEW A WART OFF A MAN'S NOSE AND BROKE A WINDOW TWO BLOCKS AWAY!" (Coincidence, perhaps, that Keaton chose the cyclone joke, given his childhood cyclone and the cyclone in *One Week*.)

Here, Keaton re-creates a native American entertainment, with which he was also closely familiar. Briefly, the "First Part" of a minstrel show consisted of dialogue between Interlocutor and Bones and Tambo (although Keaton named his end man Sambo, the usual name was Tambo, short for the tambourine he played). The jokes exchanged between this trio "existed chiefly for the sake of introducing set [musical numbers], just as a musical comedy had its dialogue built around a definite vocal programme. The songs were by no means all humorous, and in general it was a rule that the worst jokes should precede the best and more serious lyric efforts." This segment was followed by the "walk around" and "olio" ("in one") that entertained the audience while the stage was set for the second half of the program, generally a revue of sketches and parodies.[4]

The first appearance of blackface (burnt-cork) minstrels was probably February 6, 1843, at the Bowery Amphitheatre in New York City, with a four-member troupe called the Virginia Minstrels. Keaton undoubtedly heard of Edwin P. Christy, whose Christy Troupe became so popular "that their name was eventually applied generically to all Negro impersonators."[5] Keaton includes trademarks of the "First Part" in his condensed version. Interlocutor is the straight man, usually attired in full suit and "expansive shirt front," and often in white face; he speaks impeccably and pompously, serving as the butt of jokes from the end men. Keaton's six minstrels are tagged on each end by Bones and Sambo wearing blackface, curly wig, black suit, white gloves, tie, and shirt. Bones was so named for the set of "bones" or ebony sticks (they may have originated from horse ribs) that he would clack and toss to the music while his counterpart shook the tambourine.[6] Keaton abbreviates the minstrel show to a few jokes and jiggling; after all, this program only tastes of Keaton's memories. This is not theater, but a film of theatrical dreams (using the word *dreams* might be premature, but clues are being planted toward that *reality*).

This "multiple exposure to end all multiple exposures" was one of the earliest special-effects triumphs in film.[7] In the minstrel show, Keaton gives a full display by maintaining a theater-audience distance. But complying with film's demands for point-of-view editing, he inserts closer shots of Interlocutor, Bones, and Sambo each delivering gag lines, thus letting us approach the action for the best perspective. Cutting to speakers with single shots serves two key purposes. First, it mimics our eye movement toward a speaker. In a stage show, our eyes land on one speaker to the near exclusion of the others; the actual cut to a closer shot is to focus and exclude. Second, returning to the master shot builds credibility for Buster playing nine roles simultaneously. Although a cinematic trick, we accept (suspend disbelief) the exposures as reality because Buster also appears as a "single" talking offscreen to a responding "single." Thus, each Minstrel (and each Musician) is a separate entity existing in his own cubicle and in action with "others."

Keaton's self-duplication boggled his crew. Clyde Bruckman, Keaton's staff writer, recalled the skepticism that confronted the idea:

He did an entire minstrel show all by himself—nine Busters in blackface on the stage at once. Every move, song, and dance exactly in unison. That meant taping off the lens into nine equal segments accurate to the ten-thousandth of an inch.

"It can't be done," said Lessley, the cameraman.

"Sure it can," said Buster. "We won't use tape."

He built a lightproof black box, about a foot square, that fitted over the camera. The crank came out the side through an insulated slot. It was in the front that the business was: nine shutters from right to left, fitted so tight you could have worked underwater. You opened one at a time, shot that section, closed that shutter, rolled the film back, opened the next shutter, and shot, and so on.

"Keep this a secret, you lugs," said Buster. We did. Hollywood gave up on that one. No one ever tried to copy it.[8]

# The Playhouse

Keaton himself described the challenge for Elgin Lessley who had to rewind the film and handcrank eight times at the identical speed:

> If he were off the slightest fraction, no matter how carefully I timed my movements, the composite action could not have synchronized. But Elgin was outstanding among all the studios. He was a human metronome.
>
> My synchronizing was gotten by doing the routines to banjo music. . . . I memorized the routines very much as they lay our dance steps—each certain action at a certain beat in a certain measure of "Darktown Strutters' Ball." Metronome Lessley set the beat, metronome banjo man started tapping his foot, and Lessley started each time with ten feet of blank film as a leader, counting down, "Ten, nine, eight," and so on. At "zero"—we hadn't thought up "blast off" in those days—banjo went into chorus and I into routine. Simple.[9]

Once the gag peaks with the display of nine minstrels, the descent still contains aftershocks, although we know we will soon be at rest. But the first aftershock is nearly as powerful as the shock of nine Busters: Buster is also the Audience. The Audience two-shots are figuratively whittled down from the Minstrel nine-shots; we unwind by "seeing double" instead of multiple. Three specific couples, a cross section of society (upper crust/stale crust), watch the vaudeville show: (1) Husband (Buster) in suit and string tie stares numbly beside Wife (Buster) in a pageboy with a plumed fan in a gloved hand; (2) Boy (Buster) in sailor suit sucks a lollipop beside Granma (Buster) in bulky sweater and flowered hat; (3) Blonde (Buster) with plunging neckline sits beside elderly snoozing Gentleman (Buster). Buster as Audience is both Spectator and Actor. The emphasis moves away from the minstrels, although we remain aware of them offscreen–onstage by next seeing the program in close-up:

KEATON'S OPERA HOUSE
—PROGRAM—
BUSTER KEATON PRESENTS
BUSTER KEATON'S MINSTRELS

INTERLOCUTOR . . . . . . . . . . . . . . . . . . . . BUSTER KEATON
BONES    . . . . . . . . . . . . . . . . . . . . . BUSTER KEATON

| | |
|---|---|
| SAMBO | .BUSTER KEATON |
| TENOR SOLO | BUSTER KEATON |
| ASLEEP IN THE DEEP | BUSTER KEATON |
| COMIC EFFUSION | BUSTER KEATON |
| SONG AND DANCE | BUSTER KEATON |
| QUARTETTE | BUSTER KEATON |
| CLARIONETTE SOLO | BUSTER KEATON |
| FINALE | BUSTER KEATON |

The camera tilts down the remaining list for the aftergag:

**STAFF FOR BUSTER KEATON**

| | |
|---|---|
| MANAGER | BUSTER KEATON |
| STAGE DIRECTOR | BUSTER KEATON |
| MUSICAL DIRECTOR | BUSTER KEATON |
| ELECTRICIAN | BUSTER KEATON |
| PROPERTY MAN | BUSTER KEATON |
| THEATRE TRANSPORTATION | BUSTER KEATON |
| ADVANCE AGENT | BUSTER KEATON |
| DANCES ARRANGED BY | BUSTER KEATON |
| SPECIAL INSTRUCTOR | BUSTER KEATON |
| ORIGINAL SONGS & MUSIC BY | BUSTER KEATON |
| SCENERY PAINTED BY | BUSTER KEATON |
| MECHANICAL EFFECTS BY | BUSTER KEATON |
| MARCHES ARRANGED BY | BUSTER KEATON |
| TABLEAUX BY | BUSTER KEATON |

Husband utters: "THIS FELLOW KEATON SEEMS TO BE THE WHOLE SHOW."

Through this visual gag, Keaton presents one of the best in-jokes in film. So far Buster has popped up more than fifty times in less than ten minutes between visual appearances and program credits (nor is he finished). Beneath this overexposure lies a parody of one particular film director, Thomas H. Ince, who plastered his name on many a credit. "[Ince] gave a personal stamp to every Ince production, and this, coupled with an enormous ego, made him feel justified in assuming directorial credit whenever he felt like it. . . . Ince's mania for recognition extended not only to placing his name before the public as much as possible ('Thomas H. Ince presents A Thomas H. Ince production. . . . Supervised by T. H. Ince') but even to using his name subliminally."[10] One

132

critic quipped that "Ince's new picture is to be called *Modesty Is the Best Policy*."[11] In a 1958 interview, Keaton recalls his parody: "Well, we just set out to kid Thomas H. Ince. . . . We started the picture . . . saying 'This is a Keaton Picture. Keaton presents Keaton. Supervised by Keaton.' [laughs]"[12] At the time of *The Playhouse*'s release, Keaton gave credit where it was due: "Thomas H. was my Ince-spiration."[13]

Once we meet the Audience, the story shifts from onstage spectacle to in-house "drama" as audience members interact. Granma scolds Boy for propping his feet on the rail; Blonde studies Gentleman through her opera glasses, until he wakes to clap and falls asleep again. Boy drops lollipop into Blonde's lap below; instead of the glasses, she holds the lollipop to her eye. Granma peers over the rail to hear the Blonde complain, pouring her soda on Gentleman who opens an umbrella. Return to stage, minstrels rise in finale. Buster-Stagehand wields the ropes with difficulty. The stage extravaganza has brimmed over into the audience, another clue that something suspiciously dreamlike is at work. The familiar stone face still peers out, although this time through costumes; thus, Keaton darkens his cheeks to make them sunken or dons wigs, hats, and dresses. Multiple exposure now becomes a vital ingredient in an intricate visual routine, not merely a technical feat. Earlier, the musicians were in a three-shot (literally, a shot composed of three separate shootings), in which they interacted minimally *within the same shot*. Here, however, the audience members interact with their neighbors above, below, *and* sideways: in the same shot, Blonde wakes Gentleman or Boy lowers feet on Granma's command; in two answering shots, Granma and Blonde "regard" each other or Granma's soda splatters Gentleman "below." This third variation of multiple exposure creates a breakthrough of geographic space in different dimensions—or yet another illusion.

The number of Busters per shot may have decreased, but they continue to appear. Hoofers in Bustersuit now enter separately, meet center stage, twirl canes, tap, soft-shoe, kick, and shuffle. They do not cross or touch (they cannot, being in their cubicles), but their steps vary enough to assure us that we have two separate dancing Busters, not superimposition or mirror reflection. On a live stage, two dancers can shadow each other to suggest twins, or mirrors can reflect reversed images; identical twins are the ultimate reality. Here, there is no shadow, mirror, or twin; only Buster 1 = Buster 2. The greatest pleasure of the self is indeed oneself.

Keaton's soft-shoe twins represent one of many vaudeville dance acts, including "transformation dances," in which a woman wearing many costumes would dance while "strip strings" pulled from backstage removed a layer at a time; "sand jig dances" or shuffles to 4/4 time on fine sand; and "legmania," an eccentric high-kicking dance form of which Joe Keaton was master.[14] He mentioned his specialty in a letter he wrote to a Terre Haute, Indiana, paper about his showbiz entry: "I called it eccentric because neither the audience, nor Myra, who was accompanying me on the piano, ever knew which way my feet were going next. Neither did I because I never made up my mind about that until the last possible moment."[15] While Keaton documented his father's legmania in *Convict 13*, here in *The Playhouse* he pays tribute to the leg-acy in a double dose of Buster.

We suddenly dissolve. Here are the clues that this has been a dream: the telltale optical and Buster's pose (curled up in a bed, dressed, clapping in sleep) when the shot clears. Enter Joe Roberts, Buster's Nemesis, to oust him from the room. Buster shakes his head pitifully as moving men remove his bureau. Before exiting, Buster wags a threatening finger at Joe. We cut to a wider shot to see the room "disassemble": men (stagehands) kick out walls (stage flats); the back wall rises into offscreen rafters, exposing Buster (Stagehand) lowering a sandbag. Ironically, the only element in Buster's dream with any "truth" was his clumsy Stagehand; it is poignantly fitting that as a stagehand in "real" life, Buster would dream to be *everyone else* important in the theater.

Keaton's personal stage experiences, translated through the dreams of his persona, now spill into Buster's waking state as a backstage drama. First comes Buster's "eviction." His rude awakening was so carefully presented as a reality separate from his dream that we believed this catastrophe. Having been in one dream-frame (illusion), we do not suspect a twist so soon; however, it comes through the long shot that breaks the set. In essence, we have been looking at Keaton's composition of "nested boxes": Buster within the box of his dream, within the box of his "room," within the box of the stage, within the box of the Opera House, within the box of the frame, within the box of our vision. Keaton pulls us back and forth through these boxes as he cuts. Once the set breaks apart, we recognize that Buster's eviction was only an excuse for attacking melodrama again. Blesh remarks that Keaton recreated a "classic eviction scene . . . even to Buster sitting in despair, his head in his hands."[16] Buster becomes the stereotypical despairing widow with babe driven into cruel winter snows by a villainous landlord. But this illusion is shattered as quickly as Buster's nap, and Keaton wakes him to an important reality.

As he passes a time clock, Buster ponders the sign PUNCH CLOCK and obediently smashes in the face. This literal translation may well be Buster's hostility at being roused from magical dreams, as well as Keaton's eager blow to all that the scene signified for melodrama.

Another homage to the near quarter-century of his life on stage is the infamous "knothole" in the next scene, a frivolous interruption if we do not acknowledge its significance for Keaton. Sweeping backstage, Buster finds a knothole that he kicks with heel and broom; the stick slides into the hole and he crashes to the floor; he extracts the broom, stares at the hole, and sweeps on. Keaton described some of his capers in evolving the "stage knothole" routine:

> When Pop recited his "beautiful poem," I would come out behind him and make a terrible racket by banging a broomstick on the floor. I continued slamming the broom on the floor. The audience realized what I was doing when the stick went through a hole. This upended me, and when I hit the floor I made another terrible noise. Exasperated, Pop would kick me out of his way and grab the business end of the broom. On pulling this up with my unwanted assistance, we would throw it away and then calmly continue his recitation just where he'd left off. That was supposed to be the end of the routine.
>
> But . . . the other acts on the bill . . . contribute[d] new plot turns and complications. . . . [At] Keith's Colonial Theater in New York, a couple of those fellows sneaked down to the basement under the stage and tied a rope exactly 175 feet long to the end of the broomstick when it came through the hole. When Pop and I, singing "The Volga Boat Song," complete with gestures, eventually got all the rope up a dirty, tiny American flag was tied to it. The quick-witted orchestra immediately swung into "The Star Spangled Banner."
>
> The next week [another] act . . . quickly covered the stick [from below the stage] with fresh mustard. At the next theatre we played, two guys on the bill hung onto the broomstick while Pop tugged away like mad. They let go suddenly, and Pop went about three feet in the air as it came up.
>
> Once when the broom came up it had our two weeks' closing notice on it. At still another show they took the trouble to put a huge slingshot below the hole. When they let this go the broom

**135**

shot away into the flies. It traveled so fast that Pop didn't even see it rocket past him.

[At] Keith's Alhambra . . . on upper Broadway, the other acts . . . got an eel several feet long from the Aquarium [which] they brought up . . . on the subway in a five-gallon can filled with water. When this came up on the end of the rope, Joe Keaton turned green under his makeup, believing it was a snake. The eel wriggled away across the stage with the broom still tied to it.[17]

Legend has it that once Keaton discovered the knothole in Columbus, Ohio, the act made their own knotholes in every stage thereafter.[18] Only fitting, then, that one should appear on this "stage."

In some Keaton films, once nemesis appears, love must follow. Echoing the multiplicity theme, lovely twin ladies enter with identical hats, dresses, and suitcases. The use of twins—actually, two women who resemble each other, one being Virginia Fox—recalls the optical illusion that Keaton used earlier with himself. As star of his own dream-show, Buster alone would have been enough to play all the roles. Dardis entertains the idea that while Keaton was hatching *The Playhouse*, he may have recalled a jingle from child-star days: "Little Buster Keaton is a whole show within himself; he's a regular theater."[19] Blesh considers that Keaton centered half the film on himself because of a broken ankle and he needed a less physical film; Keaton said, "We don't need falls or chases . . . I'll be the entire cast."[20] To keep the focus on himself without multiple exposure, Buster must remain the focus of the action even among others. The "twins" is not only a clever sight gag for a routine on mistaken identity but each twin serves as a directional arrow. By their positions in each shot, Buster becomes more prominent and central. The girls occupy two cubicles without multiple exposure but simply with their positioning. Our perspective changes toward all other elements in the frame so that the focus remains on Buster; our view is subtly guided by Keaton. As an earlier example of this in the orchestra, *three* Busters work independently of each other, yet the cumulative effect is *one* Buster. Now, the two girls, who should be more noticeable because they are separate and different characters, in fact seem to blur because of their position in our periphery as we zero in on Buster; thus, the effect is still *one* Buster, although he shares the spotlight. As typical Keaton leading ladies, they are stepping-stones, not distinct personalities; Keaton's "ladies" in his Audience were unique because they were Buster!

# The Playhouse

The twins trigger a disappearing act in one uninterrupted, straight-on shot that makes us aware of their actions, while Buster is oblivious to them. The twins are positioned on either side so that he only sees the left one as he sweeps. She speaks and he gallantly opens the door bearing a star and number 1. He is then aghast to find the second twin on his right, spins to door 1, and leads her to door 2. Keaton gives us door numbers to keep track of the twins; without labels, we would get mixed up, no longer be one up. The twins make separate well-timed exits/entries until they step out simultaneously and bookend Buster by the wall. Knowing he is awake, Buster considers one cause of his double vision: fleeing to the prop room, he pulls out a bottle of booze from his pocket that he gravely slides away from him across a bureau.

While Buster comes to grips with the consequences of indulgence, Fate devises a trick to coincide with the multiplicity theme of the film. A stagehand sets up two full-length mirrors at angles by doors 1 and 2. We return to Buster in the prop room for an interrupting, anticipatory shot that builds the gag to a small peak, since when he steps into the next shot, he finds *four* twins (two girls, two reflections). Buster has entered a variation of his own multiple exposures, but one step beyond his control. Caught in the center of this illusion (and center of frame), Buster pinches his arm and slaps his face. We cut to the prop room into which he speeds again, to smash the bottle and write in a logbook:

I RESOLVE NEVER TO DRINK ANY MORE

B.

The period after "B" gives the illusion of conclusion when, in fact, the deliberate spacing of the line and the unpunctuated sentence are clues to an upcoming verbal gag. Before this gag's conclusion, however, we cut to a stunning medium shot bordering on the surreal: the back of Buster's porkpied head bobbing as he writes, his face casting triple reflections in three wall-mirrors before him. He raises his head to discover three more of himself. Buster's pleasant dream is now a living nightmare, not a hallucination to be cured by teetotalism. He is haunted by his pretty visions, victimized by his imagination, and punished by Fate for dreaming too much of himself. The editing that moves Buster and us from illusion to illusion implies the greatest illusion of all: Film. We fill the "screen" of our mind with surreal connections, interpreting Buster at his most vulnerable. Between full-length mirrors, he is a target; within three mirrors, he is absorbed. At the peak of this insanity, Buster runs back to confront the twins. Unlike Buster, we understand the setup (as opposed to our bewilderment at Buster's "nested" dream where *he* was in control). We know this gag has been "done with mirrors." But because now he is awake, Buster reconciles these visions: he touches the mirror and the arm of one twin and shares the joke. With enlightenment, however, comes a dire truth driving him back to the prop room. In close-up, to balance the earlier shot, Buster edits the logbook: after ANY MORE, he writes BUT JUST AS MUCH.[21] The space is filled with the anticipated gag-line; the routine closes with Buster's rueful look at the broken bottle.

The second half of *The Playhouse* consists of three special "acts" that not only recall more Keaton memories but show a sublime adaptation of theater to film so that stage-on-film becomes purely cinematic. Each act—Tarzan Jr., Zouaves, The Tank—is punctuated by scenes of background information and recurring illusions. For example, actors backstage fling their costumes at Joe in his billowy Zouave outfit, announcing, "WE'RE THROUGH WITH THE ZOUAVE ACT." Such an informative scene leads into a scene echoing the multiplicity theme. Having rapidly fallen in love, Buster kisses the wrong twin and is shoved away. Door numbers no longer help Buster since the girls switched rooms offscreen; we are as entangled as Buster in the illusions that filter into reality beyond his control. Illusion is inherent in Buster's life. Only his perception distills the truth. At this moment, though, he is too entrenched to see straight.

As the Zouave dilemma broadens, it pulls Buster in amoebically; a problem does not exist in a Keaton film without ensnaring Buster somehow. A minor equation-illusion even occurs in Joe's simple plea to "GET ME SOME ZOUAVES"; Buster offers cigarettes, thinking it a brand name. But Buster avoids total helplessness in this crisis when he creates an "equation" of his own: he bribes some lazy ditchdiggers to become the new Zouaves. The scene fades to black, an optical that Keaton does not often use except to conclude a filmic "chapter" or to signal THE END. This is a clear time lapse, a cinematic "stage lights down," leading us directly to the first of the three major acts.

The costume-change with the new Zouaves transfers to Buster himself following the next fade-in. An animal trainer instructs Buster to "DRESS THE MONKEY" in the cage. Cut to show the monkey escape; cut to show Buster's futile call to the escapee—these are brief shots leading to another fade-out. Time is constantly abridged to advance toward the most important quick-change in this sequence. Because of Fate's luring away the monkey, Buster must accept the unfair guilt of losing him. As a lowly and paranoid stagehand, he assumes the burden of replacing what has been lost. Fade out on Fate's ultimatum; fade in to Buster's hunched-over back. He turns, becoming the newest equation: Buster = monkey. A dark makeup outline surrounds his typically pale, haunted features; his guilt drives him into the cage to await the trainer. Buster is so immersed in this identity that the trainer is fooled by his swaying, crouching "pet," TARZAN JR., as the onstage placard proclaims.

Buster's dreams of being a "star" are coming true in an unusual way. Keaton gives his new persona a rich identity, probably based on Peter the Great, the "smartest chimpanzee" he ever saw on the London stage in 1909. While animal comedy acts—dogs, horses, elephants, cats, snakes, seals, bears, birds—abounded in vaudeville,[22] Keaton was impressed by Peter who "dined in full dress, biked and roller-skated to the American ragtime strains of 'Down in Jungletown,' undressed and donned pajamas, and then returned to bed"—most of which Buster does dexterously in this sequence.[23] We remember how uncannily Buster and animals adopted each other's traits in *Hard Luck*. Here, Buster *is* the animal. The radical contrast between Buster as primate and as man is emphasized backstage when the trainer adjusts the monkey's tuxedo: Buster straightens instantly to apologize, then easily scrunches into character. He knows both roles very well.

We see Buster's stage entrance first as a theater audience behind the proscenium. Keaton cuts closer, giving us "stage-seats" in order to study Buster's eerie impersonation—the graceful glide of elongated arms and curled fingers, his hobble, "grunts," and twitching face. Like his mentor Peter the Great, Buster-Monkey rings a bell, eyes a pretty maid, stabs his food with a fork (when not observed by the trainer, however, the "animal" uses his paw, then reverts to a fork when watched), smokes a cigar, and climbs into bed. Buster alternates between himself and his alter ego: as human, he knows how to improvise for entertainment (for example, he drags on the cigar and distractedly places the lit end in his mouth, then hops under the bedsheet where he plays with a bedbug); as monkey, all movements are expressed through the primate body. But like our own positioning in space through Keaton's editorial choices, Buster is "born free" to breach distance. He scampers into a theater box and perches on a rail, munching from the candy box of a portly dame. In irised close-up, masked to look subjectively as if through unfocused binoculars, we see Buster's blurry face sharpen as the dame focuses; his face grows enormous as brow and jaw pump while chewing. Predictably, we cut back to the original distance to catch the result: the woman faints. We keep switching perspectives as both theater and film audience in order to be eyewitness to what Buster and his playhouse "audience" see.

The Monkey act is assembled with shots that widen the boundaries of the stage, giving a sense of what a theater audience experiences when actors leave their stage positions and invade the house. Once the trainer pulls Buster back to the stage to continue the act (tumbling a stage flat, riding a bike between milk bottles), we watch the theater audience rise panicked at this frisky creature. Buster cannot continue his charade nor sustain the routine much longer without some conclusive "peak and descent." Enjoying the power that comes from creating a near-riot, Buster now cares little about losing the real monkey. He escapes by diving *through* the backdrop of a painted ocean—another illusion, as the slit cannot be seen until it is used. He has penetrated an illusion of real life without confusion or hesitation—perhaps even too smartly, as Buster did in *The High Sign*, since he knew of secret hideouts before we did. Here, however, Buster-Stagehand should be familiar with the set, and we can excuse him since he uses it to his advantage. Unexpectedly, Buster spits water at the trainer; he not only swims in "seawater" but also drinks deeply. Through this "baptism," Buster avenges his dehumanization. He was resigned to accept it, but as in earlier films, suppression only energizes him to rebellion. Buster declares independence, "grinning" and clapping while the last traces of monkeyhood dissolve as the curtain falls. He eyes the trainer fearlessly, then paddles his arms in the "sea" as though to freedom. Buster ironically has reclaimed his humanity by becoming the animal he empathizes with, one also "imprisoned" (caged). And ironically again, in so doing, Buster has become a "star."

Buster's plunge into the sea-backdrop is a modified homage to the memory of what The Three Keatons christened the "Standing, Sitting, Original, Aboriginal Australian native splash dive." On a vaudeville stage, Buster would take a running dive from a chair, hit the backdrop, slide to the floor, then flip and land seated.[24] Here, maintaining the illusion of the film, Buster passes *through* the backdrop. This action is necessarily cinematic, since only through the position of the camera can we see how Keaton milks this "invisible" prop (the slit) while building Buster's confidence. We are behind the backdrop, on a side that a theater audience would never see, as Buster invites Joe to look through the slit. We change sides with the snap of a cut, matching the wallop the trainer gives to Joe's face as he collapses backstage. We cut to his fall, to the trainer, to Joe's flying his fist through the slit, to the recipient of that blow: another lowly stagehand. We hopscotch to each side, matching the blows that Buster instigates without landing any himself. He has transferred his frustrated blow of PUNCH CLOCK to rivals who do his "dirty work" by proxy; the last blow is significantly aimed at an anonymous stagehand who represents a position Buster can now happily quit.

Having achieved stardom as the offspring of the great Tarzan, Buster is now destined to move up the evolutionary ladder to be a Zouave. As the latter, he plays a commander over the villain Joe, who ironically ordered his melodramatic exit from reverie. Under Buster's commands, the ditchdiggers and Joe reveal their incompetency and, by contrast, fortify Buster's control. The act opens with a strictly theatrical tableau: Zouave guards playing cards or keeping sentry. Buster-Zouave steps onstage to blow a trumpet. A slapstick Busby Berkeley–esque choreography (minus the overhead shot) ensues and the Zouaves shoulder-arm, cluster, and swing around to form the spokes of a revolving wheel with Buster as the hub (again, a composition favoring the focus of our attention). Keaton dissolves stage restrictions by intercutting to an illusion in the audience: two one-armed men sitting side by side. They "comment" on the Zouave act by either clapping each other's hand in satisfaction or by one withholding it from the other in displeasure. Meanwhile, pseudoserious Zouaves unbuild and reassemble a cannon, accidentally fitting a midget Zouave in among the pieces (another parody of authority figures). Buster fires signals and flags directions, adding to the chaos.

Another cutaway to the one-armers' reactions allows the Zouaves in the meantime to shift about onstage/offscreen. We return to MLS to see Joe alone before a brick wall; Buster searches for the others. He shoves Joe aside, exposing all the guards filed behind his giant proportions; each Zouave pops his head over the other's shoulders. Keaton has turned a stationary camera, perfect for a flat tableau, into a depth-creating device. This is an impossible illusion on stage: although a theater audience seeing the column of men would grasp the full illusion of one man in front of many, those on the sides would naturally spot the lineup because of their angle to it. The Zouave act concludes with slapstick: a human pyramid stands on a weakling "middle man" as Joe climbs to the top with a ladder. The illogic of this arrangement is only convincing to us because the ditchdiggers are clearly inept. The one-armers project our displeasure, acting as our surrogate and freeing us to laugh instead.

# The Playhouse

The last routine in the Zouave act is uniquely dimensional and multilayered because its film treatment surpasses the simple limitations of the stage. This time, to audience enthusiasm, the Zouaves toss each other to the top of the wall. Fitting his high rank and suggesting slower motion against the frenzy of the Zouaves, Buster is lifted to the top of the wall. Joe, the object of Buster's annoyance, remains below. After a cut to audience response (a transitional device marking passage of activity onstage), the Zouaves reassemble below to hoist Joe en masse on their shoulders. Naturally, the upward movement emphasizes Buster as he stands above them directing; he then offers his arm to pull Joe up, as if with Tarzanian strength. The trick backfires, perhaps because Buster is too cocksure, and the wall falls forward. Through smooth cutting, we follow Buster's roll off the stage, down the aisle, and through the lobby doors. Now Buster lives the irony at the start of the film when we first thought the Conductor had to pay admission: he staggers to the box office, hands the usher his ticket, and reenters. There is no doubt about Keaton's logical-illogic anymore; it runs rampant in this mix of dream and reality. The proscenium has also been shattered with Buster as projectile; he in essence has shattered the whole house. Buster has weakened its groundings by rolling (literally) around the theater, connecting himself to its magic and pulling it with him. He becomes full of multiple personalities, each renewing instead of sapping the other's energy.

The show must go on. Fade in to the third and last major act, with a brief prelude. Joe accidentally sets his applied beard on fire and Buster literally interprets another written command to help him. FOR FIRE ONLY, the sign reads below an ax case; Buster whacks Joe with the flat end of the ax and hacks off the smoky beard. His literalness is crucial for a stagehand, which Buster is at heart, for he must follow directions meticulously to meet his cues. Actors may improvise and interpret (and when Buster acts—as the Monkey, for instance—he does so vividly), but stagehands uphold the letter of the script. Buster as stagehand is merely performing his "role." Layered into the burning-beard gag is Buster's ongoing mistaken-identity gag: he kisses the wrong twin, who slaps him. Obviously without the proper script, Buster cannot cue the right action.

The stage curtain rises for The Tank. The twins in swimwear stand before a giant white-framed tank against a totally black background. An emcee enters, a "straight man" who turns into a prop when Buster throws him against Joe as they chase each other across the stage and among the rafters. The emcee's narration, "THIS YOUNG LADY CAN STAY UNDERWATER

LONGER THAN THE BOTTOM OF THE RIVER," evokes two fond memories for Keaton. The twins perhaps recall Annette Kellerman, world-famous Australian swimmer, diver, and fashion-setter (the risqué black one-piece tights known as "The Kellermans"). Annette originated the Original Aboriginal Australian Splash, a dive from a springboard and a roll into a ball before hitting the water, which Keaton adapted for his own act. Once after Annette performed her aquatic feat, drenching the orchestra and first rows of the audience, Keaton dove after her unexpectedly wearing his full suit.[25] Keaton's previous play with multiple mirrors may also recall Annette's dazzling act against a hundred mirrors.[26]

The second memory associated with the tank perhaps commemorates typical novelty vaudeville acts like "Blatz, The Human Fish," who would eat a banana, play the trombone, read and sleep underwater in a tank.[27] In addition, Keaton introduces the illusion of "black art," a staple of magic acts in which black on black erases itself, creating an eerie disjointedness as when a person in black against black wears white gloves.[28] The tank set against a black background is black in its transparency, with only a stark white frame. We sense the possibility of a trick behind the darkness but then face the *illusion* of reality (the baffling mix of trick *and* authenticity). Keaton walks the threshold between drama and comedy (and a little melodrama) when the twin buckles after "FOUR MINUTES." Her sister as a noncomic entity arouses genuine panic as she yells, "HELP! SHE'S CAUGHT!" This calamity creates real drama while also implying a trick: what device has she been caught in? An illusion, of course. The drama allows Buster to play another role—Hero. He is actually juggling two separate but related actions at the same time: (1) backstage dodging Joe, whom he lures into a magician's case that is the monkey cage; and (2) hearing the onstage commotion and running to save his love. Buster is an illusion creator, covering distances in seconds. He has reversed Fate by caging his nemesis (replacing the monkey with Joe, so to speak); now courageous, he braces to rescue his love from another cagelike prop, into which blackness she could disappear.

Keaton inserts a whimsical but weak gag that contradicts Buster's ingenuity: he scoops out the tank water with a teacup from the prop room. It may be another "literal" translation of how to use a teacup or scooping out a "sinking ship"; or perhaps Buster is just momentarily panicking. Still, it is a sorry gag in the midst of Keaton's drama. The gag seems as intrusive and unfunny as the one in *The Navigator* in which Buster's underwater traffic-directing postponed the girl's rescue. Buster returns to the prop room for a sledgehammer, prolonging the agony unnecessarily, especially as no one else seems to be helping the girl; he breaks the glass, pouring forth gallons and the twin into the orchestra pit. Our position is reversed to see the water gushing into the audience. The deluge is intensified as we cut to the lobby; first, the audience flees toward us; after a tense moment, the doors burst from their hinges under the flood. This spectacle "saturates" the opera house; it is the total devastation of the proscenium, the floating away of illusions. To save his girl, Buster has literally shattered the last illusion (tank) and, with it, all future illusions of grandeur. Now Buster has earned his favorite role, Lover, and no more theatrical dreams are necessary.

The film comes full circle as Buster once more enters the orchestra pit (wide awake), this time bobbing in the water, puncturing a drum, paddling with a violin, and slipping on a bass fiddle. Buster has evolved from a dreamer to a realist, from a fantasy musician to a virtuoso of every instrument he touches—ironically destroying them while using them as tools of survival. Even Joe gets his deserved final dousing; having escaped the cage, he slips into the pit where this baptism should cleanse him of his transgressions, as befits the penitent villain of melodrama. Although he ousted Buster from his "room," he has been sympathetically presented as a bumbling Zouave, and we encourage his redemption.

Once free of the theater's confines, the nested boxes, and the illusions that both ensnare and liberate, Buster can "act" normal. His immersion in the theater has been so overwhelming that he runs for dear life with the twin, only braking when he spots a painter finishing a sign: JUSTICE OF THE PEACE. Another literal reading for the ex-stagehand: Buster yearns for justice and peace, this time through wedded bliss. The twin, however, refuses to budge, and Buster experiences a reminder of his theatrical nightmares. Discovering his mistake of taking the wrong twin, he returns to retrieve her sister whose neck he marks with an "X." Again, Keaton manipulates the environment for his gags: a painter just happens to be working outside the Justice of the Peace, and Buster just happens to use his paintbrush to mark his real girlfriend. Seeing is finally believing, and he checks her neck one more time as he heads upstairs. Darkness descends like a curtain on the screen. THE END.

Buster has leaped through all the hoops (or boxes) that both theater and film conjure up. Unfortunately, when the film becomes Buster's waking reality in the second half, it weakens with a large number of characters and tangential scenes. While Keaton always focuses on Buster, the nondimensional characters dissipate the film. It is almost as if Keaton hopes to endow the multiple characters of his film with a multiplicity of roles (e.g., Joe = landlord = Zouave = bearded actor = prisoner); but none of them have the direction and dimension that Buster gives just *one* of his invented characters. Keaton's concern with being as "loud" a trumpeter as Thomas H. Ince may have been both his best joke and an obstacle. His initial desire to be the "entire cast" was never fulfilled, as he conceded half the film to a "cast of thousands." If Keaton had indeed been the entire movie, perhaps his loosely tied reality would have been as dynamic as the technically splendid tricks of his dream.

## Chapter 11

# The Boat

(November 1921)

Courtesy of the Museum of Modern Art/Film Stills Archive

Having drowned illusions in *The Playhouse*, Buster tries taming the storms of Life and literally goes out to sea to do so. *The Boat* is a near-perfect depiction of Keaton-style calamity, futility, and disaster, without total destruction. This short has been considered Keaton at his thwarted best; the epitome of the little man versus Nature, versus Machine; the ultimate question of defeat and survival. At the same time, it is not a serious portrayal but a parody of disaster (true disaster is yet to be seen). The ending is not so much Buster's utter despair, as it is comic frustration and its requisite perseverance.

The titles in *The Boat* are compact and few; most are sardonic commentaries, the kind of rich barb that opened *One Week* (with which this film has many parallels). *The Boat* begins with a title, an unusual format for Keaton, but similar to his first short: EIGHT BELLS . . . AND ALL'S NOT WELL. Knowing Keaton's modus operandi from the preceding nine films, we sense through these six words and the potent ellipsis that some dreadful nautical event is in progress. The next shot confirms this: Buster is tossed about the cabin of a violently rocking boat. Keaton has dispensed with traditional film exposition for a comedic purpose. Instead of starting with general and cutting to specific (i.e., Buster at sea ⟶ Buster inside boat), Keaton throws us immediately into the specific, eliminating the first establishing shot. His motive is simple: the establishing shot *is* the joke, so it needs to be placed *into* the sequence as a punch line.[1] When we finally cut to exterior long shot, we learn that Buster is not even at sea but on land. His boat DAMFINO is being yanked on a rope by little Buster Jr., wearing a porkpie like his father. Buster staggers on deck, tumbles overboard, and spanks Jr. while wife Sybil watches from the deck. Although Keaton has steadily used Virginia Fox since *Neighbors* and will switch to other leading ladies, he fittingly brings Sybil back in *The Boat*. Their first collaboration was a tale of married life and cyclonic disasters; *The Boat* promises the same.

The next observation, ALL FINISHED AND READY FOR LAUNCHING, further explains why Buster's capsize was on land: he has built his own Nemesis. In long shot, we see the boat through an open garage door. As Buster prepares to haul the boat out by car, he discovers that the boat is bigger than the doorway. Although Buster seems better off in property now, his luck has not changed much since *One Week*. Sybil continues her blithe wifely role, although coy kisses have now become dismayed reprimands. Sybil drags Jr. to await the master-builder in the car, which holds a life preserver, masts, smokestack, and a second porkpied lad. The Juniors extend the multiplicity theme of *The Playhouse*, both as twins and miniature mirror reflections of Buster.

Buster will stretch our credulity in this film, although, ironically, his actions will support Keaton's favorite theme, Buster versus Machine. Buster's cleverness in building always falls short of mastering the actual construction; thus, the "mind" of the invention competes unpredictably with the inventor. This mind is sparked by the creator's touch; perhaps the mind has even been sapped from the creator by osmosis. Buster's devotion to the inanimate object embues it with its own life, forming more equations: Buster = Dr. Frankenstein, Machine = Monster. With the assistance of Fate, Machine's mission is to outsmart its creator. In doing so, Machine (boat) absorbs Buster's practical nature, even his common sense. Thus, some of Buster's gestures will be nonsensical and self-defeating, particularly when his Monster becomes more imposing than he anticipated; his hoped-for "teamwork" will ultimately turn into terror.

To work with the Machine, Buster desperately destroys his own security—he breaks the door down by prying out bricks. He enters the car (with a "footnote," he swings his leg over Jr. 1 to do so) and proceeds to haul out the boat. In long shot, focusing on the two-level house, the boat breaks through; in extreme long shot, walls and roof collapse. We *knew* that would happen; it seems incomprehensible that someone as wise and precise as Buster would not have seen it coming also. The *theme* of destruction, however, is vital to Buster's survival, although the *reason* for destruction is not always convincing. Through destruction, Buster learns how to regain his control over the Machine. He can show the Machine that he has not been outsmarted or defeated but is still the boss. Buster salvages a piece of lifeboat reading DAMFINO, a bathtub, two oars, and loads them into the car. In a deep long shot with the car pointed at us, behind which is the boat, behind which stand the remains of the house, Buster readies to drive; he seeks the offscreen horizon. The composition documents this dynamically: the car points at us, forcing us to see behind them what the Buster family must leave and never regret.

Buster's determination in the next title is clear: THERE'S MORE THAN ONE WAY TO LAUNCH A BOAT. However, Keaton's commentary is a bit tongue-in-cheek because he knows (as director, he has arranged) that Buster's goal is destined to be foiled. Buster has maneuvered the boat onto the launching ramp, but Jr. 1 now chooses to lie across the ramp to dabble with the waves. Sybil screams for Buster to brake the car hauling the boat along the ramp. The "more than one way to launch" becomes a way unforeseen by Buster. The front wheels of the car dangle off the dock as Buster clings to the rope. Cut to MLS of Jr. 1 oblivious to Father's heart-rending decision; cut to Buster smirking as the decision really is not over losing the kid but the car. He opts to cut the rope, however, and tips his hat respectfully when the car drops into the water. The reliable old friend from *One*

# The Boat

*Week* days now must perish because of a porkpied instrument of Fate. As Joe Keaton carted his son by a suitcase handle, Buster picks up Jr. 1 by the seat of his pants and sets him to pull on the rope with Sybil. Buster dramatically breaks into the frame and heads to the background, never turning to us in his determination to launch this boat. He supports the tilting vessel with bare hands, secures the rope, and vaults into the boat. We cut to a startling long shot of the boat pointing at us, its name clearly DAMFINO. Buster steps into the prow, stark against the sky, while below stands Sybil and a Jr. on either side. Buster has resumed control, towering above family and machine, visually supported at the apex of the frame by these components; he speaks loudly, clearly, and nonverbally on who is in charge. Sybil wields a Coke bottle as the men doff their porkpies.

Before the christening and maiden voyage, a word on the curious name of Buster's vessel. It has appeared three times already, prominent in the camera angle as well as in how Buster isolated the name when carrying the lifeboat slat. Keaton makes it impossible to ignore the name; it is, in fact, the most important wordplay in *The Boat* and in Keaton's silent film legacy. The name also appears in the 1927 nonnautical *College*: "Keaton [a square student trying to be big man in campus athletics to win the girl] drops a racing shell into the water, then steps through the hull, sinking it. Its name is 'Damfino.' This is probably the longest running single pun in the history of the silent film."[2] Pronounced quickly with a long *i*, the word becomes a cry of frustration: DAMN–IF–I–KNOW. The name becomes an emblem Buster carries with him, *his* opinion of Keaton's subtle commentaries on his sea experience. DAMFINO is the long-awaited verbalization of how Buster has survived thus far.

The name is more richly defined in the christening scene when Sybil's bottle fails to shatter against the boat. Buster's perplexed expression reads: Damfino what's going on here! Buster bends over the side (over the name) and breaks the bottle with his hammer. The painted word is almost a subtitle for Buster's reaction. We also read more into it because of his pose in the composition of the shot: he bends directly over the word as he contemplates the bottle and we connect word, man, and situation. In the next intriguing medium long shot, Buster stands majestically in the prow with his back to us. All the shots that include Buster's back to us are like his turning away from our laughter and from Keaton's wry comments, which have been like chapter titles (just as *One Week* had "chapters"), each anticipating the curve. By turning his back, Buster remains unfazed and undistracted, determined to control his invention, undermine his children (also his "inventions"), and reverse Fate. When he continues his actions, we cut closer as though he finally permits us to join him. We are, however, at a higher angle, emphasizing his in-control position and the drama of the launch. Now the boat slips into the water—and, unfortunately, does not stop slipping.

During this latest catastrophe, Keaton switches us to various views of the sinking vessel instead of maintaining one long shot. Switching to angled and profile shots moves us all around as participants to the disaster. The technique gives us a renewed superiority (one-upness) over Buster who dared to turn from us. From this perspective, Buster "shrinks" as the boat disappears, visually implying the shrinking and sinking of his dreams. Before total submersion, only the portion of boat bearing the word DAMFINO is visible; at that point, Buster fittingly breaks his stonelike pose to glance over his shoulder at us. The name is Buster's unmouthed comment; the name and Buster's turn to us are inextricably linked, as though the boat is speaking while its owner gives a fitting facial response. When the name is "underlined" by the water right before it slips in, Buster finally realizes his pose is invalid and his effort wasted. Chest-deep in water, he stumbles along the submerged vessel and falls into the briny deep.

With one major mishap so early in the film, inevitably more will follow of greater intensity and variation. Keaton now turns from one predictable gag (boat sinking) to more gags with new twists and turns. In short, Keaton has dispensed with the simplest, most expected disaster early on, with more creative ones up his sleeve. Curiously, the mishaps of *The Boat* occurred not only on film but during shooting as well. Technical director Fred "Gabe" Gabourie constructed two DAMFINOS, one to sink and one to float. Unfortunately, the one meant to sink remained afloat, despite a "1,600 pound pig-iron weight, a breakaway stern, and a series of holes bored into the wood." After futile attempts to sink the vessel, Gabourie hauled her to the ocean floor with "an underwater pulley system hooked to an offscreen tug." The "floater" persistently sank and only with pumps below deck did it stay above water.[3] Keaton called Gabourie's job on *The Boat* his "ordeal by water": it was the first of many credited appearances of a technical director on his films.[4] During the making of *The Buster Keaton Story* (1957), the technical crew ran into similar problems re-creating gags from *The Boat*. Keaton as technical adviser told the "construction department all about the bugs, how to eliminate them and how to prepare them in the first place."[5]

# The Boat

The next "chapter" of this short reacknowledges Buster's good intentions and identifies the boat-monster as an essentially kind spirit: YOU CAN'T KEEP A GOOD BOAT DOWN. Keaton seems to admit that there are forces leading this nice personality astray and that Buster may yet thwart them. The boat has been revived, adorned with flags, and boasts the bathtub as a lifeboat. Buster sets the smokestack down—unwittingly over Jr. Keaton records the latest monkey wrench in the works by "sectioning off" the elements in the frame to stress Buster's oblivion to his action. For example, when the smokestack lowers over the kid, we see only Buster's legs in the frame; then cut to MLS of Buster from the waist up. In both "portion" shots, we see how unaware Buster is because his attentive face is never turned to the act of covering Jr. We cut to inside the stack for a dark medium shot of the shrieking kid. This shot signifies how far Keaton's first two films have come cinematically and thematically. Here we experience how it feels to be *inside* the cylinder, unlike Buster's fight with the chimney of *One Week* where we only imagined his entrapment. Both shots provide visual gags with different points of view. This shift in perspective leads to a symbolic interpretation: that the kids are just like dad, and Jr. is a miniature Buster trapped in the dark by a larger power outside him—the innocent "goat" trapped in a narrow world and hearing himself scream from within.

In addition, the kid's "ear-piercing shriek" recalls the prison whistle in *Convict 13*, when the close-up became "audible" in our mind's ear. By cutting to the kid, then to Buster's puzzled expression, we again "hear" the sound. Buster, of course, is responsible for the entrapment of his "alter ego," but because he is oblivious, he is puzzled. As he hears the shriek again (cut to interior of stack), even Buster's hat flips on his head; he taps the stack as a doctor would a chest and peers inside. The inner/outer views give us the chance to see two sides of one entity. Being paranoid, Buster is primed to expect a nonphysical opponent—another invisible hand of Fate. Since *One Week*, Buster has come to accept that he is not only up against elements of nature but all of Life itself.

When he discovers the mundane source of his haunting, Buster is annoyed. There are no normal caring words as, "Hey, Jr., are you all right?" Instead he lifts the stack, tipping it over the rail and dropping Jr. into the water. We wonder at Buster's senseless action again: Was he so rattled that he did not see he was pitching his own son overboard by his hasty moves? Or was it wishful thinking? As a paternal afterthought, Buster flings Jr. a life preserver; it sinks. In this world of opposites, Buster will not take more chances: he tests the water with a thermometer. Perhaps because of the life preserver, Buster considers Jr. not worth saving—for once he may want to agree with Fate. Buster hesitates in his fatherly duties; we notice he is never like this in romance or invention. Oddly, however, the time Buster deliberates on saving Jr. does not agitate us as did the delay in saving the drowning twin in *The Playhouse* or the girl in *The Navigator*. Juniors are natural but unnecessary offshoots of marriage, barely tolerated and worthy of perdition. Once on board again, Buster tucks Jr. underarm and lowers him below to Sybil who, also frustrated, swipes at both boys with a broom. Buster's annoyance is clear in his suitcase-treatment of the kids—a memory of father Joe, perhaps, whose rough handling became increasingly violent over the years. Keaton lost his own two sons when he and Natalie divorced; in their bitter split, Natalie changed the boys' surname to Talmadge. Following such a memory film like *The Playhouse*, we wonder at how much of Keaton's past and present intertwine with his sardonic film-lives.

On a very good day, the best partner for Keaton is a nonhuman one, particularly a cooperative Machine. The next sequence shows Buster's ideal collaboration with this "loved one." Into the major boat sequence (or, in general, the major routine of each "chapter," à la *One Week*) Keaton inserts tangential episodes as reminders that smooth sailing is not in the forecast. The latest chapter begins when Buster steers the boat from the pier—and pulls the pier and two bystanders into the water. The boat still has a mind of its own and wields its power when Buster is not wholly attentive to it.

While effecting his comic business, Keaton paints seascapes on film in which Buster and environment interact. Just as the set in *Neighbors* was integral to the comedy and atmosphere, here too the river plays with Buster and creates tone and thematic expectations. Keaton presents the horizon, the longed-for division of earth and sky. The DAMFINO glides in placidly from the left, across and out right. Buster stares off, one hand on hip and one on wheel, demonstrating ease of command; his expression changes slightly as he spots something ahead. Keaton inserts another long view of the boat's progress on the water, but *we* see nothing alarming. We return to Buster as he pulls a lever; a responding long shot shows masts, stack, and flagged canopy flatten simultaneously to the deck. The reason for this is presented naturally in the boat's journey: the camera pans along with the boat sailing toward and under a low bridge. When the boat emerges from the other side of the bridge, the verticals rise with

# The Boat

Buster's pull and the boat glides out of the frame. Keaton designs the leisure cruise as a welcome balance to Buster's tossing-about at the start of the film. He does not use dissolves for a smooth flow but instead follows the boat's left to right movement with left-right pans, creating a visual momentum across the screen. As we cut to catch the boat gliding into or out of the frame, it is as if our eyes skip to new lines of different paragraphs, as if we are reading (left-right) the story of Buster's journey and are lulled by the hypnotic horizontal pattern.

Keaton again alternates one up/one down on Buster. As captain, Buster must have his wits about him to withstand any problem situation. Predicting low bridges on his voyage, Buster obviously decided to confront this inevitability while still on land by constructing the lever that lowers the verticals. The careful glide/pan of both the boat and camera resolves the gag as the bridge creeps up on us during the boat/camera's movement. Since Buster sees them before we do, he maintains his "supreme" position over us. Now the tables turn on Captain Buster: once we know of low bridges, Keaton toys with variations on this theme. He elaborates on the gag, creating rings stretching outward in "circularity" like a stone dropped in water. Of course, he did this with the piano in *One Week*, in which the presence of the prop spawned variations until the routine finally ended. The magic number "three" is also replayed for comedy since the bridge gag is repeated twice more. Buster, however, forgets this "principle" of repetition and decides to sit back and steer with his feet. The second time the gag is repeated, we discover a low bridge at the right end of a long shot toward which the little boat steams from the left. We cut to Buster's quick reaction as he spots it and pulls the lever in time. The long shot captures the precision timing with which the verticals collapse and the boat passes safely under the bridge and out of the frame. Fate intervenes, however, as shown in a cutaway when a rear flag pole dips into the water, summoning Buster to refasten it. Through Keaton's editing, we learn again (twice up on Buster now) that the boat is heading for another bridge, the third repetition. As the boat "pans" before us, masts and smokestacks topple, with the last mast knocking Buster overboard. He has overestimated the tranquility of the ride and not accounted for the dangers still lying ahead. On the other hand, Keaton has forced us to see things "offscreen"/"offshore" through editing that Buster, in a lofty but nonetheless tunnel-visioned view, does not see. We now cut to Buster pounding the foamy water as he swims toward his boat, as though we look at him in a "boat tracking shot." A small

**153**

craft floats in the background; it provides depth as an "anchor" to mark Buster's swim against its stationary position. Again, Keaton attempts to have the background contribute to the overall picture.

We cut momentarily to Sybil and Jr. below deck, reminding us of their existence. When they join him above, we remember that for all of Fate's interference, Buster is not really alone, at least here; whatever their worth, he still has family. Better late than never, they commiserate on the damage. We cut to the front of the vessel, another angle that helps us see the action most effectively. Buster drops an anchor overboard; it floats. Here is another opposite to balance the sinking life preserver with predestined failure. He can only stare at the anchor characteristically (hands on hips), then sit contemplatively (chin in hand). The triple-bridge routine has been capped with this impossible sight gag (anchor), which, of course, recalls the whole impossibility of this little creative boat. What other vessel can flatten itself with the pull of a lever to fend off the menacing low bridges that loom ahead? Yet it does so, right before our eyes. So what seems impossible is executed logically, realistically, and mechanically. It is impossible mainly because we have never thought of it. This is, after all, the world of a man and a little boat named DAMFINO, in which none of us "no" what will happen next.

TEN SECONDS LATER . . . Fade in and all is shipshape. Keaton's "transition" title "makes fun of transitions."[6] This is another example of his economic choice of simple words that really requires deeper scrutiny. In this unfolding narrative, we move from chapter to chapter (garage ⟶ pier ⟶ river . . . ) with decisive transitions. We do not have divider calendar days, as in *One Week*; instead, Keaton marks progress by tongue-in-cheek overtones to familiar mottos. This innocuous time title takes on humorous significance when we realize it is a caption for another visual absurdity: Buster has completely fixed his boat in "ten seconds." Keaton also revives the fantasy that we accept with suspended disbelief and reinforces Buster's determination to undo all that Fate tangles up. He challenges Fate's rapid destruction with equally speedy reconstruction.

Keaton takes a brief interlude belowdecks to rekindle Buster's familial rapport. Will paternal instincts survive this latest test? Upon entering the cabin, we recall the riblike bungalow of the Buzzards in *The High Sign*, for here too the tight set draws our vision into the background, structuring depth by its design. It is like a tunnel lined with benches on the right and left of a narrow center table; walls of long narrow slats extend from foreground to background. The ceiling is scalloped, reaching away from us; pictures and light fixtures on the walls provide more depth and dimensionality. The background china cabinet appears proportionately small at the rear because of perspective: the two sides seem ready to merge in the distance. Metaphorically speaking, Buster and family are trapped in the belly of the whale. Of course, ironically, Buster has built his own whale. Yet it is still Fate's invention constructed to gobble them up.

Buster perpetuates the "eating theme" of the film with a concrete gag (and concrete is not much of an exaggeration): he introduces Sybil's inedible flapjacks. Buster and Juniors gnaw, slice, and bounce them to no avail; they finally hide the flapjacks in their porkpies. Suddenly the room tips toward the camera so deeply that the thick ceiling drops low enough to obstruct our view of Buster's head. Keaton has created a real box of a room hemmed in on all sides except the front—the "wall" of the camera. When the table slides toward us, almost crashing through this "wall," we cut to exterior for the explanation: the boat is heading upstream. Depicted through a tilted camera, the DAMFINO plows "up" the 45-degree angle of river from bottom left to upper right. We return to the same interior tilt where we left off and pause before the room drops acutely "into" the background. Why? The boat is churning downstream; the corresponding exterior depicts the river angling 45 degrees from upper left to lower right. The river, of course, remains placid and smooth, the sharp angles having no gravitational effect on the water. Keaton has simply tilted the camera (frame) to slope the landscape. This is one of Keaton's rare camera manipulations for visual effect, or what Kerr calls a "visual pun." After all, if Buster's boat is heading downriver, the river should literally be heading down. "Keaton had no qualms about manipulating the camera lens itself. To get the uphill and downhill shots all he had to do was tilt the camera. That, in his understanding of the game, was cricket. . . . If he was going to play with the camera, he would play with *it*—not with the world it recorded, not with the resulting film in the laboratory."[7] Keaton's greatest play on film in *The Playhouse* was also a play with the camera lens, not the film, and he abides by his principle of "no fakery." The literal translation of upriver and downriver is typical of Buster's world in which extremes happen in the blink of an eye and with little concern for logic—or rather, with a great concern for the logical-illogic. It is impossible for a river to be so tilted without tumult; but it is no less logical (or no *more illogical*) in *our* reality that we use the term *upriver* or *downriver* although the river appears absolutely straight to our

naked eye. Keaton wants us to *see* what happens when there are no constraints on possibility and when descriptions (e.g., "PUNCH CLOCK") become literal truth.

In a world this honest, however, Buster becomes slightly unrattled;
his response to these upheavals is to nail to the wall a painting of a clipper
ship on rocky waters. The painting is a miniaturization of Buster's troubled journey; he seems to have anticipated such a fate, since he obviously
chose to bring this work of art with him. When he nails, water begins
dripping from behind—a literal translation of the image. The flat becomes dimensional, the cliché literal. A *picture* of stormy weather becomes reality—or so Buster thinks, as he blinks at the dripping water
and even tastes it. It is as if he has penetrated the flat surface, just as he
broke through the glassless clock in *The Haunted House* or the illusions
in *The Playhouse*. But there is a "logical" explanation for this illusion, as
Buster discovers when he lifts the painting and water sprays past him: he
has nailed through the wall into the water. To plug it, Buster draws on
his utilitarian nature: he nails a flapjack over the hole, recalling the earlier prop and perpetuating his beloved equation theme (flapjack = patch).
Shortly, Sybil will pass through the cabin when cleaning and stop short
at her flapjack; but accustomed to a life of equations with Buster, she
merely dusts it off.

Fate's attack on the boat begins to break through directions and levels of space. The cabin is now tossed to the side as a speedboat rips
through the waters. We are becoming immersed in greater threats to the
DAMFINO and therefore immersed, so to speak, in the composition of the
shots themselves. The speedboat hurtles toward us and veers sharply off
left, as if we are the DAMFINO itself churned in the wake. We too feel flung
around the cabin as it (and the family within) angles sharply toward left
and right. Buster goes to nail down the steering wheel. His return to the
cabin is another dramatic "back" shot, breaking through the camera
"wall" as he heads toward Sybil in the rear. He is, in essence, stepping
away from us, the audience, who are in the most controlled of positions,
since we usually know the most as "observer." These "back" shots affirm
Buster's control.

The DAMFINO cruises left, continues center and off right as the ends
of the frame draw together, wiping the scene black with a "sliding-door"
optical. Keaton has not used this particular wipe before, although it is
reminiscent of the "curtain" wipe in *The Playhouse*, which was an optical
effect appropriate to the setting. Likewise, the slamming-door effect is a

curious visual insight into the theme: Buster is unequivocally trapped, the walls have closed in, the whale's jaws have snapped shut. Many clues have been planted to suggest this entrapment: literal uphills/downhills, leaky storm paintings, disastrous omens such as sinking life preservers and floating anchors, the speedboat of the gods and the iron fists of their bridges, the inner-belly design of the cabin, even Sybil's inedible flap-jacks—all pointing to Buster's being trapped, stranded, and starving on the high seas. A simple nail is as likely to bring security (staying the steering wheel) as it is to rain disaster (spring a leak); it is the inevitable duality. Buster is definitely caught behind trapdoors in his own home; nothing is safe or predictable except the unsafe and unpredictable. All he needs to complete the dismal picture is an albatross!

The full threat of the "eight bells" at the beginning of the film (like the bells of *One Week*) culminates in the last "chapter" title of the film: OUT ON THE BROAD PACIFIC, DARKNESS STUMBLED AND FELL. Keaton's tongue-in-cheek comment attributes great control to Buster's surroundings (control by Fate). He also suggests that the "authority" figures, the greater powers around Buster, are really as inept as ever. The curtain of darkness employed as Fate's handmaid to thwart Buster only "stumbles" along on its mission. Of course, when even an inept force "falls" on Buster, its resounding thud will hit our hero with such power that its destruction will be worse than if it had just rolled in quietly.

The "jaws of the whale" open—the optical slides apart to reveal the resilient little ship bobbing on the rough sea. Within, there is a semblance of a cozy life as the Buster family bunk for the night. Keaton gives realistic detail of the family's preparations for bed: Sybil dresses Juniors in their nightshirts; Buster lights a candle, pulls a nightshirt over his clothes, crawls into the bunk. He is really allowing time for the storm to brew. These details are interrupted by crosscutting to exteriors that show the boat's increasingly dramatic tossing in the water. It is as if the two lines of this "perspective" (interior/exterior continuum) are merging in the distance of *time*, as the physical lines of the cabin earlier merged in the distance of *space*. Keaton switches between interior and exterior to accelerate the inevitable merging of the two locations: Buster's bunk collapses under his weight; a jagged lightning bolt pierces the sky; Buster struggles with his knotted sheet. All along we know interior/exterior will unite; Buster himself expects it, for he is fully dressed under his nightshirt.

At the merging point of no return, the storm finally invades the cabin. Water bursts into the porthole, drenching Buster. Stopping for his hat and candle, Buster heads to the deck where his white nightshirt serves as our "beacon" in the pitch blackness outside. The figure of the "little man" is all the more poignant as Buster stands vulnerable in his flapping incandescent gown, holding a futile candle and clutching his porkpie to his head as he faces the dark abyss with hand to forehead. The simultaneously poignant/comic image reemphasizes Buster's "senselessness" as he stares into the eye of the storm: when the wind blows out the candle, he tries to relight it in the neck opening of his nightshirt. It seems peculiar that with Buster's "state-of-the-art" compact boat he has such primitive lighting and navigational devices. Buster's shattered concentration, his imperative to light a candle in the wind, obliterates sense; he pays for this "thoughtlessness" by toppling overboard. Buster's struggles with an umbrella and collapsible spyglass are more painful reminders of his ill-preparedness for this rigorous voyage. These accoutrements are useless: a gale steals the umbrella instantly. The spyglass droops as he looks through it and desperately tries to keep it straight by peering through it between his legs; he topples again. Perhaps Buster is weary from his combat with the cyclone in *One Week* where his body was in command at every minute. Buster's reliance on useless items detracts from his total self-dependence. Nature here not only blows him around as did the cyclone but also soaks him—he is figuratively shrunken by the drenching. Buster heads into the cabin, locks Sybil and the kids in the back room, and taps a message on the radio. Exterior long shot, a three-pronged fork of lightning hits a mast; interior, smoke issues from Buster's headset. The storm has invaded Buster's privacy; it knows where he is and follows him everywhere. The minute he lit the candle, the wind blew it out; he nailed a picture and water rushed in; he now activates the radio and lightning strikes. The "eye of the storm" is literally watching his every move.

Communication opens between a patrol boat and the DAMFINO in a graphic depiction of electronic transmission. Keaton's literalness takes the actual shape and form of the radio messages and creates a powerful sight gag with titles. Their dialogue in electric lettering: $S O S$ , Buster taps twice. *Who is it?* Buster responds: *Damfino* The stunned telegrapher angrily taps back: *Neither do I.* Buster's nonplussed stare at this abrupt response again reinforces the innocence of the boat's name—the very name he chose for it. In calling the name for help, Buster assures loss of his own rescue. Fate's jaws close for another tasty bite.

The boat is now spinning in the water, and Buster must keep up with it. In a scene that Fred Astaire might have loved (à la *Royal Wedding*

[1951]), Buster choreographs his crawl around the cabin. As the cabin revolves clockwise, Buster stomps onto the right cabin wall as it meets him, crawls along the ceiling, steps over bunk beds. After one turn, we confirm this phenomenon with a cut to exterior showing the little tub spinning in the water like a chicken on a spit. Keaton not only has designed his cabin for claustrophobia but has created a sight gag that only an enclosed box can illustrate. By intercutting between the enclosed cabin-box and the turning miniature vessel, Keaton suggests that both are one and the same. Intercutting also builds the sight gag of Buster walking over four sides to a visual fever pitch. Each time we return from seeing the hapless boat in another revolution, Buster is performing another variation on the theme. He finally nails his slapshoes to the floor and continues telegraphing at revolving angles. When we see the boat at rest (overturned), we are prepared for the third variation in the interior: Buster hangs upside down by his shoes, urgently tapping. His happy sea-life has turned topsy-turvy, and he literally portrays it. He copes with the upheaval through the impossibility of two simple nails fastening him to the ceiling/floor. Buster knows that equations eventually return to their original state of being. As much as floor = ceiling, with a mere turn ceiling will = floor again, and Buster is planning to be in position.

Buster's assaults by the natural forces in *One Week* and *The Boat* have indeed flung him through all dimensions of space. The revolving house spun horizontally like a reckless carousel; the revolving boat now spins vertically. Together, the two inventions are like a spinning atom with Buster as nucleus. The power within erupts with a force capable of destroying itself. When Buster drops from the ceiling, his common sense and all he holds dear seem destroyed as well. First affected is his family, which Buster finds in a tumbled heap when he slides the rear doors open and closed (a physical duplication of the sliding-door optical). The flapjack-patch flies off the wall with a burst of water. Buster drills a hole in the cabin floor and tries to direct the mighty leak into a funnel he sets in the opening. Buster's desperation has driven him beyond sense, even if we allow that such actions *seem* sensible in a moment of panic. But for Keaton, too, the props strain; it seems contrived that there just *happens* to be a funnel and drill in Buster's reach. True, Buster's utilitarian nature would adapt any object floating by him; but Keaton's deliberate choice of funnel and drill, followed by Buster aggravating the situation by drilling a hole in the bottom of the boat, weakens the success of the gag. Only belatedly does Buster recognize his catastrophe. He smacks the geyser with a pot and, finally, with the painting. The water throws the painting into Buster's face, a literal "confrontation" of man and nature. The painting is like a fragile bridge between them, fluctuating with every pull and push of these forces. This "head-on" collision numbs him to total sense-lessness, in a gag recalling the rescue scene of *The Playhouse*: he scoops water with a teacup, then sits on the bunk to sip it. Having experienced hope, bewilderment, confusion, confidence, insecurity, panic, despair, and abandon, the emotions cancel each other out and result in helpless-ness. Although funny on its own, the gag stunts the whole routine because it delays the rescue and prolongs imminent tragedy. Buster's in-vincible spirit is the only reason we can overlook the flaw, for he is rein-vigorated in this momentary inertia. His mental battery is being re-charged during "teatime."

Action + crosscutting = chaos, which Keaton proves with the rocking boat and the family's choreography as they discard their tangled life pre-servers. The claustrophobic cabin and the rising water parallel rising emo-tional turbulence. Visual energy is compressed and combusts, and this force must be released. The family thus escapes the inevitable interior drowning and heads to their watery end outside. The editing moves the film to its conclusion simply and swiftly. Each shot recording the des-perate action is interrupted only when the action expands beyond the frame's perimeters. For example, Buster places Sybil and Juniors into the bathtub that drifts away without him; cut to an extreme long shot of the DAMFINO and Buster drifting into the black background. One pathetic drifting is matched by a greater one. Switching to subjective perspective from Sybil and kids, we experience their deprivation; the film's strongest element, Buster, is actually drifting away. And its loss is depicted in an extreme distance shot that isolates the loss even more. The potentially heart-wringing tragedy is thwarted, however, when the next cut brings us directly to Buster on board the DAMFINO. We transcend the situation, *watching* it rather than *feeling* it; we no longer drift with Sybil but rather observe Buster distantly from a safe position. We readjust our emotional glasses with each new placement. We can no longer feel the same (or any) sentiment with Sybil. Rather, our emotion is curtailed, "deadpanned" to encourage laughter at the odd circumstances created by Buster's own senselessness.

For once, we feel the strong presence of a "tragic flaw." Buster has contributed to his own drowning and we feel this will become a disturb-ing emotional crisis. But Buster's personal response to his life-death di-

# The Boat

lemma alters our expected grief. As a result, we sidestep sentiment and detour onto a comic lane; tragedy parodies itself. As Buster waves to his offscreen family, he suddenly stops and makes an "aw-shucks" gesture, then turns, slips, and stumbles. Is this all he can think of saying in the face of wind, sea, destruction, loss of family, home, even life itself? As his past perhaps flashes before him, Buster remembers pesky Juniors, nagging Sybil, inedible home cooking, traitorous inventions—and all he can say is, "Shucks, it could've been different, but it wasn't. Maybe it'll be better where I'm going." Buster is resigned: both sense and senselessness have been used, to no avail. Fate that takes will also give, even if the gift is total deprivation. This is the Master Equation that the Master Goat will never avoid.

Buster spies his hat—his identity, his personalized anchor without which he is incomplete and drifting. The porkpie is so important that Buster bestows his offspring with junior porkpies. As will soon be seen in *Cops*, the porkpie is the essential physical presence of Buster's persona: a soft, malleable, yet durable protective covering of his energy and talent. The porkpie is also a crazy contradiction, another strange equation: it is a flat covering for a round head; it sits securely and heavily, even though it is light enough to fly off on a breeze. The porkpie looks flattened by rough battering, yet that is its natural shape. And so, porkpie = Buster. We recall the headgear of Keaton's contemporaries: derbies and rounded hats (Chaplin, Laurel and Hardy, Langdon, Arbuckle, Ben Turpin, Joe Roberts), top hat (Max Linder, Raymond Griffith), straw hat or cap (Harold Lloyd, Lloyd Hamilton)—and we see how Keaton stands out in the crowd. In most of his features, Keaton abandons the porkpie and cuts a handsome figure in tuxedos (*Sherlock Jr.*, *The Saphead*, *Battling Butler*) or period costumes (*The General*, *Our Hospitality*). His feature film hero will grow beyond the casual figure of the shorts to match his sophisticated narratives. But his spirit, represented by the porkpie, is still in each character, as a brief scene in *Steamboat Bill Jr.* demonstrates. As a silly college student visiting home, Buster is forced by his appalled father to give up his beret and ukulele for some decent work clothes. Buster tries on an assortment of hats in a store. In quick succession, the store owner replaces one hat with another on his head as Bill Jr. sits stoically. Suddenly a porkpie surfaces as one of the hats; Buster pulls it off, shocked and with a wary afterstare. Keaton has created an in-joke, reminding us that weaving through any *assumed* identity is the omnipresent Buster persona, one that pops to the surface at the mere drop of a porkpie.

# The Boat

The hat now becomes a symbol of Buster's "demise" once the DAM-FINO sinks (again) beneath the water. Buster has accepted the ultimate sinking by sitting reflectively, knees drawn up, facing the submerging end of the vessel. At its christening, the boat slipped endlessly into the water; the "life cycle" is complete as it sinks into an aquatic grave. Both times, Buster is steadfastly perched aboard. He remains unflinching, frozen, as he and the boat disappear inch by inch. Keaton holds on the still water to show no further sign of life. Given the water's tumult around a sinking ship, Buster's self-anchored position at such an angle against onrushing water is a magnificent representation of his control over the elements. Instead of toppling, thrashing, and splashing, Buster assumes a pose characteristic of a calm situation. He introspectively considers his despair as he accepts defeat and literally sinks into it. To accept it, he cannot run from it or topple into it, for either gesture is a struggle with the opposition. Buster is at his philosophical best here, in this one moment, when he maintains his character to the very end and immerses himself in the event. He is the reflective captain who willingly goes down with his ship.

Keaton intercuts between Sybil's wails, Juniors doffing their hats in tribute, and Buster's floating porkpie. His hat is our last connection with Buster in this bleak hour. But our lingering view of it is tinged with anticipation, for Keaton holds the porkpie shot for a curiously long time. Instead of fading out on the hat on its watery grave, we hold; the anticipation arouses a suspicion of the irony that has laced the film through its titled and visual opposites. Dwelling on the hat is like a pause in an interrupted conversation, when the listener knows that the speaker has not yet completed his thoughts but is catching a breath for the conclusion. After this stimulating pause, the hat suddenly springs out of the water— on Buster's head. He looks around, perplexed, and paddles over to the tub. The situation is too baffling for the family to even rejoice. The only thing "said" (by one of the irritating Juniors) is a request for a drink. Buster again is perplexed at this and solves his quandary by turning on the tub faucet to pour water into his hat. As the kid drinks thirstily, the other Jr. pulls the plug from the tub. Tragedy, overturned by Buster's resurrection, is once more inevitable, thanks to Fate's little porkpied emissaries. Catastrophe is full-circle home: Jr. tossing Buster on land has come to Jr. drowning Buster on sea. The only advantage is that the Buster family can now die together. They clutch each other silently as the tub sinks.

# The Boat

In *One Week*, a reversal of fortune greeted the newlyweds when the first train bypassed their house. *The Boat* offers the same again: Now the older married couple open their eyes to find that their tub has hit ground underwater in the nick of time. They dumbfoundedly walk through the water with their backs to us, hand in hand. The camera pans with them as they emerge from total blackness to a ghostly white ground—a beach. This time, the "back" shot does not speak of Buster's rebellion or turning away from us; rather, it seems a consolidation of the family for the first time, and we can only humbly follow as if pushing them to safe ground. Yet even with this hopeful trailing perspective, we remember the origins of this sea voyage, when Buster left *terra infirma*. We again worry about the (in)stability that certainly awaits him. The last title is a simple query from Sybil: "WHERE ARE WE?" Sybil's question is not only mouthed, but its documentation as a title card reinforces the question in our mind. We also suspect Buster's response. The only answer Buster gives is *not* provided in a title card; it is read in a close-up of his face, his mouth carefully forming the now familiar, purposely belabored, deliberately stressed word-name: damfino. With a flourish of his arm to follow him, they walk away from us, hand in hand, into the night. THE END.

This is the greatest equation of this film, and Buster fully realizes and identifies his situation, as never before articulated: DAMFINO = LIFE. The name of the boat, christened in innocence, becomes his self-proclaimed condition. It has been that all along. Buster has "grown" to recognize the resonances of this name. To become so articulate and to discover those connections within himself—in other words, to "grow," Buster has had to endure crises. Not only does his little family nearly sabotage him but his invention becomes a modified treadmill on which Buster must pace himself or lose himself. The treadmill symbolism will be developed in a later short, *Daydreams*, by which time Buster has grown into an even more poignant soul whose "journey" does not involve boat, car, or material possessions, but the pain of his failed dreams. Buster is on a journey to becoming an ephemeral, philosophical spirit, for within the filmmaking process, Keaton too is growing. His comedy now transcends slapstick and is layered with ironic symbols and hidden meanings.

For the first time in his short films, Buster has no real human nemesis (the house in *One Week*, of course, was the major nemesis, but even those disasters were brought on by Handy Hank). All other shorts have involved Buster against human *and* mechanical foes in varying degrees. *The Boat* is Buster one-on-one with his invention. Pitted against inanimate

# The Boat

objects, Buster seems more helpless and less rational, although he manages to rescue himself. Kerr mentions how gags like drilling water into a sinking ship make little sense even for a desperate Buster: "The gag is, for Keaton, not even a good gag. Keaton is rarely persuasive when he is behaving stupidly. We know that he knows better than that . . . he is underestimating the intelligence we attribute to him. He is working too hard in a new sense: fighting against what *is* instead of rolling with it."[8] In dealing with a human nemesis less intelligent than he, Buster rarely hesitates: as the scarecrow, he boots Joe and Pa; as the little ghost, he rounds up the counterfeiters; as the romantic poet, he creatively torments Joe. Buster anticipates human moves faster than they do. With the forces of nature or machinery, however, Buster is putty. Their meeting of minds is far more intimidating. Sometimes there is little else he can do without appearing helpless; Keaton himself alluded to this:

> INT[ERVIEWER]: There is a consistent character in all your films who, for instance, seems to be quite helpless with machinery.
>
> KEATON: Well, as a rule—I'll take two different comics. You take Harold Lloyd off the farm and you put him into the Ford Motor plant in Detroit. He would be afraid to touch anything, unless he was forced to by one of the foremen or something. With me, I would be just as scared of it but I would take it for granted that I ought to know what I'm doing and to get out immediately to try and do it. And of course I'd gum it up—that's what would happen to me, because I don't know what I'm doing but I'd make the attempt.[9]

Buster is initially ignorant of the mechanical mind, but his talent to think and act like a machine helps him adjust after his first naive goofs. The machine meets its match, for Buster tries hard with intelligence and wit to learn-by-doing. Since he emerges unscathed, the battle has in fact been equitably fought.

Buster fights, loses, succeeds, fights, loses, succeeds (or does he?), and finally poses his question *and* answer ("damfino") as he walks away. This endurance surpasses the staunchest survival tests of Chaplin, Lloyd, and Langdon combined. There was always a definite outcome with these three contemporaries; we never questioned where we or they were at the end. But here . . . what is this land? Are there wild animals or cannibals waiting? Are they back where they started? Is there a second train coming, as in *One Week*, a symbolic train ready to destroy them entirely? The destination of the sea voyage (never announced in the first place) remains unidentified at the end. The possibility of *Life* being Buster's only conceivable journey has never been stronger. "The real answer of Buster Keaton, both artist and man, is 'Nowhere.' His answer to the question 'Where?' is the question's echo. It broods over every voyage, large or small. It is not so much 'Is this trip necessary?' as 'Is this trip going anywhere?' For voyaging is inescapable—it is life, it is time. In *The Boat*, the question is left honestly unsolved: 'Nowhere' is both answer and non-answer."[10]

Even the other rootless Keaton hero of *The High Sign*, who came from NOWHERE and wasn't headed ANYWHERE, still ended SOMEWHERE. Buster and family are somewhere indeed, however far off course, although it is nowhere until they can identify the land. Keaton caps the film with the continuous running gag of DAMFINO, bringing the film closer to a parody or inversion of tragedy. There was greater melancholy in Buster's sigh at the end of *One Week*; he returned the DIRECTIONS with fatigue and regret. Although both films show Buster surviving, *The Boat* ends with a joke and we are relieved. At the same time, the joke is just another wry comment. Keaton has tossed a monkey wrench into our psyche, for the ending is not neatly tied up with victory or defeat, but with the unknown and uncertainty. The hero is in a state of limbo. Keaton lets us feel whatever degree of empathy we wish for Buster, for he appeases us on many levels: slapstick, symbolism, psychology, theme—something for everyone. What *is* certain is that the Fates who have let Buster build his boat also destroy it (and, ironically, with his help). Yet as the boat is sapped of energy, Buster seems replenished. There is cause for laughter, then (however fragile or uneasy), as long as Buster can walk away in one piece.

## Chapter 12

# The Paleface

(January 1922)

Courtesy of the Academy of Motion Picture Arts and Sciences

From the oil wells on the horizon to Buster's slapshoe moccasins, *The Paleface* is a study in naturalistic comedy. Surpassing *Neighbors* in which the setting spawned many slapstick routines, here the landscape welcomes both comic and dramatic situations. Some critics attribute a documentary style to this film because Keaton conveys "visual truth in both action and photography."[1] The characters still retain their comic eccentricities, and the comedy includes the usual sight gags and layered routines. But there are more subtle, real-life "colors" on this artist's palette as he grows confident in the medium; Keaton mixes rich hues from primary colors and paints on his largest canvas thus far.

The central figure will naturally be Buster, broadly defined and fitting into a panoramic landscape; but, for the first time in a Keaton short, his appearance is delayed to present instead a critical dramatic situation. The scope of the film is suggested by the opening title, IN THE HEART OF THE WEST, THE INDIAN OF TODAY DWELLS IN SIMPLE PEACE. This title reads like the start of a factual text, but the words "heart" and "simple peace" resonate emotion. The establishing shot of Indians and grazing animals on a reservation gracefully dissolves into a medium shot. The suggestion is not of a dissolve as time lapse; rather, Keaton is creating mood by blending the shots and representing a harmonious life between Indians and nature. Part of the harmony and goodwill is a complacent figure, the comic element in a serious setting. Big Chief (Joe Roberts) sits by his tepee, puffs on his pipe, and spits to the side. He is Keaton's wry comment in this documentary presentation. Then, like a pause after a paragraph in a narrative, Keaton fades out.

Abruptly, the tone changes with the next title: BUT THERE CAME THEN A GROUP OF OIL SHARKS TO STEAL THEIR LAND. With just two transitional devices and two shots, the tone has been radically altered; the story has developed a crisis within the opening minutes. Setting, character, and conflict have all been economically, boldly selected and presented. The resulting effect is the juxtaposition of tones from both ends of the spectrum: on one end, harmony and tranquility; on the other, discord and violence. By setting these contrasts side by side, Keaton controls our emotional response. The opposite actions ensure audience attention, just as if Keaton flashed a hand before our relaxed faces to startle us.

The film's villain is a distinguished figure in a top hat, next seen stepping from a Rolls Royce and entering the small building of the WESTERN OIL LAND LEASING CO. As we join him inside conferring with several men, we dissolve within the shot to a closer view of the same conference. Like the time lapse in *The Haunted House* when Joe demonstrated the staircase gadget, we now see a similar effect. By moving closer, we approach the perpetrators of the deed; we are witnesses and jurors. Keaton implies that hatching a plot takes time behind closed doors, and he measures film time in a specific physical location by "flashing forward" to suggest the duration of such plotting. A stealthy man in turtleneck next summons Top Hat, and the plot turns despicable. We cut to an office behind another closed door, where these two men confer as Turtleneck brandishes a blackjack. He speaks without titles, keeping us in momentary suspense about his gesture. The scene dissolves into a *flashback*: Turtleneck waits in a dark corner outside the GOVERNMENT LAND OFFICE for an Indian to leave with a paper; he strikes the Indian with the blackjack, steals the paper, and places a coin in the Indian's hand. *Dissolve* back to the two men and the subsequent title, making the scene more horrific: "AND THAT'S HOW I PERSUADED HIM TO SELL THE LEASE FOR A DOLLAR!" The action has been funneled through time and space (wide ⟶ narrow ⟶ wide; large office ⟶ inner room ⟶ large office), returning to its original setting where Top Hat announces: "WE'LL GIVE THEM TWENTY-FOUR HOURS TO GET OFF THE LAND!" This funneling effect not only uses film devices to layer the scene visually, but it also symbolizes the secret inner workings of criminals.

After a fade, signifying another lapse in present time and providing emotional respite from this ultimatum, a number of quickly paced titles build to a climax. THE TRIBE GETS NOTICE TO VACATE. A brave hands Big Chief a letter, which we see in handwritten close-up, a device pulling us directly into the communication as though we are the recipient: "AND YOU MUST GET OFF AT ONCE! J.C. HUNT, PRES. GREAT WESTERN OIL CO." The Chief proclaims to his braves: "WHITE MAN KILL MY MESSENGER!" The horror intensifies because we realize the earlier attack was not just striking the Indian but killing him. The tension is sustained and heightened by cutting to a medium shot of the Chief. Thus, his comment is stressed and his pointing offscreen is even more threatening as he says: "KILL FIRST WHITE MAN THAT COMES IN THAT GATE!" The white man's ultimatum has now been matched by one of Indian vengeance. The line is also a crucial stepping-stone to continue the comic action; it is a cue for the dormant comedy to hear its wake-up call. Keaton's response to the Chief's "feed-line" is typically visual: cut to the high wooden gate with a center door. The visual and the verbal join to build tension that is mostly dramatic but inevitably comic. The silent gate—the visual—is the only possible introduction to Buster, a purely visual creature entering a mostly visual world.[2]

Up to this point, the film's realism has been severe; comedy has been disturbed by the poignant social drama that launches a Keaton film for the first time. The drama has been constructed mainly of dialogue, recalling some contemporary film dramas in which numerous titles filled the screen with exposition and speech, followed by visuals to illustrate.

# The Paleface

By this careful sequence of shots and titles, we follow a dramatic continuum, with only one comic breather (Big Chief). There is no comic relief in the oil shark's office; for once, the villains are not comic caricatures but real and corrupt human beings. But because we know this will ultimately be a comedy, Top Hat and Turtleneck must become comical targets with the appearance of an avenging angel (Buster). Because of his position against the oil sharks, we assume Big Chief will be that angel's sidekick. All that follows, however, will always be tempered by the opening "docudrama." For the first time, Keaton has chosen material transcending slapstick and romance. Just as Chaplin wove the plight of the immigrant or factory worker into his comedy, Keaton focuses on the exploitation of the Indian, and within this frame plants his comic seeds. The resulting bloom will bear the traits of both parents, drama and comedy.

Buster's delayed appearance has been deliberate in order to create drama. The Chief's dictum to kill the first white man now connects us subconsciously to Buster's arrival, as his is certainly the palest face possible. Keaton develops a gag around his persona's physical appearance. His "white" makeup is like a mask; the "edge lines" end sharply under the chin, clearly separating light face and dark neck. As "the paleface," Buster's blanched features will, more than ever, suggest a vulnerable, helpless little fellow arriving from a delicate world of shadows and entering a dark and stunning reality.

The peaceful tone that opened the film is momentarily recalled by a butterfly that flutters over the gate in the anticipatory long shot; it beckons someone unseen. But because of the dramatic situation established, we feel an irreversible cynicism: the tranquility "before the white man came" will never be recaptured. When the gate slowly opens in response to the butterfly's silent call, an arm protrudes; Buster's inquisitive face completes his piecemeal introduction. In searching for the butterfly, Buster wanders in from the "other side"—literally, of the gate; figuratively, of another world. Like the distant horizon of *The Boat*, which Buster sought with hand to forehead, the butterfly is equally elusive. It also is far enough away to distract Buster from seeing the danger in his tracks. He enters holding a large net, intent on being a serious collector, but simultaneously (à la duality) appearing diminished by his own seriousness. He is like a child pretending to be a doctor because he has a plastic stethoscope. Adult mannerisms are convincingly mimicked, but the child's mind has yet to become the adult mind.

# The Paleface

Buster's interaction with the butterfly becomes a miniature portrait of Protagonist versus Nemesis: butterfly thwarts Buster's polite efforts to capture it. As his patience was exhausted by the fish who swallowed his golf ball in *Convict 13*, Buster with mounting annoyance picks at the butterfly but pinches the air, nets his own head, and tries to punch his quarry. The butterfly placidly flutters away, luring Buster into position between two Indian braves. Buster tips his hat at them. We relish seeing the hornet's nest he has entered, the unfolding alignment of Fate's plans with Buster's innocent hobby. It is like watching a frame within which a magical picture paints itself, unaware of its predetermined dimensions.

As he pursues this "big game" in unknown territory, Buster becomes distracted by its newness. Buster's butterfly-dance is a precursor of things to come, and his exploration becomes a metaphor for "looking for trouble." The gate is like the picture frame just mentioned; Buster has closed himself into the "frame"—he even locks the gate with a satisfied pat. He tastes the contents of a nearby kettle, sticking his tongue out in displeasure; the pot suggests the "stew" simmering around Buster. The interactions between Buster and braves become typical Keaton choreography; pursued and pursuer silently converse through space and movement. These two team-players, in fact, toss their roles back and forth until neither one knows exactly who the other is; the position of control is constantly exchanged like a football. The braves think Buster's hesitant steps are of fear, when he is actually pacing to pounce upon the butterfly.

With vengeance in mind, the braves do not see the butterfly; after all, it is a natural part of their environment, not a focus of attention and certainly not for capture. Buster represents the enemy, and despite his harmless pastime, he is suspect to the braves simply because he is *there*. Buster's mad dash to slam the net on the ground alarms the braves who leap at him, but they are amazed when he bypasses them to study his catch with a magnifying glass. Inserted close-up: a bee between his fingers. Buster stomps on the offending creature, kicks dirt over it, even shows his sting-wound to a brave. Buster employs one of his most important characteristics, that of the well-intentioned innocent, like the poor Goat who sought companionship without realizing just how "wanted" he really was, or the bank teller in *The Haunted House* becoming a criminal because he held a gun in self-defense. Buster is the unwitting scapegoat who will bear the sins of his white brethren. This *innate* innocence is different from *assumed* innocence (child versus adult). When childhood's rose-colored spectacles are switched to a magnifying glass, so to speak, the harsh realities of the world (e.g., angry bee, oil sharks) loom large and clear. Buster must adapt quickly—another characteristic evident from *One Week*—and mold *himself* to his surroundings. Enter Buster as the newborn adult who recognizes these cruel stingers and shows no mercy.

Even in his self-imposed "growing up," Buster is quickly diverted by the passing of a pretty Indian maid into a tepee; the prospect of a love-relationship again overwhelms all other business. The usual father-nemesis appears just as quickly: Big Chief steps out and drives Buster off. Buster as "outsider" arouses suspicion in others by his self-absorbed behavior. He displays other major characteristics: innate curiosity and oblivion. Being both at the same time has its advantages: it creates comedy and molds a deep comic protagonist. But he also finds himself directly in the line of fire. His loner status ironically invites incompatible company, as a magnet draws unwanted things to itself. Buster's persona cannot be complete without those he must oppose. His lonely spirit precludes loneliness, for his destiny is to be pursued by those he seeks to avoid. His innocent actions have an ulterior sinister meaning for these wary Indians. When he tries for the butterfly and nets the Big Chief instead, he adds yet another nail to his coffin (or potato to the stewpot). The braves lynch him, but ironically, Buster seems oblivious to their assault. He has captured his butterfly in the melee, places it in his basket after confirming it through the magnifier, and walks away, still followed by Indians.

The setting of the next shot accommodates Buster's casual search for more specimens, and it contains the very item that will test his endurance to the limit: the inevitable, preordained stake. As Buster saunters toward the stake, Big Chief cues the war dance. Buster naively watches, his body beginning to jerk a tempo; he suddenly joins the end of the line, kicking and clapping. His well-honed childlike qualities are crystal clear. The dance looks like fun, and he's that kind of guy, never realizing it is for him the tom-toms beat. Buster is now embroiled in his special brand of naive trouble, just as in *The Goat*, his innate curiosity caused him to peer through prison bars at the moment of an unfortunate photo session. Buster's oblivion is like a sheath protecting his childlikeness from reality, or his view *beyond* reality; he sees the best, the brightest, the farthest, but cannot see the up-close. In the past, by overlooking the odd construction of his house or the ocean swallowing his boat from under him, Buster only saw beyond to a dreamy promise until the last moment. At that moment, his farsightedness was corrected by the giant magnifying glass of "Reality." Of course, his preferred condition is that of a frolicking child, a play-doctor, a zestful overgrown toddler who kicks up his heels on a whim. In his view, there is no harsh reality as long as he remains alone. He does not yet know that these Indians have been plunged into a drama that has forced *our* eyes open from the start. It is merely playtime for Buster, and if these Indians are real, he will be as surprised as when the cigar-store Indian sprang to life in *The Goat*.

Mid-dance, Buster falls, and with it, his play-world is shattered, for the Indians seize this opportunity to tie him to the stake. The Indians assume a typical Keaton-authority figure; in a position higher than Buster, they are supposed to know what they are doing, but they are careless on the job. They only tie his hands behind his back and leave him to gather kindling. In the meantime, curiosity and shrewdness combine in Buster. The giant symbolic Magnifier has descended before his wide-open eyes; his fall to the ground has rattled the child's brain and the adult "genes" hiding beneath surge forward, anticipating Reality. Buster now joins the victimized world of the Indians by himself becoming their victim. Knowledge of the adult world rushes to Buster's consciousness, and he calmly, coolly, intuitively thinks of escape. In separate long shots intercut with shots of Indians bustling about for branches, Buster stands center and alone with his stake. He discovers that he can lift the stake out of the ground while it is tied to his hands. Keaton thus depicts Buster's loneliness and salvation in one shot so that we enhance our pleasure by assuring ourselves that this barbecue will be brief.

Once again, Keaton choreographs space and dimension by filling a potentially empty shot with elements that accumulate around its visual core—Buster. Keaton also endows this sequence with a naturalistic prop (the stake) in an appropriate environment (Indian reservation), again milking an object that has naturally sprung from its neighborhood; there is no intrusion of a prop for prop's sake. With the stake, Buster plays a game of tag by stepping to the left of the kindling that an Indian lays before him. When the Indian returns with more branches, he is astonished that either Buster or the kindling has moved. Buster stares front with *assumed* innocence, for now as the *adult*, he can exchange moments of innocence with cunning in order to keep his hide from being tanned. The wistful butterfly-collector is like a phoenix reborn (luckily, here, without ashes). Buster has plunged through a mental baptism of fire, hoping not to experience the flames firsthand.

The precision dance between this Indian and Buster builds to a flurry as they weave back and forth across the wide and deep spaces of the frame. The Indian collects and replaces bundles to catch up with Buster who moves whenever his opponent is not looking. At one point, Buster altogether "disappears" from the Indian by stepping directly behind him, stake still on his back, while the Indian spins in Buster's shadow. Ironically, there is no verbal communion between the two: only stares *at* or stares *away* from each other (another advantage of the silent medium). Buster's world is one of shallow logic, which perfectly fits the Nemesis's shallow mind. The Indian does not shout to his brothers to stop Buster, nor do Buster and Indian ever converse. Buster's own logic fails a bit here, though, for in discovering the means of escape, he chooses instead to play tag with the Indian. Where his logic fails, however, Buster's ingenuity triumphs to torment his tormentors, play with their minds, catch them off guard, and challenge them so that *he* may use his full adult potential to teach them a lesson. It is almost as if without staying in a dangerous situation Buster cannot grow. He refuses to remain the victim; he will *play* the victim only to become the victor. Although Fate lured him into a perilous picture frame, Buster can now *choose* his survival tactic and paint his solution. His drive is the choice to win in a no-win situation.

Buster's last pas de deux in this choreography is introduced by matching medium shots of the Indian gaping and approaching and of Buster cocking his head in feigned wonder and invitation. With these shots, Keaton forces us to look straight into each opponent's face, to see how the victim/victor dichotomy will be resolved. Buster has endured the "stake dance" to confuse the enemy who will be too exhausted to follow him. Buster conks the stunned Indian on the head by bowing and lowering the stake on him. He slides down the stake, drags the Indian and a handy blanket behind a bush, slices off his braid, and creates a "scarecrow" equation that will revolutionize Buster's existence like no adventure has yet. In *Convict 13*, Buster adopted the appearance and mannerisms of his enemy, but by being a con or a guard, he continually got into trouble for always being "one of them." Buster knows now (from his collective memory of past short films, so to speak) that he must surpass any impersonation, leap past being just an Indian, and become a force they can fear: a god.

Buster has already altered the natural order of things by reversing what is expected of an Indian confronting a white man—a "scalping." To become Indian, he scalps his "victim." When Buster steps out draping the blanket around him, he sports the braids on either side of his head,

atop of which sits his porkpie touting a feather. Total indoctrination of
Buster as Indian, with full scalping privileges, is yet to be seen when he
retaliates against the evil white men of the oil company. In the meantime,
however, Buster is still unsteady in his new identity; he must join in the
barbecue by running *with* the Indians, contributing branches to the kindling even though the victim has vanished. Buster walks tall to imper-
sonate his colleagues while trying to walk casually toward freedom; just
as suddenly and instinctively he will make a mad dash with another
branch to simulate the enthusiasm of his brothers. Cleverly, each mad
dash also leads Buster further from the stake, until he meanders among
the tepees, possibly seeking the lovely squaw, and suggesting to watchful
eyes that he is indeed searching for himself. Here is a variation of *The
Goat*: Buster's Wanted poster seemed to pursue Buster, and here Buster
is again in search of himself, although he also makes himself invisible. In
both cases, capture is predestined but, at all costs, to be circumvented.
Finally, a wary Indian suspects an oddball in the tribe (perhaps he bril-
liantly notices the feathered porkpie) and steps on Buster's blanket. Our
hero's haughty stride serves to no avail when he is de-blanketed to reveal
his white-man's suit. Tit for tat, Buster casually pauses before snatching
the blanket out from under the Indian's foot. The Indian is outsmarted
at his own game. Once more, too, Buster's typical run-fast/stop-short
movements define his physical approach to life's obstacles. It is also his
mental approach as he needs these "pauses" or "short stops" to refuel his
energy, devise secret plans, and confuse the enemy all at once.[3] Even in
the butterfly hunt, Buster's moves/nonmoves were answered by the start-
stop moves of the Indians, who never knew whether to come or go. Of
course, so early in the film, Buster was mesmerized by the butterfly and
unaware of his impact on the Indians. Now, both parties are conscious
of the other. The child has been forced into premature circumspection,
cynicism, and deliberation. This is perhaps why Wead has remarked that
*The Paleface* has the "most hieroglyphic action in all of Keaton's work."[4]
The pictures speak a multitude of words and intentions.

Keaton moves from one tight locale to broad open spaces. He uses the
physical terrain to parallel the comic peaks and nadirs of the developing
comedy and the ups and downs of Buster's dilemmas. Keaton literally
allows Buster to depict these ups and downs by following the contours
of the landscape in which he finds himself, as in the next gag. Here,
Buster ingeniously turns the blanket into a parachute as he fast approaches
a bridge over a gorge. We are first alerted to the gaping hole by the quick

cut that Keaton makes once Buster begins his flight from the smart Indian. Buster and Indian run across the bridge, action purposely recorded in a long shot to emphasize how miniscule Buster and his hunter are against the immense perilous land. Danger is highlighted by Buster's controlled stunts, as when he nearly slips off the other side of the gorge. Buster holds up the blanket to hide himself, as if standing behind a drawn curtain in the living room of a girlfriend who tries to distract her unexpected husband. He simply is convinced that the ruse works, not imagining that the Indian could move behind him. When he finally peers over the blanket with near-relief that he is free, Buster is seized from behind by the Indian and pitched headfirst off the cliff. We watch the descent in an extreme long shot as Buster's helpless dot of a body plummets through space under an impromptu blanket-parachute, a deus ex machina woven from the coincidence of Buster's life. He does not perish, as the Indian hopes, but rather descends gracefully like a heavenly spirit only to continue the endless chase. Another Indian walks along on the ground below; Buster lands on him, knocking him out and covering him with the blanket. Next, Buster discovers a log cabin after he dispenses with his braids. This superficial disguise has miserably failed, and any future disguise must be more authentic, stemming from inside, not outside—from the essence of Buster's persona. We do not enter the cabin with Buster but are left with the Indians who see the blanket rise groggily before them; eight Indians jump on it only to find a brother beneath. With a crosscut insert, we see Buster again scaling the "terrain," this time the roof of the log cabin. The chase is pivoting through every dimension—north, south, east, west—of the frame.

Buster tips over into the chimney and lands seated on the hearth beside a convenient prop, a large sheet reading FIREPROOF ASBESTOS   B. CHASE, NEW YORK. Keaton shows the "real thing" in every minor detail, even down to the name of the manufacturer of this miracle fireproofing. Whether he likes it or not, Buster is grounded in a very strange but real world, where a log cabin on an Indian reservation is lined with asbestos from New York. As soon as we absorb this ingredient of a forthcoming gag, we cut away to keep track of the chasing Indians who haul a log to ram the locked door. We crosscut in best chase tradition, except that now Buster's movements are not frenetic runs and leaps, but slow, meticulous actions, more of a mental chase offsetting the physical exertions of his pursuers. He calmly becomes a tailor, fashioning an asbestos vest and pants to wear under his suit. We check on the Indians and note their bumbling movement with the log as they inch closer to the cabin. Film time is prolonged for effect, to emphasize their ineptitude and document Buster's newfound skill as a tailor; the Indians are either very slow or Buster is breathlessly fast, for when we return to see his handiwork, he is already joining the sleeves. Title: STRICTLY FIREPROOF—ASBESTOS B. V. D. 's. The gag recalls the destiny that haunts Buster every minute: the stake. Although his quick wits outsmart the Indians, he cannot escape Fate, which will insist on fitting him into his scapegoat suit; he at least modifies his destiny with a fireproof one.

Only when Buster has completed his sewing do the Indians crash into the door that topples onto him, providing another momentary escape while the Indians rummage around the cabin. The detailed shots needed to record the passage of time and place follow in rapid succession, each joining in a crescendo that leads us back into the outlying wilderness. In apparently unfamiliar territory, however, Buster has an uncanny sense of direction. We are awed by an extreme long shot of a smooth mountainside incline. Buster trots down from its peak, accelerating into rolls and hand-springs; a few of his authentic tumbles are examined in close shots.[5] We cut into the slide with a shot of an abrupt void off the edge of the cliff. Buster skis into this shot and right off the edge of the cliff on his stomach, across the air, and smack into a tall tree. These daring feats are reserved for Buster, of course, as the transforming personality, the evolving hero, whose nature must be tested and whose rebirth is inevitable. Such a price to pay for being a dimensional character! The Indians motivate Buster's change and are kept in our periphery while we focus on him. For our breathless hero, we know the Indians are the costumed pawns of a greater Chaser. Thus, when Buster runs, he feels both the tangible and the in-tangible at his back; the latter will ultimately absorb Keaton as his work progresses. For Keaton, the Chase now resonates deeper matters involving not just body but mind and heart.

Another blanket awaits Buster, this one a tool to convey him to safety. Beset with arrows, Buster prepares to dive into a blanket held by the group of Indians, much like firemen hold a net to catch a jumper from a blazing window. But a miraculous resurrection takes place because of how irony, luck, circumstance collaborate—the right elements at the right time and place. This escape, however, also involves a cinematic trick that weakens Buster's otherwise self-reliant ingenuity: he leaps into the blanket and *back* onto the mountainside via film in reverse. The moment Buster sinks into the blanket, the almost imperceptible joining of mirror-image shots makes it possible for him to land feet first on the slope and scramble back uphill away from the Indians. His long slide down has been revoked, his power enhanced; his actions impress those who seek to capture him. Although meticulously aligned for symmetry, this device suggests that Buster is in a truly helpless situation and requires a miracle. The miracle worker must be Keaton, for no one else exists to help him out of this pickle. Buster's butterfly hunt has lured him between life and death in treacherous terrain. When he nets his own head trying to catch his quarry at the beginning, we are amused but not reassured of his chances for survival. Yet the nature of comedy, and of Buster's inner spirit as we know it, now convinces us that he can balance on the dangerous precipice of life. The Indians run around the base of the cliff after him. They are not amazed at this display of stamina but are desperate for their prize. Through film manipulation, Keaton has reinforced the curve motif by retracing the road that once led to escape. Instead, in typical curve fashion, the road has led to disaster $\longrightarrow$ salvation $\longrightarrow$ disaster, but it will ultimately lead to regrowth. Going backward is sometimes the only way to move ahead.

Big Chief has been watching from the site of the stake, scanning the horizon for Buster. The hand-to-forehead scan is a Buster trademark; because the Big Chief also does it, it implies a brotherhood between the two—if and when they become friends. Buster crawls backward out of a bush into Big Chief; thinking all is safe, he stands, only to fall into rigor mortis against Big Chief's protruding stomach. Buster's zero hour has struck, but his flight has sapped him of energy at this vital time. Symbolically (and comically) speaking, although his body will be "consumed" by his funeral pyre and the asbestos underwear will be his "shroud," Buster's spirit will be purified and reincarnated. He will become a force to reckon with and, fittingly, master of the supreme duality: he "dies" and lives at the same time.

Once the Indian fire dance is under way, Keaton lets us feel the rhythms visually; he carries us along its ritual and mystery. He intercuts shots of dancing feet, pounding tom-toms, and hopping shadows, filmed from dramatic angles as the Indians dance toward us; or as they fill the background, flames lick the foreground with Buster trapped in the middle. The situation is too ghastly realistic. Only the "deadpan" peering out through bodies and flames rescues us from total despair. Never has the "great stone face" served a more ironic purpose for blending drama and comedy than in this quasi-documentary burning-at-the-stake. Buster refuses to wince at the tongues of fire. Instead, he puffs and stares quizzically; his mouth blows little blasts of air to redirect the smoke. The rest of his body waits patiently for the denouement. There is obviously no need to worry with asbestos BVDs.

Keaton subjects Buster to his most daring and frightening adventure, one that pushes us to the brink of the drama/comedy threshold that haunted us from the start. Buster helps us through, reminding us with his stone face that he will be unscathed; he literally blows smoke from our eyes, for he has prepared us for his redemption. In medium shot, his eyebrows join his mouth activity, fanning up and down when a flame bursts before him. As Keaton approaches the climax of this scene, Buster gets hotter until his whole body begins hopping to the heat. The fire reaches its apex, then dies. Buster too reaches a peak and regenerates with relief that the worst is over; almost like the old saying, he stood the heat *and* remained in the kitchen.

During this sequence, Keaton remembers Buster's other reason to live besides life itself; he cuts to the pretty Indian maid who stares at the dreadful scene and steps hopelessly back into her tepee. She represents our nagging doubt about Buster's survival, but her view is limited while *our* hope springs eternal because we have known Buster longer. Shadowy dancing figures before a drummer add a ghostly air to what the Indians see as a "supernatural" conundrum in an otherwise predictable event. In the great chain of Fate, Buster is forging a link between his destiny and that of the Indians that will help them both in their hours of need.

Time passes whenever we cut from dance shots to Buster; his suit is more shredded and his face gradually darkened by heat and soot. He resembles one of the Indians now and, in so doing, touches their souls— he has outlived their flames. The Indians stop and stare in disbelief particularly when, in a sublime ironic gag, Buster steps forth among the ashes with hands on hips, reaches for a smoldering twig, and lights up a cigarette—one good smoke deserves another. He has reached into his own ridiculous torture and illuminated the simple minds around him. He has surpassed the uncomfortable "face-coloring" gag in *Neighbors*, where Buster became black with paint. Here, he does not use a different color to get off easy, for now he will become even more embroiled in the Indians' dilemma; Keaton has stressed this plotline above all by opening his film with it. Buster's coloring takes on an added meaning because of *how* and *why* it has changed. Saving his skin will become secondary to saving his new "brothers under the skin." He sacrifices his pale face for something greater, which has nothing to do with outward appearances. Buster will become a "paleface" again once he washes off the soot, but in the meantime, he has attained a high rank among those he once could not understand. He is his own butterfly freed from a box and ready to soar. The Indians fall on their knees and worship the survivor of their fiery ritual. For them, Buster cannot be a typical paleface but a transcendent deity. For us, in all his onionskin layers, he is still a Keaton Kontradiction, the child-adult who has quickly learned the laws of Reality while retaining his innocence. As this mortal-immortal looks down upon the hunched shoulders of his adoring subjects, Buster is haughty and casual. He has worked hard for this moment and relishes it with combined disbelief and certainty. He raises the bowed Chief and offers a peace-puff on his cigarette. Unlike Buster's quest for a relaxing, private smoke in other films, he now transforms a plain cigarette into a symbol of brotherhood and harmony. The Chief lays down the tomahawk as Buster leans on his back, surveying all with a relieved, slightly rambunctious look. Fade out. Buster's solution has indeed been up his asbestos sleeve the whole time, and what they don't know can't hurt them—or him.

HAVING BEEN INITIATED INTO THE REDMAN HE IS NOW A MEMBER IN GOOD STANDING. Fade in to the next major chapter in this epic saga on the reservation. Buster now has privileges of both worlds for having proven himself invincible: he emerges from a large tepee in a quilted robe and pipe to confer with the Chief. "WHITE MAN SAY WE MUST LEAVE." Buster shakes his head and answers: "US INDIANS MUST STICK TOGETHER." With the help of his Indian valet, he removes his high-living costume and promptly becomes one of "us Indians" by donning his feathered porkpie. After typically slapstick business of the Chief mounting his horse with the assistance of four braves, after which he promptly crashes to the ground, Keaton presents Buster's approach to horse riding. He lifts his maneuvers beyond the merely physical into a characteristic play with space. Buster's horse stands facing right, midsection covered by a bush. Gazing dreamily into the far right, Buster rides off—to the left. He has mounted *a second horse* that contributed the other half of the "one" animal we think is behind the bush. Not for Buster to simply mount a horse and fall off; when he rides, he must tumble between planes of illusion. As Kerr states, Keaton "lay[s] bare the simultaneity" of two planes in space after having neatly tricked us into seeing flatness.[6] The bush was so natural a camouflage for both horses that we never suspected any duality with one animal. Buster himself does not even notice, for his eye fixes on the horizon filled with threatening oil wells.

When he rights his pose on the horse and gallops into a long shot of the assembled tribe, Buster and Chief ride toward us and fade out. Aside from the dramatic impact of forward movement, Buster is symbolically heading into our domain, the Real World. From Buster's ride, Keaton fades into a panorama of oil wells as Indians ride in from background to foreground. Unlike other films shot on a set, this film is steeped in realism because it is filmed on land with real mountains, trees, sky, oil wells, and smoking tepees stretching to infinity. We are familiar with Keaton's adroit spatial choreography in limited spaces, but soon he will mold crowds to fit into and collaborate with his natural playground.

Like another slap in the face, we cut abruptly to the interior of the office, which contrasts sharply with the freedom of the great outdoors. Buster adamantly (and colloquially) addresses deaf ears behind the desk: "IF MY TRIBE DON'T GET WHAT'S COMING TO THEM, YOU WILL!" Buster points to his hat of authority and welcomes Big Chief and tomahawk, towering with menacing strength over a rattled Top Hat. Buster asks, as if second nature now, "ON WITH THE DANCE?" Buster mimics an Indian stereotype, patting his mouth for a whooping sound to summon his comrades in to begin the war dance. Like a bandleader, he gives a downbeat with his hatchet and directs the circle of dancing Indians. Buster has come a long way from his fumbling butterfly-hunt to choreographing a war dance; he even stops the performance to demonstrate to one Indian with two left feet what the proper steps are. Buster's earlier visual play with two horses was more than just a sight gag, in a symbolic sense: he is in fact now facing two different directions at once, like the previously mentioned two-headed god. He is more powerful than Big Chief, master of the war dance, and spokesman for the entire tribe because he is a "Redman"; but his face provides entree to the pale world where he can work miracles to preserve all that is natural, fair, and free.

On their behalf, Buster adopts the traits of his brethren; eagle-eyed, he spots a paleface slipping out the side door, crawls after him, surefooted and swift, spanks him with the flat end of his tomahawk, and reaches for his hair. Ready to invoke his scalping privileges, he is slightly disappointed when the enemy stops him with a shaky hand and relinquishes his toupee. Buster only stares, then accepts the artifact and hands it with pride to an admiring Big Chief. However, he angrily notices, as we do in an exterior long shot, that Top Hat is escaping on horseback. Thus begins the climactic chase that will harvest the screen with comic gags growing out of a natural terrain, like carefully planted wildflowers. This is Keaton's sketchbook for the sophisticated landscapes he will paint in his features, particularly *The General*.

Keaton crosscuts between the advancing Indians and the escaping villain, until they merge in one shot: as Top Hat rides up a slope into bushes, the Indians continue up the incline past him. Meanwhile, Buster has been having his share of difficulty with his steed. He watches in awe as his horse folds its legs and rolls over; just as silently, he stares at the gun drawn by Top Hat who has stealthily overtaken him during Fate's equestrian interference. Buster innocently touches the gun, accidentally fires it, and immediately raises his arms in surrender. Has the folding horse made Buster regress into inexplicable naiveté? For all his privileges among the Indians, does he believe that his survival is only luck and that without Big Chief's bulk, he is vulnerable to the enemy? Why has he forgotten that a gun is no more formidable than a well-aimed hatchet? He has lost the bravery of a brave and fallen back into his routine of the susceptible little man against the world.

Top Hat orders him to disrobe and Buster first discards his Indian beaded vest. Then as he reaches for a suspender, modesty overwhelms him and he plants a puny sapling between himself and Top Hat before removing the rest of his clothes. His regressed state revives his shy, gentlemanly behavior in which he cannot handle too much exposure in emotionally revealing situations without blushing and dodging. The meager tree hardly covers anything, but Buster needs to preserve the dignity he has left and is compelled to use the setting—literally—to cover his inadequacies.

We crosscut to Indian scouts in the hills as a time passage device; by the time we return to our hero, we find the men have exchanged outfits. Top Hat in Buster's clothes bullies him into walking ahead in his place, and Buster, fairly pleased with the elegant hat and overcoat, rather agreeably raises his well-cuffed arms overhead. He forgets the devotion that his tribe now holds for him. Within seconds, the keen scouts point to their subjectively viewed quarry: a top-hatted figure strolling jauntily in front of a little porkpied and vested person firmly wielding a gun. The Indians think their redeemer has single-handedly toppled the enemy and needs their help. An Indian fires the first arrow.

Keaton paces the launching of these pointed missiles against Buster's

181

curious reactions to them. From a frontal view, we see Buster stride in from the left when suddenly the first arrow lands at his feet. Opposite visual movements—his entering one way, arrow flying in the other—meet in the middle of a static frame. Buster looks up innocently, holds out his hand to test for rain, examines the unusual "raindrop," twirls it, tucks it under his arm like a walking stick, and walks off right. We watch more Indians gather as one shoots another arrow; the little crowd warns us of a real "downpour." Following the multiplicity or repetition principle, Keaton lets Buster walk into another landing projectile; this time, as he picks it up, suspiciously eliminating the rain theory, a third and fourth land at his feet. In his regressed state (and obviously distracted by his fancy new clothes), Buster is taking an unusually long time to size up his dilemma. As he peers around in a medium shot, another arrow pierces his top hat. His wide-eyed stare ironically fails to notice the new appendage to his chapeau, but then again, Buster has never recognized the up-close very easily. Only when he tiptoes away in the next long shot and removes his hat in the process, does he find the arrow there. All at once, Indians launch more missiles in a separate shot, like the outburst of an orchestra reaching a sudden furious crescendo in a quiet piece of music. Buster holds up a helpless hand to stop them but flees as the shower descends. Even in this predicament, Buster fulfills his equation philosophy: he turns an arrow into an handy walking accessory. However, his atypical dim-wittedness nearly turns himself into an equation as well: as Lebel suggests, Buster = "arrow-quiver as he becomes an unharmed, serene Saint Sebastian."[7]

We cross wide distances and enlarge our cast of characters by groups rather than individuals. As Buster traverses a rocky road from left to right, another Indian scout watches him, then follows the Indian tribe also pursuing left to right. The scout claps to summon *another* tribe who emerges from behind boulders: A RIVAL TRIBE OF SAVAGES WHO WENT BROKE PLAYING STRIP POKER. These Indians race downhill, joining the chase that now throbs with crosscuts. Our eyes flow left-right as Buster moves across one shot, matched by another shot of left-right-moving Indians, as if we are reading the narrative of an epic Western. When one direction is exhausted, Keaton introduces another, so that Buster will then slide *down* a vertical slope and race toward *us*. He suddenly brakes and pauses to stare as if there is something baffling in our midst: when we finally see the object of his concern, we learn that his Indian pals are retreating without him. Buster's stare at us not only creates drama but suggests that he addresses us and that we as omniscient audience can answer his question. We have seen the rival tribe and know that Fate is never too far behind in dropping unexpected monkey wrenches (or arrows) into Buster's landscape. But because the camera lies between us, Buster cannot hear our answer. He simply scratches his head at our silence and secludes himself behind a tree to think for himself.

When he emerges, Buster presents himself to the offscreen retreating tribe, exhibiting every side of his body and calling, "IT'S ME—LITTLE CHIEF!" Meanwhile, in the so-*far*-yet-so-*near* background, the Strip Poker Indians loom up over the hill behind him. The planes of depth fill with tension and ironic geometric beauty as danger lurks behind Buster in his supposedly safe foreground. Buster leans wearily against a tree trunk when suddenly a hatchet lands into it with a definite thud. Buster eyes the unwelcome visitors behind him, and the chase continues.

The pièce de résistance of the chase, which has filled virtually the whole film, now caps the remaining minutes. The climax is not frenetic action and crosscutting, but breathless danger in a taut escape scene. Against a bright sky, a fragile bridge of wooden staves, most of which are missing, hangs between two cliffs. Buster must crawl on it to reach safety on the other side. We cut to an advantageous medium long shot to examine just how Buster plans to cross this bridge. As he makes his way over some staves, he picks one up from behind and places it over the gap stretching before him. When three angry Indians creep close enough to reach out to him, Buster swipes the stave that one Indian was about to take, slaps him with it, and lays it ahead of him to further his progress across the chasm. We cut to the opposite cliff where Buster's tribe convenes. In the meantime, Buster has reached the scary midpoint of the bridge, which is totally bare of staves except for those on which he kneels and switches from back to front in order to cross. Buster has finally abandoned his naive outlook. Fancy clothes certainly did not make this man; when the arrow pierced his top hat, his bubble burst along with it. Buster must unleash his survival instinct, although perhaps nothing less than another miracle will help him now.

The chase is still under way, although the chasers are immobile, watching their quarry from a distance. The three parties in the chase have formed a triangle over the jagged territory, with the two tribes at the two lower points racing up toward the third point, Buster. As the lower angles move up, the triangle collapses into a straight line of tension—the bridge itself—with all three parties now on the same plane. "Like a human

Caterpillar tractor laying his track,"[8] Buster enlivens every bridge metaphor ever concocted by humans in a desperate moment: crossing a bridge when coming to it; burning bridges behind; bridging a gap; and so on. Buster graphically, silently epitomizes the human condition, proving that we do not have to run to be caught up in a chase. The Chase, the capital-letter kind, is an internal one—against ourselves and whatever we perceive is behind or before us, moving or not. It is the desperation to flee even with nowhere to go.

Keaton's realism has hit its height, so to speak, with the suspension bridge, which spanned ten to twelve feet over a chasm estimated at between sixty and seventy-five feet.[9] The stunt was a blueprint, perhaps, for Keaton's future daredevil feats that rivaled even Harold Lloyd's clock-hanging, building-climbing stunts (which, although on dizzying heights, were guarded by scaffolding below him). One of Keaton's more perilous "documentary" stunts was in *Our Hospitality* in which Buster's character was to rescue a girl (Natalie Keaton) helplessly rushing toward a waterfall. Keaton was tied to a security wire on a sixteen-foot log on the shore, but the line broke while he was in the middle of the rescue and the log fell into the rapids. Keaton avoided drowning only by reaching for low branches as he passed the bank. The footage, used in the film, was captured by his cameramen because Keaton insisted that the camera never stop cranking until he said cut, no matter what happened.[10]

Danger has menaced this short from its beginning, and Keaton capitalizes on this with his harrowing finale, which may have prompted critic Robert E. Sherwood to remark: "It is strange that the silent drama should have reached its highest level in the comic field. Here, and here alone, it is pre-eminent. . . . *The Paleface* is a veritable epic."[11] The real danger of the bridge stunt (not to mention the implicit tragedy of the Indians at the outset) has nearly precluded laughter; we find it only in well-timed and appropriate moments during the action. This comic relief is like a cool sponge on feverish skin, and it arises out of the land itself, tailor-made to its look and texture. Buster is at a stalemate, literally dangling in a life-death choice. Fortunately, Big Chief halts his arrow launchers and announces: "STOP! IT'S LITTLE CHIEF PALEFACE!" However, Buster does not realize that his home tribe waits for him, so intent is he on escaping the enemy. When Big Chief suddenly plants a hearty hand on his shoulder, Buster instantly undoes all that he so painstakingly accomplished: he plunges between the cables, free-falls through the air, and splashes into the river below. There are concluding splashes and dives between Buster and rival Indians, until the last physical chase across land brings Buster home.

Back at the reservation, two Indians walk out the famous high gate as Buster runs in from the right. As one Indian turns to him, Buster swings the lock bar down, knocking him on the head. When he sees the second Indian, he swings the bar up under his chin. Buster has lost all perspective of home and safety; his last desperate steps in Top Hat's outfit frighten even the Indian women and children. He stumbles to lean against his tepee and falls into the entrance. Braves on horses break across the grounds in a cloud of smoke. Buster tries to sneak past Big Chief but is caught under his giant restraining hand. Certain of his execution at last, Buster is amazed that Big Chief and tribe kneel humbly before him. His relief intensifies when he discovers a paper in Top Hat's coat pocket, which we read in a masked close-up:

GRANT DEED. THIS INDENTURE, MADE THE <u>THIRD DAY</u> OF <u>JUNE</u>
IN THE YEAR OF OUR LORD NINETEEN HUNDRED AND <u>TWENTY–TWO</u>. JOHN
SMITH. THE CROW FEET TRIBE OF INDIANA.

Big Chief kisses his cheeks and offers Buster anything he wishes. Eying the Indian Miss, who in close-up flashes a smile, Buster announces: "ME LIKE INDIAN SQUAB." Big Chief nods and Buster goes to stake his claim. He kisses her hand, they hug, and with unleashed passion he drops her low and kisses her. Fade out. Suddenly, a title: TWO YEARS LATER. Fade in. Buster and "squab" are in the same passionate embrace. He straightens, gasps, and resumes kissing. Fade out for real.

"Two years is a long time for a kiss to last; but above all, one has the impression that Keaton has sustained it for two years because the position in which he found himself with the young Indian maiden was of such visual beauty, was so perfectly placed in space, that two years seemed a suitable duration for it."[12] The last gag holds us in suspense also, not the way the chase did, but by resolving the film in an unexpected way that speaks of Keaton's approach to revealing emotion. Winning the girl is a fair reward for Buster's dangerous, at times unjust, adventures, but how is it funny? Keaton's primary concern has always been to cap a film with humor or a surprise punch, like Buster's return from China in *Hard Luck*. We have cause to wonder now if Buster's hard-earned happiness will ever last. We are relieved to know that it has already lasted two years and that it seems frozen in time—which is perhaps the only way happiness *can* last.

Buster's frozen stance plays not only with visual space (the happy couple has not budged) but with progress *through* time. Time stands still when Buster embraces his desires. With love, there is no further need for a Chase. Buster finally dispenses with his scapegoat outfit (and for a while, it *was* a real outfit). The magic picture frame closes at last around a serene landscape with Buster in a permanently perfect pose. It is a frame that both secures and liberates a happy heart.

Despite the ending, however, Keaton's experiment with realism in *The Paleface*, and to a farcical degree in *The Boat*, touches disaster and tragedy too intimately to deny their existence in Buster's comic world. What would happen to the little man—and to his comedy—if the world became too large for his frame and his pursuits too distant for his reach?

## Chapter 13

# Cops

## (March 1922)

Courtesy of the Academy of Motion Picture Arts and Sciences

*Cops* has always been more than just a chase film. It is a self-portrait drawn from a reflection in a fun-house mirror, it is a ripped Valentine's Day card, it is a cherished dream from which one sadly awakens to call it pointless. *Cops* is a stunning and stark comedy that lifts us all the way to expect the usual ending, only to hang us in disbelief that we have stepped too far over the tragedy threshold—and that Keaton has closed the door to keep us from reentering.

187

# Cops

A symbolic entrance is implied from the very first title: LOVE LAUGHS AT LOCKSMITHS—HOUDINI. On the title card, a drawing shows Cupid aiming an arrow at a padlock. An iris opens to a medium shot of a woman (Virginia Fox) shaking her head at Buster who stands behind bars dolefully shaking his head too. He resignedly shakes her hand and tips his hat. As soon as we admit that our hero must be in jail, we cut to a long shot informing us that Buster is actually holding the bars of the front gate to Woman's palatial residence; he is not behind bars but in front of them—barred from entrance. Here, then, is one interpretation for the cryptic opening title: Buster is denied access to his love by a wrought-iron enemy (padlock); yet, if industrious Cupid has his way, love will triumph with a key. As Woman walks off, Buster suddenly wags a finger after her, to which she huffily turns with uplifted chin and proclaims: "I WON'T MARRY YOU UNTIL YOU BECOME A BIG BUSINESS MAN." Buster mocks her nagging, then turns to us and sulks, stuffing his hands in his pockets and shuffling away with a last look behind him. Cupid has obviously misfired.

The main quest in Buster's many short-film lives has been that for love. As love is the first verbal and visual image we see in this film, it will influence all that follows. Just as the drama of the Indians affected our perception of comedy in *The Paleface*, so too will locks and bars temper our vision of a happily-ever-after ending. We anticipate a triumphant ending anyway, but getting there will be the challenge. After all, *One Week* promised sour echoes along with the wedding bells, but Buster and his mate stuck it out, even into *The Boat*.

*Cops* proceeds with what Lebel calls a "cascade of gags"[1]—a torrent, in fact, that pushes Buster into symbolic rapids (or more appropriately, as will soon be explained, a rough sea of blue). Although the theme is love, the title is *Cops*, and that will be the predominant figure through which the theme is developed. The first "cascading" ripple in the film recalls both *Convict 13* and *The Goat* in the way Buster chances upon good fortune and loses it in the blink of an eye, usually in the presence of a menacing bulk who is revealed as a police officer. A stocky man (Joe Roberts) hails an offscreen cab; as Buster shuffles into view, Joe pulls out a handkerchief and drops his fat wallet. Buster kicks it over to him, checks within, then taps Joe's shoulder. Joe berates Buster, who futilely explains his innocence. He sets his porkpie on straight with a slightly intense look, as if now that he has been rejected by Love, what else matters? Buster shadows Joe as the cab pulls up; Joe slips off the running board, with Buster too eagerly helping him. They grapple, Buster dusts him off, and

Joe pushes him aside to drive away. Buster pauses, with a penetrating stare at the offscreen cab, then subtly picks up his porkpie and stares at the fat wallet in his hand; just as slowly—and innocently—he extracts his newfound fortune.

We cut to the interior of the cab as Joe checks for his wallet and, in horror, discovers it missing. We suddenly cut to the rear of the cab as it U-turns and roars up to where Buster stands; a stocky hand reaches out of the window and swipes the wallet from our hero's unruffled grasp. Inside the cab again, Joe smugly opens it, then gawks and shakes his empty wallet upside down. Like a reflex, the rear of the cab U-turns again. Transfixed by his fortune, Buster is unable to leave his lucky spot— or is he predicting Joe's reaction to his loss and waiting to play another sticky-fingered game? He stands counting the money as the cab this time enters to obstruct Buster from our view. Joe lumbers out, tugging his sleeves fiercely, only to turn and find the cab drive off—and Buster no- where in sight. The silent invisibility with which Buster leaves the scene is the punch to the routine and to Joe himself who gazes angrily after the cab. Buster's short stature and nimble moves have protected him from Joe's overbearing but clumsy girth. However, while Buster's cleverness usually helps him out of trouble, Fate usually thwarts his best intentions. Buster justifies his "theft" because he had intended to return the wallet to Joe but was unfairly threatened; therefore, Buster "earned" the money just like a good "businessman." But Fate thinks Buster has no business meting out his own brand of justice or changing his impoverished destiny without fighting the preordained battles of his daily life. Buster has struck a match and now must play with fire: when Joe stares after the cab, he draws back his jacket to reveal a police badge. His identity is an "aftergag," a surprise whetting our appetite for more cop-revelations that (judging from the film's simple, emphatic title) will soon inundate Buster's life. His romantic frustrations and social transgressions are now set to haunt him. The hopeful quest that propels him into good deeds will lead him only into an endless chase.

Buster begins accumulating misfortunes like flypaper, for as he exits the cab at a corner while counting his dollars, a hawkeyed loafer rivets his attention on the bills. Buster already is blasé about wealth by waving away the cabbie's change; he unconsciously signals a green light to Fate to abuse his naive (probably hopelessly naive) grasp of financial matters. The shrewd onlooker connects Buster's money to another event nearby that is shown in a long shot: a family hauls their furniture into the street.

# Cops

In two-shot, the family man tells his mate: "I'VE TELEPHONED FOR THE EXPRESSMAN." The onlooker's pinched face glows with invention as he prepares for Buster by sitting on the curb in front of the furniture and snapping into an effective wailing/rocking act.

Buster's entire demeanor thus far has been unusually contemplative. He walks as if in a dream—and of course, love has that palliative effect on his otherwise attentive behavior. Coupled with (1) his beloved's heartless ultimatum, (2) the "crash course" in high finance that he must take to become a businessman, (3) his perplexity on how to even begin, and (4) the sudden fortune and imagined business acumen that has seemingly descended upon him, it is no surprise that Buster is dazed. He is at heart the gullible child who cannot understand why his "caretaker" does not accept him as he is; but he must impress her with his adult potential dormant beneath the hairline. He must rise to her expectations to win her affection while forcing himself to believe it is for the best. After all, his retort to her was rebellion against her demands that, on some level, he recognizes as contrary to his nature. However, Buster now opens himself to opportunity since he is at a loss to understand, much less solve, his dilemma. Primed by a life-full of coincidences, Buster hopes that every corner will burst forth with solutions; but he forgets that in Life's devilish games, no gift from Fate is without its price tag. Love, a cherished gift from the gods, has been obstructed from view by the furiously fluttering wings of Cupid (Fate's little messenger), and Buster is having difficulty distinguishing between fact and fraud.

Keaton provides a dialogue of titles intercut with two-shots of Buster and the con man, starting with his sob story: "I'M BROKE AND THEY THREW ME OUT." Buster nods in understanding—he has been there himself. As the con man flails his arms, he knocks Buster on the head; although this gesture symbolically reduces Buster to mere object, our hero remains sympathetic. "IF I DON'T SELL MY FURNITURE, MY WIFE AND BABIES WILL STARVE." That line hits a soft core in Buster who, without hesitation, reaches into his pocket with his reasoning intact: "I'LL BUY IT AND PROVE I'M A GOOD BUSINESS MAN." Buster's simplistic rationale for believing such melodrama from a total stranger is oddly acceptable to us. His logical-illogic is in keeping with his personality and with the ache in his heart that can be soothed once the padlock is opened. Ironically, Buster has stepped on the big-business road to success with the wrong foot, starting with "theft" (wallet) and continuing with fraud (con man). With these two crimes, Buster also exhibits his two-sided nature: as clever, even conniving, as he can be (as with the wallet/cab), he is also gullible. To make the road more perilous, Buster has also coated it with a heavy sprinkling of self-justification.

The con man takes the entire wad, to Buster's dumbfounded amazement, but as an afterthought returns a few dollars and shakes his hand. Buster regards his purchase with his back to us, always an unusual position for Buster as it usually reveals his state of mind. Buster turned from us in *The Boat* to assume his captaincy; he turned away when regarding his house in *One Week* and thus emphasized his small stature against the behemoth. Once again, Buster's back tells a woeful tale of duality: he thinks he is in control, aloof to our dubious stares (and from the "sucker!" glance of the con man). Yet, at the same time, Buster has lost his fortune and is visually dwarfed by the giant heap of furniture. Keaton's commentary is more poignant now that his Fate-ridden hero is trapped in a perplexing duality; his two halves, innocence and shrewdness, vie for success because of a frustrated love. So desperately motivated, Buster agrees to any golden opportunity because it is justified by his "good cause."

Nagging Buster is always the flickering intuition that, whatever the motivation, he falls into the strangest of situations; even now, he scratches his head and ponders the furniture. Buster enters the next unfortunate circumstance with a horse and wagon standing across from him; a tag reading FOR SALE $5.00 hangs from the horse's back. Buster hurries over to hand his last bill to an (honestly) dejected man sitting on the curb beside the horse. As Buster leads the horse and wagon out left, the price tag slides off and drops to where it originally hung—on the sleeve of a mannequin blocked by the animal. The astonished man studies the $5.00 tag on the jacket as the shop owner appears to snatch the money from him; the man struts off with his spiffy apparel. When we see the circumstantial trickery at work, we laugh uneasily at how convincing each setup is. How deft the hand of Fate to lay the sleeve upon a perfectly placed horse! Keaton's camera secures this illusion by holding us in a frontal position so that we are as fooled as Buster is. However, because of this objective view, the trick is revealed only when the horse is led away, dropping the missing piece into the jigsaw; or in other words, as the horse walks off, another tableau is uncovered as if Keaton slides a second painted panel across the one we are watching, with only slight but crucial changes to the image. Middleground shifts sideways (horse/wagon led out frame right) to reveal the dense layer of trickery prepared by Fate. Ironically, with his back to us, peering directly into the "truth" before him, Buster still does not see the machinations at work. His tunnel (of love) vision destroys a panoramic view, just as Keaton limits our view through his lens by revealing only certain planes at a time. But the ever-present irony (and imminent tragedy) is that Buster's proximity to the truth does not help him find it any better than we do. More than ever, Buster is turning his back to us, no longer seeking our guidance or sharing our sympathy. Rather, like a determined novice at a job for which he was hired by mistake, he seeks the tacit approval of his boss (Woman) who waits in an iron cage for a progress report; nor will he ask for help as he musters his worth with shaky self-confidence. He seeks, hoping to find, but the easy choices he makes are not the right ones.

Fate's "torture" of its hapless goat is successful because each character in the plot unquestioningly accepts very obvious mix-ups and misrepresentations. Buster, of course, sets the precedent, and if he cannot spot the incongruities, who can? The shrewdest one in the lot seems to be the con man, which is one reason why his "business" booms. But the other un-business-oriented people (Joe, the man at the curb, the family man, and soon the entire city of cops) win or lose randomly because they do not question what befalls them. As Buster loads a chest onto his wagon, the family man unblinkingly joins in with parts of the bed. The man reasons: Why shouldn't Buster be the expressman since the family was expecting one? Buster reasons: Why shouldn't he be helped with the loading since so far he has made all his wise business dealings through the "kindness of strangers"? Why didn't the shop owner ask the man with $5.00 if he wanted the jacket but just assumed it from the combined presence of man and money? And why didn't Buster question the man about the horse and wagon in the first place but merely figured they belonged together? This senselessness is bearable only because the characters have hidden agendas that fit into the unrelated ingredients of each situation they enter. Each agenda is executed silently, unlike that in the extended "dialogue" between con man and Buster. The con man is Fate's articulate spokesman, setting up the clearest duplicity upon which all hidden ones are modeled. When Fate speaks, everyone listens.

Buster is stunned at yet another lucky break as the man, followed by wife and children, heave their furniture onto the wagon. Buster decides to sit, ponder, and watch. Fade out, fade in to the man tying the knot that holds the mountain of furniture in place. Buster shakes his hand, only to be eyed dubiously, then flings his chair to the apex where it lands securely. The wife returns to hand Buster a suitcase, large vase, and pitcher for the load. Buster puts the vase into the suitcase but, unable to shut it, stomps on the luggage, smashes the vase, and locks the case. This senseless gag is another illustration of Buster's incompetency for the "job" and for handling emergencies, as depicted in *The Boat* and *The Playhouse* during the rescues. While there is no burning peril here, there is the nerve-racking distraction of lost love, if not lost life. Still, this weak gag, plus the "taken-for-granted" attitudes of the characters, detract from the power of the film. But Buster's demeanor and motivation help somewhat to suspend doubt and disbelief. With this view, the shards of the vase are still the vase, it now fits in the suitcase, and Buster can move on to more important matters. He next hangs the pitcher on a folding tie rack; the pitcher pulls the rack down and it crashes on the ground. Buster carries the rack to the driver's seat, an action that will have impact on a future gag as it is too deliberate and incomplete at this point. The family man emerges a last time to hand Buster a card that we read in close-up: 4 FLUSHING PLACE. Oblivious to its meaning, Buster tosses the card away and drives his wagon toward us and off left.

The plodding horse personifies Buster himself at this point. Buster too wears blinders and clomps along as far as his reins allow. Though he sits in the driver's seat, a force greater than he clucks the horse on to an undetermined destination and works in obtuse ways. Buster's entire routine with the horse encompasses many symbolic gags. Dynamically composed shots of Buster and horse together suggest their equality and oneness. At times, the horse (or just its ears) occupies the foreground as Buster sits directly behind; or when the horse's head breaks into the side of a shot, its passage across the frame always leads to Buster following behind, linked and inseparable. Like *One Week*'s house on barrel-wheels, Buster and horse develop the potentials of the wagon as a major prop. The previously isolated tie rack now becomes a rich prop in itself. When Buster draws up to a parked vehicle jutting into the frame where a dog peacefully slumbers, he stretches out his arm for a right turn. Man's best friend suddenly lunges at his arm. In defense, Buster slips on a handy boxing glove to continue the signal. To avoid similar problems, Buster nails the folding tie rack to the wagon and sets the boxing glove on the end. The dramatic result is depicted in perfect uncluttered composition: as we watch the rear of the wagon gently roll away from us, the rack and glove burst out to the side signaling a left turn. The planes are in subtle motion, complementing each other: wagon heads to the background, glove aims to the side, wagon answers with the turn indicated by glove.

Buster's utilitarian nature has won again. On the one hand (the bitten one), Buster protects himself from harm. On the other hand (that of Fate), Buster's invention is destined to curve back on him. Sure enough, just as the wagon rolls around a traffic cop, Buster turns, flexing the glove directly into the cop's head. The curve of the wagon and the curveball of Fate are inextricably linked. Buster replays the action as he concentrates on turning again around the cop. While he may have been unaware of the first thump, Buster notices the groggy cop flapping directions the second time and slaps the reins to leave the scene. Although the cop is too dazed to identify what hit him (a Keaton Cop cannot necessarily identify it anyway), we have finally met another policeman after a long stretch. The title's warning is revived and the promised cascade—not only of gags but of cops—is revitalized. Buster's effort to counter his Fate (the dog) turns him into a symbolic punching bag. His solitary silhouette bobbing along on a wagon to Somewhere recalls critic Rex Reed's description of Buster Keaton sitting in a last interview "looking for all the world like the kind of man dogs kick."[2] A fitting picture, for in *Cops*, one dog even takes a bite.

Being too long in the driver's seat has a subtle pernicious effect on Buster's general attitude. His whole business venture has been straight into unknown territory, emphasized by his action of discarding the address of the family man. He measures progress by the accumulation of wealth and property, but what to do with it is beyond him. His business skill seems restricted to mastering U-turns with his wagon. His journey through love is no more directed or profitable. Yet Buster feels that his material assets are lifting him to new heights (driver's seat = symbolic control), and as we see him in close-up, he fidgets restlessly at his too-slow speed. In profile view, the old nag clomps exhaustedly onward. Buster shades his eyes to stare ahead of him and, finally, fluffs up a pillow and stretches out to doze. He is bored, annoyed, even dangerously aloof to the humility of his situation; his lucky entrepreneurial streak has made him too comfortable in the control seat. For a dash of realism, an automobile whizzes past the wagon. Perhaps it is a peripheral comment that Buster's business is hardly state of the art, contrasting "old" and "new" or "horse" and "horseless carriage," and is therefore doomed.

With the next cut, we arrive on a street shortly before the horse does as if we have outraced the poor creature, at which point the tired animal decides to stop in its tracks. Buster awakens and jumps off with a set of earphones and a wall telephone, pulling more tricks from his magic prop-wagon. He covers the horse's ears with the headset, then returns to his seat where he rings up the phone, speaks into it, and waits. Resuming the shot with horse, the nag suddenly clomps out of the frame, and Buster nods and returns to sleep. Buster has communicated with another animal again, as he did in *Hard Luck*; he should, after all, develop a rapport with his business partner. The animal responds to his call and, again, the humanness of nonhuman characters infiltrates Buster's intuition, distancing him further from a comfortable niche in a human world.

Buster's progress is interrupted for an update on the family at 4 Flushing Place; the wife conjectures, with innocent irony: "MAYBE HE WAS ARRESTED FOR SPEEDING." Far from that destination, Buster plods on, suddenly awakening to stop the horse and demonstrate what a *real* business gait should be. He dons the reins, sets the bit in his mouth, clomps at an angle to the ground, and pulls both wagon and horse out of the frame. The equation is complete: Buster = horse. As businessman, he has rolled up his sleeves and stepped into his employee's (horse)shoes to show how the job should be done. As amazed pedestrians watch, Buster hauls his cargo with equestrian strength into the next shot. He removes the gear and retrieves a fallen object, which we see in close shot to be dentures that he unsuccessfully slides into the horse's mouth. The routine is capped by an offscreen visit to DR. SMITH   GOAT-GLAND SPECIALIST. After a pause as we wait on the sidewalk, Buster suddenly skids downstairs, followed by a revitalized horse racing out of the building. Given his affinity with the horse, it is not surprising that Keaton once commented that his favorite memory of *Cops* came from this "spiritless, broken-down horse" named Onyx, which was bought for the wagon scenes.

One of the last scenes was supposed to show the horse riding in the wagon with me between the shafts pulling it.

The horse was the soul of co-operation until we tried to get her to walk up the ramp into the wagon for that scene. Then she balked. I had a crane brought to the studio, planning to hoist her up by putting a veterinarian's saddle under the horse.

We got the vet's saddle under her all right, but the moment we tried to lift her off the ground Old Dobbin started kicking away viciously at everything and everybody.

We were on location. It was Saturday, and we took her back to the studio. I decided we would have to find another horse that resembled her to double for her on Monday. But when we returned to work on Monday we found a new-born colt standing beside her. As has happened in many another case, mother knew best in this instance.[3]

The situation was ripe for punnery and Keaton knew it: " 'The baby's name,' I said, 'is Onyxpected!' "[4]

Buster's quality time with his four-legged partner reveals more crystal-facets of his personality. The horse sequence emphasizes his preestablished childlikeness: communicating with animals, inventing, equating, innocently falling into trouble. This last "facet" is vital to the rest of the film, as it will open the floodgates of cops promised from the start. Keaton's story has been floating along a linear surface, like Buster's straight-arrow trek along flat streets. Every once in a while, a gag floats to the top like a cork in water, reminding us of the nearness of cops either through the presence of a real officer or Buster's brush with risky business. By now, he has exhausted the horse routine and changed his tired nag into an energetic charger. As a result, he convinces himself that he is even more successful in business; wherever he goes, he can now get there faster. His symbolic destination, naturally, is the land of cops. With all systems go, it is the perfect moment for Fate to lead Buster onto another detour in his journey.

ONCE A YEAR THE CITIZENS OF EVERY CITY KNOW WHERE THEY CAN FIND A POLICEMAN. At the policemen's parade, of course, which we now see in a long shot marching from background to foreground. Keaton lavishes several shots on the precision platoons passing before blocks of cheering crowds. These orderly formations are ironic, given Keaton's cynical lampoon as the sequence begins. This "heritage" of ridicule stretches back to Mack Sennett and his Keystone Kops. In his autobiography, Sennett stated unequivocally: "Reducing authority to absurdity was a standard formula."[5] With the first appearance of the Keystone Kops in *Hoffmeyer's Legacy* (December 1912), their trick-photography stunts and cliff-hanging chases became a standard for film comedy, particularly as a visual way to reduce authority to buffoonery. But Keaton's depiction of huge crowds of men in blue gliding along the streets in neat and tidy lines suggests a new approach to ridiculing the cop figure. No longer will the cop be one person against Buster nor will there be a rattly chain of dodging cops with Buster crawling around them; now, the collective "Cops" is one giant of a body pitted against a little man. "Cops" has become another house as in *One Week* or another threshing machine as in *The Scarecrow*, ready to swallow the little fish frantically swimming in an ocean of blue. Earlier in *Cops*, Keaton launched an inventive blow with a novel gadget (tie rack/boxing glove) on a single member of this team; it was an appetizer to the upcoming feast and a tribute to slapstick comedy. The prop, however, was a creative step-up from the traditional billy club that Buster used on the cop in *One Week*. Dispensing with a preliminary cop, Keaton now floods the screen with multiple attacks on his parody-figures through controlled space and crowds, a technique successfully used in *The Paleface*. Keaton turns authority absurd with sophistication:

> No well-placed whacks with clubs or bricks in the style of the
> wildly mischevious little tramps that were pursued by the Keystone
> Cops mar this minor masterpiece. Keaton follows Lloyd and many
> of the polite comedians by hanging in the attic many of the stock
> gimmicks of the 1910's that he had used while working with Fatty
> Arbuckle. Later, in 1924, he expressed his view on the older slap-
> stick devices: "A comedian today no longer finds his dressing room
> filled with slapstick property bricks, stuffed clubs and exploding
> cigars." Comic situations have taken the place of these veteran
> laugh getters.[6]

How Keaton regulates the tumultuous flood of cops with Buster in their midst will define the theme of the film. The theme of love conditions and is conditioned by the chase. After all, Woman has not yet reappeared in this film, but her presence is Buster's driving (or is it chasing?) force. This multidimensional theme involves complicated questions that can only be answered by the last echoing footsteps of the runners.

While presenting cops on parade, Keaton ties the disparate strands from the first reel together. For example, in the flag-draped reviewing stand, the Chief of Police greets the Mayor and a young woman—*the* Woman of the iron gates: "I'M PLEASED TO MEET THE DAUGHTER OF OUR MAYOR." At this point, Keaton reintroduces this pivotal character now that familiar paths are about to cross again. Seemingly endless bands of officers and mounted police glide past in separate long shots that bracket internal action scenes, such as the Mayor's greeting or a recap with Buster accidentally sitting on the horse's dentures. Police shots are fluid and ongoing, like a gently undulating river, mesmerizing us until Keaton pounces with an unexpected but inevitable surprise.

As more police march around the corner of a building in an extreme long shot, a tiny horse's head suddenly pokes around as well; a wagon follows. Behind the wagon enters another squadron in blue, unaware of any interruption in their rank and file. Movement fills the frame to capacity as Keaton maximizes continuity and matches complementing angles and perspectives. When the visual flow is interrupted to advance the story, it is as if "microcosms" are set off to spin within the larger world of cops. For example, with a cut, the microcosm of the reviewing stand appears before us; Woman is aghast at Buster's eye-catching float. Buster is oblivious to the parade, but he notices the unusual ovation and assumes it is for him. Again, he invokes his own agenda: because he is pleased with his business, he believes news of his success must have reached the public. Buster slaps the reins importantly and nods to the cheering throng with uplifted porkpie, acting even more haughty. The horse stops when the parade stops; cops march in place. By this time, *everyone* is wearing blinders, seemingly wrapped up in their own self-important and isolated little worlds.

Another microcosm spins on a rooftop where an anarchist hurls a lit bomb over the side; with a cut, it promptly lands on Buster's seat. He is, coincidentally, searching for a match to light one of his longed-for cigarettes; as usual, smoking gets him in trouble. He lights up with the sizzling fuse and stares at the unusual lighter. Woman in the stand screams; frozen panic fills the grandstand. Keaton builds with tension-pacing cuts between Buster and bomb, grandstand, Buster, and finally a long shot of the wagon and troops around him. Buster disposes of the bomb with an explosive toss. Smoke fills the screen like an opaque mask, a natural time-lapse device, a cloudy silence-before-the-storm. The explosion is not only the anarchist's dream come true but Fate's keg of dynamite breaking the dam. The macrocosm is ruptured; the separate self-absorbed little planets within it fall off their orbits. Two mortal enemies (Buster, Cops), who have avoided each other with private reveries and personal agendas, are stirred into a maelstrom. Chaos is in order, so to speak; now is the supreme test of Buster's real talents and Fate's raison d'être. The explosion shatters all traces of security. As the smoke dissipates and cops in tatters spin in the streets, discipline is scattered to the four corners. The animated horse races madly past the grandstand, but instead of serving business, the animal wreaks havoc by ramming a hydrant and letting loose a geyser (a literal cascade). The anarchist's incidental role has truly been forceful, for his handiwork now propels the wild throngs to loot the strewn furniture as cops bumble with the hydrant.

# Cops

The anonymous endless streets become the ultimate racetrack for Buster and the cops who have been set in motion by yet another fateful act. The steady marching now becomes a furious acceleration through time and space; the flowing river becomes a turbulent flood coursing unleashed through every avenue. When one gush subsides, another follows. Between gushes, Keaton again inserts scenes of internal action, like those corks rising with a will of their own to the surface. Likewise, each internal action set between the waves of cops is like one tenacious breath-bubble after another floating to the surface above a drowning man. Each bubble reflects many of Buster's typical responses to his life: a stare, a shrug, a blink. After a melee shot, for instance, we cut to two peaceful open umbrellas on the empty bleachers; one umbrella rises and Buster, cross-legged beneath it, holds out a hand for rain. Gush intrudes: a torrent of cops climb the bleachers, destroying it with their weight as Buster escapes through a building window. Another shot reveals a solitary garbage can on wheels in the background center. Gush: cops pour from our position into the background. Ebb to silence. Gush: cops pour across the frame; silence. Slowly, the can lid rises on Buster's head; he looks in every direction and leans forward too far, toppling the can. He crawls out, looks around, and runs toward us and off right.

Offsetting the visual momentum, Keaton inserts two verbally ironic titles, uttered by the Mayor and the patiently waiting family man. These are the last two references to the microcosms spinning out of control—the last words, in fact, ever to be spoken in *Cops*. The Mayor desperately orders the Chief of Police to "GET SOME COPS TO PROTECT OUR POLICEMEN." His is another sarcastic remark on the shaky reputation of authorities. Shortly after, the pacing father at 4 Flushing Place wonders aloud: "DO YOU SUPPOSE ANYTHING COULD'VE HAPPENED TO OUR FURNITURE?" With that, another revelatory gag takes place: he reaches for his jacket and police hat. All along, Buster has been playing with more matches than he knows: his business has unknowingly been subsidized by his fateful nemesis, cops. His biggest (and most literal) match, the bomb, has finally sparked the animosity that was smoldering, primed to explode in his face.

By now, Keaton is faced with the challenge of concluding his film in a hail of cops, balancing the filled-to-capacity frames with more well-placed, well-paced gags that use his hero's favorite traits. There is no turning back from cops now, and Keaton will punctuate each current in the flood with Buster's idiosyncrasies. Keaton mixes choreography with spotlighted gags until the end. When he captures the long view of the chase, he teases the space with crisscross movements and plays crowds against single figures. In one beautiful composition, for example, Buster runs toward a building in the center of the frame; streets stretch away from us like an extended V on each side of the building. Buster skis to a stop as cops head up each street to the foreground, and he *strolls* into the building. Cops pass each other, switching to the opposite side street they were on, and head back into the distance. Buster reemerges and runs straight toward us. One of his typical approaches to danger—to walk casually—is the rich pause in the middle of another onrush.

Keaton also reaches into his repertoire from past films to give Buster a chance to improvise on survival instincts—and to remind us that he has not yet lost his sense of humor. As in the cop scene in *One Week* or the one at the beginning of *Cops*, Buster hides behind another traffic cop after being chased up the block; he throws the traffic cop on his pursuer, inciting both to follow him. In another sequence, Buster disappears into a row of cars spanning foreground and background. After cops run by, we cut to a close-up of Buster at the wheel of a car, his arm draped nonchalantly over the window. Like his odd disguise in *Hard Luck*, we see that Buster again hopes to melt into anonymity by dangling his clip-on tie under his nose. Lured by the quiet, Buster removes the tie and hurries back down the silent row. A mass of cops begins to funnel out behind him. Suddenly *one* cop pops out of the foreground and confronts Buster. Still unaware of the wave behind him, Buster avoids the *one* cop by streaking into the cars before the rest descend upon him. In this confrontation, the convincing silence of the silent film makes the crowd scenes work for comedy. We supply our own sound effects and volume to the tramping feet, aided by Keaton's toying with his shots through the motion or nonmotion in them. Each whirlwind past a stationary object enunciates the calm that follows, usually with a refreshing sight gag. The clatter of running, breathing, and shouting would be deafening in real life. But for Buster, only the visual determines his detours in this race; he *sees* one cop before him and does not see (much less hear) the *hundreds* behind him. In playing tag with one, he makes himself vulnerable to many, but by *not* hearing them, he is alert to what looms ahead. There are never any verbal quips between chaser and chasee. There is always the "emphatic play between bodies because of the difference in mass":[7] Joe is to Buster as the Rock of Gibraltar is to a pebble; or a horde of cops is to Buster as the Pacific Ocean is to a raindrop. The battle is immediately defined, waged, and won by sight. As will become clearer in the last minutes of the film,

Buster is propelled on the chase not so much by what is behind him but by what beckons before him.

Inevitably, the threads dangling from the beginning of the film are pulled into place during the final laps. The family man wanders through the furniture-laden streets. This important figure is reworked into the picture at the peak of Buster's catastrophe, and he and the furniture symbolize the devastation of our hero's enterprise. Buster runs through the furniture and hops into a trunk. Pause, then gush: hundreds of cops blot out the space as they tramp left to right. Pause, and cut closer to the family man angrily rolling up his sleeves as Buster lifts the lid. He sees the cop and promptly lowers the lid. The cop locks it and tries to haul it away, but Buster crawls out the unattached bottom. A flight ensues, followed by more confrontations down alleys, around corners, bodies striking—a gallery of hits and misses that reprise the same story. The sequence is capped by an incredible flight of fancy in which Buster grabs onto the tail end of a car that races across middleground; he snaps off the ground and flies out parallel to the road while racing cops serve as his backdrop. Buster is showing a desperate need for greater sources of locomotion to remove him from disaster.

His prayer for a miracle at this point is revealed en suite. We look down into a yard cut off from the street by a fence (reminiscent of *Neighbors*). On the street side, Buster climbs a long ladder leaning against the fence. As he reaches the top of the fence (the center of the ladder), Buster swings his legs over and seesaws the ladder into the yard. Cops soon emerge on both sides of the fence as Buster balances on the ladder perpendicular to it. A little too deliberately (but setting up the miracle), Buster crawls along to the yard side of the ladder; as cops pull on both ends, the ladder becomes like a rocking ship on rough water. In an extreme long shot, the ladder is yanked so forcefully on the street side that Buster is shot off like a projectile and flies over the fence. The previous little flight of Buster on the tail end of a car is now magnified into a full arc over the streets in the land of cops. This is a desperate cap to his predicament. Outer space is, of course, the one dimension that Buster has not yet entered, and what better medium for a "flight" from the cops than through the air? Yet unquestionably, Buster has become increasingly frantic—from clipping on a tie mustache, to hiding in a bottomless trunk, to sailing into the unknown on a deus ex machina. An emotional danger exists here, and Keaton as all-knowing filmmaker is aware of Buster's vain chase. Outside assistance—ladder (possibly a wire) catapulting

**201**

Buster through the air—is imperative for he can no longer do it alone. Not surprisingly, this ticket to freedom is a boomerang. When Buster lands in a long shot, it is directly into Joe from the cab-and-wallet routine. Buster's dreams are annihilated as his past meets him head-on. Caught between a stocky devil and the deep blue sea, Buster knocks Joe over and continues his flight on foot.

We gaze at a wide empty street. A tiny Buster runs from around a building. Again, one cop meets him in the foreground. A mass of cops oozes around the corner as Buster scurries beneath the one cop and out foreground left. Keaton repeats the same confrontation in nearly the same configuration of one in front and hundreds behind. He has surely not run out of choreography, but more likely he has run out of hope. The elements are nearly identical to the first composition of this event, but now the distance makes Buster even more miniscule, diminished by space, by crowds, by emptiness. All has failed, it seems, as Buster constantly curves back to the beginning, to the same rut in the same bad dream. The use of space and bodies has elevated the chase to a plateau on which we no longer expect the victim will be saved but only wonder how inventively he might postpone his loss. Pictorially, Keaton emphasizes the irony of how an open-ended street can still be a dead end.

Buster races up to a large open door and, after a few starts and stops, runs into its darkness. Cops from every direction clog the entrance. We cut back to a longer view to learn that cops are pushing themselves into the 5TH PRECINCT POLICE STATION, as the sign above the door announces. Gush: the endless stream billows down this final street and trickles through the door. Pause: one cop emerges and locks it from the outside. He turns—it is Buster in uniform. With hands on hips, he reads the sign and dumps the keys in the trash can. Woman suddenly appears, the strongest (yet infrequent in appearance) thread binding the whole. She snubs Buster as he stands plaintively with hat in hand. Setting his hat on askew, Buster pulls out the keys and unlocks the door. Hands reach out from the darkness and yank him in. Fade out.

Fade in to a sketch of a tombstone with THE END carved on it. Buster's porkpie hangs on the corner.

Although Keaton's realism in *The Paleface* proved to be a workable component of comedy, he inspired a new question that is appropriate to ask again: What would happen to the little man—and to his comedy—if the world became too large for his frame and his pursuits too distant for his reach? The final shocking tombstone with Buster's unmistakable epitaph-porkpie is the answer. But why is it the only alternative here when Buster has managed to elude "the end" much more happily before?

Some critics offer explanations for Keaton's grisly final shot, although Keaton never proffered a reason. Blesh mentions the third Fatty Arbuckle rape-murder trial as a possible influence; it occurred at the start of filming *Cops*. He writes that *Cops* "betrays Buster Keaton's growing sense of the hopelessness of Arbuckle's predicament."[8] Dardis bases Keaton's outlook on an unhappy childhood as the onstage "human ballistic missile" in the hands of a temperamental father,[9] although Keaton thought otherwise in his "as-told-to" autobiography: "Because of the way I looked on the stage and screen the public naturally assumed that I felt hopeless and unloved in my personal life. Nothing could be farther from the fact. As long back as I can remember I have considered myself a fabulously lucky man. From the beginning I was surrounded by interesting people who loved fun and knew how to create it. I've had few dull moments and not too many sad and defeated ones."[10] Whatever biographical reasons may have formed Keaton's dark tone and strange conclusion, it seems safest to trace these changes through what Keaton has left us in his artistic portfolio.

The tombstone appears at the end of a chase that has lasted virtually the length of the film. The chases are not only physically active ones involving a pursuer (the cops) and a pursuee (Buster). With Keaton's system of equations, the "chase" also equals an internal pursuit that exists mentally, awaiting an opportunity to materialize. Thus, while the "cop ⟶ Buster chase" constitutes the greater visual part of the film, the chase framing the film is a symbolic, thematic one: "Buster ⟶ love." Buster never actually runs after the girl; in fact, she is hardly present. Real bars prevent him from moving closer in the first place. But as this love chase goes on *within* him, Buster is kept from his goal because of the very route he chooses (or has been forced to choose): big business. The detours on this route lead him into the physical chases with cops that will bar him from his goal forever.

The "cop ⟶ Buster chase" begins with Joe, which to some degree is a lengthy mental chase as well because he only reappears at the end. Joe has kept the hunt alive in his mind, waiting for the chance to grab his man. His fervent desire eventually expands into the desire of every cop in the city; he "multiplies" into hundreds of cops, and each cop is his proxy, until only a solid faceless mass pursues Buster. Thanks to the explosion, the chase switches from a mental pursuit to a nonstop physical one, coursing into every street.

**203**

# Cops

All chases—physical, mental, emotional—merge through Keaton's masterful control of space and crowd at the end of the film, when Buster seeks refuge in (of all places) the precinct. Hundreds of policemen enter the single door from all directions. A later parallel is a similar chase in *Seven Chances* (1925), in which Buster (who places an ad in the paper for a wife by 3:00 P.M. so that he may inherit a fortune) attracts hundreds of willing brides, all shapes, sizes, colors, and ages (the girl of his dreams has refused him). He awakens from a nap in a church pew to discover the throng behind him. Immediately upon his escape, the irate spinsters begin one chase that leads into a second consisting of numerous boulders following him down a steep incline. Keaton presented the rock chase in a few shots and without a double. What was initially planned as three boulders following Buster developed into hundreds of specially constructed rocks (one, eight feet in diameter).[11] The feature chases, and certainly their forerunner in *Cops*, echo Keaton's concern with movement of masses. In *Cops*, the single plainclothesman at the start of the film unintentionally spawns an entire population. After the physical chase ends with the intensity of numbers and speed, Buster remains alone, collected and unscathed. The mental chase for love also reaches a climax at this point in Buster's face-to-face confrontation with Woman. For *that* chase, however, it is now the moment of actualization.

We have been led astray by the title, by the plethora of cops, and by Keaton's fondness for cops in previous films to conclude that cops must be the only "chaser" of the film. The opening shot of Buster through bars also immediately suggests a direction toward a law-and-order story (according to Sarris, "law and disorder").[12] In addition to establishing direction, the first visual joke is a twist: "jail bars" are only "gate bars." Because of "bars," the viewer expects an ending in which Buster resumes his position behind them, whether he deserves it or not. He does indeed return to them the minute he retrieves the keys from the trash can. But his place behind bars has nothing to do with justice, freedom, crime, or anarchy. For all his efforts to succeed in business (and in the business of surviving), he gives himself up willingly at the end. He does not sacrifice himself for guilt at disturbing the peace. His surrender has nothing to do with police matters, but with *affaires d'amour*.

And in these *affaires* is found the ultimate "chaser," identified by the opening title, which also disguises the theme: LOVE. Buster is as pursued by the vision of love as much as he pursues it. It is as if Buster runs before a mirror with Cupid flitting above him; because of the illusory reflection, Buster imagines he runs toward Cupid, but in reality, Cupid runs after him. We can easily see why Buster more than once dodges the single cop before him but overlooks the mob behind him: in his crazy mirror, they are both the same and it doesn't matter which direction he faces. Because of love, Buster embarks on the folly of Big Business and not only falls into another "stationary" chase (with the con man "running" after Buster's wealth with his sad story) but indirectly into a chase with the anarchist (a race against time) and ultimately with all the cops in town. Love is the invisible "carrot before the horse." In *Cops*, Buster ironically "becomes" a horse as he dons the reins and demonstrates the proper gait to his spiritless nag. The "carrot" might have been suspended all the while before his inner eye as he led his stubborn horse. When Cupid catches up with Buster as he confronts the object of love, he is unabashedly spurned. Just as the horse had no real reason to move on (until his doctor's visit), Buster has no reason at the end either, for his medicine of life has been terminated with one swift blow. His personal chase was futile; the cops' chase, victorious but not through their devices. The key that Buster has been seeking to open his heart becomes the door key to his doom. It was Cupid all along, in league with Fate, who held the carrot.

For each face of sadness or confusion that Buster wears (through the bars, at the con man's story, at rejection), there is an equally snappy look (the nag at Woman, the lordly regard of the crowd, the wiser-than-thou look when counting money). This was a dilemma with the hero in *The High Sign*. The latter expressions, making Buster complexly human and laughable, deserve a sobering dog-bite to keep him from abandoning the expression of the eternally hunted. As the film whirls to conclusion, Buster loses his haughty demeanor. He fetches the key with the look of a puppy that has been spanked too often with a newspaper. No guise can protect him now that his heart has been trampled upon. With the tombstone, deadpan takes on a brand-new meaning.

In *Cops*, Buster faces an unusual predicament for the first time: he is given an ultimatum by Woman. For once, she is a strong-willed female, stronger by far than the Nancy Drew–inquisitive of *The Haunted House* who contented herself with cradling Buster's head at the end. But the *Cops* girl keeps a gate's distance, and so Buster's work will always be futile. Her hardness to him is clear from the outset and she gives no A for effort. Buster faces an imbalanced set of odds—not merely the normal bout with man, animal, object, or fate, which he has handled with wit and endurance. He has met a new Nemesis: the rejecting heart of a woman.

In this light, the opening title (an in-joke that also pays tribute to Keaton's "godfather/uncle" Harry Houdini) now becomes multilayered: " 'Love laughs at locksmiths—Houdini,' an almost musical alliteration that parodies the use of famous quotes as prefaces. Its humorous point seems to be made when the opening shot shows the hero behind bars, which turn out to be the gate of his girl friend's estate. Actually, however, the play upon the opening title is not completed until the film's final shot, when the hero, spurned by the girl, allows the police to yank him into jail. It is a sardonic reversal. Locks laugh at lovesmiths, after all."[13]

Buster never gives a clue that his last shot will be so startling, for throughout *Cops* he shines with the unflagging verve that characterizes *The Scarecrow*, *Neighbors*, and *The Goat*. Especially when working alone, Buster masters the situation at hand: commandeering the horse, inventing the glove signal, acknowledging the crowd, finding new ways to hide. Buster, however, acts stupidly when he breaks the vase or accepts the bomb. This is not frenzy as in *The Boat*, but an undercurrent of sad distraction and preoccupation. As considered earlier, there is indeed a life in jeopardy—and it is his own.

Yet Buster never acts smarter than when he leads his favorite foe, the police, into the station. It is a perfect lure, to be sure, and a perfect finale for the cops who think they have caught him. What better way to trick the cops than to slip by them in their own uniform (vestiges of *Convict 13*). Buster can dispose of them with one turn of the lock. He is in jail, where we expected him to be, but he seems to have the last laugh by walking out. This is the usual Keaton twist that insures comedy. Femme fatale, however, will set matters straight. Her rejection becomes the opposite of comedy, for it contradicts the traditional happy ending and fulfills the bitter irony of the opening title. Woman not only rejects Buster's love but all he represents; hence, nothing remains for him but to surrender to the imprisonment that was echoed from the start. Yet what *is* the crime that requires his life sentence?

It is tempting to rely on the tragic Arbuckle scandal as a reason for Keaton's moroseness. For once, both Buster and Keaton seem to admit that there is no perennial happy ending, for the world contains much to prevent one. In the endings of *One Week*, *The Boat*, and *Cops*, Keaton concludes with a twist on what we anticipated: although Buster is chased, the house is wrecked, and the boat sinks, our hero is ultimately reprieved and moves on. But the twist of *Cops* is twisted: Buster goes to jail; he walks out; he goes back to jail, forfeiting his reprieve. If that double helix isn't enough, we are dealt one final stunning blow: the ultimate twist from which there is no return. With Buster now out of the picture and his "presence" depicted only by a bleak headstone, his hat ID, and the double meaning of THE END, there is not even the inkling that this is just a dream and a happy ending will follow, as in *The Haunted House*. Whatever afterworld Buster is visiting is most definitely closed to us.

Keaton uses another tombstone at the end of his feature *College*, but it is presented with a vastly lighter tone (as much as a tombstone can be light): Buster has married his girl, they "are shown in a rapid series of shots moving through marriage and children, middle age, old age, and death, represented by *two* graves this time."[14] They will continue to be together in the expected progression of a happy marriage. Whenever Buster works alone, he does so out of immediate necessity, motivated by the reward of a female at the end of his struggles; he obviously prefers companionship or, more often, a lifelong mate (*One Week, Convict 13, The Scarecrow, Neighbors, The Haunted House, The High Sign, Hard Luck, The Goat, The Boat, The Playhouse, The Paleface, Cops*). For a soul who has lost the will to live—and to be loved—there is nothing else but loneliness. It is more than coincidence that *Cops* is united by drawings at the beginning and end that cancel each other out: the symbol of vitality is replaced by the symbol of mortality.

There is no mate for Buster in *Cops*; this film is a quest that fails. Buster blatantly feels his business venture is not worth pursuing if Woman will not accept him. He gives up thinking of what else to do, except to offer himself back to the wolves, simply *because* she has not accepted him. Perhaps Buster will make friends in jail, but since the mass of cops sought him with a vengeance, it seems unlikely. Luckily, Keaton spares us any more of Buster's death than the stunning shot of his tombstone with its wryly perched porkpie. "We *know* the hero cannot be killed—but he is. We don't *see* him die for that would rupture the comic stylization beyond repair. The drawn headstone distances us from the fact of death far enough to keep us within that extremely subtle generic terrain we can still call 'comedy.'"[15]

Never does the precarious balance on the threshold of comedy and tragedy tip toward the latter than with the single crashing final shot of *Cops*. Yet when Buster learns that the final joke is on him, he still reacts typically: ponders with suppliant hands, backtracks to the trash can without further thought, straight-facedly yields to his fateful decision; even hops to help the hands pull him in. The gestures are more poignant because he relies on what little he has left that belongs to him alone—his personality, his character—even though he has been deemed a failure. Buster walking away from Woman and Cops would leave the image of a living but deeply lonely man on the horizon. Ironically, returning to the cops is his only dignified alternative. "The cops did not win. Fate did. But, even then, it was not overt disaster. Fate, rather, moved a final piece, checkmating hope. It was the victim, as if made mad by the gods, who then destroyed himself. Had there been an epitaph on the little stone, it might well have read: 'He Did the Right Things. He Thought the Right Thoughts. Wha' Happen?' "[16]

Buster's porkpie alone remains to pay tribute to the pursuer-turned-pursued.

## Chapter 14

# My Wife's Relations

## (May 1922)

Courtesy of the Academy of Motion Picture Arts and Sciences

*M*y *Wife's Relations* is seldom mentioned with the ardor of other Keaton "classic" short films like *Cops* or *One Week*. Even the title seems to clash with the roster of his other relatively simple titles. Blesh called it, "Like an early Keystone, . . . little more than good slapstick with the Keaton comic personality."[1] For sure, the little man's presence among the proplike characters who are his "wife's relations" elevates the slapstick from the Sennett style to a *thematic* sophistication that it lacks on the visual level. With all its shortcomings, particularly the uncomfortable ethnic humor aspect, *My Wife's Relations* contains sequences that encapsulate the themes of Buster Keaton's world to the nth degree.

FOREWORD IN THE FOREIGN SECTION OF A BIG CITY—WHERE SO MANY DIFFERENT LANGUAGES ARE SPOKEN, THE PEOPLE MISUNDERSTAND EACH OTHER PERFECTLY—THERE LIVED A YOUNG ARTIST WHO WAS PULLING TO GET AHEAD. Fade out. Fade in to find Buster with his back to us, distancing us by his concentration as he molds a claylike wad hanging on a wall hook. He stretches and twists it temperamentally, then steps back to study it, breathing hard with exertion. We cut to two observant kids nearby munching on peppermint sticks. Keaton opens up the punch line (as he did in *The Boat*) by cutting now to a long shot; the visual exposition reveals the wider world into which we were thrust with the misguiding title. The "young artist," it turns out, works in a candy store and the wad he molds to perfection is taffy. As the kids run out and peer through the window of the BUSY BEE CANDY COMPANY, Buster waves and continues pulling.

Keaton has fooled us with his exceptionally long, multithought title. Our focus falls easily on the last phrase about the young artist, as Buster always conjures up wistful occupations by his very nature. Watching his act of creation, we quickly forget that the narration is also setting up the environment, the macrocosm in which the artist works. Only until the location is visually altered, that is, with a long shot, do we remember the "misunderstanding" buried in the middle of Keaton's title. Language will not be the only source of "perfect misunderstanding," but visuals promise to be the same. As Keaton has "stated" many times in other films, seeing is not believing, and the truth is not always what it first looks (or reads) like. Even we who are fluent in English will perfectly misunderstand Buster because his world is full of crazy equations and unknown variables.

Elsewhere in this Tower-of-Babel town, a happy couple telephones a balding man who sits at a book-covered desk. Their dialogue captures the ethnicity through their native language. Keaton conveniently deciphers the long sentences so we can "understand" what is being said. The male partner asks: "MOZECIE NAM DAC SLUB PO POLSKU . . . ," which dissolves into "CAN YOU MARRY US IN POLISH AT ONCE?" The man at the desk responds in a medium shot: "TAK—JA NIE MUWIE INNYM JEZYKIEM," which dissolves into "YES, I SPEAK NO OTHER LANGUAGE." From this simple communication, we see how language will now be a barrier for anyone *not* speaking this tongue, and obviously Buster, whose vocabulary is filled with symbols and equations, will be sorely in need of a polyglot interpreter.

Buster's taffy has become a masterpiece of a prop as he drags it the width of the store, from background to foreground, and skips over it twice like a jump rope. When a postman, befuddled by the words on envelopes and store signs reading things like s. f. kowalski & spa sklad kolonialny, enters the candy store, Buster draws him into his three-dimensional art by swinging the taffy around his neck. As the postman fights with the candy, Buster quietly retreats; by stepping outside, however, he creates even more havoc in the larger space. His calamitous energy spreads outward the minute it is released; his artistic "genius" for creative mishaps fills any space it enters, like a goldfish growing relative to the size of its bowl. Outside, Buster steps on an envelope, blotting its address with the sticky grime from his shoe, and innocently hands it to the postman who is exasperatedly picking off taffy threads from his uniform. In a domino effect, the postman hurls a bottle at Buster who ducks; the missile crashes through a store window behind him; Buster flees and trots directly into a truck of a woman (Kate Price) who has stooped to retrieve groceries from a broken bag. They topple and Kate, not one to take an assault lying down, hoists Buster back to the scene of the crime. The store owner looking at his broken window is the balding man of earlier appearance, a justice of the peace, who is reintroduced at this crucial moment for the sake of the newlyweds he is awaiting. And indeed, a couple—Buster and Kate—are hurrying anxiously toward him. Even sign and body language fail to bridge this communication gap, for the justice believes their haste is impatience to join in wedded bliss. Kate's speed, of course, is propelled by her amazonian desire to rid the world of miscreants like Buster. In the fracas, Buster slips the envelope into his pocket for safekeeping, a fateful choice that will have its impact later.

Keaton lines up his events for cause-and-effect, bringing together separate and unrelated units to create chance collisions and life-revolving confusions. Is Buster's contribution as an artist "in name only," whose life circumstances keep him from his true vocation? Is his role to unite the different clusters around him by becoming the magnetic core to which all differences are pulled? (After all, his artistic medium is a sticky one, and he is perfecting the art of "pulling." An envelope of unknown but undeniable importance has already stuck to him.) This sequence illustrates Buster's facility to bring many pieces together into an ensemble that will become, to his surprise and disadvantage (à la curve), an all-swallowing Machine. This implement of Fate has already been operated in *The Scarecrow*, literally as a thresher, and in other films as more symbolic "machines" (boats, houses). The Machine of *My Wife's Relations* will be operated by—in fact, is made up of—human agents. Buster's artistic qualities, which are misplaced in his lowly position as candy maker, will be annihilated as he passes through the cogs and gears of this Machine. As he grows up, however, and leaves the art world to enter "Reality" outside, he will learn how to pull the plug.

The justice of the peace (an average-witted authority figure) fails to notice the couple's obvious lack of fluency in his language; duty calls and he performs the service. "CZY BIEZESZ TEGO CZTOWIEKA ZA MIEZA?" (dissolve to "DO YOU TAKE THIS MAN TO BE YOUR LAWFUL WEDDED HUSBAND?"), he addresses to the bride-apparent. In close-up, Kate's roly-poly face stares befuddled from under her outrageous flowered hat. After a pause, she nods vigorously, *assuming* she has understood the gist of his statement if only because they both witnessed the window-breaking. She gives the only possible response in the circumstance: "SURE! HE BROKE YOUR WINDOW." The justice questions an equally puzzled and paranoid Buster, who suspects he is being accused although he did not directly commit the crime. "CZY PRZYZEKASZ GO KACHAC HONOROWAC I MITOWAC SO SMIERCI?" Typically wordless, Buster's face gives a full spectrum of responses: uncomprehending eyes, dubious blinks, perplexed raised eyebrows, doubtful glance at Kate. Urged by an assistant's solemn encouraging nod, Buster manages a reluctant nod back. The justice waves a hand over the couple, then gives each a pen to sign a paper, which they do blindly. The justice kisses the bride, to her horror, and shakes Buster's hand. The paper is given to Buster and finally revealed in a close-up masked to stress the dreadful words, CERTIFICATE OF MARRIAGE. Curiously, the certificate is printed in English as Kate and Buster read it without a translator. Keaton obviously manipulated the gag to resolve it and, of course, to place Buster in a worst-case scenario as quickly as possible. We have been led into the misunderstanding theme so forcefully that we too accept this inconsistency with little problem. Buster's responses fluctuate between melodrama and a realistic, though subdued terror. He cringes, double-takes at the paper, rolls his glance along Kate's arm to her face before lifting his eyes to heaven, then closes them and plasters himself against the justice's desk. Kate flies a fist and brandishes the paper like a weapon as she drags her spouse out by the shoulder. Buster lays a timid hand on his cheek as the iris closes.

With the title's focus on wife and in-laws, and with the wedding occurring so early in the film, Keaton is surely establishing marriage as the butt of his ridicule. He uses absurd figures to personify this nightmare milestone, in particular, juxtaposing the dominating, masculine matron Kate with Buster's otherworldly spirit. Keaton already lacerated marriage in *One Week* mainly through biting titles, although the mate was an object of desire, perhaps even passion, and certainly simple romance. The wedding ceremony was mocked mercilessly in *Neighbors*. By *The Boat*, the institution had created an enormous change in Buster's life: the wife seemed more of a nag, the kids were pests, and possessions caused as much pride as frustration and despair—they even threatened his very well-being. Marriage now no longer gradually spirals down from an ideal, where for one brief but shining moment the knight and lady are happy. Marriage is an assault, an imposition born of chance, misunderstanding, and confusion. On the heels of *Cops*, in which Buster abandoned all hope of attaining love (much less marriage), *My Wife's Relations* offers a logical sequel for Keaton's attitude to this frightening institution.

Embedded in a neighborhood where verbal communication is stymied at every corner, marriage becomes even more unbearable. Keaton situates Buster in a predominantly Polish neighborhood, but not to contribute another "Polish joke" as there is no mockery of anyone from that heritage. After all, the Polish judge appears no different from the American one in *Neighbors* (the latter, in fact, was more of a cartoon character); this judge simply speaks a foreign tongue. Rather, Keaton makes use of distinctly Polish-sounding (or here, Polish-looking) words and names so that anyone alien to the language will still derive a sense of being lost in a foreign land. The words hint at but adequately disguise the vows for Buster, Kate, and even us, although we have been prepared for the marriage by the earlier sequence with the happy couple. Keaton uses language to create separation between people, the barrier he enjoyed in *Neighbors*; language is as much of a divider as race. In *My Wife's Relations*, the helplessness of being "illiterate" only adds more dread to that abysmal feeling of an unwanted union. Keaton will continue to draw upon the ethnic (Irish) differences of the in-laws so that these characters are not only grotesque stereotypes of inherited relatives but they offer the added complication of a tradition into which Buster will never fit. As long as there are barriers, Buster will always be (perhaps prefer to be) on the outside looking in.

HOME OF THE BRIDE AND FAMILY. Iris opens on the men of Kate's family scattered about a well-lived-in room. Each has special physical traits and is here nicknamed by them. A man wearing a cop's hat (Cop = Harry Madison) reads a paper with his feet on a table. A burly man with mustache (Burly = Joe Roberts) enters with a lunch tin and shovel, and hangs his hat on a wall lamp. The patriarch of the brood (Papa = Monte Collins) reads by the window. Another chap with a pickax (Pickax = Wheezer Dell) enters, removes Burly's hat, and caps the lamp with his own. A fourth brother with a bowler (Bowler = Tom Wilson) enters, flexes his muscles, and discards the hat on the lamp to place his bowler. The men go about their private business with indifference, unless one infringes on the other as with the prized wall lamp. Each individual functions in a niche or cubicle unto himself. Therefore, everyone needs a good reason to join forces, to merge into a large smooth-running unit, like cogs and gears precisely assembled in a large chassis; familial devotion is hardly a good enough reason. Without each person, however, the resulting machine cannot function; with parts in the wrong place, it will go haywire.

These in-laws give us pause for thought on the title. The pronoun "my" makes this film an unusual personal possession; not only is Buster talking to us as first-person narrator even before the film begins, but perhaps Keaton is alluding to his own marital "relations" in the Talmadge clan (this biographical fodder will be discussed later). "Wife" as part of the title zeroes in on what Buster must contend with, even though he begins as a bachelor. Wife soon barrels in and literally hauls Buster from his artistic vocation to a new, hard-hitting fate. Wife is the instrument of Fate; ethnic issues have only been the means to bring Reality to the forefront. Keaton also uses the curious word "relations" as opposed to "relatives" or "family." Dictionaries define "relations" as both mutual connections and/or dealings of persons or groups, as well as sexual intercourse. The second definition gives the title a wildly suggestive meaning that a pretty wife for Buster (like Sybil or Virginia) might naughtily complicate their married life. Yet with a battle-ax like Kate, this definition can be promptly eliminated; Keaton makes this clear in a forthcoming "wedding-night" scene. "Relations" implies impersonality even in human interactions, the businesslike way in which people "connect" because they are forced to by marriage. Connections are imperative to begin "relations." Thus, when Buster finally appears, the in-laws will connect into the perfect machine that sucks their intruder into its workings and churns him around. With a life of dull routines and deep ruts, the only way this "family" can work is mechanically and superficially, just like a well-oiled robot with no depth or emotion; in fact, robot and emotion are contradictions. Given that the family is visibly working-class, the machine image is richly significant and Buster is the "plug" that charges this machine with current.

Keaton's next title warns us and evokes sympathy at the same time: DANIEL NEVER ENTERED A DEN LIKE THIS. Kate sails with Buster into the midst of her brood and, with convoluted English that again belabors the ongoing language confusion, blurts out: "PAPA! SHUT YOUR EYES AND SEE WHAT I MARRIED!" Instantly, the start button is pushed, Papa dispenses Kate to the kitchen (her territory in this male land), and The Inspection begins. In a methodical exchange of moves and gestures, the brothers and father alternate their respective duties in "La Machine." Burly smacks Buster forward and opens his jacket; Bowler looks over his head and hat; Burly thumps his chest; Bowler shakes his head; Burly checks his teeth as Bowler feels his legs and arms. As one phase of inspection stops, another begins, followed at last by a cumulative effort: the group hoists Buster up for communal search. Burly announces: "HE WON'T LAST A DAY IN THIS FAMILY." Buster lies on his side, stretched across their width, as they hold him and confer among themselves. Ensemble, they drop him, opting instead for dinner. The four brothers have inflicted a nonstop automated appraisal of Buster's physique, like an octopus grabbing its prey. He has been literally manhandled and discarded, in a variation of the thresher that moved his body through space and ejected it when done. That, of course, was accidental; this machine is frightening because it is composed of humans who have lost their humanness in a flat existence. But typically, Buster strikes a casual pose as he lies horizontally in their eight arms, realizing how useless it is to fight or even question the current; he knows he will be released in due time.

Buster must now begin to exert adult thoughts, pushing even further into the attic of his mind the artistic sensibilities that were being lost in his taffy work. The "universal language" of art fell silent the minute he stepped outside his store; now his only language is of survival against a foe, Machine. His first rebellion goes unnoticed by the hungry crowd at the dinner table, which juts into the right end of the frame. With an abrupt look at them, Buster squashes the bowler as he steps up to the wall lamp to hang his porkpie; he discards the cop's hat with gusto and claims the lamp as his own. The hat routine occurred before Buster ever witnessed it; however, he gravitates to the lamp as if he knows intuitively where his porkpie goes; after all, home is where you hang your hat, and Buster has been brought home. He understands the discarding nature of these in-laws by the number of chapeaux on the floor as well as by how he himself has been discarded. Buster will fit into their schemes, if only to challenge them at their own game. As usual, both innocence and adult perspicacity unite for the battle.

The machine functions well in any aspect of daily life that corrodes into a routine or mundane operation, and dinner is no exception. Each unit (relative) is peripherally aware of when its counterparts start and stop their "roles." The comic essence of this scene is sustained by the relatives' rapid-fire actions and their nonstop manipulation of Buster. He does not integrate easily into the works because his "part" is not designed to fit into their equipment; he does not, to repeat the opening message, speak their language.

Keaton seats us at the long dinner table across from Buster who is sandwiched between Burly and Bowler. The brothers pound the table with their knives; Kate in the background hollers back and carries a pot to the sink; impatiently, Papa and Burly smack their hands on the table. Their primitive mealtime behavior recalls Joe in *Neighbors* whose gross size and manner contrasted sharply with Buster's refined and gentle ways. We cut to medium long shot for a natural framing device, using the brothers around Buster to suggest entrapment; he is "framed," trapped by the shoulder of Cop who sits across from Buster but with his back to us, as well as by the shoulders of Burly and Bowler on each side. Mixed in with their show of a ravenous appetite is the comic frustration of Buster trying to get a bite in edgewise. As he directs food to his mouth, he is systematically disturbed by Bowler for the bread, Cop for the butter, another for the peas. At the fourth interruption, Buster lays down his silverware, closes his eyes, and hands over another plate. Scarcely gripping his utensils again, Buster is interrupted by Bowler for the salt, not to mention the pepper, which Buster delivers with his right hand as his left takes the butter. The fork inches closer to his mouth in little climactic ascents toward satisfaction, only to be interrupted at each step by cream, peas, and bread passing through in different directions. The flurry increases until Buster throws down his fork and turns, draping his arm over the chair. He is clearly able to survey his in-laws' gastronomic feats, each captured in a "solo" medium shot: Burly slices off a third of a stick of butter but smashes the larger chunk into his bread; or sweet-tooth Bowler drops twelve sugar cubes into his coffee until Buster stops him to pour the coffee into the sugar bowl instead. Buster's ingenuity also helps Bowler deal with the troublesome spoon that sticks his eye each time he drinks from the bowl; Buster bends the handle and hangs the spoon on the rim. Bowler gratefully whacks Buster in the back—past the fork aimed at his open mouth. Buster learns that neither working with the machine nor against it gives him a chance to eat. He must devise a plan that will dismantle the machine and give him room to sate his appetite.

The opportunity arises with the main course. Kate brings in the meat and Papa halts Bowler's overeagerness to eat in order to say grace. All bow, armed with utensils; after a solemn pause, everyone except Buster (who remains bowed) stabs their respective portions. Startled by the rush of the attack, he finds he is left with an empty pan. Keaton cuts closer so that as Buster examines it, he is again framed by claustrophobic shoulders. Buster turns disgustedly, becoming a directional arrow toward a wall calendar that reads: TODAY IS 8 THURSDAY. As the devouring machine operates at full steam, Buster surreptitiously pulls off the Thursday page to reveal TODAY IS 9 FRIDAY and nonchalantly informs the God-fearing Catholics of their transgression. The relatives shamefacedly return their meat to the tray and Buster, with a feigned sympathetic headshake, forks a large hunk for himself to eat in peace. Keaton records his victory in a shot that is similarly composed of the entrapping shoulders around him, but which now offers a significantly different interpretation to the same scene. He sits within the confines of his captors but indulges in a celebration feast. His adult machinations have finally turned the barrier into a benefit and a reward.

Buster has met and outwitted his opponents on their level and using their ethnic/cultural differences as weapons. By not being of the same Friday meat-abstaining religion, Buster is illsuited to fit into their machinery. The family's ethnicity has screamed out to Buster, although we have only seen the exaggerated physical appearances that are more cartoonish than human. This Irish family is never so named, but they are identified by subtle trademarks. Buster is aware of these from his view; for us, Keaton plants informational signs, as with the biblical reference to Daniel and the den (strains of "Danny Boy" also filter in), followed by the unmistakably Catholic abstinence from meat. Keaton uses specific cultural markers that assume his audience also recognizes these group distinctions, for the resolution of this gag depends on audience understanding. There is no gag without these differences between Buster and clan; there is no solution without the barrier. Of course, although Keaton finally demonstrates that the barrier can achieve personal gain (getting the meat), it will always separate and ostracize, with potential for either comedy or tragedy.

The title that begins the next "chapter" in Buster's marriage tale is another biblical-sounding quotation, adapted for Keaton's comic motives and reinforcing the Catholic strain. He also uses this line to introduce the anticipated "wedding night" scene: AS A MAN MAKETH HIS BED, SO SHALL HE SLEEP. Kate is already fast asleep in her isolated bed, without having prepared the companion twin for her mate; there is only a bed frame with a peculiarly (deliberately) placed broom standing against the headboard. From a side door, mattress, springs, pillow, and blankets suddenly move toward us; as they turn, Buster is revealed awkwardly setting his sleep-ware on Kate before he sweeps his area and absentmindedly sets the broom across the frame. A predictable gag follows when he lays the mattress across the broom, turning the bed into a seesaw. Buster has made his bed into his nemesis as he rallies to lie on whichever end of the bed comes up first but always crashes into the opposite end. This is another of Buster's regrettable acts of distraction (like drilling a hole in the bottom of a boat). Symbolically, however, the scene is a beautiful, wry, visual comment on Buster's bed-making and his fateful circumstances.

Intercut with Buster's bedroom adventures are glimpses of the male sleeping machine, each component unconcerned with the odd noises from the bridal chamber and focusing on individual agendas. Papa and Burly knock each other out of their respective sides of the same bed; Bowler adjusts a pair of earmuffs to drown out the snoring of his bed partner, Pickax. By recording the sleeping routine of the family, Keaton begins to segment the second half of the film into defined, specific, and separate routines. The film acquires a distinct "chapter" feel, but without the repetitive devices of calendar pages and helpful hands as in *One Week*. Instead, the routines that follow (The Big Sleep, The Sneeze, The Photo Session, The Beer, The Chase) epitomize the family as a faceless mass, an "individual" confronting Buster, a well-oiled Machine. The latter image characterizes the family best because of their ensemble activity, their oddly integrated give-and-take nature as they unconsciously merge against Buster the intruder. These routines are minor spin-offs of The Dinner and The Inspection, but they now clearly become evidence of an emotionless and automated lifestyle. Every waking (and sleeping) day is segmented into team-machine efforts, usually of a brusque and self-centered nature.

After Keaton cuts to the men's quarters, he returns to Buster's doldrums for updates on his progress with his bed and on his growing animosity toward his darling. As Buster slowly rises from the collapsed bed, falling over Kate in the process, she with braids a-swinging like a Wagnerian goddess of vengeance drags Buster up by the hair, slaps him, pitches him offscreen, and flies a fist at him before turning over to sleep. Not once in Buster's history so far has even a *male* opponent displayed such overwhelming battery on his person. Keaton interrupts to let Buster recuperate and ponder; we see Pickax who is disturbed by Bowler's raucous snores and removes the earmuffs for his own use. Back to Buster sitting in bed, crumpled but with a new and frightening look in his eye—that of murderous intent. His adult mind has now grown to such dimensions that it extends into very dark borders, nearly obscuring the wide-eyed innocence that Buster had moments before when crawling under protective covers. Now he feigns sleep, periodically delivering a hearty whack onto Kate's back as if deep in restless slumber. Kate spins to attack, but the sight of his peaceful dozing face warms her heart into believing his innocence. The "magic third" delivery of a well-deserved whack rounds up the routine, which backfires on Buster as he accidentally peeks at Kate while she suspiciously eyes him, waiting for his arm. Buster, of course, falls quickly back to sleep as if nothing is wrong. Kate shatters a pitcher on his head, the bed sinks under the impact, and Buster lies numbly still. Kate smugly switches off the light, and the scene fades out to the next title: MORNING.

Buster's resuscitation from unconsciousness comes about through the next "chapter" involving a curious home remedy that the handy housewife conjures up. Buster has not budged an inch among the shards, even with Kate's commands to rise. When vigorous shaking fails to rouse the lad, she shrieks for her family with the doubled-meaning explanation: "HE'S BEEN OUT ALL NIGHT." Such obtuse conversation with its own logical-illogic triggers the equally obtuse relatives back into their familiar role of Machine, pulling Buster into its equipment. Instantly, the cogs and gears revolve: Papa climbs over Buster, each brother takes an arm or leg, carts him to the floor, and pumps. Back in her kitchen, Kate grabs her cure-all, as the irised close-up reveals: PEPPER. She first grinds it into Buster's nose, then pours the bottle as the Machine steps back to watch. Buster's typically graceful responses choreograph this latest chapter, The Sneeze. Like

The Inspection and The Dinner, one behavior is contagious to the next; sneezing infiltrates the entire lineup of relatives. The storm of sneezing bursts through the group, starting with Buster's first delicate sneezes, his quivers of sneeze-anticipations, his expressive body forming triangular poses as he performs a litany of sneezes. Burly at the head of the sneeze-line is followed by Cop and Bowler, each with their quirks (Papa with little spurts, Burly and Bowler in duet, Bowler falling forward with every powerful blast). Buster once again becomes visually and physically caught between the blasting in-laws. As he chokes on the pepper, he steps between Papa and Kate who shove him into other relatives as they counter their own sneezes. Buster is a ball in a pinball machine, with each relative the flipper tossing him against another obstacle. The choreography swirls him around the room so that if the sneezes die down, his stumble into another relative repeats the same chorus. Eventually, he separates from the Machine by rolling feet over head onto his stomach and landing with two little sneezes, like an accent mark in a peculiar song.

The Machine transports itself into the kitchen where The Sneeze routine is abruptly abandoned for a plot complication desperately needed to bolster the flagging story. As amusing as the routines are that highlight the mechanical operations of this group, they really do nothing for the content. The routines are abstract paintings of a cluster of relatives, a gallery of unusual family portraits in different daily activities. The pictures show us how they look, pose, and integrate, but nothing courses through their existence with lifeblood, much less a rich story. By this point in the film, the clan's ethnicity and its position in an ethnically diverse environment have been minimized. Keaton has taken the potentially rich, albeit uncomfortable, frame of ethnicity (as with race), stamped it flat into comic stereotypes, and dropped it.[2] Perhaps it has become too flat, too difficult, too unnecessary. His usual themes of Buster versus Fate, Machine, Rival, and Self have always been more intriguing to him than the use of stereotypes. Keaton, however, finds himself juggling multiple flesh-and-blood characters who are meant to remain in the picture; he decides that they best work in chapter-like routines as an ensemble. They become a machine, but they are repetitious (certainly unattractive and unsympathetic) even when the scenarios change. Thus, *My Wife's Relations* suffers because Keaton's best themes are diluted and overshadowed by the slapstick predictability of a very limited cast.

There is also no upward movement of Buster's character, particularly in collaboration with his surrounding crowds, as there was in *Cops*. Even though the family group works in unison to thwart Buster, just as the cop crowds did, Buster is strangely laconic, resigned, compliant to his horrific marriage to a termagant and her kin. Buster's honor in *Cops* against the sea of police (or the police Machine) derives from his quest toward a goal (Love) and toward the freedom to achieve that goal. *My Wife's Relations* lags because Buster's determined flight and fight are missing. The family challenges him, for sure, but it does not inspire. Buster/Keaton even loses sight of his art (taffy/film) that drove him to temperamental devotion. Now weary with the repetitious family, he slides through his "kidnapping," not just thinking of eventual freedom but perhaps equally thinking of eventual doom. He is unusually quiet, even for a silent film character, and his own behavior seems to resist both the family and his own aspirations and dreams.

The Sneeze routine ends when the missing thread from the beginning—the sticky envelope—reappears. Searching for a handkerchief in any coat pocket, Burly unearths the letter in Buster's jacket and opens it unconscionably. Its typewritten contents appear in close-up:

JOHN BROWN

ATTORNEY–AT–LAW

WOOLWORTH BUILDING

NEW YORK CITY

DEAR CLIENT:

    THE ESTATE OF YOUR LATE UNCLE
HAS BEEN SETTLED. PLEASE CALL AND COLLECT
THE $100,000 HE LEFT YOU.

YOURS TRULY

JOHN BROWN

Despite the unrealistic generic salutation to such important legal news—which obviously accommodates the gag, since the "client" will become Buster by association—the whole family falls under the spell of wealth. Burly staggers and announces to everyone: "KAT'S HUSBAND IS RICH . . . NOW WE MUST BE NICE TO HIM." The brother thus acknowledges the crude, self-absorbed behavior the relations have inflicted on Buster; *now* they must be nice to him because of his valuable price tag. Buster is suddenly different by mere suggestion, just as earlier, Buster was a criminal because he stood near the broken window. The contrast between the family's future behavior and what they *really* feel is demonstrated by Papa who has not yet learned this news but suffers the last of the sneezes privately with Buster; he finally gives his son-in-law an impatient high-kick to the mouth and sets an alarm clock beside him as an afterthought when he leaves. When the alarm rings (in close-up), Buster groggily rises, shuts it off, and dizzily returns to sleep, covering himself with a mat. Although Buster has suffered many well-aimed assaults from other close encounters (*Convict 13* and *The Haunted House* particularly), our hero has never experienced the onslaught that he does here. The attacks prior to *My Wife's Relations* ironically recharged Buster's batteries or led him into dreams in which his "flight and fight" became even more fantastical than his waking life. Buster here is, pure and simple, a punching bag whose purpose is to absorb the blows as they come. He is not overwhelmed by odds or numbers, for he was up against the greatest of both in *Cops* but still outwitted, avoided, and evaded them very nimbly. Rather, Buster is a straw in the wind, embracing his unsteady fate with scarcely a question mark, and becoming wildly, almost willingly manipulable.

This surprising wishy-washy aspect of Buster is clear when the newly loving relatives burst into the room; Kate pours her love over Buster in a shower of coos and kisses. Buster's deep-rooted common sense will not readily accept this about-face, of course, and he responds with a curious stare. But when Kate shyly swings his hand in hers and gaily skips out like a teenager in love, with pigtails flapping behind like come-hither gestures, Buster suddenly skips out after her. Between *Cops* and this dire marriage, has Buster become so starved for love that he will settle for any momentary show of affection? But then, what is one more conundrum, Buster thinks, so he might as well skip along with it. He does not rebel against, question, oppose, or escape the extreme behaviors that have victimized him, although he tried earlier to outsmart them at dinner. But as the proverb said, he made his bed and he is now lying in it, either by choice or by force, and this Machine is too overpowering to fend off right now.

Back in her kitchen, Kate digs out a roll of money from a coffee can and breaks through the male barricade to give it to her spouse, with the warm suggestion: "GO RENT A NICE PLACE, WE WANT TO MAKE YOU HAPPY." The brothers also make contributions (Pickax from savings in his shoe; Cop donating, then retracting one bill from his donation). Papa merrily shakes Buster's sleeve-draped hand while our hero focuses on the loot, extracting his hand to count the bills while Papa obliviously continues shaking the sleeve. In this group portrait, with Buster fully absorbed into the loving household because of an unknown (to him) circumstance, we note Buster's increased disdain for his kin; his look is more assaultive than a physical blow. He gives the illusion of shaking his father-in-law's hand while occupying his own with a more important matter. Buster intends to profit from his mishap, feeling perhaps that he has earned it. But therein lies the same troubled character trait as in the pseudo-Buzzard of *The High Sign*. Buster is contemptuous of his imposed relations, yet he becomes comfortably settled in this asylum with the mere lure of wealth. Keaton is obviously making a harsh statement on his hero's priorities here, even though any number of reasons can excuse his impaired judgement: bad marriage, jaded outlook of a life-weary traveler, confusing social background. All these elements roll in and through the film, creating an artificial and uneasy melange from which Buster must choose his values.

The allusion to an impoverished society, which was cradled in the original title, surfaces again with the next title: FROM THE ALLEY TO THE AVENUE . . . WHERE THEY BOUGHT THE PLACE EVERY TIME THEY PAID THE RENT. Reenter the "art" that Buster as struggling artist was attempting to mold; now it assumes the form of high living, obviously designed by Buster as artist and master of finance. His lavish choices include fireplace, grand piano, chandelier, and a Venus di Milo. The gap between great art and an uneducated audience's reaction to it (as well as the barrier between classes underlying the whole scenario) is emphasized during the next sequence. Papa studies the Venus and asks, "WHO BROKE THE ARMS OF THAT MONUMENT?" Buster might equally look at Papa in his new clothes, or Kate reclining like an elegant dame on a sofa sweeping a large plumed fan, and inquire: How do you make a silk purse out of a sow's ear? Buster's own pretense at high living is at least based upon his struggle to be an artist; his newly acquired elegance is really a manifestation of what he innately possesses. But old habits die hard for persons plunged into circumstances beyond their background, as with Kate: although waited on by her maid, she pours her cup of coffee into her saucer to drink from. Buster likewise makes a regal impression when he enters; as the butler opens the door, a walking cane appears first, followed by Buster in a light porkpie, dark suit, white polka-dot tie, boutonniere, and pocket hankie. His man-of-leisure stroll is accompanied by stereotypical moves like bouncing his cane on the floor before tossing it to the butler, removing his gloves one meticulous finger at a time, or smoothing his jacket with a lordly facial expression. But Keaton quickly reminds Buster of his humble beginnings and his real priorities that he has obviously forgotten. He gives him a symbolic kick to the rear: as he enters, Buster slips on the Oriental rug. He is mocked by one of his pretensions to wealth. As the first title said, Buster wants to "get ahead," and he is certainly capable of high living; he has just not earned it honorably.

Buster shakes his head at Papa's ignorance and prepares for what is the next chapter, The Photo Session. The clan primps in their new clothes including Cop in uniform, Pickax with top hat, and Burly in long coat and checkered vest, which is padlocked closed but which still rides past his ample stomach with every move. A photographer sets up a large camera and tripod. Ever curious about mechanical things, Buster peeks through the lens, pulling the curtain over him, and dislodges the tripod. As the frustrated photographer rights the camera, Buster squeezes between Kate and Papa for the group portrait. The gag triggered casually by Buster during his slapstick accident with the tripod leg is now completed in a "delayed reaction": as the photographer readies to shoot the posed family, the camera slowly lowers as the tripod slides to the floor. With it, the photographer stoops; with *him*, the family stoops to stay within camera range. When everyone lands on the palms of their hands, smiling all the while, the photographer frantically orders them back up. Buster has unintentionally switched on the Machine again by his act of curiosity in investigating the camera. Although its descent is contrived, the gag is anticipated because of what Buster has established. Sinking to the floor for the sake of a photograph is unquestioned by anyone, and as a unit, the Machine agreeably sinks together. Buster, who should know better, is again absorbed into the works; his uniqueness is chomped into oblivion by the hungry jaws around him. As with the sneezes, Buster is bounced between relatives as he vies for a central position for the shoot; but Bowler shoves him to the back, Pickax steers him behind Cop, and Burly picks him up and drops him in the rear. In a last-ditch effort to claim any spot, Buster crawls between Burly's legs and tilts his wide-eyed head at the camera. Although the family tried to hide him, Buster ironically becomes even more noticeable in the portrait because of his odd position.

The enormous explosion of flash powder topples and disorients everyone (Papa and Pickax cling to each other; Cop fastens himself to the doorjamb; Buster gropes blindly). For once, the loathing of the clan for Buster is directed to the hapless photographer, and they stalk him. For the first time, perhaps, Buster works with the clan to rid them of this incompetent person. With Kate's mighty punch, the photographer flies (with a cut) through the living room into a slowly rising heap; suddenly, Buster flies out horizontally after him and into the rear end of the photographer who (with a cut) is rocketed out the door opened by the butler. Buster returns proudly to the congratulatory pats of his in-laws. He has either voluntarily become "one of them," himself resenting this unprofessional photographer and offering his body to "fire" him in slapstick fashion; or, given his projectile entrance, Buster may well have been launched by force as though from a giant catapult, not only because he is the only young and agile member of the family but because he is also putty in their hands. Perhaps he has suffered too many blows and is totally punch-drunk. His "good dog" response to the praising in-laws is disturbing; he seems to be on their side and is willing to beg for approval and belonging.

As a reward, Kate bestows on Buster a great family responsibility. She commands: "GO PUT A HALF A CUP OF YEAST IN THE HOME BREW." This is, of course, another reference to a kind of cultural heritage, stereotyping the Irish as hearty home brewers and convivial drinkers. In the kitchen, Buster tastes from a vat of beer, then carefully opens a YEAST box from which he picks a cube. In this close shot, we see the other end of the box open over the vat, unbeknownst to Buster, spilling all the cubes into the brew. In long shot again, Buster meticulously breaks his cube in half, returns the unused portion to the box, and leaves. Fate is intervening in a peculiar way: having set Buster into a frightening situation, Fate is now maneuvering to have Buster possibly kicked out as an "unprofessional," just like the photographer. Perhaps in some logical-illogic way, Fate is showing a little mercy for Buster who has obviously lost his drive and humility in the midst of these mediocre nonentities. Fate may be pulling Buster back into a game more worthy of his talents.

The last sequences of the film become swamped in more ways than one: (1) literally, by the flood of home brew that will shortly invade the living room where guests have arrived for a nouveau riche party, and (2) figuratively, by even more nonessential characters who flood the scene to create additional chaos for Buster to swim through. And both people and suds are frothy, insubstantial nemeses for Buster; it is as though Buster is bumping against a massive jellylike blob, fighting for a breath of life. Unfortunately, so is this film.

Before the brew reaches the party, however (and through minimal crosscutting, we receive tension-building updates on the progress of the brew as it seeps through the rooms), Kate and guests exchange incidental banter. One guest stares intently at a small horseshoe tattoo on Kate's back, visible in her low-cut gown: "THE MULE THAT KICKED YOU MUST HAVE BEEN A PONY." This comment is one more example of the large number of one-liner vaudeville-type titles that fill this film. Another guest marvels at the house, commenting with an almost discernible brogue: "HOW DO YOU DO IT? 'TIS A HOME FIT FOR A BOOTLEGGER." Kate answers by extracting the infamous grimy letter from her bosom; as she dusts it off, she is horrified by the real address now appearing beneath the dirt—

MISS ROSE ROYCE

I 2 PARK AVE.

NEW YORK

—an obvious pun on status and wealth. Her scream summons the family; symbolically, the shattering of their "dream" is concretized in Burly's appearance: his too-tight jacket has finally ripped, and a gaping tear runs down his back. Kate announces the dreadful curve that was, in fact, inevitable from the deliberate way the envelope was obscured since the beginning: "THIS LETTER IS NOT FOR HIM . . . WE'RE RUINED." After an angry conference, Burly announces in perfect convoluted logic: "LET'S MURDER HIM FIRST AND THEN BILL HIM."[3]

Back in the kitchen, foam fills the frame and threatens to explode its confines. Meanwhile, an innocent Buster reentering the social circle is puzzled by the spurns of clan and company. In one menacing medium shot, the clan congregates, a seething machine about to attack, a massive tank crowding the frame with their bulk. Kate wordlessly smashes the letter in her hand. Buster, still seemingly unaware of its contents (or if he ever learned its contents offscreen, then guiltily), shivers and draws his collar up at the sudden chill; he animates the stock phrase "cold shoulder." The stalemate breaks: Buster strolls, then blasts into a run, initiating the final chapter, the requisite Chase that will set the Machine in motion again. The chase, evident so far in Keaton's films and in the history of chases in any film genre since the concept was born, is the bullet that speeds through a story at the moment of highest tension and conflict, leading to resolution and conclusion. For Buster in *My Wife's Relations*, the chase has been uneven and halting, almost as if Buster cannot decide whether to start one or not. The chase for Buster has always been one for self-preservation, as many preceding films document; in *Cops*, it was a mirror-image chase—chasing love while he was being chased as an enemy.

The weak chase of *My Wife's Relations* consists of reliable slapstick, a cause–effect run throughout a house that falls somewhere between the undeveloped chase of *The Haunted House* and the sophisticated one of *The High Sign*. As usual, Buster inserts variations in his personal approach to the chase. Unsure of whether to come or go, he strides toward Kate and brothers in his hat, cane, and gloves but then strides away from them as if he is merely going for a walk. Blocked from escape, he backs into the kitchen and disappears into the sea of foam that now obliterates everything but the high kitchen cabinets. Only Buster's head and pleading hands poke through the lather. Keaton adapts the rambling rooms of this rich home more successfully than he did the wide-open spaces of the haunted mansion; but he does not use the technical (albeit gimmicky) split-screen effect of the Nickelnurser residence. Rather, he gives Buster props to drive through his space with the train of stereotyped characters behind him. The beer foam becomes a protective screen for Buster as he seeks refuge from the Machine. When Burly opens the kitchen door searching for Buster, he breaks the dam, so to speak, and the brew floods over the clan. A hide-and-seek chase ensues that would otherwise be pointless in the large simple room, but now the chase holds more twists and turns because the foam wipes out the room and Buster can hide from the crowd without even trying. Buster's face breaks through the lather on the right side and the family rushes right; his deadpan then appears left, cuing the family to that side through the bubbles. But just as quickly as the rich foam gag erupted, it is abandoned (without further trace, ironically) for more prosaic runs and collisions in adjacent rooms. We can easily attach symbolism to the next incident in which Bowler breaks from the glaring crowd and hurls the Venus di Milo at Buster; when it crashes against the wall, Bowler then flings a shard at his target. There goes Art; it was never understood by the uncouth clan anyway. In an ironic way, it doubly assaults Buster who himself failed the art test by misplacing an obviously passionate talent in the wrong milieu. Papa joins in the destruction by prying bricks from the fireplace. What little elegance Buster chose to share with his "family"—misappropriated funds notwithstanding—has turned into a weapon against him. Buster assumes his dodging pinball role as he whirls through cowering female guests and armed male guests who fling bricks or beer bottles as Buster flies by. Despite the crowds, the emphasis is on Buster's creative efforts to foil the various chasers with any props on hand: (1) he propels a serving wagon into three guests and pins Cop against the door; (2) he lifts the piano top to slide off an attacking guest; (3) he jousts with a hatrack, slamming against Pickax and Burly. Recalling his thoughtful nature in *The Haunted House*, Buster hits Cop with a brick, then gently lays his head on the brick as a pillow. Together, the clan and Buster pull apart the house of cards that never had a secure foundation.

This chase yearns for a momentous episode to cinch it, and the best that happens is Buster's interplay with another staircase, this time a simple one unlike its counterpart in *The Haunted House*. Buster positions himself at the head of the stairs and begins his descent rolling down, pulling the carpet with him. With a couple of shots, recalling Buster's flight down the heavenly staircase of *The Haunted House*, Bowler and Pickax leap over the snowballing carpet as it tumbles flight after flight of the apparently high staircase. Yet another peripheral figure, a carpenter, is found sweeping the landing between flights; when the carpet roll drops with a thud at his feet, he propels it with a kick the rest of the way downstairs. Keaton seems restlessly tossing in people for the sake of confusion-by-numbers. The unexpected carpenter suddenly appears in a presumbly finished house for the sole purpose of continuing Buster's flight down a winding staircase. Of course, he is the only character with no motive to attack Buster and thus sends him on his way rather than assaults him. But Keaton could have simply kept Buster rolling down any number of flights by his own momentum. In a strange way, it is Buster (or is it Keaton?) who has lost his momentum and needs outside help to free him, if only from a stick figure.

Buster's last dealings with this family are odd little hems-and-haws, trying to prove his ingenious bravery against the mob when he would be better off with a self-preserving honorable discharge. Instead, as the carpet unrolls at the foot of the stairs before the waiting family, Buster lands seated. He heads back up the stairs (to escape them?), then slides down the rail (no way out?), and lands in a wing chair (part of a plan?). He picks up the end of the carpet and pulls the clan off its feet (did he really have to go upstairs to do this?). He escapes from the foyer door as an iris mercifully closes.

A long pause and the iris opens, facing the end of a train. Buster leaps over the rail and sits, propping his legs up on it. The camera tilts down to a medallion on the gate: RENO LIMITED. Buster breathes easily as the train pulls away from us. THE END.

Buster is visibly relieved at untying the knot because it had entrapped him in a cruel curve beyond his choice and desire. "He leaves for Reno, thereby leaving his wife and her family forever (grounds for divorce: mental cruelty, no doubt)."[4] The final gag is another Keaton witticism and a play on the audience's knowledge that Reno is the quick-divorce city. The gag is contrived and punctuated by the tilt quietly revealing the surprise solution, almost like a deliberate afterthought and certainly a revelation to us since Buster must have spotted the train from *his* distance and knew its destination. The last scene is also a powerful reminder (almost like the morbid coda of *Cops*) that Buster has no one to ride home with; he has only managed to elude another nemesis.

This Machine has proved to be an incredibly vicious one, launching low blows with no compunction for any *assumed* misdemeanor. Keaton's blueprint for this Machine never focused completely on the issue of ethnicity, which floated insecurely in and out of the story, unsure of its own existence. Rather, he just wanted to situate Buster in a *large family*, Irish or otherwise. It may well have been Keaton's (sub)conscious effort to depict and satirize the clan into which he himself married. There is an unavoidable coincidence between the bizarre events of *My Wife's Relations* and happenings in Keaton's marriage. Blesh describes a hectic life: "househunting under the Talmadge clan," Natalie's eagerness for the wealth and luxury she would not achieve as a star like her sisters and husband, and Buster's growing obligations to stardom by wearing the mask of Hollywood host.[5] Not much of a social climber, Keaton's "creativity dropped under the strain,"[6] and when taxed, resulted in substandard films such as *My Wife's Relations*. Keaton was trying to ridicule an uncomfortable subject, and his efforts reflected his discomfort.

Dardis makes a blunt parallel between the characters of this short and Keaton's own relations:

> The only evidence of what Buster may have thought about the clannishness of the Talmadge family can be seen in his film called, aptly enough, *My Wife's Relations*. Produced just a year or so after the marriage, the film is a wild caricature of home life in which he depicts himself as a piece of human refuse found in the street and taken home to live with the members of a particularly vulgar Irish

family. He is harassed and victimized by everybody in the house, but he eventually emerges victorious over all of them. Buster's treatment as a child is recalled here as well as his position with the Talmadges. The film gives us a glimpse of what he thought of both families, for, after all, he was only a comedian.[7]

In writing of his marriage to Natalie (to whom he never refers by name in his autobiography), Keaton describes his newly acquired relations: "In my entire life I never knew a family so devoted to one another as my in-laws were. They all worked and thought together as a team without conflict or jealousy. They all liked me, I think, and I certainly liked and admired them. But there were times when I had the disquieting feeling that I had married not one girl but a whole family."[8]

In her own story, "Peg" Talmadge, the matriarch of the family, who strove for the success of her girls, described Buster with reservation: "He looks at strangers out of his straight brown eyes in an almost disconcerting fashion" and mentioned that Buster was "not really a great reader."[9] Peg claimed that the happiness of the sisters came from their *not* marrying actors. When Keaton objected to this, Peg informed him, "You're not an actor at all. You're a comedian."[10]

Kate does not resemble a nagging spouse as much as a nagging mother-in-law. As a brash, independent, older woman, she is the target of Buster's antipathy because of her gross size, looks, and manners, and perhaps even because of marriage itself, which, thanks to Kate's untimely presence, was foisted upon Buster in a horrible misunderstanding. Kate has none of the sweet, silly, naive, or strong wills that Buster seeks in his women. Her one indulgence to cuteness, when she pays sudden affection to Buster, is an exaggerated sight gag (Wead calls this the "termagant['s] . . . maidenly dance copied from winsome heroines of D. W. Griffith").[11] Here, we also have a wonderful reversal of what was at work in earlier shorts: Buster was usually towered over by Joe; now he is dwarfed principally by Joe's sister.

Because Buster for once is pitted against a woman who matches his comic instincts instead of playing in his shadow, the situation is open for some of Buster's best routines with the opposite sex. The woman is finally not a desirous, delicate object nor, because of that passive role, a dull element in the film. Instead, Kate is an instant sight gag, just as Joe often was, or as the Buzzards were, or as Kate's brothers are in this film. Wead mentions the "rarely used bizarre face" in Keaton's films, which is employed here by the brothers with a "crosseyed actor and [a] toothless bearded one."[12] Because we reduced their "essentials" to one term (Burly, Cop, etc.), they are certifiably one-dimensional. Every Keaton film character, except Buster, has been such a flat type, fading further into the background under Buster's shine. For all her hustle and bustle, Kate too is nothing more than an overweight stick figure.

One of the many problems with *My Wife's Relations* is that Buster so frequently shares his scenes with these types that he risks becoming one himself. This is especially true during The Chase, when many of Buster's usually inventive escape ideas are missing and he falls into a slapstick trap. His runs are frantic, uneventful, and routine; there are only a few of his thoughtful "signs": the kind pat on Cop's head after he sets it on a brick; the meticulous measurement of the yeast. He plays off the group occasionally with his own unique flair, as with the superb solo demonstration of the "cold shoulder." But the extras contribute little for Buster to use. The carpenter's only function, for example, is to push the carpet down the remaining flight; he seems a trivial insert in an elaborate set that Keaton might have used more effectively. Some members of the crowded cast offered more than usual. The photographer was sufficiently mined for comic potential, as a conductor of an ensemble dance poking fun at the phony rich. The justice of the peace presided over the running gag that comprised the entire film. Essentially, though, the guests fall out of the picture after brief and generally unnecessary donations (frozen stares, the piano-top slide, witty banter about a mule), all of which might have been handled by members of the clan instead. With more brainstorming by Keaton, the guests could have added delicious chaos to the film with high-style choreography (like the precision dancing of the bank customers and the ghost traffic in *The Haunted House*) or with punctuated repetitions (the turbulent guests during the storm in *One Week*; the same-but-different group chases of *Cops*). As the film stands, the six-member family could have adequately handled the gags of the guests, tightening and freeing the film from its final disorderliness.

Keaton was no doubt trying to repeat his triumphs in steering faceless masses in *Cops* and *The Paleface*. With a nebulous identity, the crowd becomes a giant prop or a giant straight man; important offshoots (usually Joe) keep personal distinctions and idiosyncratic gags in their own dim spotlight. Here, however, the guests and even some brothers are not around long enough to matter; they distract and hinder. The end of *My Wife's Relations*, like that of *The Haunted House*, becomes a jumbled heap,

**231**

lacking the solid mass movement of *Cops*, or the simple Buster-versus-one-or-two that pulls the best comedy from each character. Instead, this film aptly demonstrates the old adage, amended for obvious purposes: too many cubes spoil the brew.

Of all the flaws in *My Wife's Relations*, the weak character of Buster is the most crucial. When Buster is weak, the film follows suit, no matter how creative and dynamic the choreography or gags are. As has been noted already, Buster has been unusually quiet in this film, particularly given the high number of titles, which coincidentally are uttered primarily by the characters around Buster. He speaks to the clan only when he holds a winning hand, for instance, the calendar page. His lack of speech all the more accentuates the Machine to which Buster is wedded, an entity that does not involve him in normal conversation. Because of it, he must choose between a marriage made in hell or living in solitude. Although Buster's character is less than admirable, the themes that infiltrate his life float to the surface as the film progresses, particularly his confrontation of overwhelming forces for the sake of love. In this short, Buster chooses gladly to head off on his own. He does not—cannot—work best with people for whom he harbors hatred: "Keaton's characters are outsiders in the sense of spectators, not of nihilists or anarchists. He isn't at his best when he hates people (unlike W. C. Fields, for instance . . . ). . . . *My Wife's Relations* has some of the Fields ingredients, but Keaton muffs the loathing."[13]

De rigueur in Keaton's films, there will always be someone Buster will not agree with (Joe the rival, the Buzzards) and someone he will always try to thwart or outwit. But usually balancing this struggle is the reward of someone for whom he cares greatly and whom he will usually win. That has been Buster's essential life goal. In *My Wife's Relations*, there is no one he even wants to like. The people are either machines or incidentals. Because he agrees to play along with the family when they treat him civilly, Buster stays in a situation that always wavers between hate and tolerance; it is never love or anything remotely resembling it. This is the greatest flaw of *My Wife's Relations*. Not that Keaton can't break the mold or deviate from the characters we are accustomed to. But what he provides here does not work, for it fails to reflect the unemotional-emotional character that Buster really is. Keaton introduces A YOUNG ARTIST whose description signifies a struggle to come, bordering the comedy-tragedy threshold. But Buster's pursuit of art is shallow, the emotions he displays are negative or nonexistent, and his circumstances are so abysmal that even Fate gives him a ticket to freedom.

" 'Tis better to have loved and lost, / Than never to have loved at all."[14] So Tennyson ended his poem. Mrs. Talmadge may have doubted whether Buster ever read anything like it, but ironically, the line fits Buster as we have come to know him. In *Cops*, Buster is even willing to sacrifice his life for an unrequited love. If love means that much to him, he should never settle for anything less.

## Chapter 15

# The Blacksmith

(July 1922)

Courtesy of the Academy of Motion Picture Arts and Sciences

Falling right on the spike heels of *My Wife's Relations*, *The Blacksmith* is a refreshing, although regrettably weak, return to Buster's innocent punnery, "old-fashioned" rivalry with Joe, and romantic boy-wants-girl fare. Keaton lets Buster master his own destiny after the requisite bouts with Fate, and the hero seems a bit more like his old "little man against the world" self. He does not sacrifice life nor lose his spirit to another's domination. Buster returns with the verve of his first films and, for the most part, minus the paranoia and bitterness of *Cops* and *My Wife's Relations*. Unfortunately, Keaton does not situate Buster's latest exploits in a consistently challenging and sophisticated frame, and so *The Blacksmith* echoes the heavy-handed slapstick of Keaton's less skilled shorts. Some of the routines, in fact, feel contrived for effect. Perhaps it is only Keaton awkwardly reacquainting himself with Buster's carefree outlook before "life" became too serious.

The opening sequence is an unusual one for Keaton—a parody, in particular of Longfellow's poem "The Village Blacksmith." Keaton chooses three lines from the verse to establish the who, what, and where of his film. Fade in to the title set on a painted landscape, looking down a road bedecked by houses and chestnut trees: "UNDER A SPREADING CHESTNUT TREE THE VILLAGE SMITHY STANDS." Fade out; fade in to a real-life diorama, of Buster in long smithy apron leaning a hand on a tree trunk. With mock seriousness, he looks slowly around, swings his porkpie, and slaps it cocked on his head before dropping back into his original pose. The camera begins a slow tilt—which lasts almost seven seconds—to the top of a *palm* tree; suddenly, cut to an extreme long shot of this huge tree with a now tiny Buster at its base, and fade out. Maltin remarks, "There is something about [Buster] attempting to strike a heroic pose beneath the silliest-looking tree in California that is irresistible."[1] Besides creating an incredible sight gag with the tree, Keaton has hurled his first javelin at a venerable American hero.

Fade in to another Longfellow line and the drawing of a flexed muscular arm reaching into the frame: "AND THE MUSCLES OF HIS HAIRY ARMS ARE STRONG AS IRON BANDS." Fade out and in to a medium shot of Buster, still posed by the tree, now flexing his right arm into a huge muscle under his rolled-up sleeve. While in the Atlas stance, he casually takes a pin from his tie, pops the muscle like a balloon, and haughtily drops back onto the tree. Buster is willing to deflate his own muscle and is not just a passive character used by Keaton to parody a chosen subject; Buster actively parodies himself and presents a combination tongue-in-cheek/arrogant acknowledgment of the satire.

The last line to be poked, "AND THE CHILDREN COMING HOME FROM SCHOOL LOOK IN AT THE OPEN DOOR," is set beside a black square representing the "open door." Iris opens on exterior of the shop advertising BLACKSMITH & AUTOS REPAIRED, with a large horseshoe over the door. Framed by the doorway in middleground, Buster works the bellows with typical hand on hip, then hammers a smoky object on the anvil as school children peek in at right. The boss blacksmith (Joe Roberts) stomps into the tranquil frame, shoves the kids to the ground, then scares them out. Buster never blinks; he is more preoccupied with pumping the bellows—and lifting a frying pan with three eggs to show us that his industry is devoted to breakfast; with tongs, he holds a plate for the eggs and pulls a saltshaker from his pocket. Under Joe's angry eye, Buster casually lays the plate on the anvil and hammers it as though it were a horseshoe.

With Joe's entrance, the poetry of the opening minutes is as quickly shattered as Buster's muscle. We almost wish Keaton would continue with line-by-line tableaux of the poem because they capture in sight-gag language the essence of parody, with the lines "translated" into comic visuals. The rest of the film, however, consists of separate skits, which by the end hastily merge into a final group chase. Robinson calls *The Blacksmith* "a series of gags arising not out of a developing story situation but exploiting the comic possibilities of a particular setting."[2] The gags coincidentally resemble those of the Keaton-Arbuckle short *The Garage* (1919), which was "closer to the Keaton shorts than to any of the works with Arbuckle that preceded [it]," a sign that Keaton may have contributed much to the stylization of Arbuckle's slapstick in their collaboration.[3] But, of course, an advance over Arbuckle or even early Chaplin is not necessarily Keaton up to par.

The most obvious prop to "milk" in this setting is the horseshoe, the symbol that surfaced in *One Week* after the storm and that also appeared on Kate's back for some Irish luck. It is not meant for its fortune symbolism here (although Buster will need as much luck as he can get), but rather as a symbol of blacksmithing. Buster's rapport with horses, as in *Hard Luck*, will enable him to communicate with the animal and develop gags of a personal nature, unlike those with humans. He builds up his routines by first playing with horseshoes, then with people, *then* with the horse, which in Buster's world is working his way up the evolutionary ladder.

Buster dunks a red-hot horseshoe into a water barrel and hangs it on the narrow end of an anvil. He is diverted by curiously comparing a second horseshoe to his slapshoe but accidentally burns his sole and sticks his left foot in the water; staggering back, he steps on the hot shoe with his right foot, which he dunks; then as "third" repetition, he himself tumbles, sitting on the hot metal. With his "delayed response" trait, he thinks, then yells and turns, exposing the horseshoe outline burned into his trousers; he dunks himself in the steaming water.

Buster's next routine expands into the exterior, widening to include others who will eventually accumulate for the finale-chase. The giant horseshoe is magnetized and creates havoc for Buster as he helps Joe with work, for as they exchange anything remotely metallic, it flies up to the horseshoe before either realizes it: two sledgehammers and a wagon wheel head north when neither looks and each thinks the other has grasped it. Impatiently, Joe demands the item, only to find Buster pointing to the space where he thought he left it. Characteristic nonverbal expressions punctuate Buster's spoken replies or in fact become his only responses to the conundrum: he about-faces, stares with mute worry, lifts questioning arms. Joe responds less subtly and chokes Buster. This episode recalls a statement that Keaton made in a 1964 interview about a situation depicting Buster's favorite way of responding—silently. Keaton himself felt strongly about silence, as interviewer Gilliatt indicates: "He wouldn't want to stop anyone else using words in the cinema. It is just that he personally doesn't think you need to talk much, in life or in art or anywhere else. He said between long silences and coughing fits and stompings around the room: 'Say I'm working in a blacksmith's and I'm the blacksmith's assistant. It's perfectly natural for me to work with him for hours without saying anything.' Two minutes' pause. 'When I hit my nail, I don't *say* I hit my nail.' "[4] With a blacksmith like Joe, one would not want to say much anyway; with a blacksmith's assistant like Buster, one does not have to say anything.

A crochety old sheriff draws up to the fracas, especially when Buster pokes Joe for emphasis and the boss smacks him to the ground. The sheriff scans their incompatible height and weight and reprimands Joe as Buster nods with a martyr's look. The sheriff holds out his star as authority, and while each gazes aside, no one notices the star take off en route to the horseshoe. The sheriff pats his star, only to find a void; he draws his revolver to Joe's stomach. When each again looks away, no one sees the gun fly north. The dim-witted sheriff only sees his pointed fingers and demands the gun back. When Joe threatens, the sheriff blows a whistle for help. We expect the whistle to go the way of all metal, but ironically it does not. Rather, four deputies abandon their checker game outside the SHERIFF'S OFFICE and race over. Joe visually towers over these weaklings who land their share of punches, only to be walloped in turn. Meanwhile, Buster as innocent bystander casually looks up to find the real culprit and climbs a ladder to it. An extreme long shot records the simultaneous actions: Joe's fight below, Buster's drop from above with the accumulated metal on the group. Joe is knocked flat and the sheriff (who had been directing the fight from behind a wagon) gleefully cuffs him. As they drag him off, the group reveals Buster, sitting behind them watching.

Buster dislikes his boss, who with his brusque nature destroyed his daydream of being the legendary village blacksmith, but he has been tolerant. He might "rebel," that is, make eggs instead of horseshoes, but he rallies quickly back to duty even if he must ruin his meal. So Buster knows that as long as the brute is around, he needs to toe the line and abandon his poetic visions. But Fate's magnet, which causes trouble for Buster at first, actually curves to his benefit, and Buster uses it as a weapon in the circumstances leading to Joe's removal. Thus, Buster can perform his job like a good assistant (by climbing the ladder, he was "helping" to retrieve the lost objects for his boss) and still ensure his freedom through Joe's arrest. Now as his own boss, the way is clear for Buster to live up to the legend.

Buster inserts a "serial" gag reaffirming his expertise: he drives his nonworking pocket watch into the hot coals as he pumps the bellows. We assume he knows how to repair his watch by such drastic measures, but the solution is unresolved for the moment; this does not even seem like a gag but rather a diversionary insert just emphasizing Buster's smithy know-how. In fact, the watch will surface again to close the frame to a longer, thematically relevant routine. Enter a customer, an elegant lady in riding apparel (Virginia Fox), who disarms Buster with her aloof, upper-class charm. "MY HORSE NEEDS SHOES." Obviously smitten with her legs rather than the horse's, Buster eyes her as she walks around. But service with a smile (or deadpan), and Buster's business continues to spoof blacksmithing, even though not as deliberately as the opening scenes did. Posing as a shoe clerk, Buster questions the horse on preference and size; when he stretches his hands to indicate size, the horse nods. While sitting on a shoe clerk's box designed to measure feet, Buster measures the width of a hoof with a special slide rule. His designer merchandise is arranged along the walls in shoe boxes, and he swings a rolling ladder around the shop until he lands at the right pair. He adorns each ride back and forth on the ladder with a picturesque pose, arm and leg bent just so to dance on the air, carefree and content. Dissatisfied with the selections, the horse nods to something offscreen. In medium shot: a display case with six "latest" horseshoe models. Buster retrieves the

# The Blacksmith

Roman sandal model and fastens it to the horse's feet with all its leg straps. Buster even fetches a half-length mirror, which we cut to in medium view to see the horse scrape approvingly. Buster and horse nod in easy partnership. Were humans only as agreeable! Fade out.

Curiously, Keaton suggests time passing rather than presenting a continuous series of shots cut together. After the fade, he opens an iris on Buster brushing the horse's side facing us and powdering its nose. The time passage perhaps suggests the rapport that Buster and horse have developed as he tended to its grooming—or with the beauty salon powder-puff, its maquillage. The suggested rapport is important as it will be a direct contradiction (and a major weakness) of the lengthy routines that constitute the next sequences of the film. In a complete reversal of the detailed care and attention that he lavished on the horse as customer, Buster now cancels out his fastidiousness by demolishing his "work of art." And Buster performs it with stilted moves, as if Keaton himself knows this is entirely inconsistent with his persona's nature, but for the gags to work, the "stage business" must be carefully blocked.

This behavior begins as Buster leads the horse to stand parallel to an old jalopy jutting diagonally into the right, and then he stands between the two. As Buster proceeds to "repair" the jalopy, he rips out parts and attempts to oil up the car with a jammed can. So engrossed with the car, Buster fails to see (or feel or hear) the catastrophe he wreaks with every turn: laying a smudged hand on the horse and imprinting a black palm on its pure white coat; squirting squiggles on the horse, then into his own face and blinding himself so that he further staggers about and stains the horse's body. With his face blackened again, Buster pats the horse, aware of its anxiety yet never looking at it and discovering his handiwork. When the elegant lady returns for the horse, Buster leads it out so that its dark side, like the moon, is turned away from us, from her, and from him; the side that is revealed is pristine white. The woman pays and casts an arrogant head-to-toe appraisal at the very dirty Buster. An exterior long shot provides a subjective view (Buster's POV) as the horse trots off, now exposing its dark side. He stares befuddled at the offscreen black steed, even looking around the smithy as if for its white twin. As the horse turns once more, Buster realizes the "double vision," although he cannot explain the reason for it until he spots his grimy hand and wipes his face.

The routine immediately recalls the bisected-face of *Neighbors*, in which the illusion is revealed either as black or white pieces or as black-

and-white. There, his bisected face was a clever disguise, making the most of a fateful paint accident to baffle and lose the arresting cop. However, here, Buster slowly realizes the horse illusion is not a bizarre trick of Fate but his carelessness on the job. Nor does the bicolor horse serve any real purpose other than first as a sight gag of Buster's self-absorbed behavior and then as a capping illusion to fool Buster. This routine neither reinforces Buster's ingenuity nor offers an attack on the usual clumsy authority figure. His self-blackening as the oblivious blacksmith ends up minimizing the care with which he groomed the horse and destroys an object of beauty for some forced slapstick routine. Buster's moves also lack the spontaneity of the black-white face in *Neighbors* and its complex development as a mind-boggling, thematically (race) curious event. Wead maintains that the racial question is again at work in *The Blacksmith*, as the elegant lady shows her disdain because Buster has become "blackened."[5] It seems more likely that her disapproval arises from his oiliness threatening her spick-and-span appearance.

The next gag "on the list" (this film appears to be a roster of blacksmith gags) enters the space that Buster deliberately leaves gaping at his side as he wipes off the last of the oil. He even stares offscreen through the space, as if anticipating what will next enter. Buster is noticeably dividing and blocking his surrounding space, consciously controlling the movements for the sole purpose of executing gags. A painfully bowlegged rider hobbles into this void, leading a dark horse behind her; Buster follows them into the background of the doorway. She demonstrates her bouncing problem vividly to him; he nods sympathetically and raises a knowing hand. Buster replaces the saddle with a large, hexagonal-shaped spring gadget from a display case marked TRY OUR SADDLE SHOCK ABSORBER and straps it on the horse. The woman pays Buster; then puzzled about how to mount such a lofty device, the woman flings split-body highkicks to reach it without success. Buster rolls the ladder beside her, and she climbs up to perch herself on the absorber. He watches with hands on hips as she bounces away on her steed. Other than the visual humor of a unique prop and the woman's gymnastics, Buster dispenses with this episode just as any blacksmith would send off another satisfied customer. The gags are minimally played out; they are randomly episodic in their presentation and execution rather than concentrated for comedic highs and lows. It seems that Keaton's strategy is to "serialize" the gags in a "to-be-continued" format so that although an audience may ask, "Where's the punch line?" the gag will have a delayed resolution. This is the pattern at work, since Buster now concludes some earlier "unfinished business": he extracts his watch from the fire, hammers and dunks it, fits it into the case, listens to it, and pockets it as good as new. He resumes bellowing and whistling, as one last update shot shows the woman bouncing on the dark horse down a road away from us. Keaton is no doubt offering vignettes that fill a blacksmith's day: repairs take time and customers must try out their merchandise. And if a gag needs to be resolved, it will be so in the appropriate hour of the "workday."

Just as Buster returned to his watch, he now returns to the jalopy. One of the "village" kids stands by the open door, armed with a giant balloon and lollipop, to watch Buster work. His legendary fame is reduced to idle curiosity on the kid's part, and Buster's desire to be adored is now replaced by a desire to be left alone. With each turn, the kid interferes: Buster pulls out a headlight with an incredibly long wire directly into where the kid stands; he asks the kid to step out of his way, tipping his hat impatiently; when he pries off a tire, the kid obstructs his view. A single look from Buster drives the kid back a few steps, but not enough. As he holds up the car with one hand, he searches for a jack, opting instead for the balloon. Incredibly, befitting a dream world and certainly one of poetic hyperbole, the balloon that he ties to the axle holds the car up. We might rationally inquire: if the balloon is so powerful, why didn't it lift the kid out of Buster's way altogether? The balloon works as a literal suspension not only of the car but of our disbelief. The kid fires a slingshot at the balloon; the jalopy drops to the floor; a plank flies up, propelling a loose tire into Buster's face as he holds it. The brat runs out as Buster fumbles to pick up the car.

This balloon recalls the earlier "ridiculous" but intriguing sight gag of the balloon muscle. The muscle gag was set in a specific parody frame, to comically distort a serious, venerable subject. Thus, with the spreading chestnut/tilting palm tree and the curious children terrorized by Joe, the balloon muscle sustains the sarcasm of the introduction. However, when the poem-as-frame is abandoned for slapstick prose about "a day in the life of a blacksmith," such a fantastic "tool" is not as easily absorbed into the new structure. Given that the film has not been incredibly realistic anyway, there is still a logic to even Buster's silliest activity; that is, magnets do attract metal; horseshoes can be stylish *and* functional; bumpy rides can be made shockproof. But the balloon jack taxes the imagination, particularly as the lightweight child has not taken off with the balloon. A dream would justify this unreality, but any remotely dreamlike visions were shattered at the beginning. The string of the balloon appears stiff and straight, as though an invisible wire leads from the car to the ceiling, suggesting outside technical assistance. Equally important, Buster does not burst this balloon (or visionary bubble) as he did his balloon muscle, but rather works with it very seriously. The kid instead bursts the balloon, not only because he is a pest but to mock Buster for believing in the impossible. Buster earlier spoofed himself with a twist of the wrist, providing a comfort zone of laughter. Now, however, he really believes in his balloon jack even though "reality" precludes such a law of nature. Keaton has not provided enough "magic" in this smithy by which we can believe it also.

Keaton inserts another view of the woman rider along the road—another segment of the serial in which no punch is made, but just progress to some ultimate goal. She does, however, serve as a directional arrow toward the white Rolls Royce that rounds a corner toward us and backs into the shop off left. A dapper driver with straw hat and cane steps out and summons Buster who wipes his hands carefully on a rag before checking out the loose bumper. He lays his rag absentmindedly on the Rolls for closer inspection; the driver hastily snaps the rag away, flicking a hankie at the spot. Buster apologizes with a gentle wipe and a pat to the whitewall tire. Just like the woman with the white horse, the driver leaves Buster with his charge. The parallels between the two "props," of course, are obvious: snooty woman and man; white horse/white car; both elegant objects juxtaposed to the old jalopy; Buster's absentminded treatment of both horse and car leading to their "destruction." In fact, Buster almost repeats the same gestures and positions with the Rolls as he did with the horse, except that now he (more consciously?) inflicts physical blows to the car because it is inanimate.

Buster chooses to work on the jalopy over the Rolls, thus showing his preference for the challenging old heap rather than the easier Rolls job. Unlike past films, Keaton now repeats a similar major comedy act within minutes of its predecessor. He has always managed to find a variety of possibilities in either staged sets or exteriors, but here he seems to have run dry. The repetition does not have the impact of the "magic three" pattern, when a gag is repeated twice quickly and the third time provides a punch. Such a gag is brief, concise, and swift, being only one gag *within* a larger routine. This, on the other hand, is a routine replayed only after the same one concludes. The method of destruction differs, but it is nonetheless predictable, as Buster works with the same materials indigenous to his setting. Hence, after another greasy hand is placed on the door of the Rolls while he studies the jalopy, Buster begins a methodical, at times senseless, step-by-step destruction of the Rolls. In order to place an oil-filled tray within easy reach, he shoves it into the back seat of the Rolls with much sloshing. He tries to hammer a bent nail straight on a loose jalopy tire but becomes conscious of the damage he might do; instead, he hammers it on the hood of the Rolls. He continues nailing on the floor and arcs his hammer over his shoulder into the Rolls window. Even when he turns to extract his stuck hammer from the window frame, he does not react with the concern he shows for the jalopy's tire. Rather, he tosses the hammer through the broken window and proceeds to get a blowtorch for the bent nail. Suddenly, he spots the palm print on the Rolls and tries to brush it away while also scalding the fender with the torch. Buster sets the blowtorch on the running board, and the flame burns off the paint as he works at removing the smudges. His short-term attention is diverted by the rope that holds the jalopy's engine; by loosening the rope, he begins to "dance" with the wildly swinging engine that rams the Rolls four times. Once he controls the engine, he lays it gently on a floor mat and dusts it carefully.

During this sequence, Buster's stilted moves to wreak unintentional havoc on the Rolls become distracting and detract from the predictable, repetitive gag. Each stoop, each laying of a hand on the white body, each ignorant smudge or bang seems contrived. Of course, there is a conscious contrivance to every act on Buster's part; except for unforeseen mishaps and improvisation, Keaton entered each scene cognizant of what he must do to play his props and characters in a routine. But his gestures then became so natural that he seemed to experience this "unknown" as if for the first time. In the horse and car sequences of *The Blacksmith*, Buster seems to think aloud: Now I'll place my hand on the car door just so and bend this way to reach it while looking at the jalopy—even though I'm not supposed to realize what I'm doing. His awkwardness overshadows all other business and becomes obtrusive and unnecessary as he twists his body in an overly complicated fashion. Keaton's obvious objective is to mark up the horse/car, and all movements in this limited space must be directed (indirectly) to those two objects. Perhaps Keaton is even trying to suggest Buster's woebegone fate: that as soon as he does one good thing (clean the smudge), another worse situation (torching the paint) occurs. But Fate is not smudging the paint or wielding the torch; these are all Buster's careless, perhaps even confused, choices. His movements are

# The Blacksmith

unconvincing because of their deliberation. Buster is overconscious in aiming the oil can at the horse or misaiming the hammer. It is hard to believe that Buster, even in concentrated oblivion, would not turn to see what is catching the hammer; or that when he finally discovers the problem, he only reacts listlessly and moves on to other business. The earlier magnet scene was similarly restricted in that everyone's moves required a fixed position directly below the horseshoe with measured projections of each metal object so that they could "drift" up to it. Yet with the flurry of activity in the fight scene and each party's intense reactions before and after an object disappeared, we noticed the deliberate positioning less and could accept it more easily. That routine was encased in a logical, although silly, rationale. Here, Buster's premise is senseless even at his most absentminded. Given his graceful choreography of falling walls, ghost traffic, human machines, and racing Indian tribes, these routines pale by contrast.

Keaton himself reflects on another problem with the destruction of the Rolls Royce and the painting of the white horse. When Keaton's staff had to determine the fate of the ocean liner in *The Navigator*, they thought of sinking the ship. Keaton recalled *The Blacksmith* to them as his rationale for not doing such a radical act: "Sink her? 'I'll say not. No, it's not the money.' He reminded them of the Rolls Royce he had beat up in *The Blacksmith* only two years before. The scene, considered surefire, had met a cold, hostile silence. 'You guys remember *that* dud,' he said. 'If we sink a beautiful ocean liner, they'll hiss. You could do it in a tragedy, where it's serious, or in out-and-out farce, where it doesn't *really* happen, but you can't do it in comedy like that. Those same people who wished *they* had a Rolls would be wishing they could inherit a liner just like I had, or even just a trip on one.'"[6] Keaton's reasoning is similar to that of W. C. Fields, who wrote in 1924: "You usually can't get a laugh out of damaging anything valuable. When you kick a silk hat, it must be dilapidated; when you wreck a car, bang it up a little before you bring it on the scene."[7]

The battered jalopy hardly gets a dent compared with the treatment of the horse and the Rolls. Ironically, as Buster lands yet another blow on either body, he takes every precaution to preserve the heap, carefully brushing at each mark and transferring it instead to its counterpart. Our discomfort with the gag may indeed lie with the destruction of such an elegant object; Kerr even likened the destruction of art (as the Man O'War statue in *The Goat*) to a tragic death. But Man O'War was not a finished sculpture, only a clay model already sagging before Buster even sat on it.

244

# The Blacksmith

The Rolls and the horse, however, arrive in pristine beauty; to mar that for comedy comes close to a crime. Coupled with Buster's stilted movements and his oblivious destruction, the horse/Rolls routines slow the film and lose comic potential. It is unfortunate that Keaton chose to include two such similar, weak routines in the same film.

The most interesting aspect of these routines is Keaton's shooting of them. He will often angle our perspective into the scene so that we focus most on the object being attacked, usually the largest element in the background of the composition. Usually, Buster stands between the jalopy and the horse/Rolls, thus mastering the job from a pivotal central position while at the same time being trapped between them. He is trapped in essence by the damage that he creates, and this is crucial to the final chase in which all the parties he has offended by his "incompetence" will seek revenge. Buster's fixing/damaging business would become even more stifling in its long duration were it not for the layered look of shots that move us more into the action than would a straight-on perspective. Keaton's usual lineup is: jalopy in foreground, Buster in middleground, and horse or Rolls in background, all shot from an angled perspective. Interestingly, the horse routine has the following layered composition:

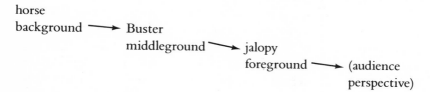

while the Rolls routine becomes its mirror image:

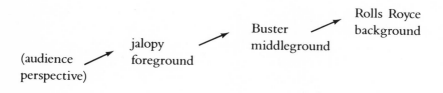

But again, Buster's business in these curiously composed shots does little to convince or surprise us, as he is not as much trapped by these "nemeses" as he is thwarted by his own overconscious movements.

Suddenly, Keaton cuts to a trucking shot of the shock-absorbed

**245**

woman stomping toward us with murder in her eye and a large branch in her hand. Cut to the smithy entrance as her horse enters riderless and steps before Buster. In a delightful medium shot that breaks the shallow dark setting, we view Buster's head staring dumbfoundedly at us through the absorber, its hexagon shape framing him. He warily looks out of the corners of his eyes, lays down his hammer and apron, dons his jacket, and leaves. As he heads out, however, he shuts off the still-flaming blowtorch, never noticing (or caring to notice) its devastation on the car. When Joe returns to survey the damage, he and Buster begin an interior chase that further utilizes the props already animated. Upon seeing Joe, Buster reacts in an unusual manner: his porkpie flips into the air and lands on his head. This is another remarkable antigravity feat, like the balloon jack, that carries the idea of the ridiculous to the extreme. Yet because the porkpie is Buster, his identity and self-expression, it is an odd but sweet addition to his nonverbal vocabulary.

Trapped *and* protected by the Rolls from Joe, Buster tries to slip away but instead begins a roundabout, back-forth series of steps to avoid flung hammers (they crash through the windows) and the engine-on-a-rope (it lands on the Rolls, of course). Joe begins a furious attack, using a Rolls door, but Buster nonchalantly steps out of the car through the other door. With echoes of the falling wall in *One Week*, Joe swings the door at Buster but fits the open window frame over his body to the floor; he simply walks out of it as Joe falls on his face. Buster secures the rope hook to Joe's belt and yanks him up to the overhead beams. Buster calls the horse over and aligns him deliberately under Joe before he begins to cut the rope with a knife. Buster's excessive torture of Joe is puzzling, especially as he could simply leave him dangling after all the trouble of hoisting him up. He also forgets the impact that the horse will receive when Joe comes crashing down. In a destructive bent, Buster stabs at the rope with almost devilish delight, parting the frays as if sharpening the knife on a strop, and lands the decisive blow. Overhead, however, Joe has moved along the beam and drops not on the horse, but on the Rolls. Buster turns to leave; by now, the Rolls owner has returned along with the stomping woman. No amount of hiding behind furnace or doors will postpone Buster's fate—nor should it, given his peculiarly careless attitude toward work and property.

The chase continues outside now that most of Buster's principal opponents have converged at the site. Joe, dapper driver, and stomping woman are all revved up by their desire to hurt Buster. He meanwhile flees in the horse and wagon that was parked outside all the while. The horse takes off, pulling Buster alone on his stomach over rolling country. As the horse veers, Buster skids and tumbles into railroad tracks; his shoe catches in a split rail and he cannot extricate it.

Keaton reintroduces the final pivotal character—the first customer who is now the last one to reenter Buster's life for better or worse. She has driven up to her estate, but her rich parents discover the black-white sides of her noble steed and the mother faints, agitating the horse into a bolt. Buster, suffering from incredible oblivion, does not notice the on-rushing train that roars toward us as he bends toward us also, fumbling with his shoe. The train screeches to a halt right behind him. We switch to a frontal view to see just how few inches from his posterior the train actually braked. As the engineers approach him, Buster suddenly glances up, around, behind, and leaps out of his shoe. He races into a road just as the horse rams into him; he staggers from the impact into a haystack with the woman conveniently in his arms.

It has taken a chase with its usual domino effect and rigorous physical exertions to bring out the best in Buster. Now he stumbles flexibly into traps or tumbles instinctively in and out of danger. His responses are natural and secure because he is self-preserving in his flights from the enemy. He is in a familiar mode again, not the mindset of careless destruction that is antithetical to his nature. Now in a potentially romantic haystack setting with a woman who has captivated him, Buster abandons all pretense of being a professional blacksmith and works his charm at his favorite role: young lover. He fans her with her hat, and she, astounded at being saved, bashfully slips him money as a reward. He looks her up and down, perhaps remembering her attitude earlier, and hurls the money into the hay. She shakes her head and leaves Buster to pause slightly before he leaps into the hay after the money. When he finds it, he retrieves his love, spots a diamond ring on her right hand, and moves it over to the left. Noticing also that the train is about to leave, he pulls her to it, but she stops him in his literal tracks.

Keaton makes the most of a set again, although it has been somewhat purposely concocted for a specific outcome. There is no obvious reason to expand into a train sequence when the setting is a blacksmith shop. But Keaton likes trains, and such a setting frees him from the dark interiors that so limited him to the point of repeating a routine nearly "verbatim." Now Keaton will use a train to carry his hero to a new life, away from the constraints that shackled him to an unnatural existence. The train setting allows Buster to dispense with his annoying followers for good: as he and his fiancée debate, the small angry mob (now including the wagon owner) stealthily draw up the rear. Buster casually takes hold of a rope as he speaks, accidentally pulls it in a gesture, and releases gallons of water on the unsuspecting pursuers. An extreme long shot reveals the opened engine-watering spout. Buster lifts woman up to the departing train and is dragged after it before leaping in himself. The four scowl as the train rolls away from us, with Buster and woman waving goodbye.

The seemingly pat happy ending has a tag resolution that for Keaton usually epitomizes the best of a film that suffers from numerous flaws. This happened in *The Haunted House* with the dream tag and, to a lesser degree, with the last capping shot of *My Wife's Relations*, also another train denouement. Now with a fade-in, a title: MANY A HONEYMOON EXPRESS HAS ENDED THUSLY, wise words set against a sketch of a train landscape (bringing full circle the opening picture/title tableaux). Fade out, iris opens partially on elevated tracks above a small town. A train rolls in from right to left center and abruptly falls over into the town. Pause, and Buster in a robe and pipe enters the irised shot from behind the tracks to upright the cars. As he winds the toy engine, he speaks offscreen. The woman in the next shot lays a baby in the crib; Buster walks straight toward us and yawns. Upon hitting front center, he reaches up and pulls down a surprise window shade on which is printed THE END.

Keaton gives a double meaning to his simple title: How does the honeymoon express *really* end? In a crash, as the immediately ensuing event implies? In a placid domestic scene? Or is it both, given Keaton's acid views of marriage? Whatever Keaton's commentary on marriage is in this case, more important is what Buster does. He has left his ill-suited lifestyle behind to play with toys. His baby is not even as interested as Buster is in the train set, and after playing, it is time for bed. His genuine aptitude for blacksmithing (which was clear for "personal" business as making breakfast or fixing his watch) will now serve him well to repair his train. Free of the blacksmith environment, Buster is once again a humble persona craving a simple, playful life. Working for someone else has always crimped his style.

In both *My Wife's Relations* and *The Blacksmith*, which contain enough flaws to wonder about Keaton's focus at this time, we need to sift out those parts of the film that reaffirm Buster at his best. No film has ever been devoid of that. On the whole, *The Blacksmith* lacks the vitality and parody of the opening and closing sequences. The car and horse episodes, even the chase itself, lack Buster's usual grace, for he does not add instinctive slips, slides, or other embellishments but dives and ducks like the next guy. At special times, however, when he is left alone to "be himself," charming moments of self-expression occur: the porkpie somersault, sharpening the knife on the frayed rope, rolling along the ladder, communicating with his kindred horse. Keaton adds a few shining stars in effective composition: highlighting Buster's dread by the hexagonal frame; the long tilt of the palm tree to diminish the "legend"; the layered perspective of the otherwise endless horse/car routines; a dynamic view aimed at us followed by an objective profile view to stress the proximity of the train to Buster; juxtaposing the real train with the toy train to segue into Buster's new life; and the natural wipe of the window shade to end the film. (Kerr calls this shade another "shutout" like the hand in *One Week* or the cowcatcher scene in *The Goat*, used to intensify the experience of movie-watching.)[8]

The pièce de résistance, however, is the ending, commencing with the haystack scene; it is "a *Reader's Digest* speed denouement."[9] Buster is gallant in rejecting the girl's money but also practical at the last minute when retrieving it. He is romantic and clever in instantly finding an engagement ring. As Buster solves a private problem with his fiancée, he also manages to dispense with his professional problems—employer and customers—with the accidental pull of the water tank. Robinson finds the typical Buster persona on "home ground" at this point with his beloved toy, the locomotive.[10] With this toy comes the nicest trick (or equation) of the film: blacksmith = family man. Even with the jab at marriage implicit in the wreckage, Buster himself fixes the wreck and seems content with his quilted robe, pipe, baby, and wife (although he pays the most attention to the train). This is more than Buster was ever able to do as a blacksmith. His unhappy disillusionment at *not* being the great poetic hero only caused him to destroy the very things he should have repaired. He exposed an unnatural incompetence that belittled his character most uncomfortably, and it became evident in his movements.

Yet when Buster gives a slightly contrived yawn at the end, is he merely tired, mocking us, laughing with us, or bored with his lifestyle? Keaton is truly on home ground in this scene and, as a result, our search for the real Buster ends. We find our hero divorced from slapstick, as he should be, and leaving us once again with the silence of a two-sided coin.

## Chapter 16

# The Frozen North

## (August 1922)

Courtesy of the Museum of Modern Art/Film Stills Archive

Keaton escaped the bustle of the Talmadge household to film *The Frozen North* on location in the High Sierra (where he would also film *Our Hospitality* and the underwater sequences of *The Navigator*).[1] One reviewer stressed its wintry setting by calling *The Frozen North* "a broad burlesque on the prevailing 'snow' picture" of the time.[2] Burlesque, unadulterated parody, giant in-joke—all are apt names for this unusual short that expands the "spoofery" that

Keaton has to this point only inserted in small doses into *The Blacksmith* and *The Playhouse*. Here, he revolves the entire film around that comic form. Keaton spoofs three silent-screen contemporaries, each with easily recognizable features that became their trademarks: William S. Hart, Theda Bara, and Erich von Stroheim. A little Ben Turpin is thrown in, and because of the locale, there are echoes of *Nanook of the North*, the "father" of the film documentary. As imaginative as *The Frozen North* is, with many memorable scenes hinging on the surreal, it is a film that lacks overall consistency and energy. Above all, because Buster absorbs the idiosyncrasies of other characters into himself, the film misses the one driving force that should give it depth and anchorage: the "little man" figure against the world.

LAST STOP ON THE SUBWAY. An iris opens on a subway kiosk in the middle of snow country. Buster, in knee-high boots, long fur coat, and porkpie punched out to look like a Mountie's hat with a string tie, swaggers out boldly to center foreground. He pauses and turns, revealing (in medium close-up) his socks clothespinned to a laundry line draped across his back. He continues walking toward us and out. Keaton instantly presents absurd sight gags that parody the hardy life of the outdoors law enforcer: Buster comes to work in the woods via urban transportation. Keaton also picks the silliest laundry items to adorn his back for visual amusement. He will continue to hang out and dry, so to speak, the simplest images that constitute a whole genre—in this case, Western and "Yukon" pictures—and twist their basest, most incongruous forms into sight-gag burlesques of what is otherwise serious and dramatic.

Buster approaches a saloon, the main site of "civilization" in the wilderness and the anticipated landmark of every Western. He stops short at the window and, in a reverse interior shot that frames Buster leaning on the sill, we see a man operating a roulette wheel. Suddenly Buster scratches his left palm—a superstition of impending fortune. As a variation on one of his trademarks (a self-spoof perhaps), Buster puts his hands on his holsters instead of his hips. Peripheral information is conveyed through the odd advertisement of a life-sized bandit, a bandanna over his mouth, suggesting that professional bandits USE BULL'S EYE AMMUNITION. The poster gives Buster an idea; he sets his clothesline on a snowpile and begins to cut out the bandit with a dagger.

Keaton records Buster's every move as he places the cutout at the window and juxtaposes that action to the dancing and drinking of the saloon patrons. Buster ducks behind the figure as he shouts "HANDS UP!"

In an interior long shot that directs our vision to the bandit in the window through the crowd, Buster confers with his "buddy" and swaggers in to collect guns and loot. Thus, Buster dispels his earlier image of a Yukon law officer for one of a snow rustler, even though this latter "career" was spontaneously chosen when he spied the gambling room. To be convincing, Buster yells out his plans to the bandit as everyone stands petrified. One fearless man, happily drunk, swipes at the board to find the gun is flat; he stares into the paper nozzle, then pulls the cutout in through the window. As he counts his money, Buster is slowly surrounded, visually trapped and diminished, by angry gamblers *and* his cardboard comrade. He stares, he thinks, he dumps the money on the table and pushes it away as if he cannot imagine how it got there. He tips his hat, heading for the exit; the patrons assist by pitching him headfirst out the window into the snow. He abruptly sits up, stares at the saloon, and staggers around the corner.

The best parody of the genre took place in the saloon in a gag that may well have been lost, as it is not in the version studied. According to Blesh, at Buster's order of "Hands up!" all hands rose—"even those shyly concealing ones of the famous bare-skinned calendar beauty September Morn who hung framed behind the bar. Buster had had this choice bit of pop art specially copied from the Chabas painting but with mobile arms."[3] The Yukon must be dreadfully lonely for the romantic likes of Buster, if he is the persona we remember, the thoughtful fellow struggling against the planet. His holdup, however, does not lend credence to this noble character; we keep his "little man persona" in check since this obvious satire offers a new interpretation to Buster's adventures, as the next episode demonstrates. After Buster clumps away from us through the snow, he enters one of two adjacent cabins and locks the door from within. He turns, stopping dead at what he sees: a man and woman embrace before a roaring fireplace. Buster displays an unusual burst of melodrama, as in *The Scarecrow* when he chanced upon Joe and Sybil: he presses his heart and flings an arm to the doorjamb. In close-up, Buster adds a brand-new reaction: tears stream down his deadpan. (Keaton remarks on how much trouble he had "crying" in this scene: "I could only cry from one eye. So I took my finger and moved some glycerine over to the other eye.")[4] When the couple kiss, Buster slowly pulls out his gun and fires twice. He steps between the sprawled bodies, turns them over, and does a double take. "I MADE A MISTAKE . . . THIS ISN'T MY HOUSE OR MY WIFE," he admits, glancing guiltily around. He tips his hat and tramps back out to the other cabin.

We can rest assured now that though the face is the same, the character is not Buster. Under the modified porkpie lies the spirit of the silent Western, the target of Keaton's burlesque, William S. "Two-Gun Bill" Hart. Hart became a film star and director when he was forty-nine years old, moving from the stage to work with producer Thomas H. Ince (an earlier spoof victim for Keaton in *The Playhouse*). An essay on Hart in a volume of his complete films by Koszarski describes his character's "most authentic embodiment yet of frontier virtues in the movies."[5] Disappointed by seeing a Western movie that failed to capture what he felt was the Old West, Hart embarked on a new career. "None of the impossibilities or libels on the West meant anything to [the theater manager]—it was drawing the crowds. Here the reproductions of the Old West were being seriously presented to the public—in almost a burlesque manner—and they were successful. It made me tremble to think of it. . . . I had to bend every endeavor to get a chance to make Western motion pictures."[6] Koszarski describes Hart's character and acting:

> Hart took his work in Westerns most seriously because they were ideal vehicles for the expression of his personal art. . . . The cowboy protagonist emerges as a methodologically potent mediator between wilderness and civilization. Hart brought to the melodramatic commonplace of the 'Good–Badman' role unprecedented personal charisma. His physical presence incarnated Western virtues: he was tall and lean (6′2″, 180 pounds), he wore the rumpled, bulky costume of the cowhand or prospector or faro dealer with authority and grace, he could ride and shoot pretty well. His face was a most extraordinary icon: its hard planes evoke both the wild wolf and the Puritan forefather. It was a face made for expressing the dark emotions: Hart gave portrayals of cold, murderous hatred and unbridled fury. . . . Melancholy and a certain dryly understated humor with sardonic peaks also became him. . . .
>
> Hart suffered his greatest creative problems in the expression of tender emotions. He prized their importance as a director and as a storyteller; as an actor he was limited physically and emotionally, relying more heavily on classic gestures and mise-en-scène from the stage. . . . Hart quelled too many strong feelings with blinked

tears and repressed gulps, vowed vengeance too often with a quivering clenched fist.[7]

Blesh offers a less reverent description of the Western star, calling him a "dour, horse-faced, and horsey hero," and referring to Keaton's "field day doing a takeoff on Hart's thespian peculiarities," he adds: "[Hart] was unique as a cowboy who could weep. He was the sensitive type—a kind of poet in chaps. . . . Bill Hart had cleaned up the rowdy, roistering frontier and made it fit for women and children. He virtually originated the sexless, ascetic, he-man sort of horse opera. He never kissed the girl though he always threatened to up to the last moment. . . . And, of course, he never stole."[8]

Keaton admits to doing the burlesque (including opposites of his "ascetic" behavior) of W. S. Hart, who once was fourth in popularity after Chaplin, Douglas Fairbanks, and Mary Pickford. In Keaton's words:

> As a boy [Hart] had lived on the Frontier, and he tried hard in his pictures to show the Old West as he remembered it. . . . The saloons in Hart's pictures looked like the ramshackle bars he had seen there. The people who sat laughing, playing poker, and had gunfights in them behaved like human beings, equally capable of good and evil. Bill himself played what came to be known as a good bad man.
>
> . . . If Bill didn't romanticize the Old West he sure gimmicked up his good bad man. . . . He rolled Bull Durham cigarettes with one hand. He kept his Stetson on with a leather string tied under his chin. On his gaunt eagle face this looked good. But no real cowboy ever wore one, to my knowledge. Real cowboys also didn't blaze away at human varmints with guns in both hands as Bill did on the screen. But the main thing he did in his pictures that they didn't do in real life was cry. After about 1918 there was at least one scene in which Bill broke down and unashamedly let glycerine tears roll down his thin, leathery he-man cheeks.[9]

Keaton states that he fumbled with one-handed cigarette rolling in the film, tied his hat on with a string, and carried two six-shooters, all from his first appearance in the snow. In addition, Keaton claims the supposed wife and lover "whirl around" when shot and "kerplop dead on the floor," at which Buster strides over, kicks the lover's body to the side, and is about to boot the woman when he discovers his error.[10] Keaton's main burlesque of Hart here was the crying. This scene seemed to have angered Hart most of all the burlesque mannerisms. Keaton believed that "what really got him . . . was my kidding his crying. My guess is that he knew in his heart just how fake that was. Perhaps he did it just to prove that his fans would accept anything he did on the screen. Bill did not speak to me for two years after he saw that picture."[11] Keaton could not understand Hart's reaction since he felt "you can only burlesque successes, never flops"[12] and he "judged top performers for their ability to laugh at themselves."[13]

It is surprising that Hart would have taken such offense, unless of course he could not appreciate Keaton's teasing admiration or else lacked a sense of humor. But perhaps Keaton's bad elements of his good-guy image were too bad even for Hart. Buster's lecherous behavior is a realization of a baser self that Hart would have repressed for the woman's sake. And if Hart's characters hardly stole, Buster's parody does so with ease, with trickery, and with a subtle yellow streak down his fur coat.

Offsetting such machismo is a woman driven to passionate fire for her man. Buster's wife here (Sybil Seeley, making a brief reprise as another spouse, this time spurned) runs to embrace him, hanging from his neck as he stands aloofly; he casts her aside and sits on the bed in dramatic profile. She hurries to him with outstretched arms, but he banishes her (Sybil has indeed served the full gamut of marriage with Buster, from bride to reject). Then in an odd response, puzzling for a Keaton heroine, she sighs, then screams in a vivid close-up, followed by flailing of arms and knocking a shelf from which falls a vase that flattens her before his feet. Buster breaks his statuesque pose to regard her, the shelf, and her in that order, then resumes his manly pose with hand to chin. Cut into this peculiar reaction, between her scream and knockout, is a shot of a patrolling Mountie (Freeman Wood) who runs to the door at the sound. To fool him, Buster picks up the unconscious woman and begins to dance with her to the music of a gramophone. When the Mountie queries him, Buster stops dancing, his innocent face framed by his wife's shoulder, and the Mountie leaves. Buster's "adulthood" has taken on a devious arrogance under his parody persona. His present behavior as a stereotype or caricature (reducing a human being to mere trademarks) becomes evidence of how dimensional the *real* Buster is when he is not spoofing. In contrast to the character here who is constantly subsumed by Hart, we see how genuine Buster is in such environments as *One Week* and *Cops*, when he is in no one's shadow. At such times, he exudes emotion while being deadpan; he is richly dimensional against flat backgrounds. The Buster/Hart figure turns out to be a paltry shadow of both men, a cartoon built of shallow symbols meant purely for parody.

Buster drops his wife when the Mountie leaves and angles forward, one hand on hip and the other arm straight to the wall, to look out the window. Suddenly he stares eagerly. Framed in a door across the way, with snowbanks on either side, stands a vampish lady (Bonnie Hill), hand on hip, arm on jamb, eyes on Yukon. Buster responds to this luscious sight by ripping off his vest and unfastening his tie. In this image of the alluring female, Keaton is parodying another celluloid celebrity manufactured by Hollywood as the answer to the "lady-killer" typecast forever by Valentino: her name was Theda Bara, an anagram for "Arab Death," better known as "the vamp."[14] She spelled evil and doom for any unfortunate man in her path, unlike Valentino who was more of an excuse for exotic love fantasies rather than the cause of dissipation and death. This woman's first appearance calls the vamp to mind, and her presence brings out the beast in Buster. She will eventually cause his demise, as any good spider woman should; but she does not have a "leading-role" display of her parasitic nature beyond the first show of a sensuous body. The outcome of their "affair" must instead spotlight Buster as hero and Hart impersonator, and he cannot be usurped by any other strong type, particularly by a woman. She portrays someone teetering on the brink of fidelity and fire; the vamp would not have thought twice about this.

We could also associate Keaton's burlesque of wild lover types with that of fellow comedian, the cross-eyed, mustachioed Ben Turpin, who did an outlandish spoof of Valentino's *The Shiek* in the 1923 comedy *The Shriek of Araby*.[15] Though *The Frozen North* preceded *Shriek* by a year, both comedians were heading in the same direction. Likewise, just as Elinor Glyn's novel *Three Weeks* was "fractionally" spoofed in Keaton's first short, it also served as a Turpin spoof, *Three and a Half Weeks* (1924), and included a parody of Erich von Stroheim (who will also appear in *The Frozen North*).[16] Turpin once modeled a spoof on W. S. Hart, showing how these icons of the screen, who represented the serious side of emotion, passion, and the American way, were rich grist for the spoof mill by comedians who enjoyed good-natured ribbing.

An iris opens on a long shot with the Mrs. still on the floor and Buster buttoning his dapper white jacket. With a spiffy white porkpie and a tap of his cane, he steps bootless into the snow to pay a visit to his flame.

He strolls across a long shot of a snowscape, white against white, swinging his cane with every other footstep into the deep snow. Brimming with passion, he turns his back to the camera to breathe in the far dark pines and leans on his cane—which sinks into the snow and he with it. The camera pans next as he passes six flowers growing tall in the snow; touched by the loveliness, he picks one, sniffs deeply, and walks on. Pan as he passes a sign reading KEEP OFF THE GRASS and thus takes giant strides over that snow-buried patch and exits right. Keaton has adapted for the Yukon the image of a young man in love strolling through a pastoral landscape. Buster keeps a springlike feeling in his mind; he is warmed by fiery passion and is thus impervious to snow and cold in his lighthearted walking suit. Nature too seems indifferent to the snow by poking its flowers through the icy surface. Although snow prevails, Buster still acknowledges the presence of a warmer season by treading carefully over the grass that lies somewhere beneath.

The Mountie takes leave of his mate, the vampish woman. As she closes the door, she is startled to find Buster behind it, leaning on the cane and holding out the stiff flower. He bows, also tipping the flower into a lit candle on the table, and presents the blazing bloom to her. They both stomp it out, she stepping on his foot in the process; he hops in pain, pauses, and steps on her foot in return. As the stalwart hero, he will not be "stepped on" by anyone, particularly a female. His is a macho passion, personified by the fiery flower, and he needs no help to light or extinguish his flame. His ferocity in *affaires d'amour* is clear when the Mountie returns, bumping Buster's stooped rear end with the door. The Mountie grabs his wife's coat and pushes her out, but Buster pulls his hat low and slowly bares his teeth in a snarl. The Mountie double-takes at this—as do we, seeing such an uncharacteristic facial expression, which is again the influence of the parody figure and not derived from Buster's own persona. When Buster follows them out, he slams the door behind him; a ledge of snow crashes on him, a fall anticipated both by the switch to exterior and by the ponderous ledge. After a pause and preparatory cut moving closer to the cabin, Buster breaks through, ready for action.

Beside a dogsled, a grizzly bear of a man (Joe Roberts) bows awkwardly in his heavy clothes as Buster angrily points offscreen: "AFTER THEM!" Buster repeats the order twice more, but Joe only bows in reply; when Buster threatens, Joe backs off. Joe too spoofs Buster through his obvious dim-wittedness made dimmer by the extreme cold; at the same time, his unusually meek behavior emphasizes Buster's authoritative he-man stance, giving an odd switch to their usual roles. In one last update shot, the Mountie's dogsled races toward us and around a big pine. Buster looks even more lordly as he prepares to pursue his flame across the Yukon in a variation of the usual "chase" adapted to a snow setting.

Fade, then an iris suddenly opens on Buster's mode of transport: a four-seater with windshield and engine. The modern conveniences of life in the frozen north are sight gags in themselves. They spoof Buster's character who is already a misplaced "Westerner" in north country, who must snarl his way unconscionably through trickery and bravado. The "taste of the good life" undermines the ruggedness of Buster's survival; he has always wanted an easy "out" to facing these rigors—after all, he took a subway to get here. Now we see his streamlined vehicle, equipped with a golf bag and clubs, which dangle on Joe's back (obviously serving as caddy as well as guide). The team, however, is a desperate lot, made up of retriever, whippet, boxer, dalmation, and dachshunds. As they mush, the dogs veer off, breaking from the sled that continues sliding toward us and flings Buster into the snow (the dogs, of course, head for the trees). Buster presses snow into the steaming radiator, gives a "shucks" gesture, and calls out "CAB!" A white horse leads a hansom cab and top-hatted driver directly to Buster and Joe—another vision of transplanted urban life, Buster's desires coming true at the snap of his fingers.

Great wastelands of snow are rapidly crossed now as we cut between the speeding vehicles caught up in the chase. The Mountie's sled passes by a sign reading L—LINCOLN, NEBRASKA, and they park and alight before a cabin. Meanwhile, Buster is stopped by a well-furred traffic cop for another dogsled cutting laterally across. The cab then races off to catch the attention of a vigilant motorcycle cop who records this traffic transgression on his speedometer and follows on his propeller-driven cycle. When they meet up and the cop writes a ticket, Buster secretly screws the propeller on backwards. As Buster drives off, the cop revs his cycle, but roars in reverse into an icy pond. Buster's cab next stops at a small sign reading a foreign tongue, reminiscent of *My Wife's Relations*: SEVERNT TOCNA 3 MILE JUZNEJI. Joe relates this to Buster who thoughtfully points to different directions, then scratches his head. As Buster ponders, realizing he has made a wrong turn somewhere, Joe steps up to the driver's seat, toppling the cab under his weight in a shot carefully composed to anticipate the gag by providing ample frame space on the left side. Buster flies feet over head with the cab, then stands considering with hands on hips as Joe heads off left. Clearly, Buster and Joe and their requisite pursuers (cops in any disguise) continue the perennial chase, just as if they have never left the big city. The chase must go on, relocating car or train to new terrains. As a result, the Chase is perpetuated and Keaton can develop sight gags of greater absurdity.

The following sequences postpone Buster's pursuit of the girl who, true to formula, will resurface by the end of the film. Instead, Buster yields now to some comic business that milks the setting for all it is worth. The frozen north offers a collection of props that cannot be found in any other place; although Buster easily transplants a subway to the woods with peculiar comic logic, moving an igloo onto a city street has a less convincing, hence less acceptable, justification. Perhaps because the north is more extreme and "foreign," its landmarks work less in a city, for instance, while urban life more easily fits into the north because it is "home" for us and fills us with comfortable associations. So as Buster tramps through the north, he now has the opportunity to "do as the Romans do" and partake not only of his previous lifestyle via cabs and trains but can rough it like a hardy traveler, enjoying the best of both worlds.

Buster and Joe enter an igloo through a draped doorway. The igloo is a curious home that strives to be cozy inside, with a moosehead over a woodpile, a guitar that seems to float on the white wall, and a table with a checkered cloth. Like other Keaton sets that capture a whole room within the frame, such as the Buzzard bungalow or the DAMFINO cabin, the dome of the igloo curves gracefully at the upper corners of the frame, giving not only a closed-in feeling but a beautiful composition that defines and highlights the objects within its parameters. Buster drops his gunbelt near a bearskin rug and hangs his hat on an antler, which snaps down and drops the hat when he turns away. Buster thrusts another guitar at Joe, ordering him to play so he can close his eyes dreamily at the sweet strains. He unfortunately leans too far back in his chair and crashes through the ice wall. Buster crawls back in, spots his hat on the ground, and throws a puzzled look at the moose. In such a subtle reaction, given only moments after the gag (antler dropping hat) occurred, Keaton keeps the comedy consistent and fluid; he does not let the gag happen and end but rather keeps it alive if only by Buster's delayed reaction when he discovers the unexpected afterwards. It is not often that Buster prolongs a gag with a reaction after the punch has landed.

Buster calls Joe to action; Joe steps into a pair of tennis-racket snowshoes and stomps out of the frame. At a loss for footgear, Buster removes the two guitars and slips each foot into a sound hole, crunching down the wood. His footwear offers an ingenious sight gag complemented by the comical gyrations of his arms keeping balance or his various falls, runs, staggers, and slides to follow Joe. Once again, his utilitarian nature adapts another object to an odd equation. As he plods into the long shot of Joe hacking through the icy surface beside an Eskimo fishing at his private hole, Buster pauses for one precarious second of dubious balance and falls promptly out of the guitars. He settles in for a long episode with the ice hole, including a brief repartee with the Eskimo who is pulled (literally) into the routine with his troublesome neighbor.

Buster stands mid-center of the newly hacked circle in the ice and logically steps aside, knowing the consequence of falling through; illogically, however, he decides to jump onto the circle and falls into the water. Buster emerges, flapping his long sleeves like a seal; even now, Buster translates his reaction into one befitting the arctic habitat: he "becomes" a seal when he emerges from the water. For the whole scene, Keaton maintains a frontal objective camera position, interrupted only a couple of times for detailed close-ups to clarify small business. This perspective maximizes the routine, which is based on the symmetry of the two bodies (Buster and Eskimo) sitting back to back, hunched over their respective fishing holes, absorbed in their work. They are mirror images of each other, even halves of an inkblot spread open on a folded sheet of paper. This routine is a prime example of Buster's special persona in the world, not as parody symbol but as his own man. Here, he is once more tricked by Fate, made vulnerable to the curve, beset by obstacles, alone even though with another, industrious while his efforts garner no reward, and punished although he is innocent.

Buster perches on the side of a guitar, readying to fish; all the while, the Eskimo is transfixed by his own activity, unaware of Buster. In close-up, Buster fastens bait to the end of his line and drops it into the hole. The Eskimo attaches his latest catch to the large pile of fish that is refrigerated in the water; in close-up for clarity, we see the peg that holds the pile in place fall in as well. Back to the long shot, Buster, munching on a small fish, is puzzled at a tug and reels in a big one—the Eskimo's pile of fish. He offers a baffled but grateful stare at the hole and continues. Each man resets his line and, within seconds, begins a tug-of-war between them as their hooks link beneath the water. The resulting choreographed tugging displays a surprisingly soothing visual that balances each half of the frame with its alternating actions: as Buster pulls his pole up, the Eskimo's pole drops and vice versa. The tugs get more desperate until the men stand, hearing nothing from each other, but concentrating on the enormity of their catches. With one final pull of the pole over his shoulder, Buster pulls the Eskimo into the hole; when he turns, he sees the Eskimo's legs disappear into the water. Buster hauls in the Eskimo, then casually heads off—also stepping into the Eskimo's snow-rackets on the way—as the irate fisherman hurls snowballs at Buster. One knocks his hat off and, as he stoops for it, Buster arms himself with a racket and swings some dexterous backhands at the snowballs. The Eskimo stalks toward Buster, but he brandishes the racket with a whoop. The Eskimo flees, and Buster twirls his racket with satisfaction just as a camera pan right reveals a bear behind him. Buster turns with a pause as the news sinks in and he runs off. A lone wolf jumps off a snow mound and knocks Buster to the ground.

Keaton's interest in utilizing the wide-open landscape for gag development and atmosphere is never greater than in these outdoor routines or even the interiors of the igloo. This unusual setting allows for a dreamy quality that could never be achieved in a tenement as in *Neighbors* or in any mundane locale common to most of us as the audience. The strangeness of this location, plus its endemic flora and fauna, are miles from our everyday humdrum existence. Thus, when Keaton transplants the contrivances of our daily lives into this dreamscape, the sight-gag potential intensifies immeasurably; gags seem unreal while being extremely real. Robinson claims that Keaton makes "greater use of snowscapes here" than even Chaplin would employ two years later in *The Gold Rush*.[17] The land creates a dazzling white canvas of sprawling barrenness and pine-fringed edges, against which the Eskimo, dog sled, hansom cab, igloo, lone wolf, and so on, suspend in eternity. The snow gives a sense of groundlessness, heightening all that is already bizarre and surreal, although also strangely logical. (After all, guitars are shaped like rackets, why not use them the same way? Cabs and motorcycles are fast, why not ride them here?) Keaton also uses effective pans to traverse the snowscapes, either for a punch, as in revealing the bear as the source of the Eskimo's terror, or to layer one sight gag onto another while condensing time. Thus, we pan to follow Buster sliding his cane into the snow as he walks, to the tableau with the flowers, to the tableau with the grass sign. The camera is as much of an adventurer as Buster is.

Inside the igloo again, Joe busily pushes a carpet sweeper, an irony that recalls another possible target on Keaton's hit list. Wead mentions the possibility of a spoof on *Nanook of the North*, a "primer" documentary that captured the life of the Eskimos.[18] For all its ground-breaking work by Robert Flaherty as a slice of life, "[it] was not free of charges of falsification for the purposes of color and melodrama. Nanook's igloo was often a mock-up to facilitate camerawork, and the Eskimos featured in the film were reported to be highly amused at Nanook's dramatic use of the harpoon when they themselves found a high-powered rifle much more practical."[19] Thus, these two films are linked by their obvious contrivances. Buster's igloo is certainly a mock set. His companion Eskimo is the straight man who, as Nanook's "brother," goes about his fishing but becomes the butt of a comic spoof. The igloo was a symbol of Nanook-style life upon which was superimposed all the "refinements of urban living."[20] Buster himself obviously recognizes the incongruity of such refinements, for after he studies Joe carpet-sweeping the floor of ice, he applies a swift kick to him. However, all Buster gets for questioning the oddities of this world is a painful stubbed toe.

Perhaps Buster is more annoyed at Joe's focus on housework rather than on helping him pursue his love. Suddenly, he cups his ear, harkening to a distant sound. We cut to Bonnie sweeping her doorway. All sense of distance is destroyed as Buster hears the faint whisk of her broom in what was previously established as two remote and separate locations. Buster the frontiersman has obviously acute hearing tempered by his rugged life of survival. He stoops to exit the igloo and, in matching reverse angle, steps out of it. Bonnie notices his ardor from afar and tosses her broom aside before swaying aloofly into the cabin. Befitting his he-man behavior, Buster pulls a bottle from his jacket and takes a bracing, lip-smacking swig; in close-up, the bottle of soda pop becomes obvious against the white background. Buster scrunches his face—another uncharacteristic expression that clearly indicates he is not his usual persona but an adaptation of other more facially emotive characters. Buster stalks past a puny tree semiburied outside the cabin, takes swift steps toward Bonnie's door, and slips on a snowbank; he wraps his coat around him and strides sideways into the doorway. Bonnie, playing solitaire, starts at his offscreen presence. When we finally see him darkening her doorway, his eyes bore into her as he stands immobile, snow-covered, then flings his hat across the room. Each move tries to impress, master, control. Suddenly he spots trouble outside: the Mountie heads home after gold-panning. Buster becomes an equation to save himself: he inserts his brawny arm into the bands of wood on the door that hold a log to bolt it shut. Buster braces

himself for the inevitable struggle that only his arm of steel can withstand. Keaton intercuts between exterior and interior, twice each, to increase the tension of the approaching Mountie juxtaposed to Buster's firm
stance. The Mountie opens the door, but Buster "opens" with it, his arm
merely bending at the elbow with the door hinge. As the Mountie counts
through his gold pan, Buster studies the door as an item of perplexity,
opening and closing it and scratching his head. The reason for his sure-
fire/backfire is temporarily more intriguing than either danger or passion.

The Mountie drops the pan at seeing Buster and throws his gloves on
the floor. As Bonnie hides under the staircase, Buster nonchalantly ducks
under the banister and runs upstairs. What seems like a recurring yellow
streak is in fact Buster's wavering between cowardice and bravado. Thus,
Buster evades the Mountie by climbing out the upstairs window, onto
the roof, and slipping into a deep snowpack below. Not anxious to risk
his neck for this pest, the Mountie heads downstairs. This turnaround
also provides a time lapse for Buster to hide—and he does so, imagina-
tively using what the landscape has to offer, while again demonstrating his silly habit of remaining in place when he should flee instead.
When we return outside to see Buster, we find instead a snowman with
a pointed head holding Bonnie's broom. The Mountie races past it; the
snowman turns slowly, the snow breaking apart to reveal Buster. For
once, his evasion tactic of staying put works to his advantage. Stranded
without guitar-boots, mutt-sled, or any other getaway vehicle, Buster
seems forced to be a victim of the elements and eventually of the Mountie. Rather, he has fooled the Mountie (himself a rather obtuse authority
figure for not seeing the new snowman on his lawn) and positions himself
back where he began his chase of Woman.

As he stands at the door, Buster tears off his snow-thick coat. Bonnie
has been dazzled by the snow too long, it seems, for she gradually leans
forward, wide-eyed and smiling slightly. From her point of view, we see
Buster, his ordinary self suddenly dissolving into an officer bearing a
white uniform jacket adorned with medals and a band across his chest;
he holds a riding stick and a cigarette in a holder; a military hat sits tilted
on his head as a monocle gleams in his eye. The vision puffs extravagantly
as he swings his arm with regal grace and stares arrogantly. The vision
dissolves back to Buster the ordinary, slightly hunched in his drab suit.
Pushing off the wall for momentum, Buster lands before Bonnie and
swings her around. What he lacks in appearance, he makes up in moves.

This particular target of parody is Erich von Stroheim, whose first directorial and starring vehicle was *Blind Husbands* (1919), which might well have been the source of Keaton's gag here: "The unconventional yet straightforward plot line dealt with an American doctor vacationing in the Alps with his wife. The man is a decent man, but dull, taking his marriage—and his wife—for granted. The wife, likewise an honorable person, is nevertheless sexually frustrated and thus prone to be receptive to the seductive advances of an Austrian army officer, played by Stroheim."[21] The villain naturally pays in the end for his lascivious ways. *Foolish Wives* (1921) essentially used the same plot, but it was "set this time in Monte Carlo, with an American diplomat and his bored wife [who falls] prey to the attentions of the bogus Count Karamzin, again played by Stroheim."[22]

Affected no doubt by snow blindness, Bonnie succumbs to the aloof, august Buster von Stroheim in her vision. As plain old Buster, he has no alternative but to unleash a tornado of passion because she has seen a remarkably alluring, burning coldness in his physique; Buster becomes her desire. Nonetheless, she struggles with Buster after slipping out of her short-lived delusion; he, like Stroheim, will pay for his sins, not at the hands of the husband, but those of another, nearly forgotten figure.

The film is wound up swiftly, again typically pulling all characters back into action. Joe waddles about on pliable skis that quiver with every step as the Mountie searches with hand to forehead. When they meet, there is a vivid scuffle with actual bloodshed: Joe stabs the Mountie on the arm, but he bolts and flings Joe through the air; in fluidly matched long shots, Joe plunges into a snowbank with only his skis exposed and cycling for help. The Mountie places a tourniquet on his arm and rushes back to hear his crying wife who has been tossed onto the bearskin rug. Buster meanwhile has disguised himself again, camouflaging his face while making it blatantly visible; this time, he attaches Bonnie's fur hat to his chin like a beard and carefully turns to greet the Mountie as if a cordial visitor. But the film assumes a startling reality all in a flash as the heat of passion and betrayal overwhelms the principals, for the first time in a Keaton film. The Mountie lunges at Buster with a knife; Buster pulls off the beard and blocks his adversary. There is no room for levity or comic distraction with a silly disguise; the knife is real and Buster's life is at stake. The drama of all the movies Keaton has been spoofing has finally seized control of his own comedy.

We cut to the window as Buster's estranged wife Sybil passes within its frame and looks in. She steps forward with a pistol pulled from her dress. We reverse angles to an exterior medium long shot, with Sybil's back to us. We look past her through the window to Buster, whose back is also to us as he works over the Mountie. Buster is perfectly framed, both as the central character and Sybil's target. She slowly points at his back and fires; a bullet cracks the glass; Buster stiffens; Sybil runs off as Buster turns to us in pain and surprise. We recall the earlier saloon window frame that began this film, with a remarkably different effect from the framing device in this tense sequence. In the saloon, the patrons split to the sides, directing a path of vision to the window framing the bandit, just as Buster himself was framed as he surveyed the gambling. Now in contrast to this light tone, Buster is seen through the cabin window as a bull's-eye. There is a shockingly real bullet, the glass fractures, Sybil flees guiltily but avenged, and Buster/Hart/von Stroheim drops, perhaps mortally wounded, in a haunting, breathless moment. Cut to interior as the Mountie comforts Bonnie and Buster falls face down. He rises wanly on an elbow, fist clenching with ominous jealousy. From his subjective angle, we see the Mountie holding his wife. In his close shot, Buster pulls out a pistol and aims it at them, anger rushing from his eyes. To the very last breath, Buster must be the tough guy.

Dissolve. We are in a litter-strewn movie theater. Buster in his normal apparel sits asleep among the empty chairs, the last one left. He jerks his program several times as though firing a gun. A janitor watches him amazed, then announces: "WAKE UP—THE MOVIE'S OVER." Buster looks at the janitor who points to the blank screen for verification. Buster asks again, to be sure. The title confirms it for all of us: YES, THE END.

We have been at the movies in more ways than one. In Keaton's typical layered fashion, we have watched his film product, a story about his hero's adventures; yet we have also been watching a gallery of recognizable film stars who were reduced to Buster's frame of reference, and always tempered by his persona's idiosyncracies. Above all, we finally learn that the film adventures of Buster of the Yukon are in fact a dream that Buster the Regular Guy had while he was at the movies. Thus, we have a movie-in-a-movie-in-a-movie. This complication even transcends Buster's amazing layered dream in *The Playhouse* where he was numerous stage actors. Here, Buster is as if caught between mirrors, reflecting the same scene over and over no matter where he looks—a film is a film is a film. This "special effect" will be played to the extreme in *Sherlock Jr.* where Buster dreams that he enters the movie screen to become a part of the film he was projecting before he fell asleep.

The revelation that this burlesque/parody/fantasy has only been a movie-infested dream for Buster the audience member is a welcome relief, as his dreams usually are. When they occur in Buster's life, dreams contain such grim events that they would be unbearable in "real life" (the revolt in *Convict 13*, the heaven/hell dilemma in *The Haunted House*). But because they are only nightmares, life with all its problems is a welcome antidote. Within the dream context, all that Keaton deems impossible is permitted. Thus, Buster can assume new personalities, live with bizarre contraptions that mix lifestyles on a whim, and reveal emotions and instincts that in "normal" waking hours he would bury beneath his deadpan like a squirrel hides nuts for the winter. It is winter now in the frozen north, and Buster digs up his supply, relishing the variety of expressions he can wear for the first time, like a kid with Halloween masks.

It is not easy to dismiss *The Frozen North* "as a lark," as some critics do, simply because it so vividly breaks the mold that Keaton has set up in previous films.[23] On the one hand, *The Frozen North* seems a logical progression from the vague Buster character in *My Wife's Relations* and *The Blacksmith*, in which his spirit disappears under thick slapstick. But despite the several masquerades here, we find slapstick blended rather discretely with Buster's sophisticated style. If *The Frozen North* suffers, it is because the strength of Buster's usual adventures is being pulled in different directions, with slapstick, parody, and Keaton-style comedy all vying for central position. Fortunately, each affects the other positively: the character is more slapstick because of that comic genre, but slapstick is more stylized because of the character. And both fit snugly under the umbrella of "parody," emphasizing *and* eliminating Buster, as Keaton's best ironic equations and transformations would do.

Perhaps the greatest irony in *The Frozen North* is that Keaton is not only parodying his contemporaries but is in fact parodying the parody! Because Buster as the thoughtful, pensive character is the last important character we see, we realize that he has been the mastermind of these visions. Because he *dreamed* them, the film is his unique possession. Fifteen short films later, his imagination has grown bolder; he implants a stark reality into his fantasies. We now not only witness a repertoire of expressions, from snarls to tears, that Buster performs within the constraints of his immobile face, but we also indulge in the taboo that the ending of *Cops* would not depict—actual death. We see the passion "murder" of the wrong wife and her lover, as well as Buster's fatal wounding by his spouse and his struggle to revenge. We have no choice but to zero in on his "murder" through the cabin window and then in the medium shot of his fall. But before total destruction overtakes the dreamer in his nightmare, Buster awakens. Perhaps Buster intended to change his dream-movie ending and allow iron-man Buster to survive. After all, as an avid moviegoer, he knows the excitement of the "cliffhanger." But for us, the shock of Buster's "murder," Fate's merciless retribution through Sybil for the hero's bad-good (mostly bad) ways, can only be eased by Keaton's admission that this is but a dream. Now the worst that can happen is Buster's firing his program at the janitor.

*The Frozen North* may fall short of Keaton's "best" films because it mixes together many different elements that dilute and reinterpret the Buster persona. Spoofing was Keaton's occasional treat and not his usual fare. He would always return to the essence of Buster's world, aiming to expand it in the features where his silly/serious persona would be based in sophisticated, sometimes historical narratives with dimension and definition of character.

With its shortcomings, *The Frozen North* remains a strong comment on what Keaton expects of film. What has been screened is not just a dream but a film suggesting technology and art in all its hallucinatory and illusory facets. One of the most tantalizing images of all in *The Frozen North* is the surrealistic vision of Buster wearing white against a white background. Almost like its counterpart of black-on-black magic as seen in *The Playhouse*, here all that is not-white seems to float in space against the splendor of the snow. Buster in a light-colored suit becomes no more than a ghostly outline of his former self—or perhaps an ephemeral spirit of a timeless world where flowers bloom in snow and the impossible happens with a simple wish. The power of Buster's mind to conjure up such visions is, of course, enormous. It is enough to make him ask twice for assurance that he has not been left caught in its grasp.

## Chapter 17

# Daydreams

(September 1922)

Courtesy of the Museum of Modern Art/Film Stills Archive

*Daydreams* is like an album with photographs of Buster frozen in time, a collection of scenes-with-variations from his past films. Many episodes in *Daydreams* connect to earlier films, as if Keaton is reviewing the early stages of Buster's life with the jaded eye of an older, maybe wiser man. Each image is complete in what it shows to us of a special moment, while ensemble, the photographs convey the story of a whole life. As a result, *Daydreams* is a curiously reflective work, a meditation on Buster's quest along a road he has been long traveling. As much as he seeks to conquer the world, his actual rewards are uncertain, given the vagaries of fate and his own fluctuating drive. Unlike any of Keaton's films thus far, even the gloomy *Cops*, *Daydreams* provides the most poignant view of Buster "on a bad day" (or series of bad days) when his world falls to pieces even as he wields a glue pot.

We first meet Beloved (Renee Adoree) replacing fresh daisies in a vase. Elsewhere, Buster stands dreamily plucking off daisy petals and murmuring with each; we recall *Convict 13*, with a similar moment of romantic sanity in Buster's insane chase. With the last petal, surely she-loves-me, he opens his eyes with a faraway cast. As Beloved pitches the old bunch out the window, Buster (who we discover has been outside her house all along) catches them and adds them to the few he carries. He and Beloved exchange shy kisses and hold hands under the increasingly annoyed attention of her father (Joe Keaton). Buster is up against a typically difficult situation for any young man in love: approaching his intended's father for permission to marry. Ironically, Keaton has given this role to his own father rather than to Joe Roberts, the usual father-in-law nemesis as in *Neighbors*; and so there is an unusual personal conflict in that Joe Keaton challenges the worth of his future "son"-in-law. The repartee they share here is remarkably long-winded. Cut into by reaction shots appropriate to the content of the lines, Pa-in-law presents the idealist Buster with a solution to his proposal.

(Buster)   "I'VE COME TO ASK FOR THE HAND OF YOUR DAUGHTER. I'VE THOUGHT THE MATTER OVER CAREFULLY AND I THINK I'M A SUITABLE MATCH FOR HER."

(Father slams paper down; Buster heads for door; Beloved blocks him.)

(Father)   "WELL, THERE'S JUST ONE QUESTION—CAN YOU SUPPORT HER?"

(Buster stares at floor; determined nod after a pause.)

(Buster)   "I DON'T KNOW. I'LL TEST MY ABILITY BY GOING AWAY TO THE CITY AND PERFORMING GREAT DEEDS. IF I'M NOT SUCCESSFUL, I'LL COME BACK AND SHOOT MYSELF."

# Daydreams

(Father nods.)

(Father)     "VERY WELL. I'LL LEND YOU MY REVOLVER."

Possibly these titles were rewritten over time by those who found the film in various phases of nitrate deterioration (*Daydreams* was especially damaged and even considered "lost" altogether for years). Buster's excessive verbiage may well be a casualty of this rewriting process. His persona speaks at atypical awkward length, without pun, punch, or jibe. Buster's responses are juxtaposed with the snappy, pointed retorts of the father; as a result, Buster sounds wishful but insecure. He seems uncomfortable in the role he has selected for himself as Beloved's future spouse. His main concern is a fantasy proposal; his main occupation is petal-picking, not a salaried job. When *he* is popped the question by the practical father, Buster's only reply is an unconvincing "I DON'T KNOW." His plan to make it big in the big city seems more a last resort than a personal choice. Buster is now distracted from his pursuit of love by life itself, by the reality of paying bills (and getting the job to do so). He does not trust his own abilities, for by announcing "I DON'T KNOW," he invites failure. With failure, however, comes severe punishment, which Buster volunteers and accepts as his fate, and which the father heartily endorses. Buster has revealed more about himself than he realizes: he shows how "conditioned" he has become to failure. His speech and gestures lack conviction and belie self-doubt. Ironically, Keaton himself set these facets into his persona in order to play out a comedy contingent on Buster's failures. How will Buster live up to his agreement to shoot himself? By failing, pure and simple. On the other hand, Buster could be a success and win the girl, despite the father's disdain. But the comic promise to "COME BACK AND SHOOT MYSELF" is too strong to ignore or reverse now that it has been announced. It becomes an expectation of the end, and in order to fulfill that, Buster must fail.

Though slightly buoyed by the semi-approval of his marriage, Buster leaves the house already courting danger. He walks out backward as he flings a kiss to the girl. A reflection of an approaching car appears in the glass of the door; the car materializes moments later, whizzing by laterally and knocking Buster off his feet. As exhaust envelopes him, he falls into a bush. Fade. In this intriguing layered composition (which Wead calls the "very complex spatio-temporal play" of Buster's backward steps across planes, and time lapse between reflected and real vehicle), Keaton recalls the depth-of-frame issues that he treated on grand scale in *The Paleface* and *Cops*.[1] Moreover, the composition nonverbally depicts Buster's entrapment with every step he takes, the real and reflected threats to his well-being. His preoccupation with measuring his self-worth by deeds is obstructing his otherwise alert attention to details. In the past, Buster has always been overwhelmed by Fate's gambling with his life from some far-off Mount Olympus. But this time, Buster seems to be throwing snake-eyes with his own pair of loaded dice.

The remaining film, except for the very ending, is Buster's journey on a search for success. His activities will replay many experiences he has already faced but that were far more determined and self-assured. Perhaps Buster has been once too often forced to measure his plaintive wish for love with the slide rule of business. For Buster, love and business are incompatible bedfellows. His emotional life tends to oppose his utilitarian nature, especially when one is contingent upon the other. Left to his own devices, Buster as his own boss masters all that he sets his mind to; but given an ultimatum by a Significant Other, his nature splits into two opposing camps, with nary a twain between them.

In *Daydreams*, Buster's test of marital worth occurs in three separate occupations, each trying to tap unique latent talents. The outcomes, however, indicate Buster's lack of talent for anything but chaos and incompetence. Buster writes optimistic updates to Beloved with every new venture. His letters introducing the major job sequences of the film form "chapters," similar to *One Week*'s calendar and *The Boat*'s nautical logs. Each new chapter is prefaced by a pastoral scene that captures the contemplative girl in the country reading excerpts from Buster's missives. The series of letters is introduced by an objective title: SOME WEEKS LATER THE FIRST LETTER ARRIVED. Fade in to the girl in a rocking chair beside a roaring fireplace. Buster's note in close-up: MY DARLING, I'M NOW HEAD OF A BIG SANATORIUM LOOKING AFTER 200 PATIENTS. I'VE GOT OPERATIONS TO DO THAT YOU JUST COULDN'T IMAGINE. She rests her head on the back of the chair, dreaming of being a doctor's wife. Fade out.

Each fade serves as a pivotal pause between "daydream" and "reality." This discrepancy lying "between the lines" of Buster's epistle now fades into view. We see a large shut iron gate of the DR. RICHARD M. SCOTT DOG AND CAT HOSPITAL, as the sign over the entrance reads; a small dog lies outside awaiting admission. The gates open (Buster "operates" them from inside) and he follows the dog in. This could be a good job for Buster because of his affinity with animals, as in *Hard Luck* and *The*

# Daydreams

*Blacksmith*. Keaton briefly introduces some of Buster's "patients": after a view of a long row of kennel cages, we see a mutt and her puppies, a St. Bernard beside a wild-eyed Pomeranian, and a dachshund with four wheels strapped to its belly to roll itself along. In this chapter, we watch Buster exact his "incompetence" through sophisticated and slapstick performances. But the question always arises: just how much is his incompetence regulated by Fate's gleeful interference? With the canine lead of this sequence, we recall Luke of *The Scarecrow*, who was both victim and instigator of Fate's plan to torment Buster with a "rabid" dog. Although there is no elaborate chase here, Buster is the pawn again in the following fateful trick that brings two natural enemies (cat and dog) together, with him in the middle.

In the animal examining room, Buster loads a cat into a straw basket that sits in the middle of the floor. Although he secures the lid, the bottom of the basket and the cat remain on the floor when he carries it away (recalling *Cops* when Buster's trick trunk exposed him after being lifted). A dog lying nearby approaches the hissing, arched-back feline. Meanwhile, a skinny goateed doctor reprimands Buster for the empty basket. Buster offers sublime stares and a lovely view of his puzzled face framed by the bottomless oval basket as he holds it up for inspection. Buster acts a little illogically, no doubt because he cannot believe his hard luck; he shakes the basket, checking every inch for signs of the cat. His meticulous search is more desperate because deep down he knows his job hangs by a wisp with every wrong move.

As the dog and cat follow each other out through panels in the front door, the doctor demands that Buster find the feline. Buster flings the basket, which bounces against the doctor, who in turn hurls it impatiently and shoos him out. If Buster's carelessness is already threatening his job, his apparent insubordination will equally damage his chances. His odd response seems to arise from much pent-up frustration broiling inside too long. Outdoors, Buster sees the dog staring at a barrel that turns and shakes on its side. By association, Buster believes it to hold the cat. Tucking the dog under his arm, Buster gropes blindly into the barrel—and extracts a skunk. He scolds the chagrined dog as he dangles the skunk by its tail, then reenters the building. Fade out, fade in. Buster backs out the door in a long robe and bare feet, turning to reveal that he carries his well-skunked clothes at arm's length. He seizes a shovel previously set by the door and begins digging a hole in the center of the frame. We cut to the same angled view of the door through which Buster came; now the dog exits, sheepishly carrying its collar in its teeth and joining Buster at the hole. After a pause, the dog drops in the collar. Fade out as Buster mutters while he digs.

The two understand each other very well; both have been victims of misunderstanding (so the cat *wasn't* in the barrel), but Buster naturally is more upset since the dog had time to discern the different odors and not make a mistake. Yet both are gullible creatures and both have failed to handle their respective jobs. In addition, Buster has been undermined by his own "patients," a cruel disappointment since his camaraderie with animals has been genuine. All the while, beneath the misunderstanding is Fate, chuckling as it pours salt in the wound; Fate exaggerates Buster's "incompetence" with the cat by tossing in a circumstantial skunk to further mock him. We can imagine that during the fade-out/fade-in (Buster and boss conferring behind closed doors), our hero was rapidly stripped not only of his offending suit but of his job as well.

Buster is now faced with explaining the job change to his Beloved. When the next chapter opens, she has received another letter, which she reads while leaning against a country fence with a shepherd dog at her side. Excerpt: DUE TO A SLIGHT MISHAP I'VE HAD TO GIVE UP MY OPERATING. I'M NOW GOING BY CAR ROUND THE STOCK EXCHANGE DISTRICT DOING A BIT OF CLEANING UP. I FREQUENTLY MEET UP WITH DISTINGUISHED FINANCIERS. Beloved adapts: if not a doctor's wife, surely a stockbroker's. She pats the dog and gazes into the mountains. Fade out.

Every communication from Buster tries to be hopeful, to say the truth while doctoring the reality. As each job is played out, we realize that the daydreams do not belong to Buster at all; they have been neither initiated nor designed by him. Overblowing the truth makes it harder for Buster to fulfill the demands of the job and the daydreams that Beloved conjures in her cozy environment. She is always seen contemplating the future, as if in an ivory tower of some distant castle. She is encouraged by words that conceal while they also reveal. But Beloved has not mastered the art of reading-between-lines, for she has not been exposed to a life of dualities as Buster has. He must paint a pleasing picture for her (and her father) in order to achieve the sole daydream that he cherishes: having someone to love for the rest of his life. Thus Buster struggles through half-truths to save face, to boost his ego, to keep his character intact by convincing himself with guarded words that there are good reasons for moving on and up. Still he knows, with his dual mindset, that her daydreams will only become his nightmares.

# Daydreams

Buster's next job, "cleaning up" round the Stock Exchange, is just that: he now wears a white sanitation uniform and helmet and pushes his "car," a wheeled trash can, toward a clump of dirt. By hiring Buster for such a menial and unchallenging job, Fate has the opportunity to torture him further with the curve and make his duties even more unpleasant. As he sweeps up the dirt, a coal wagon passes alongside, spilling a trail of dark cargo and running over his broom handle to boot. Buster stares at the lane of coal and throws his shovel so exasperatedly hard into the can that (as we see in close-up) the bottom breaks out, dropping its contents in a puff of dust. Buster proceeds to sweep up the debris a little at a time across the length of the frame; with each dump of waste into the can, Buster creates yet another pile that he must pick up later. When he looks back over the distance he has just swept and discovers new heaps of refuse, he stares at them with hands on hips and simply starts over.

Buster is the modern Sisyphus here, rolling his garbage can back and forth just as the star-crossed Greek rolled his rock. Perhaps neither one ever fully understands why his best efforts are so eternally taunted by the gods. Buster does not seem to question his fate or think it through for a logical answer; he must simply return to square one and try again. He fails to notice that the round metal disk that he collects with the trash is the bottom of his can; he merely throws that into the bottomless receptacle as well. By now, Buster too readily accepts the curves of his life and does not even see that some of his self-defeating tasks are "man-made." He is sadly oblivious to the solutions of his problems and continues to generate more problems by this oblivion. Case in point: he overlooks that he has parked the can over an open manhole, a fact that we see clearly when Buster moves the can and a begrimed worker suddenly arises. Even though Buster positioned the can precisely over the gaping space and dexterously avoided falling into it himself, he acts as if it is all news to him. The angry worker punches Buster flat to the ground; in the time it takes him to stand, his assailant vanishes into the earth and Buster is amazed to find no one around. As he ambles about seeking an explanation, he steps into the manhole, further enraging this nether god. Buster's attitude is a little disdainful (probably tired of taking the blame for things beyond his control), and he waves his broom toughly. The worker hurls a rock and Buster swings his broom, but for all his revenge, he spins twice on one toe and crashes onto his back.

Buster is remarkably less tolerant than he used to be. Although he still stares or shrugs habitually, he is now quick to rebel, to be angry, to swipe with his broom in self-defense. Buster is growing exceedingly impatient at what he must put up with. His "death" in *Cops* and his unhappy association with his "wife's" relations have so darkened his view that even a small rock is a violation of his spirit; in better days, Buster would have been happy to start a "ball game" with his opponent. Buster has too often been humiliated and fallen onto his back like an overturned turtle; his sacrificial-lamb skin becomes more threadbare as it passes through the machinery of experience. But rather than give up and die, Buster chooses to express his annoyance, regardless of consequence.

Fate regards his belligerent attitude as reason to further punish him. Buster is no longer the silent toy in a large game; when he snaps and resists, he isn't as much fun to play with. As he resumes cleaning up the little piles he has inadvertently created, Buster must pay for his attitude in an appropriate way. The source of Buster's next trouble comes from a confetti-spewing crowd and bandwagon rolling along Main Street, campaigning for their man (Joe Roberts); as the posters say, WE WANT J. O. GRADY ALDERMAN 3RD WARD. We cut back to the placid street to which Buster gives his final touches. Suddenly, small flurries of paper flutter into the shot, followed within seconds by streamers and clumps of confetti. Buster sees this latest enemy and reacts in a new but understandable manner: he angrily points to the mess, as if reasoning with it while accusing it of thoughtless behavior. Grady also hears the offscreen harangue as he speaks to his constituents but ignores Buster like a true politician. We continue to intercut between Grady and Buster to compare the effects of one action on the other. Buster's shots are filled with his mounting fury as he struggles with the widespread litter. Streamers attack his head and he fights them as he would an octopus that grabs him with its tentacles. Grady orates to the enthusiastic crowd, marking a time lapse for more paperwork to accumulate around Buster. As Buster diligently resumes sweeping, a gale of confetti and streamers blows against him, knocking him flat. As Grady speechifies, a storm of paper also swirls around him (perhaps Keaton is commenting on the "paperwork" and red tape that politicians generate with all talk, no action).

Back to Buster who has a solution of dubious logic that acknowledges how he has been driven to desperation and must fight fire with fire: he lights a heap of paper with a match. The conflagration rapidly spreads, especially as Buster industriously adds more paper to the pile. The bandwagon ignites. Cut to Buster, who has somewhere found a fire hose and is high-stepping with it as it flaps recklessly with the powerful water.

# Daydreams

Like the storm in *One Week*, all the pivotal players of the sequence merge at the climax: the sewer worker reappears, and sprays of water from Buster offscreen burst into the shots of Grady and the hapless bandwagon musicians. Buster continues to man the hose in his separate shots, still at a distance while his "handiwork" shoots directly into every shot of Grady. Reminiscent of the flood in *The Playhouse*, a bass drum becomes a weapon in this deluge: Grady throws it at Buster (still offscreen), but a blast of water drives it out of Buster's shot and back into Grady's shot. Meanwhile, Buster takes refuge behind the toppled trash can, aiming the hose through the cylinder. Grady sneaks up behind Buster, closing in on him visually and hitting him on the head with a rock. As the hose snakes wildly, Grady hauls Buster over to the manhole now brimming with water. Buster hangs pathetically limp in Grady's huge arms. The band clusters around their man, who asks for a democratic vote: unanimous, thumbs down. Buster only stares front, beaten and broken, as he is dropped into the open manhole. Fade out. Ironically, in "cleaning up," Buster opened the door (or manhole) to his own (mis)fortune.

Buster now has two strikes against him, with a third foreboding one presumably not far behind. The predictable "magic three" principle is at work again, this time presenting three long scenarios instead of three quick gags. The final outcome for Buster is now a punch that knocks him out rather than gives him an upper hand over his opponents. Each knockout reinforces Buster's words of doom at the start, that even his best shot will end in failure. Buster cannot seem to find a career niche that uses his talents wisely. In other films as well, Buster's job skills were sorely limited and often caused his own trouble: bank teller (*The Haunted House*), sharpshooter (*The High Sign*), sea captain (*The Boat*), stagehand (*The Playhouse*), businessman (*Cops*), artist (*My Wife's Relations*), and village smithy (*The Blacksmith*). It appears that Buster's aptitudes for the job become misplaced the minute things go awry. He has thwarted himself on occasion, to be sure, but more often than not, he *is* thwarted and desperate because of on-the-job mishaps. Pressure, like a runaway horse, makes Buster lose control of his skills. When unpressured and left to his own devices, however, Buster approaches each challenge creatively, quietly relishing invention as he does his duty (the mechanical house in *The Scarecrow* is the perfect example of Buster as his own boss having fun at work). Although being a sanitation man clashes with his artistic sensibilities, Buster and job have an oddly appropriate fit. He wields his broom and trash can like a Roman on his chariot, preparing for a battle ride into glory. Buster may not be content sweeping up, but he is un-threatened and alone with his reveries, for each wave of the broom sweeps him closer to Beloved. According to the "reality" he describes in his letters home, he regards his jobs (for *her* sake) as successful and lucrative. In his most poignant equation yet, Buster turns a mundane job into a proud profession. His eyes read "between the lines"; by convincing Beloved, he hopes to convince himself too. His greatest aptitude, then, is turning the ordinary into the sublime, if only in his heart.

Still, sixteen film-lives later, whenever his efforts are mocked by a power beyond his control, Buster's first response now is to feel crushed. His reward depends on the smooth operation of his duties, and that is simply not happening. Buster's exhaustion at sidestepping catastrophe is clear in his next letter. Beloved reads while standing beside her sad-dled horse: "I'M TIRED OF CLEANING UP," the letter announces in close-up. "Tired" is a pivotal word: Buster gives the impression of being sated and bored, tired as on the level of the idle rich, and ready for more stimulating success. Deep down, he knows that his real tiredness is of the struggle in every job he tries. He describes his next opportunity: "I'M BACK AT MY ARTISTIC GIFT, AND TODAY I'M MAKING MY DEBUT IN SHAKESPEARE'S HAMLET." By way of explaining his job choices, Buster makes a surprising reference to his "gift" in the artistic arena. We remember his aborted foray into "sculpture" in *My Wife's Relations*, and wonder if he too remembers it when he writes "I'M BACK." In *Daydreams*, like a survey of his life, Buster retries the major career avenues he has stumbled onto in earlier films—as if this is his final chance to succeed in big-business, blue-collar, or artistic enterprises. Buster propels himself toward any setting, appropriate for him or not. Life has become a revolving door, and he will gladly step into any slot if only it will stop spinning long enough for him to enter.

We gain more insight into Beloved's perception of the "truth" of Buster's letters. As she absorbs the message, her daydream manifests before our eyes: dissolve to Buster in Shakespearean garb, a sword at his side, bowing with Yorick's skull in hand. In an extreme long shot that graphically encompasses the success of Buster's soliloquy, we see this deadpan Hamlet dwarfed by a large stage and cheering audience. When we cut close again, Buster slips through the curtain, but returns to encore with Yorick. Dissolve back to the girl, who continues to daydream.

Meanwhile, Reality. Keaton presents extremes to illustrate the utter irony (and ultimate tragedy) of Buster's life in this film. From Beloved's vision of theatrical grandeur, we turn to Buster's real job: a two-bit extra in a peculiar stage show. The daydream bursts like another blacksmith's balloon-muscle, and we share the disappointment with Buster. Far from the scrutiny of Beloved's rose-colored glasses, Buster bares his truths to us as audience, confessor, even therapist. *Daydreams* could have been a simple comedy: Buster trips into a typical madcap situation as in *The High Sign* or *The Blacksmith*, earns his keep, and finds love after a series of clever comic routines. But like *Cops*, a trap has been set for Buster in this film, too: love will only be his if he proves himself. This is not coincidence or quest but reward or punishment, win or lose. *Daydreams* and *Cops* present the reverse of a carefree existence. Buster's life becomes a cross-examination of his every flaw and weakness. His need to succeed rattles his steady hand and corrodes his resilience. Every pretty picture of Beloved taunts Buster's Reality, humiliating and minimizing himself in his own eyes. Not surprisingly, to report his progress, Buster does not telephone his girl, but writes instead. Letters help shield him from the disappointment *she* would hear in *his* voice.

Buster's theatrical venture is a jumble of classical/vaudeville/slapstick/drama/amateur talent show. Against a painted backdrop of trees, Buster is the palest and shortest in a row of Roman soldiers behind a woman in hula skirt, beads, leotard top, and Indian headdress. As the soldiers march to the star's soliloquy, Buster has severe problems keeping up: he falls, knocks off his helmet, awkwardly brandishes his spear, drops his shield, then drops the spear while lifting his fallen visor. The actress gives lethal stares at Buster before walking off. During the ruckus, Keaton also cuts offstage where a bereted director chomping on a cigar clenches his fists as a stage manager paces. We recall the clumsy Zouaves in *The Playhouse*, whom Buster commandeered with authority and elegance. Here, Buster cannot even hold onto his spear, much less follow a simple marching format. Every possible mishap—from falling visor to unlaced Roman sandals—occurs in rapid sequence, disabling the steady Buster of old. He who secured Roman sandal straps around a horse's leg in *The Blacksmith* cannot tie his own laces. He bumbles with incredible dexterity. We who know better recognize his pressure to succeed; his anxious distractions to "make it" only ensure his presentiment to fail.

Buster struggles in a last-ditch effort to salvage the show. He ducks under the lowering curtain and offers a feeble "encore" of a spear-twirling, highkicking solo dance for the baffled audience. Buster has turned comedy *and* drama into a misplaced hybrid, which neither audience and crew nor Buster himself can identify. The dreaded hook emerges from the wings to pull Buster offstage. In this film-life, Keaton allows Buster to fall victim to the hook that never once appeared in *The Playhouse* where it would have been appropriate, nor which The Three Keatons ever experienced in their vaudeville career. The hook speedily removed miserable stage acts from the sight of unsympathetic audiences; to get the hook was humiliation for a vaudevillian. Buster cannot dodge this hook and is yanked into the unwelcoming arms of the irate director, who drags him out the stage door. We cut to exterior long shot, where within seconds, Buster somersaults to a seated position, his helmet flung out after him. Coincidentally, Buster lands directly before a Constance Talmadge poster. As a peripheral in-joke, Keaton juxtaposes Buster's flop against the popularity of a movie star who specialized in comedy and was, in fact, his sister-in-law. We recall the (sub)conscious disdain Keaton felt from (and toward) his clan of in-laws, particularly the matriarch, which he tried to purge in *My Wife's Relations.* Yet by choosing this poster, as opposed to one of a more celebrated contemporary (Douglas Fairbanks, Mary Pickford, even Charlie Chaplin), Keaton emphasizes the "personal" dilemma in *Daydreams.* Near his sister-in-law, his alter ego cannot live up to her (family's) expectations as an actor, even needing forced removal. Keaton has already presented father Joe as one judge of Buster's worth. Thus, Buster (Keaton?) is surrounded by others as close as his own family who will pummel his unique talents with their arrogant evaluation.

The next sequences blend the best and most typical Buster-Cop chases of nearly every film thus far. They rehash tried-and-true formulas as well as insert variations and new angles to familiar routines. One novel twist derives from Buster's costume, which lends him an odd aspect as he walks casually yet despondently past a cop. When Buster tugs his skirt below his bare knees and fluffs it out nervously, the cop is suspiciously hesitant. As in other films, Buster's paranoia overwhelms him; he assumes guilt for an unknown crime, without defense or question. Wouldn't the cop be satisfied by the explanation that the luckless Buster has just been fired, is wearing his former "work clothes," and doesn't know what to do next? The cop is not expected to be sympathetic; cops are only animated figures used to propel chases and offer chaos to the world. Buster himself anticipates no more or less, and so the wary cop initiates a typically illogical and unnecessary chase. It *is,* of course, necessary only as an integral part of Buster's gullible psyche. After all, the physical chase represents the eternal Chase that is his destiny.

In another traffic-cop gag en route, Buster and the first cop wait at the corner, side by side yet aloof to each other, until the traffic cop signals "Go" and they resume their pursuer-pursued roles. Buster enters a distinctly ethnic neighborhood, evidenced by a chop suey and noodles restaurant and a Chinese man in a straw sunhat who balances shoulder poles with dangling baskets. The "ethnicity" is circumstantial and provides visual gags such as the collision of Buster, Chinese man, and cop. Their action remains unresolved, while Keaton cuts to another event that promises to involve Buster in some unfortunate manner. A thief steals a cash roll from the proprietor of a secondhand clothing store; when the proprietor summons a policeman, the thief slips the roll into a folded pair of pants. As the cop pushes the thief out of the frame, the camera pans the cop walking away. It pauses suddenly as the chasing cop races up to him to describe his quarry. The camera again pans, shifting the stationary cops to the right so that, on the left, we have an exclusive view of a long coat hanging on a stand—with Buster tucked inside. We have purposely been distracted and excluded visually from Buster's offscreen disguise in order to experience a smoothly evolving gag that merges the unexpected collision with the seemingly unrelated thief episode. Buster has now taken environmental disguises one step further than in previous films: no longer is there a tie-mustache or a fur stole-beard, but an entire coat hangs waiting by some predestined hand. Buster has pulled his legs up out of sight and stares blankly, like his companion mannequin, from under a turned-up brim. In such a disguise lies yet another ironic depiction of Buster's total worth: a $2.95 ticket hangs from the coat. In more ways than one, he has become a valueless mannequin.

When the baffled cops depart, we are left with the two "dummies," propped eerily against the building. The only movement—Buster's wide eyes slowly looking off left—becomes as monumental a gesture as any frame-filled crowd action. He opens the coat to reveal him kneeling on a table, then hurries over to put on trousers, jacket, and derby. Both cop and proprietor reenter the scene to prolong Buster's dilemma. Buster gulps when the proprietor extends his hand to be paid for the clothes. He looks like a patchwork quilt of all his troubles, with his Roman skirt hanging pathetically over his pants like a helpless child who cannot dress himself. Recalling past characterizations, Buster looks like a scarecrow, but without the freedom of self-expression; he is a nowhere man with lost ambitions; he is the goat again, vainly seeking comfort from a hard world. The scene also recalls *Cops*, except that now Buster is the poor guy on the curb who finds himself with cheap clothes provided by Fate.

Buster is no longer the entrepreneur deciding his business; he is the one decided upon. Sandwiched by the cop and the proprietor, Buster freezes in indecision—until he puts his hands in his pockets and unearths the thief's money roll. A moment of good fortune and Buster is cocksure again—a fatal reaction, for in giving the cop a cordial handshake, Buster walks off, leaving the cop shaking the hand of the dummy. Buster spotlights his own flaw, instigates his calamitous destiny, fails to leave well-enough alone. He has encouraged the hesitant cop to pursue him anew. We wonder about Buster's logic, concentration, and desire for freedom. Perhaps the chase, where he can outsmart his pursuers and propel his body like a sleek missile, is Buster's favorite pastime. He thinks it the true test of his talent, unlike any job could be. By now, perhaps, he has given up on career, success, girl, and love, knowing that for others he will be a failure. He may as well stick to what he does best: run.

After a slight jog, Buster's pants drop as he stands before the Hop Sing Cafe. He dashes around the corner, misdirecting the cop after him; instead, Buster steps out of the cafe, having entered an unseen side door, and retraces his path. Back at the clothing store, Buster searches eagerly through more trouser pockets. Fade out. His situation has made him anxious for any kind crumb tossed by Fate, and he hopes beyond hope that fortune will smile twice in a row. It is no coincidence that Buster tries to succeed in what is revealed as a Chinese neighborhood. For Keaton, ethnicity often signifies an impoverished setting (*My Wife's Relations* as prime example); by contrast, Beloved's elysian backdrops stress the laborious problems that Buster must face to reach her epitome. In this neighborhood, we especially wish that Buster would also find a fortune cookie that promises him happiness.

Buster's last letter to Beloved is breathless in tone and expression. FANTASTIC SUCCESS! THE CROWDS WERE SO ENTHUSIASTIC I JUST HAD TO MAKE A CLEAN GETAWAY. She rests her head against the back of her chair as a soft light reflects on her face. Elsewhere, in an extreme long shot, the enthusiastic crowd (of about twenty-five cops) chases Buster onto a deserted street and veer left. Between his search for money and his next letter home, Buster has obviously been in flight, with only spare moments to pen an update of his activities. We can almost imagine Buster scribbling a note on foot and distracting cops long enough to drop it in a mailbox. The breathlessness of the letter—meant to be read as an overwhelmed reaction to his marvelous achievements—combine with Keaton's cut to the chase-in-progress for an important effect. We find it no longer necessary to consider what Buster's career choices will be, or how his adventures lead him to be fired, or even what provokes the hostility of the cops. It is all a fait accompli. None of the details that filled the first three episodes matter anymore, for Buster has failed and struck out; he has exhausted the job market and must pay the piper.

All the great car-train-foot chases that filled the shorts till now merge in what will be the quintessential Chase of Keaton's short works. The remaining three two-reelers will have no chases in them with the dimensions of the *Daydreams* chase. Although *Cops* is considered the exemplary Keaton chase film, the physical chase here contains a remarkable image that surpasses even the rolling blue seas of *Cops*. Physically and thematically, that image encapsulates the meaning of the Chase in Buster Keaton's world. After the shattering finale of *Daydreams*, Buster in the three remaining shorts revitalizes and reaffirms his life like one who is constantly on the verge of losing it.

Certain visual designs in *Cops* and *The Goat* are replayed in Keaton's characteristic race into an isolated street, followed by a swarm of cops breaking the frame, just as the second pulse of a heartbeat immediately follows the first. Buster again runs toward something in the foreground, a person or object that demarcates his territory as he crosses through it. He now encounters trolley tracks and willingly waits for his vehicle to freedom, although cops infiltrate the rear. When the trolley crosses laterally before Buster, he snatches the back rail and snaps off the ground, his arm a spinning propeller. However, now he is lifted off his feet and flies parallel to the ground like an unfurled flag. We track along in a medium long shot, witnessing his acrobatic pose over four blocks, until he pulls himself aboard and waves farewell to the cops. Unfortunately, the trolley reaches its terminus shortly thereafter and is turned by the conductors for the return trip. Buster has settled in to read the funny papers, oblivious to the boomerang he is riding. Cops pour into the frame in a jumbled mass, watch the trolley exit, and resume pursuit. Two cops, however, have climbed aboard and tap Buster on the shoulder. Buster hands over his ticket, then realizes the truth and flips over the side as the trolley rolls dramatically toward us and out right.

Cops crisscross with Buster in nonstop spatial play. Reminiscent of both the ladder gag in *Cops* and the vertical-space play with the three-man totem pole in *Neighbors*, Buster now uses another three-story building as a major prop. He races up the long fire escape ladder of a building that faces front in an extreme long shot. As cops disappear into the building,

# Daydreams

Buster maneuvers the vertical planes of the frame by lowering himself from a third-floor window on a counterweight, pulling the ladder 45 degrees past the window. He attaches the balance line to a truck that shortly drives off, pulling the ladder (and the cops who have climbed on it) to a vertical position. With a snap of the cable, the ladder plummets into a sidewalk cellar that Buster has opened, anticipating the break. Keaton demonstrates again that Buster's best talents flare when the landscape becomes his playground. He devises a vivid interplay of dimension and direction within the frame and creates a possible/impossible world, where in one instant he pulls apart all that seems securely fastened. Controlled chaos and disaster are the only visually comic solutions to his predicament. The ladder becomes a giant weapon in a personal battle/game under Buster's command. Remarkably, only days before, Buster was incapable of holding a spear and following cues. Now free of stage audience, director, and diva, his instinctual genius rises to success. Unfortunately, his achievements here have nothing to do with business or marriage and will be overlooked by those whose approval he seeks. As in *Cops*, he outwitted the entire police force like one "in the business" for a lifetime, but none of it mattered to Woman. Thus, Buster ultimately discards his true talents for those Significant Others. *Daydreams* reflects Buster's reliance on the opinion of others, but it is also a turning-point film in his growth (or reincarnation, considering his "death" in *Cops*). His fate here pushes him to a decisive brink and will color his remaining short film-lives.

At an intersection of streets (again, Keaton's continued concern for intriguing composition of backgrounds), Buster waits for the return of the empty trolley, which rolls in left and stops. All at once, heads of cops pop up in the windows, like the guards' heads in *Convict 13* over the wall during the rock-ball game. With rare insight, the cops have fooled Buster by hiding until the last minute. The chase proceeds as cops pour out, driving Buster into the foreground; in a matching reverse shot on another street, Buster runs from foreground to background, pursued by a wave of policemen. The visuals seem to ebb and flow with the chase; they insist on the notion of endless pursuit through all dimensions.

The drama of this chase is heightened by the feat that Buster performs once he chooses between being caught and saving himself. He runs along a pier toward an offscreen goal: a ferry pulling out, as we see in long shot. Buster scratches his head and decides to run for it. Looking from a high angle as though on the upper deck of the ferry, we have a bird's-eye view

**283**

of Buster vaulting lightly over the widening gap between pier and ferry deck. We cut to stand behind Buster—another shot of his back—to emphasize his distance from us. Again, he masters the elements, assumes control of his fate, revels privately in victory. He proudly salutes and bows to the cops on the pier, receding as the ferry steams off. As he did often in *The Boat*, Keaton switches us to a crucial profile perspective that reveals subtle information reversing Buster's good luck in the blink of an eye. The movement of the background landscape stops suddenly in its seabound direction, only to glide back over the same route—back to the pier. This fateful switch is confirmed by the presence of a passenger in this profile shot with Buster. He is not just any passenger; he is a worker on board surveying the docking of the ferry as it pulls in. Thus he reinforces the irony of Buster's escape. Nonetheless, Buster blindly lights up a leisure-time cigarette. As the grumbling cops leave the pier, a clever one peers back to see the worker heaving a rope over the side. The chase resumes immediately, with cops pouring into the ferry. Still unaware of the shifting background and land ahoy, Buster randomly peers over his shoulder to discover the terrible equation of this moment: ferry pulling out = ferry docking. Buster has again been misinformed, arriving too late to know that he was jumping onto a returning ferry. Another plan is destroyed beyond repair; his job failures were evidently not enough to appease Fate. Buster must face the truth that has pervaded his shorts as he finds his "job" in the world: he is merely the pawn of the gods as they "do business" together.

Buster can neither run into the cops nor out to sea, so he stays on the ferry, believing in a secret niche somewhere *between* land and water. Buster finds such a spot on the *side* of the boat: the giant paddle wheel. As cops mill about the decks, Buster settles in between two spokes of the wheel. This paddle wheeler recalls Charon of Greek mythology, who manned his private ferry to deliver qualified passengers to the "other side." Buster likewise is ready to be transported to an unknown destination as the ferry's giant wheel suddenly rotates clockwise. He looks right and left, disbelieving yet resigned to his hard luck. Buster simply stands and steps into the next cubicle between the spokes—and the next, and the next. His cool-headed handling of yet another life-threatening force only proves his familiarity with the twists and turns of Fate; the details may change, but the essence is the same. The wheel turns faster, lowering Buster to the water's surface; suddenly, spokes = rungs of a ladder, and Buster maintains a steady climb. He steps inside the wheel closer to the hub, stumbling once but quickly resuming his gait within its revolving circumference. Buster has worked his way into the wheel, symbolically absorbed in its irony and creating another powerful equation: paddle wheel = treadmill.

The Chase, as it has occurred in Buster's film-lives, is summarized and defined in this one intense shot. Buster has become a rat in a maze, a hamster on a treadmill. He thinks he is free to protect himself, to survive undetected by human chasers, to exert his willful independence against the Machine. Yet he is only constrained, trapped, doomed, and ultimately resigned. His supposed freedom is in reality limited to choices of turning left, right, back, or forth. Buster does work well within these confines, however, as a closer shot reveals: after five revolutions, he pauses, rides up with the turn, slides to the bottom; he walks on, stops, gets carried away again; he grabs a spoke and rides up before tumbling head over feet; after more similar mishaps, he simply hangs from a spoke and travels with the wheel for one-and-a-half turns, dunking his head in the water as he spins. We remember the revolutions of the house during the storm in *One Week*, where Buster followed its gigantic momentum, absorbed its power, almost collaborated with it in order to control and defeat it. Buster learns the moves of the wheel, struggles to ride it, and by covering every inch of it, exhausts its possibilities. Unlike the clumsy employee of the three previous job sequences, Buster now masters his "work" on board by fully using the "tools" at hand. But to what avail does a hamster run through its course? It is only the same futile trap day in, day out. That frustration saps the creature's spirit and motivation, even though years of the same drudgery may pass before the hamster simply gives up.

Ironically, Buster willingly entered this disguised treadmill as a solution to his problems since he believed the ferry was docking. His logic once again failed to consider the curveball that not only returns him to the water with a boatful of cops but binds him lockstep in an endless circle. Buster's choice to hide has become the sad culmination of his twisted daydreams. From the start, his visions of success (seen through Beloved's eyes) have been warped into chases of the impossible. And his personal quests—or chases—for the good life only equal the Supreme Chase. Defeated and caught in the eternal treadmill of life, Buster, like the hamster, finally sacrifices his will. For both of them, to exercise it in a vicious circle is a fate worse than death itself.

Once the cops spy him from the decks, Buster physically gives up all resistance: he stops his gait, leans against the arc of the wheel, and with the momentum of the turn, shoots out into the water. A cop throws him a farewell kiss, a gesture oddly reminiscent of *Buster's* reaction to the defeated cops. For once, the cops seem smart and Buster seems dazed and stymied. A fisherman on the pier reels in a big catch: Buster's hooked rear end rises from the water. The fisherman dangles him with an evaluating eye, and as Buster rolls over lifelessly, the fisherman strings him through the lapel to his pile of fish and dumps them back into the water. The fisherman crosses his legs, awaiting another bite.

Buster = a fish out of water. He kicks when he is reeled in but then turns still and glassy-eyed. Buster knows he has willingly crossed a threshold from which there is no return. In the following sequence, Buster devolves further, from lifeless creature to inanimate object. Back at Beloved's home, a mailman checks tags on his two truck deliveries: a goat and a sack. He extracts a pair of legs (Buster's) from the sack, checking another tag on them (like a tag on a corpse in a morgue), then carries Buster's bruised and tattered body on his shoulder toward Beloved's house. The goat watching intently provides animated contrast to Buster's moribund state. Inside the house, the postman drops Buster on the floor as the father reluctantly signs a receipt. Buster has become a flesh-and-blood letter; the very mail that linked him with Beloved now gives her the "bad news" that will sever their relationship. His cherished letters home have turned on him with a cruel twist. In an ironic equation, Buster becomes his own correspondence; he can no longer hide between the lines of his handwriting, for he now blatantly personifies all his failures in a battered presence. Beloved bows her head in shame and disappointment. In a confrontational two-shot, Buster vainly outstares Joe with a haughty "I tried!" look but soon yields to a timid stare front and shuts his blackened eyes. Even his porkpie sits crumpled into a pathetic point on his head. Father lays his revolver on the desk and leads Beloved out. Keaton creates visual tension here now that Buster's idle promise at the start has become a gruesome reality. Buster blinks at the gun; cut to father and daughter waiting in the next room; cut to Buster prolonging the agony by raising the gun to his waist, regarding it numbly, then slowly drawing it toward his head.

We learn of the grisly sacrifice through Beloved's reaction as we are spared details of Buster's self-inflicted death. As she stiffly holds her father's hand, she suddenly cringes at the awful gunshot "sound," which visually reverberates in a puff of smoke billowing into the room. Beloved sinks against her father who pats her shoulder sympathetically. Though crushed by his failures, she despairs even more now that he has had to die for them. Suddenly, Buster walks in, announcing with astonishing complacency: "I MISSED UNFORTUNATELY. FORGIVE ME. HOW SHALL WE PUT IT RIGHT?" Again, his awkward speaking voice and bumbling efforts label him "failure"; he becomes wordy, stifled, hesitant, and insecure. Perhaps his verbal ostentation all along was to impress the obviously well-bred girl. But Buster's behavior only aggravates father and Beloved as they eye him impatiently. Her father promptly directs Buster to a window where he bends him, lifts the flap of his jacket to clear the target, and kicks him out. Cut to the flowerbed: where Buster began, so he ends, landing amid the posies. THE END.

And so, Buster completes his vicious circle. His spirit has died like a fish without water; he becomes inanimate (mail) and then endures a physical death(-like) fall in the garden, as if altogether eliminating his body and spirit from the human race. Throughout the film, Buster has appeared lifeless, uneasy, awkward, and self-effacing. Now at the end, he easily regresses to this behavior, for he is indeed back where he began. Though he outran a crowd of cops, Buster, now devoid of stamina, cannot fend off one kick from a Significant Other. His failures have not even bettered him through experience, for he only fell into a mediocre mold to please Beloved. Buster cannot explain his failures, except perhaps to admit that he cannot live a life of imposed contrasts. He is a soloist who must choose his path and wage his own wars.

*Daydreams* has struck some as "an unexpectedly sad, rueful, self-deprecatory little film," reflecting Keaton's "own deep underlying feelings of apprehension and inadequacy."[2] Indeed, the constant contrasts between Beloved's dreaming and his doing support this view. Buster ensures his own failures by denying the truth of his life: he cannot achieve the daydreams of another. Keaton purposely distinguishes between the "dreams" that Buster has (particularly his subconscious visions where everything is possible) and the equally frightening images of an unrealistic-Reality. Keaton expressly called his film *Daydreams* to make sure we see the difference. Buster's *dreams* were always extensions of his waking life: the extravaganza of *The Playhouse* derived from Buster's stagehand job; he was W. S. Hart by falling asleep at the movies; he dreamed imprisonment because of the real Convict 13's escape; and he dreamed of falling from heaven after his real encounter with a "devil" in *The Haunted House*. But none of these dreams affects Buster beyond a sigh of relief that he has awakened from his struggles. On the other hand, daydreams are more shattering. With them, Buster cannot distinguish between imagination and failure because they both occur while he is awake. He would like to sleep it off, but his obligations will not allow him. There is an almost schizophrenic Buster at work: Buster I (the dreamer) and Buster II (the doer).[3] One has difficulty separating from or merging with the other. With the pressure of Beloved's ideas added to his predestined conflicts, Buster is often at a loss to act, work, even speak. He cannot "wake up" into either of his half-selves until it is too late and *someone else* (as whoever mailed him home) reminds him that he is indeed a total wreck. It would be even more tragic to imagine a scene in which Buster totally gives up, stamps his own body, and drops himself into a mailbox, admitting in utter sadness that this is his last letter home.

The endings of *One Week*, *The Boat*, *Cops*, *Daydreams*, and (as will be seen next) *The Electric House* are often cited ensemble by critics who dwell on the tragic nature of Keaton's work. Their anticomedy seems to overwhelm the fourteen shorts that end fairly happily. *Daydreams* is especially somber in its closeness to Buster's suicide, almost surpassing the ending of *Cops*. The tombstone in *Cops* was an instant shocker, but it was a *tag-ending*, reminding us of Buster's woeful choice (but *choice* nonetheless) to surrender to the cops for the rest of his days. The tombstone altered the overall reading of *Cops*; without it, Buster's return to the precinct would have ended in a lighter slapstick tone. But as the final image, it reinterprets and reinforces Buster's shaky position on Fate's scale. In *Daydreams*, however, a pallor settles over the film from the start. The die is cast by Buster's promise to shoot himself, and all roads lead to that inevitable resolution. Buster aiming the gun at his head, the puff of smoke, the girl's reaction all conjure images too grisly for comedy. While we still suspect—wish for—a comic catch, the eerie situation forms an even greater nightmare as Buster's lifeless body tumbles into the flowers that had once inspired such hope and promise.

The greatest irony of *Daydreams* always points to the role that Fate plays throughout Keaton's shorts. On a good day, Buster fights problems arising from a Higher Control with an intuitively stoic talent, through which he easily wins his chases and attains his goals. The five "different" films, principally *Cops* and *Daydreams*, force us to accept that our hero is painfully human and that sometimes he loses. As bleak as this truth is in comedy, where we prefer not to project mortality onto our "role model," Keaton's wry humor and hypnotic choreography help make this film comically intriguing. Even though we disappointedly question Buster's choices and ask, "Why did he do that?" we can find some vaguely consoling entertainment in asking, "*How* did he do that?"

Alas, *Why?* ends up being the only important question to ask of *Daydreams*, for it is a quest doomed to failure from the start. There is no guarantee of a girl, a job, or even a death, for Buster flubs that too. *Daydreams* totally lacks the reversal of fortune that *Cops* continually suggested, at least until the last scene. The ending of *Daydreams* is a letdown because we want Buster to keep running, to become the Hamlet of his *own* daydream and ride out the "slings and arrows of outrageous fortune." In short, to keep out of the treadmill. Buster slipped into one by mistake, reminding us how easy it is to lose spirit, heart, and life itself without a dream to pursue. Neither woman in *Cops* or *Daydreams* supported Buster in his hour of need; perhaps they were too demanding to even understand what his needs were. Because of them, however, Buster abandons his own aspirations and rejects himself in the process. We only hope that, if he hasn't broken his neck in the fall, Buster can muster enough self-esteem to crawl out of the flower bed and try again.

## Chapter 18

# The Electric House

(October 1922)

Courtesy of the Academy of Motion Picture Arts and Sciences

On the second day of shooting *The Electric House* in the spring of 1921, Keaton was riding his newest prop, an escalator, to develop gags when without warning, it began to speed up. "Before he could jump clear, a slapshoe caught between the steps. Instantly he was jammed at the top. 'Shut it off!' he yelled. Before the stagehands could rush to the switch, there was an ominous splintering sound. It was a compound sound—of a 2×24 brace breaking and Buster Keaton's ankle snapping. The slapshoe was torn from his foot. Shattered ankle and all he got his hands down to the upraised floor and made a good shoulder roll. As he came over on the broken ankle, he fainted."[1]

Keaton was in a plaster cast for seven weeks, followed by a period on crutches (injury notwithstanding, during this time he married Natalie Talmadge). Heavy work was ruled out for five months, and Keaton was reluctantly compelled to release *The High Sign* to fill in the gap. Perhaps the most positive result of this accident was that Keaton conjured up the "simple" film, *The Playhouse*, in order to avoid excessive physical activity on his broken ankle. This bad-luck "electric house" was torn down and rebuilt for later filming with technical direction by Fred Gabourie. Not a nail from the original construction was allowed to be used for the new set, and even the original film footage was destroyed.

With a freshly built prop and new impetus to create a totally mechanized world for Buster, Keaton also used his own Hollywood home on Westmoreland Avenue for some exterior shots in *The Electric House*.[2] Given his luxurious lifestyle at that time, Keaton seemed eager to suggest an impressive "house that Buster built." Reviews were favorable and filled with puns: "one of the best with some most ingenious mechanical contrivances"[3] and "charged with dynamic sparks which generate a large amount of humor . . . novel, bright, and uproariously funny."[4]

*The Electric House* can be added to Keaton's list of disaster films. Ironically, in less than one year, the basic theme of destruction runs through four shorts: objects are demolished in *The Boat*, a man is sacrificed in *Cops*, hopes are annihilated in *Daydreams*, and now in *The Electric House*, machinery backfires and is destroyed while its inventor is promptly "fired." This film does not end as unhappily as *Cops* or *Daydreams*, however, primarily because objects, not a person, are destroyed. The impersonality creates a distance that keeps us genuinely laughing, instead of chuckling uneasily at disturbing afterthoughts. More like *The Boat*, *The Electric House* comes full circle to conclude with a gag that runs through the entire film. Keaton seems to have learned from experience in *Cops* and *Daydreams* that life is more than a sentimental, quixotic quest for a mate. Keaton finally reintroduces Buster's self-reliance as he discovers anew his greatest pleasure: invention. Keaton spares our emotions and concentrates on the comedy from Buster's greatest impersonal nemesis: The Machine. Operated by Fate, the gadgets foil Buster as much as they challenge him to rise to his best behavior.

# The Electric House

Buster's entry into the world of electrical engineering is a curious gift from the gods and, true to form, meant to torture rather than benefit him. The opening scene is unexpected: an elderly man, a curly haired girl with a rose behind her ear, and Buster are graduating together from an unidentified institution of learning, all garbed in traditional gowns and caps. Buster stares mesmerized at the rose as his two fellow grads converse; from the folds of his gown, he pulls a magnifying glass to scrutinize the flower. His fascination is explained when the title identifies his specialty, as noted on his DIPLOMA. THE STATE UNIVERSITY HEREBY CERTIFIES THAT THE HOLDER OF THIS DIPLOMA IS AUTHORISED TO BEAR THE TITLE OF DR. OF BOTANICAL AND ALLIED SCIENCE. STATE UNIVERSITY. Irate at Buster's behavior, the man begins an argument, during which the three scrolls fall and each graduate retrieves one randomly. At the side by a row of mailboxes (suggesting that this "state university" is more of a cut-rate correspondence school) stands Joe Roberts, who announces to the offscreen class, "I NEED A TECHNICIAN TO INSTALL ELECTRICITY IN MY HOUSE." The man smiles, knowing he is fully qualified, and joins Joe as Buster offers a rare show of disdain. Joe reads the diploma with a double take and replies: "I REGRET, SIR, I CANNOT EMPLOY YOU." Buster meanwhile studies the rose with botanical expertise, much to the annoyance of the girl and the rejected electrician. He angrily shoves Buster out of his seat—and directly into Joe, who believes Buster is proffering his diploma for consideration. The mistaken identity is announced in a close-up of Buster's substitute diploma, this time reading: THE STATE UNIVERSITY HEREBY CERTIFIES THAT THE HOLDER OF THIS DIPLOMA IS AUTHORISED TO BEAR THE TITLE OF ELECTRICAL ENGINEER.

Adjusting his mortarboard, Buster tries to explain the mix-up to Joe, who is joined by his daughter (Virginia Fox). As in previous films, a lovely face is a determining factor in Buster's life-changing decisions. Thus, when Joe asks, "WELL, DO YOU ACCEPT MY OFFER?" Buster coincidentally looks at her (a ravishing close-up as his point of view) and nods as he tugs his robe and rolls up *his* diploma. He also nervously glances offscreen at the real electrical engineer (hereafter known as E. E.). As Buster heads off to his new commission, E. E. unrolls his scroll to read: THE STATE UNIVERSITY HEREBY CERTIFIES THAT THE HOLDER OF THIS DIPLOMA IS AUTHORISED TO BEAR THE TITLE OF PROFESSOR OF MANICURE AND BEAUTY CULTURE. The girl squawks as she grabs her rightful sheepskin and throws at him the last remaining scroll—Buster's former Doctor of Botanical Science. E. E. grumbles as he sees Buster escorted into a fancy car. Strains of

**292**

revenge fill the frame, just as Handy Hank's scowls visually suggested his plot to ruin Buster in *One Week*.

Indeed, *The Electric House* is similar to Keaton's first film, most obviously with the prominent "character"—soon to turn nemesis—of the house. Both domiciles surpass that of *The Haunted House* in their attachment to Buster's dreams and creativity. That rambling mansion was merely an elaborate stage on which Buster chased and won his victories; but he was only a visitor, not an owner or a hired worker whose input might have changed the house to resemble his own personality. Both houses in *One Week* and *The Electric House* receive and control Buster's efforts. In both films, too, his involvement with a house is completely by chance, as he acquires each through unexpected opportunity. Uncle Mike gave him the first as a wedding present; similarly, the "electric house" is a fateful gift. They both promise wealth and position, garnered by the luck of the draw. But true to the curve, these houses are only Fate's playthings to lure Buster into exposing his ingenious but vulnerable side. Through his creativity, Buster reveals his core. His genius for mechanical puzzles is the intellectual counterpart of his emotional side, which is equally opened up by another of Fate's alluring agents, Woman.

Yet while Buster the bridegroom voluntarily selected his role in *One Week*, here our hero is thrust into responsibility by being forced to pick straws (or scrolls). His one connection to the science of electricity is the science of botany—he is a "scientist," however dubious his accreditation. As a result, we expect him to find his way through this unchosen profession with some know-how. On the other hand, the real E. E., who earned his degree in electricity, is lampooned by a degree opposite to his brainy career—a "professorship" of Manicure and Beauty Culture. His effeminization roils him to the breaking point, particularly as Joe assumes that the scroll is his simply because he holds it. E. E. is insulted that he should be branded with a woman's role through this mistaken identity. Buster, though, is not outraged by this twist of destiny. First as Fate's gullible "victim," Buster eventually realizes that he must play along with this masquerade, exhibiting a larcenous trait reminiscent of his pseudo-sharpshooter in *The High Sign*. Buster knows the truth, but this fortunate misfortune seems too good to pass up, if only because Woman is in the picture. Thus, Buster willingly exposes his inadequate skills to his employer and his heart to someone who barely knows him. Once he steps into the fancy car, he seals his fate; he ensures revenge from one he has enraged and becomes susceptible to defeat. In short, Buster creates yet another disaster film.

We survey the house—A MODERN HOME WHERE ELECTRICITY IS TO BE IN-STALLED—which will remain the setting until the end. The car rolls in right and parks in the center of the frame, dwarfed by the enormous mansion with its sculpted hedges, numerous windows, and long front walk. As Joe alights, he announces, "RIGHT, SO THIS IS MY HOUSE. GET DOWN TO WORK AND I HOPE THAT I SHALL BE PLEASANTLY SURPRISED WHEN I RETURN FROM HOLI-DAY." He nonchalantly waves goodbye as he turns to the car, leaving Buster standing before his "charge" with his back to us. Before the car speeds off, however, Virginia slips a thick book through the window. The cover, shown in close-up, reads ELECTRICITY MADE EASY. Buster sits on the front steps, diploma beside him, hat firmly adjusted, and opens to page one. The sequence ends with an extreme long shot of the mansion, appropriately diminishing Buster in the very center as he begins to cram.

Buster as accidental E. E. is, visually and literally, on a path to prove that experience is the best teacher of all—the experience of reading a how-to book, that is. Because Buster has graduated with some higher degree, we feel that his intelligent "research skills" will guide him through this crash course in a science that is alien yet oddly akin to him. Buster's persona here may have been especially endearing to Keaton, who in real life claimed only one day of formal schooling. Virginia herself seems remarkably astute as she not only sees through Buster's embarrassed bravado in accepting Joe's offer but also secretly locates a book on electricity while presumably being the whole time in the car from school to house. This glitch in the "circuitry" of the plot strains the film. But Keaton may well be presenting a small wry comment on the educational process, with both the kind of school that its eclectic graduates represent and the irony of "being hired" immediately upon graduation—in fact, *at* graduation (a myth perpetuated to this day with even the most hopeful graduates). The satiric tone is intensified when clearly the job, the "applicant," and the degree do not match, yet the three are joined in one quick opportunity. Ironically, for all of Buster's "credentials," he has yet to learn what he needs for this job. Keaton may not have planned to lampoon education, but he does paint a curious caricature of what the revered sheepskin is sometimes worth in a lopsided, unpredictable world.

The time that Buster spends cramming and developing his inventions is suggested filmically by a simple cut. Keaton instantly joins the shot depicting the first phase of his process (settling in with the book) with a

# The Electric House

title and group shot: THE FAMILY RETURN FROM HOLIDAY. THEY ARE IMPATIENT TO SEE ALL THE SURPRISE ELECTRICAL DEVICES. We have not needed to follow Buster's learning process—we know he is already knowledgeable in botany and will apply his discipline to electricity. Thus, the one cut linking the shot of Buster and book with the shot of the family suggests the flight of time, the speed with which Buster masters electricity and executes his duties. The following sequences then serve to exhibit the gadgets Buster has devised during "holiday" to modernize this house. It is almost a "show-and-tell" in the giant classroom of Life, with a proud Buster in a symbolic spotlight that he himself has plugged in.

Greeting the entire family as the car pulls up are Buster, a butler, a small boy, and a dog, all with a WELCOME HOME sign. From this point on, the film takes on a particularly disjointed look in its presentation of the spacious surroundings and Buster's inventions. In part, this is due to the extensive nitrate deterioration of this once-lost film. The titles also seem a casualty of rewriting, with a distinctly British flair. In rapid succession, peripheral characters (butler, maid, Mrs. Joe, and soon some dinner guests—the little boy is not seen again in this version) will flutter in and out of the film, registering the success and failure of Buster's demonstrations. Much like the guests in *One Week* and the ghosts and pursuers in *The Haunted House* (not to mention the visitors in *My Wife's Relations* and other films with clusters of stereotypical, unnamed figures), these characters only serve to show Buster off at his best or worst (depending on Fate's twist at the time). Initially, these character "appendages" flatter Buster simply by their awed reactions to his magical yet functional devices. These characters will suffer backfires of these devices when Fate (through the E. E.) tosses a (literal) wrench into the works. What happens to them because of the backfires matters little to us. Their calamities, however, stir little whirlwinds around the cyclone that is Buster, accentuating his struggles and refocusing our attention on his success and failure.

SURPRISE NO. I. This specific title follows shots of (1) a maid sweeping around the large swimming pool (a delayed establishing shot of sorts, familiarizing us with a setting that will be crucial later), (2) the family gathering around the pooltable in the book-lined recreation room, and (3) the butler carrying luggage inside to the staircase on which the Mrs. and Virginia stand. We have thus been led to the most vital prop in the film. Buster's omnipotent hand is next seen in a close-up turning a lever. His is once again the strong hand separating order from chaos, as it did with

**295**

the WELCOME mat in *One Week*. We need not see him perform this function; we only need to know his hand guides its smooth operation with a simple move. Cut to staircase, and it turns into an escalator, which the women ride with delight. Next, Buster in the poolroom presses a table button that slides an arrow-pointer along the top of a bookcase. Joe signals stop and, with Buster's push of panel button 5, a mechanical arm shoves out the chosen book on the fifth shelf for Joe's amazed approval. Cut to the girl's bedroom, where the butler (obviously trained by Buster) presses a wall button, which activates a bathtub to enter and exit the room on tracks around the bed. Virginia also eagerly tries a button, which raises the bed into the wall.

In yet another part of the house, Buster shows Joe how a button can open and close sliding doors. But the focus returns to Buster's pièce de résistance, the escalator, which began this exhibition with success and now ends it with a dire omen. As Buster works the control, Joe unsteadily rides to the top of the escalator and is propelled out the window and directly into the pool, as an exterior long shot shows. Buster tries to stop the runaway escalator but pushes the control too hard and sprawls backwards. He begins a limb-risking dance with his mechanical partner, a pas de deux echoing *The Haunted House*. He futilely runs down as it goes up; he jumps to the floor but lands on the first step and ascends; he momentarily gives up, reclining lengthwise on a step and accepting the ride. He tumbles and lands on his knees; he stands and topples, riding upside down. All efforts to balance, escape, restrain, or control the escalator fail and Buster too flies out the window, joining Joe still splashing about. To appease his employer ("DON'T UPSET YOURSELF—THAT WON'T HELP. LET ME SHOW YOU THE NEXT SURPRISE."), he helps Joe out and demonstrates yet another marvel: a lever hidden in the shrubs that drains the pool in seconds when yanked one way and refills it in seconds when yanked the other way. Joe is impressed and Buster—despite his awkward speech, despite his cocksure stance, despite Fate's warning that things *will* go wrong— rests his arm on the lever, looking quite pleased.

From the giant pool to the indoor pool table, the next demonstration is ELECTRICAL SNOOKER. Time has passed and Joe is dressed in a tux, awaiting his turn to play pool with Buster. The jagged continuity of this film has abridged the day spent exploring the many inventions in the cavernous house. Any footage lost to deterioration would probably only display more electrical successes that will be overturned in the second half of the film, bringing it to a disastrous conclusion. In any event, the marvelous day of discovery has drawn to a close, and the family has adapted to its technological luxury. Instead of staged demonstrations, many of the electrical gadgets will now "perform" within the ordinary activities of the family. For example, during an actual pool game, a ball that Buster has hit into a corner pocket rolls out from under the table into a floor track, and rides a mini-elevator cubicle up along the side of a wall rack; a small arm pushes the ball into a row of the rack, ready for the next game. Joe smoothes his mustache as he concedes defeat to Buster, who then racks up another game the "electrical way." In close-up again, Buster's hand presses one of four buttons on a table panel. In a large view of the room, we see little arms push the balls out of their cubicles and down a longer arm leading into the triangular rack on the table. To impress his boss, Buster pushes another button: rising out of the floor is a cigar box, from which they help themselves before it descends. Buster's hand, controlling the arms of each gadget, emphasizes his superior position of "creator" who merely waves a hand, points a finger, twists a wrist to set things rolling. The close-ups not only cinematically magnify how Buster engineers an unexpected device but, more important, they symbolically focus his genius into one simple controlling shot. The very hand that turned the pages of his how-to book now commands his inventions, and with that power comes the confidence to win at anything he controls. We are not surprised that Buster wins the pool games; Joe may be distracted by the gadgets, but Buster does not win just because he knows the blueprints. He has simply proven again that he is the best.

The elaborate and lengthy snooker sequence is a curious combination of human expertise and electrical genius. In fact, the sequence seems more of the former than the latter, despite the film's title. Some scenes feel more appropriate for the hand-operated home of *The Scarecrow*, particularly at the end of the game when Buster creates an odd equation with his cue stick. Studying the balls, he holds the cue perpendicular to the table, then shoots straight down, bending the stick into three sections; after some manipulation, Buster turns his cue into a golf club. Standing on the table, he mouths "Fore!" and whacks the ball into the corner pocket. Winning the game with this sleight of hand almost turns the notion of an electric house into nonsense. We feel that, for thematic consistency, Buster should have used some electrical connection to win this game. The special truth, however, is that for Buster, the human element is the only final answer to life. The human element invents the gadgetry and the games in the first place. It seeks to understand how to work with the machine as companion and friend as well as master. We can easily consider this snooker game as an experiment for a mind-boggling sequence that appeared a few years later in *Sherlock Jr.* Both sequences essentially define human genius as victorious over all things mechanical. Clyde Bruckman described the *Sherlock Jr.* story in Blesh's biography:

> We had a pool-table shot where [Buster] had to pocket a number of balls in one stroke of the cue. The camera at high level had to show it all happen. Set up the balls, Whang away and miss. We worked an hour.
>
> "You know, Buster," we said, "this thing can't be done."
>
> This made him mad. "It *can* be done. Give me fifteen minutes with those stupid goddamn balls." He coated each ball with white chalk, then shot it *separately* into the proper pocket. Each ball left the line of its path on the green felt. Then Buster placed each ball exactly where the line indicated, called, "Camera!" and took one shot and pocketed them all. Publicity men would call that genius; to Buster it was all in the day's work.[5]

It was another testimonial to the little guy facing great odds, who believed there are some things machines will never replace.

The butler enters to announce, "GENTLEMEN, DINNER IS SERVED." Buster and Joe step from the poolroom to join Virginia and the Mrs. by the staircase, once again the dominant eye waiting to wink at Buster as his problems start. Buster offers his arm to the pretty girl, but the mother snatches it, much to his dismay. One problem of this film is its stagy look in demonstrating Buster's technical wizardry. On the one hand, the gadgets are becoming more integral to the situation rather than just "show-and-tells." Yet, a kind of invisible proscenium here clashes with the intimacy of the film medium. Even Keaton's close-ups have so far existed for the main point of showing-and-telling; despite their implications for Buster's "creator" role, they still interrupt this fluid cinematic journey. Adding to the theatrical look of the film, the family deliberately spaces themselves around the long dinner table that stretches the length of the frame. Like an emcee, Buster displays his entertainments to them. The film becomes a guessing-game of how many gadgets fill the space or where will the next amazing device emerge from the ordinary furniture. Through their purposeful placement, we clearly witness the effects of the inventions on the family with Buster's every flick of a switch or push of a button. Among the special treats are chairs that slide in as each person sits at the dining table; a "drawbridge" lowering tracks to the table so that a toy train carrying soup bowls rolls out from the kitchen and stops to unload at each person's "station"; and a gently spinning lazy Susan in the center of the table. SOMETHING FOR THE HOUSEWIFE announces a cutaway to the kitchen; there the cook loads a conveyor belt with dirty dishes riding into a box from which they emerge clean and dry. (In other inserts, the cook shoos away some cats playing with the soup train, although extant versions of the film leave this action mysteriously incomplete. Unfortunately, this means that Keaton's favorite memory of the film, as related by Blesh, is missing. As the cook loads the train with food, a kitten crawls under a covered dish. When the train stops at Joe's dinner place, he is presented with the kitten dish. The accompanying title reads, "HERE IS YOUR DESSERT, SIR.")[6]

Buster basks in the family's praise as the dinner devices run to near-perfection, tempting Fate to challenge them. It indeed does, the minute that the operations prove deceptively foolproof. Ironically, Buster himself triggers the "goof switch" in another close-up, visually counterbalancing all the close-ups that touted Buster as an infallible power. When the family stands for the Mrs. who went to peek into her modern kitchen, Buster accidentally activates the button that slides the chairs *away* from the table at the precise moment everyone sits. As they fumble to their feet, Buster apologizes and redirects the chairs, also derailing the table tracks. Unaware of the impending crash, Joe speaks too hastily: "THIS IS A REALLY WONDERFUL INVENTION! JUST LOOK!" His preparatory line heightens the expectation that we already have in being cued by a close shot of the derailment. The family and Buster, however, do not suspect the catastrophe until the train dumps its cargo onto the Mrs. who promptly falls again. An iris closes on Buster nervously switching off the train as she stands and places her dish on the table. Of course, this little wreck foreshadows greater disasters to come in the second half of the film. We also recognize a forerunner of the famous wreck that Keaton displayed in *The General*. He went so far as to blow up an actual bridge with an authentic locomotive on it in Cottage Grove, Oregon (legend has it that parts of the bridge and train still lie rusting in the water).[7] Though the first minor wreck was triggered by Fate's amusement/Buster's carelessness, and the second was a Civil War fatality, both still exhibit Keaton's lifelong fascination with trains and his whimsical desire to control their destination.

The titles lumber along in *The Electric House*, spoon-feeding us with laboriously worded statements: THE FOLLOWING DAY SOME FRIENDS COME TO LOOK AT THE NEW FANGLED GADGETS. Brief shots of family members greeting three couples, Virginia engineering the train with cats as passengers, and Buster examining the staircase are followed by the title: BUT THE *REAL* ELECTRICAL ENGINEER IS PLANNING HIS REVENGE. Again, possibly due to the fragmentary nature of the film, it became necessary to insert titles to clarify sequence or intention. Whether this explains the wordiness or whether Keaton was falling short of his usual punnery, these titles show the weak effect of heavy-handed verbal expression on comedy. Expository titles hinder our subconscious process of "reading" the visual punch lines. With these cumbersome titles, pace and rhythm (hence, the punch) are "off-schedule." We need to reread them, almost translate them, and weed out their essence since they lack the "swift kick" needed for the gag. For example, the title on the *real* E. E. follows with shots of his bitterly wadding up his wrong diploma, peering into the window, entering with a wrench, and approaching the circuit panel:

| CHAIRS | TABLES | DRAINS | POOLTABLE |
|--------|--------|--------|-----------|
| STAIRS | BOOKS | BATHTUB | DISHWASHER |

Visually, his intention is clear as he gleefully begins snipping wires. The title, however, almost defeats itself by excess description. A simple MEANWHILE . . . might have been sufficient to recall the E. E.'s earlier rejection. Such brevity would stress the film's visual nature and better use our imagination.

Keaton's uneven "punch," his surprising lack of creative snap, and his rehash of prior films into an inferior hybrid are especially clear when we meet the cook as a witness to the E. E.'s intrusion. Frightened, she runs to hide inside a trunk. Our memory flashes with other Keaton films that thrived on tangential crowds and mysterious goings-on in different rooms at the same time (*The Haunted House, The High Sign, My Wife's Relations*). The weak cook-in-a-trunk gag is also an example of Keaton's reliance on a prop for prop's sake. The trunk does not advance the plot or even add a necessary gag; it appears out of the blue with the odd introductory title: HE PUTS SOME THINGS IN A BIG TRUNK AND GOES TO FETCH IT. The coincidence that Buster must retrieve something from a big trunk that the cook just happened to hide in is too great to be shrugged off as logical plot development. It seems instead a desperate grasp at some substantial prop that should draw Buster back to the staircase; unfortunately, it becomes a forced rather than a natural use of the house's potentials. Given Keaton's masterly control of wide-open spaces in *The Paleface* and *Cops*, he falls short of the same control in this vacuum of a set. Each major house that Keaton has ever used is meant as a little stage for Buster to work out his comedy routines. Unless the house becomes a multi-unit cutaway (as in *The High Sign*), however, it tends to be a confining stage set that detracts from the comedy. Still, while the house dims, Buster excels at performing in his little "spotlight."

The trunk now becomes Buster's stocky dance partner in his struggle to lift it. Recalling the cutaway of Buster Jr. inside the smokestack of *The Boat*, Keaton inserts a couple of "interior" shots showing the cook folded within and crashing to the sides with Buster's moves. Fighting its weight, Buster teeters and slams into walls before falling beneath the trunk; he trips over his own slapshoes; and in one delayed reaction, he contemplates the trunk from one side of the room before suddenly leaping across to pounce on it with a vengeance. When Buster finally arrives at his intended destination of the escalator, it is expectedly with the trunk in tow. Just as these two props have joined in one shot, the simultaneous actions of Buster's struggle with the trunk and the E. E.'s hanky-panky with the circuitry also merge, through crosscutting between each action in each respective room. For once, Buster's turn of the dial fails to prompt the required response from the escalator. Resigned to walk up with the trunk on his back, Buster falls prey to the whims of a higher god who has assumed human form in the E. E. In turn, Buster is the modern Sisyphus with a rectangular "rock" on his back, going nowhere fast because he is the butt of this predestined joke. He tramps along, only to step in place when the escalator descends as he ascends. Ironically, when Buster pauses to look out from under the trunk, the escalator also stops as if in mocking response to his nonverbal questions. Like a reprise, he resumes climbing up and the escalator good-naturedly rolls downward. As the best of Buster-Machine routines show, the staircase collaborates with Buster for the sake of comedy, while it obviously thwarts him for the purpose of defeat. This divine collaboration, in which the staircase joins its actions with those of our forlorn hero, lines up a series of ironic obstacles to ensure his doom. And so, once again, the perfect paradoxical equation: collaboration = conflict.

Shots of Buster's progress (or lack thereof) alternate with shots recording the effect of the E. E.'s interference in other "electric" rooms.

Here again is the collaboration/conflict dichotomy, extended into the lives of the film's peripheral characters. We first witness Joe having a heated finger-pointing discussion with one guest. This isolated incident precedes the E. E.'s timely snip of the BOOKS and TABLES wires, recorded in a cutaway. Almost like a retort, the mechanical arm soars out from the third shelf and knocks the guest in the back of the head, withdrawing before anyone can identify the culprit, and the argument flares. Notably, these catastrophes are beginning to occur *without* Buster in the same scene. The house is destined to fail whether he is witness or not; it will, in fact, be a greater insult to Buster when he learns that his trusting boss is suffering the backfires of his cherished inventions. Fate enjoys tormenting Buster directly; its wish to humiliate Buster will be more painful to him if he cannot defend himself in person. This new aspect of control in Keaton's films is now played to the nth degree. It seems that Fate is acknowledging Buster as a formidable opponent, and one guarantee of his defeat is simply not to have him in the arena.

We return to the escalator to find Buster still running up the stairs—a callback to the treadmill image of *Daydreams*. Aware that disaster is pervading the whole house, our return to Buster at this time provides even greater irony, for he thinks his *only* problem is an erratic escalator. The stairs abruptly stop and Buster is propelled toward the window, braking in time to keep from flying out; unfortunately, he drops the trunk onto the top step, which instantly conveys it back down to the ground floor. He innocently walks down, inspiring the stairs to lift the trunk up past Buster, out the window, and into the pool. Playing it safe, Buster slides down the banister and heads outside for the trunk.

The cook, all along sequestered in the trunk, reaches a hand out of a side hole to undo the lock. Buster recoils upon seeing this hand and perplexedly examines his own. The cook emerges, falls into the water, and crawls poolside to wrap a sheet around herself. Not seeing the actual cook because of his own confusion, Buster looks up in time to see a sheeted figure and thinks he is now haunted by another ghost (physical sheets obviously being the only sign of such phenomena). This ghost, he reasons (if reason it is), must be responsible for the inexplicable mishaps with the escalator. Buster's incredulous regard of his own hand—as if it has transmigrated from his body over to the trunk in the pool—is a weak reaction, despite his sublime facial expressions. Of course, in its most extreme translation, the "hand" symbolism supports Buster's position of control, as it did in *One Week* and in earlier sequences of this film. Buster has confidence in the power of his hands and thus must earnestly question where his control has gone. Desperately, he is compelled to check if he still has a "grip" on his own hand, for it certainly feels as if his control has slipped away altogether.

The remaining scenes create a cyclonic-style progression that only a disaster film, such as *The Electric House* is promising to be, can allow. All that flowed so smoothly will now collapse, undo, spin in tumult under the winds of Fate. Nearly every invention presented so securely at the start will individually replay its inverse or opposite purpose. All that can go wrong with a device will—and with the same amount of "successful failure" that it once had in its perfect efficiency. For Buster, the calamities are first attributed to the supernatural; this is a contrived association, opposing the idea of an "electric house." Perhaps Keaton simply drew the ghost from his roster of gags in *The Haunted House* (with which this film has much in common). From the window, Buster sees the trunk sink and deduces that the hand belongs to the drowning "victim"—now ghost. Because Buster carried the "victim," his guilt-ridden conscience works overtime, feeling responsible and thus deservedly haunted.

Like *The Haunted House*, Buster and ghost now perform a few well-timed run-ins in a room eerily lit by a wall lamp flicking on and off. Buster's illogical reasoning and this ghost sequence weakly adapted from a prior film feel inappropriate to the electric house and to what Keaton has tried to establish with this novel locale. After all, ghosts fit in a "haunted" house; why would a ghost be tampering with electricity? Why wouldn't Buster (albeit self-taught on the subject) automatically consider a natural, rather than supernatural, glitch in the circuitry? The ghost-capade also interrupts and delays the more important confrontation between Buster and E. E., and the film's resolution. This meeting must happen for dramatic reasons, of course, once the disasters throughout the house are executed, and only when the cook ("ghost") is exorcised—simply by never reappearing. But the supreme battle between Buster and Machine/Fate has, unfortunately, been diluted by this unfulfilling insert. In retrospect, we might reconsider the one major purpose of the cook: as the burden Buster must carry in his unending fight against the unknown, and as the cause of his helplessness, eventually dooming him to self-sacrifice.

The frenetic action in the concluding sequences plus the accumulating characters will, as usual, add to the slapstick chaos that seems requisite for any Keaton film with a "crowd." A distinct difference between Keaton's treatment of cop crowds and his treatment of peripheral characters is readily apparent. With repetition, the masses of policemen become blurred until, ironically, they turn into one single body—as if melded into one entity during a hot chase after Buster. There are few, if any, distinct personalities or features among the cops; they all look the same and thus turn into one amorphous power in Buster's life.

On the other hand, Keaton aims for uniqueness among the characters who fill such populated films as *Neighbors*, *The Haunted House*, *My Wife's Relations*, and now *The Electric House*. Yet while inundating his films with multiple bodies to become a single entity as with the cops, these characters retain their individual facets. They are clearly branded with idiosyncratic looks or habits (e.g., Bowler, Burly, etc.), and so we remember them as such. They imply greater dimension and development as Buster's nemeses. Unfortunately, as is the fate of such clowns, they never pass their cardboard perimeters and settle somewhere between dimensional antagonist and (slap)stick-figure. They never even attain the *symbolic* proportion of a sea of cops. Rather than fill the screen with a throbbing manifestation of Fate, these rambling characters chop up the energy of the screen and dilute Buster's focus on his own struggles. Thus, the greatest weakness of these less "famous" or popular Keaton shorts—the ones that always elude lengthy critical discussions in favor of *Cops* or *One Week*—is essentially Keaton's own weakness in losing his hero in the crowd. The themes of survival, destiny, and courage are always present, of course, even in the weakest shorts. But the audience involuntarily roots for the strongest presentation of its hero and loses interest in anything less cohesive. Thus, the strength—therefore, success—of Keaton's films resides not only in the themes but more so in the quality and power of the figures who play out those themes.

Against that yardstick, *The Electric House* concludes by depicting the popular theme of Buster against mechanical disaster, but with myriad distractions that fling him throughout space. His struggle is real, but the theme is drained by slapstick; at the end, we want to sweep away a pile of dusty, lifeless characters to find the essential Buster beneath them. Only then do we discern the struggle that is uniquely his, that is best highlighted in one-to-one encounters with a force beyond his control.

Keaton now lets this force run rampant in the bedroom, where the boss's daughter and Buster meet. As the E. E. flips a switch in a cutaway, the bathrub rolls in, crashing against Buster who tumbles into it and rolls out. Meanwhile, the Murphy bed rises into the wall, lifting the girl with it. As her legs kick out from between the bed and the wall, Buster assists her, only to be knocked flat to the floor when the bed descends. Spooked, Buster runs out through a draped doorway and begins an uncontrollable jog. As the shot cuts wider, we learn the reason: that he is unknowingly caught on the descending staircase while running to the top. Buster has become the automated Sisyphus, the same mythological victim transported into the technological era. This is virtually the same shot as Buster on the spinning disk while held by a laughing "ghost" in *The Haunted House*—a gag which, again, was only divulged by a cut to a wider shot. This time, Buster's "capture" and "imprisonment" on a vehicle that goes nowhere takes on greater symbolic resonance: now no "physical" ghost holds him, only an invisible hand that controls his every step.

With a splay-legged fall, Buster breaks clear of the run and dashes into the dining room, where more characters and haywires beckon. He first races *across* the top of the dinner table as four complacent women sup, and bursts into the kitchen. Catching his breath, Buster inadvertently leans against a hot stove, yowls in delayed reaction, and leaps to the top of the dish-conveyor belt. Typical of forced scenarios, Buster's actions seem contrived to place him in the oddest locations just to highlight certain props. Thus, rather than logically move aside to nurse his burn and play out a gag on his plane, Buster jumps *up* onto an invention that is out of his way and tumbles to the floor again. Because Keaton has introduced inventions as fodder for this film, he may have felt obligated to use them in a variety of ways, whether intrinsic to the situation or not. Thus, Keaton painted himself into a corner—or rather, blocked himself into one by overfilling his room with inventions. Like the crowd of peripheral characters, each invention distracts us with its unique malfunction and defeats Keaton's goal of a "blur of disaster" as powerful as a sea of cops. Buster's face-to-face confrontations with each backfire become only the inversion of his early successful demonstrations—another gallery of exhibitions, another collection of niches that divide and separate the film instead of uniting it into one overwhelming mass of failing energy. Buster simply tries shutting off the switch while, in a cutaway, we see the E. E. still wire-snipping. A gratuitous title informs us: THE FUN HEATS UP. Cut: the women diners suddenly slide from the table in their mechanized chairs. Cut: the lazy Susan flings food.

Surrounded by the devastation of his creativity, Buster sits in the middle of the kitchen floor, pensive and nonmoving. After a pause, he suddenly, simply screams, then props his head on his hand to think some more. In the midst of chaos, Buster has finally unleashed his suppressed frustration, perhaps even anger (remembering *Daydreams*), and lets loose with an uncharacteristic reaction. It is so unlike him to scream, to move his mouth in such a vivid expression of despair and outrage. Yet, it is only human and most fitting. Buster has for once broken the straight line of his mouth to howl, however briefly, at the giant discrepancies he cannot fathom. For a moment, he is unrepressed, vocalizing his subconscious in which are stored all the screams he has never uttered. By yielding to this primal urge, he regains control of himself to confront his rival with a burst of renewed energy. He recognizes the villain as Fate alone, no matter what ghost or human hand pulls the switch. In a film beleaguered by slapstick, rambling characters, unwieldy space, and nitrate deterioration, *The Electric House* offers one of the best sparks of Buster's persona. He encapsulates a dictum of Life in a flash action: Scream, but persist. Indeed, if we, like Buster, ever lost total control and never rejoined our battles, we would be screaming forever.

Catastrophes rain down on Buster in rapid succession now, as if his scream has cued the onslaught to begin. Plates fly from the conveyor belt, hitting Buster in the head; he travels along the train tracks and lands on the reckless lazy Susan, spinning just as Sybil did on her piano stool in *One Week*. Skidding into the poolroom, Buster tries warning the guests about the bizarre events; the next shot adds further to his obsession with supernatural interference. The butler, leisurely smoking nearby, rests his hand on the diamond-shaped window of a door. As Buster narrates his eerie tale, he spies the hand in the window. He is obviously naively convinced of a floating, omnipotent hand—and clearly a *physical* hand on an *ethereal* entity that wears a sheet to identify itself! Buster has once again abandoned his clear-headed, nearly scientific thinking for some inexplicably primitive, misplaced notion to explain his lack of control. With the ghost as option, Keaton has also unfortunately diluted the potent theme of invisible Fate as the host of this party-gone-amuck.

Buster does not notice that he is rising on the cigar stand as he speaks, and as he hurries to get to the "bottom" of his problem, he falls on the floor. The book-pushing arm, the pool-ball rack, and the balls themselves all begin to "perform" without restraint, assaulting Buster and guests. Toppled by a ball, Buster crawls out of the poolroom, stopping warily on the threshold just as the sliding doors close on his neck. He collapses when they open, caves into the arms of the butler, and revives quickly enough to proceed. With this sliding-door gag, we recall *The High Sign* when one hapless Buzzard was caught in the doorframe. While Buster underplays his wide-eyed stare at being trapped, unlike the Buzzard's grotesque mugging, the entire gag has a bothersome unreality to it. It offers the shock of a sight gag, in and of itself laugh-provoking, but in Keaton's more naturalistic repertoire, the gag strains. We can almost see the contoured neck-holes collapse around his neck as Buster stoops deliberately in place for the business. The entire cut-wires sequence is, in fact, as contrived over the space of the house as the horse-and-car-blackening sequences were in *The Blacksmith*. In order for the gags to work, Buster needs to be in the exact room with a particular gadget that the E. E. (unaware of Buster) short-circuits at that precise moment.

Naturally, coincidence is crucial: if the E. E. cuts the snooker wires while Buster is in the bedroom, there will be no connection and no gag. Hence, the comedy is derived solely from the *deliberate* control of coincidence—and in that contradiction lies the problem of a forced scenario. The causes and effects of Buster's life in this film are all predictable; even the imposed ghost as the source of the problems fails to convince us of its spontaneity. We accept the imposition mainly because it is brief and because the deliberate slapstick is tempered by the welcome idiosyncracies of Buster's nonverbal language. We are also spared complete spoon-feeding that would destroy such a cause-and-effect film; at times, we are allowed to assume for ourselves the presence of the E. E. without actually seeing him. Thus, when the cigar stand lifts Buster, we do not have to first see the E. E. snip that wire. Keaton's editing in part rescues this film from the redundancy that already exists because of gratuitous titles. We are also far enough along Keaton's record of shorts to know what lies at his heart. We know that coincidence is the fateful engine driving Buster's life, but we recognize the times when it is masterfully executed and successful: those times when Buster meets it head-on, without cluttering characters or contrived gestures and events.

At long last, the confrontation: Buster spies on the E. E. through a transom. Buster now wishes to match wits in order to defeat the E. E. on his own terms; as a title informs us: HE TOO UNDERSTANDS ELECTRICITY— BY TREATING HIS ENEMY TO A LITTLE REFINED TORTURE. The refinement is only a tongue-in-cheek thought, for Buster fetches kitchen pots and pans and flings them through the transom, creating sparks that vividly attack the E. E. from all sides. The resilient E. E., however, begins to chase Buster through the house, providing a last summary glimpse of some of the haywire devices. They end up at the showpiece of the film, the dreaded escalator, whose malfunction finally serves a good purpose on Buster's side. As the E. E. races up the steps after Buster, our hero flips the switch that accelerates the stairs and propels the E. E. out into the pool. Now this less-than-perfect vehicle undoes all its prior wrongs by offering to Buster the solution to his problem. As an equation: malfunction = solution. By ridding himself of the villain, Buster has actually adapted to the technical imperfection of his star-invention—and even enjoys it. Once the E. E. flies out, Buster too wishes to dive into the pool but elects to slide down the banister and propel himself into a fancy dive with the momentum of the reckless escalator. Buster has made friends with it, much as he tried with the staircase in *The Haunted House*. Buster has a collaborator, however hard-won, once he understands its "mind." The escalator, he now realizes, never was a threat to him; it too was only an unwilling victim. Once that cause and effect is made clear, Buster shapes it to his advantage, and even entertainment.

Buster's dive, however, is curtailed by Joe striding along the top of the stairs. The collision sends both Joe and Buster out the window and into the pool. Exterior: with the E. E. noticeably absent, Buster helps Joe out of the water. Joe points a wet paper at him and says, "HERE'S YOUR DIPLOMA. AND NOW CLEAR OUT OF MY SIGHT." The daughter who has joined them despairs as Buster hurls the paper aside, ties a handy rope around his neck and to a large rock, and leaps into the pool after throwing them a goodbye kiss. The shocked girl pulls the lever, draining the pool in seconds, revealing Buster curled like a baby asleep on his pillow-rock. He suddenly sits up, outraged that his plan to end his life is interrupted. But Joe is anxious to help and pulls the lever in the opposite direction, submerging Buster in seconds. When Joe stomps off, Virginia once more empties the pool, but both Buster and rock are gone.

During *The Electric House*, the intended glory of each of Buster's wonderful inventions turns into misery for its creator. So, too, the pool, for it deprives Buster of a swim in happier times and of his suicide in desperate times. Its miraculous accelerated draining and filling (one of Keaton's rare manipulations of film speed) is also the ultimate ironic joke. As a sort of "revelation shot," the quick draining is presented with enough of a pause, or enough beats, to create a visual punch line. With the immediate repetition of this gag to show Buster has vanished, we are clued in to the inexplicable disappearance of the E. E., last seen splashing about in the water. Buster too has obviously gone the same route. The pool and the escalator are both bittersweet costars for Buster: as much as they seem to be his allies at the end by ridding him of the E. E., they have also dealt the final blow that costs him his worth.

Where exactly has Buster's fate taken him now? It is not merely figurative language to say he has "gone down the drain." Cut: a long shot of water gushing out of a sewer line. After a pause, Buster pours out with the flow and rolls onto a bank with the rock still tied on. Pause, and the camera pans to show the E. E. sitting beside him. THE END.

Another cliché comes to life: Buster is "all washed up." Indeed, the film promises a painful ending from the start, for this is a film based on deception and a surprising bit of egoism on Buster's part to undertake a job for which he is not truly qualified. Yet Buster proves his genius for mechanical invention, considering he is a "botanist," and the only monkey wrench in the works is, in fact, sabotage. As usual, the saboteur is Fate through a human agent. With Joe's daughter pulling the lever to rescue him, it seems that *The Electric House* should have another happy ending—she clearly wants him back, even if no one else does. But Fate must dispense justice for Buster's daring ego. From *Cops* on, we are too leery to assume that Fate's torture will always be reversed in favor of Buster's happy ending. Now that we end on another "failed" note, we must backtrack over the film to make sense of it again.

The ending of *The Electric House* resembles those of the "tragic four" because Buster has left the film without anything or anyone of value. We even wonder what his motivation really was for jumping into the pool: was he depressed or was he more than ever angry? This anger has been evident and impossible to ignore since *Daydreams*; it is a new and unusual facet to a personality whose harshest reaction has usually been to shrug off challenges as if they were pesky flies. Buster flings his waterlogged diploma to divest himself of any further association with this experience or these people, but he does not simply walk away as he would have earlier. Just as his creativity has been destroyed, his anger must now destroy the creator. Buster chooses to "go out" with one of his prized inventions, and thus the only way "out" is a watery one. He accepts this choice with full control, for this is one instance where he can regain the control that was usurped and sabotaged all along. Perhaps he even remembers the trunk-victim, for which he felt responsible and haunted by another watery death. He is now trading that "murder" with his own life. Although Buster eventually learned that the ghost did not cause the haywires, it seems he never learned who *was* in that trunk or how a sheeted figure came to wander in his path. His childlike belief in such things drills a big black hole in his otherwise sophisticated, adult reasoning. His only way out of any hauntings, humiliation, and misunderstanding is to leave life through the most permanent door available. This will not be a magical pool as in *Hard Luck*, which offered him a victory dive and a new family life. This pool is his chosen undoing, brought about by the E. E.'s jealousy and Joe's inequity. Imagine his outrage when his welcome sleep at the bottom of the pool is again sabotaged by Joe's offspring.

Flushed through the pipelines of the city sewer system and landing ironically next to his enemy, Buster is again victimized by Fate and humanity. Both of these "saboteurs" even thwart his plan for suicide. In *Hard Luck*, too, we remember that Fate had better things in store for Buster and so tortured him with aborted suicide plans while also saving his life. At least in that wildlife adventure, Buster eagerly embraced his reversal of fortune and celebrated with a journey through the world. Buster's travels here convey him to a foul and depressing land—more like limbo perhaps, for he has already been through the "hell" of the electric house. In essence, then, Buster has again died and been transported to a plane that contains both the refuse of Life as well as the release he seeks. He is finally free of Joe, the house, the deceiving diplomas, and no doubt, he can easily outwit and outrun the E. E. Being with him, though, in the final moments of the film is a last-jab reminder of what has brought Buster to this stage of life. Before he can undertake a new, more worthy adventure, one that will lift him far above these depths, Buster must remember what caused his failures.

In contrast to Keaton's stronger, more intact films, *The Electric House* struggles to add its own phase to Buster's continuum. The sharpness of some isolated gags is, unfortunately, not enough to carry the film to the top of the Keaton list, for its slapstick and disjointed weaknesses encumber it mercilessly. Yet, if only for the overriding theme of Buster versus Fate, Failure, and Machine, *The Electric House* stands out as an important transitional film. Its mishmash of "used" gags, new ideas, and feelings of anger and despair are in fact a pivotal culmination in Keaton's new outlook on comedy—an evolution that began dramatically with the bleak, shocking finale of *Cops*. *The Electric House* is like a giant stewpot into which Keaton has thrown the best, the newest, and the weakest structures to date, and offers a meal brimming with the unpredictable. Like the hapless diners at the mechanized table, we too have had our chairs pulled out from under us, not knowing why the startling mishaps are happening nor how they will ever be fixed. As we look at Buster in his final shot, bedraggled and in sore condition from another botched attempt at Life, we are oddly enough not entirely hopeless but rather mixed with expectation and optimism. His scream, still "echoing" in our mind's-ear, has offered us an anchor in his rocky world so that we can steadily search for the answers to our Why and How questions. We remember what Buster is really capable of; and as he sits in limbo, with no choice but to continue living, he will remember it too. Keaton as Master Fate does not let Buster die this time. His chance to undo the mess of Life is coming, and with it will appear a new, free Buster Spirit—one unshackled by a scream and extremely weary of tombstones, flower beds, and sewers.

## Chapter 19

# The Balloonatic

## (January 1923)

Courtesy of the Museum of Modern Art/Film Stills Archive

O NCE UPON A TIME THERE LIVED A YOUNG PRINCE WHO SEEMED TO BE IN TROUBLE. With the first four magical words of this title, *The Balloonatic* becomes a fairy tale. This is not a particularly comfortable genre for Keaton; he has experienced too much "reality" since *Cops* to be so naively immersed in whimsy alone. But the fairy tale, like the dream, is Keaton's license to play at fantasies without a penalty for surviving them. *The Balloonatic*, then, is a dream film without a dream-frame. It is also a weak film, floundering for a foothold in either fantasy or reality, and it is a film that Keaton himself hardly ever mentioned. But in the wake of several sobering films in a row, Keaton now presents a welcome fling. Buster the child/man has been given a reprieve from Life to romp through its forest primeval, free, wide awake, seeking a distant land wherein lies some longed-for happy kingdom.

Setting a lighthearted adventurous mood, the opening line is immediately followed by a matching title that presents the vital counterpart to every fairy-tale prince: THERE ALSO LIVED A YOUNG PRINCESS WHO WAS FOND OF OUTDOOR ADVENTURE (PHYLLIS HAVER). Already the Prince's quest is inextricably tied to a potential love interest—Buster's eternal source of both frustration and joy. Given his quest for Woman and the nature of fairy tales, there can seldom be a prince without a princess.

The opening shot is immediately involving in its unusual composition: it is almost the inverse of the stunning shot in *The Goat* of Buster's round porkpie. Now we look closely at the supple roundness of his porkpie again, his "crown" identifying his rank among peers. After a pause, Buster raises his head to face us, inviting us into his thoughts with a rare close-up. His features are illuminated by the lit match he holds as he surveys the surrounding darkness. When he blows out the light, his pale face continues to "glow." Buster is confronted with choices, represented by different shadowy doors behind which lie mysteries. We think of "the lady or the tiger" dilemma—the frightening moment of making a fateful decision that either enriches or ends one's life by simply opening a door. When Buster opens one door, he hurriedly slams it shut when the "wrong prize" appears, then runs to another, only to find a greater threat: first a skeleton, then a roomful of fog. By slamming the door, he tries to thwart disaster and stop the entity dead in its tracks. Before Buster opens his third choice of sliding doors, he arms himself with a handy white statue. Surprise: a dragon lunges forward, flapping its hungry tongue. Is this the dragon that the "Prince" has come to slay? Buster only drops his plaster weapon and slides/rolls onto his stomach to stare at the closing doors. Without winning a prize, Buster strikes out—falling through an unexpected trapdoor.

Cut to exterior: we learn that all of these shots add up to a "revelation" sequence explaining exactly what "trouble" Buster is in. Filling the screen in an extreme long shot is a fun-house facade named HOUSE OF TROUBLE. A ticket booth, with a peripheral sign inviting GET INTO TROUBLE 10 CENTS, stands center in a gaping black void, from which Buster suddenly slides out to land with an unprincely thud. This revelatory sequence has been a Keaton surprise, based on a principle of comedy that he articulated in a 1930 interview: "The best way to get a laugh is to create a genuine thrill and then relieve the tension with comedy. Getting laughs depends on the element of surprise; and surprises are harder and harder to get as audiences, seeing more pictures, become more and more comedy-wise. But when you take a genuine thrill, build up to it, and then turn it into a ridiculous situation, you always get that surprise element."[1]

The tension began building with each of Buster's rapid-fire encounters in the dark. The final surprise, arising from a "ridiculous situation," hit us when we learned that Buster was not in a dream or a haunted house but an amusement park fun house, which he voluntarily entered for a dime's worth of "trouble." Although the revelation now offers a sensible explanation for these weird creatures, it still catches us offguard, for an amusement park has not been a comfortable Keaton setting; it was underused in *The High Sign* and not repeated in any other of Keaton's independent shorts (he and Arbuckle well covered Coney Island in a 1917 short of the same name). In *The Balloonatic*, the setting throws us because the first titles intimate a loftier playing-area. The surprise element works mainly because of Keaton's preference to invert exterior with interior, to move from small scene to large scene—in other words, to reverse the traditional expository sequence. He did this in *The Boat* to create a puzzling situation for his hero, only to explain it with a larger view in which the solution played out before our eyes. As much as it is a surprise, this inversion also twists the fairy-tale structure that Keaton has introduced, for what appears menacing to the hero seeking glory is, in fact, a harmless bunch of papier-mâché creatures in a playland full of fun-lovers paying to get scared. Furthermore, it highlights Keaton's layered, cyclical perspective in which the fairy-tale world is first suggested, only to be reduced to the bustle of the real world, from which everyone (especially Buster) wishes to escape—in order to return to the fairy-tale world.

Before he walks off, Buster is mesmerized by a rotund woman who buys a ticket with giggly anticipation and disappears into the dark entrance. The irony of Buster's escape into a fantasy world is depicted now with his being on the *outside* looking in and once more becoming vulnerable to real-world dangers. He plans on being amused by the spectacle of the fat lady plummeting to the ground, even brushing the landing-spot

**314**

clear with his shoe. In choosing to be entertained at another's expense, he will in turn be mocked and reprimanded by the force that metes justice in this "outside" world; Buster can no longer slam a door to stop his destiny. His "punishment" begins with the arrival of a potential princess—a flapper who trots by him. He straightens his tie and casually strolls after her, easily falling into the tempting trap set by Fate. Buster as Prince is ready to rescue her from calamity, for he wishes to protect his chosen one from the vicissitudes of life as he knows them. He forgets, however, that the curveball strikes *him* when least expected, and there is no one around to help him divert it. Having escaped the "trouble house" unscathed, Buster probably feels in authority; he has been dubbed "prince" from the beginning, and with this privileged title comes some superior, albeit unconscious, attitude that he is invincible. Unfortunately, he is rejected by the flapper as a masher. His eyes blaze, his nostrils flare, right before he is mocked and doled out the final punishing blow—this time by the forgotten fat lady, who slides directly onto Buster. After the crash, she skips laughingly back to buy another ticket. Dazedly watching her, Buster remembers where he sits and scoots off to avoid a replay. He catches up with the flapper who hesitates before a curbside puddle. Like Sir Walter Raleigh, Buster spreads his jacket on the water, bows, and doffs his hat. Curveball: a car rolls in over his jacket and picks up the girl while Buster is left to wring out his jacket and heart.

Finding his princess is no easy task—like trying to fit a tiny glass slipper on a giant foot. Buster so far has been crushed (in more ways than one) in dealing with the fair sex, yet he seems willing to try any romantic route if it will lead to his princess. At YE OLD MILL, a second pretty damsel purchases a ticket for a boat ride through a dark tunnel. She seems adventurous, just as the second opening title suggested, for she embarks solo on a ride that usually requires a companion; in fact, her solitary fling is asking for "trouble." Sufficiently attracted, Buster dons his wet jacket, buys a ticket, and sits beside her. While she eagerly looks forward to a fun excursion, even seemingly unaware of the fellow next to her, Buster's expression recalls the "innocence" of the wolf in grandma's nightgown while eying Little Red. Like *The Playhouse*, where Buster the stagehand followed his directions to the letter, here he would probably happily comply with the peripheral warning sign—KEEP ARMS INSIDE OF BOAT—and plan all kinds of mischief with obedience as an excuse. The vessel drifts off with a push from the attendant and slowly rounds the tunnel, with a fade-out to suggest the beginning of the trip. A quick fade-in ends the trip in seconds: the boat floats in from the final bend in a shot that counterpoints the earlier direction. The girl's demeanor has changed; both passengers stare sullenly ahead of them and sit far apart. Buster's porkpie is crumpled; his black eye becomes visible as the boat turns and glides toward us; one end of his collar juts out like a broken Cupid's arrow. The boat moors with an ominous "thump" and the girl stomps out, with only Buster's eyes following her.

This girl's mettle has proven to any man less than a gentleman that she is not to be trifled with. Buster's lapse into wolfery in the mill's darkness has only backfired. Unlike the opening darkness filled with scary figures, this darkness that he thought he controlled held another source of "trouble"—his own untempered freedom to snatch the Princess for himself. While destined for royalty, Buster is still punishable by Fate, battered and rejected by women, and very much alone. He cannot yet merge the license of the fantasy world with the rigors of the real world. He is due to forge even greater battles to match the stamina of his comrade in arms (or so he wishes her to be). This girl seems worth her weight in royal jewels; as much as she welcomes the exhilaration of adventure, she fends off its perils with an unhesitating blow. She acts quick, stands firm, takes no nonsense, while also seeming demure, tender, and romantic. Without really knowing her, we easily identify her as the Princess of the opening title, not to be mistaken with any other lady who has so far crossed Buster's path in this kaleidoscopic world of reality/fantasy. While bruised in this battle, Buster also has his second thoughts about her, for as he hobbles away, he turns once to see her drive off in a car well loaded with camping gear. He may be angry, but he is intrigued; in his purest innocence, he probably admits that his grasp of the inside and outside worlds—make-believe and harsh reality—is just a dichotomy that punishes him in the end. His has never been a simple world, but one always split and "between the lines," one fluctuating between two equals. With this confident and feisty girl, Buster longs to share her adventure, learn how she tames her Fate, and settle into *one* world of romantic bliss.

A huge hot-air balloon dominates the fairgrounds in the next extreme long shot. Buster is dwarfed by its enormous size, as if insignificant next to such a colossal combination of human enterprise and natural force. The balloon represents the perfect blend: it is a fantasy come true, the magic of soaring over clouds complemented by the reality of science. With hands on hips, Buster stares at a crowd of top-hatted men and suddenly darts toward them. Again, Buster is fascinated, drawn to adventure, and probably hoping for a chance to balance fantasy and reality. In just these few opening scenes, Buster has been asking to belong, to join someone or something that challenges without risk, pleases without penalty, controls without threat. He fluctuates between finding his independence and merging with a Significant Other to fill his empty life. And unlike any film since *Cops*, Buster now enters these situations with a confidence expressed through crisply enunciated nonverbal gestures. In fact, *The Balloonatic* will continue to the end as entirely nonverbal. Buster's interactions with Machine (balloon), Nature, and Woman will be articulated through a gamut of physical poses and facial registers. Fittingly, the silence of action dominates this film, for Buster is immersing himself in a purely physical test that will not only make him worthy of a Princess but will also earn his long-elusive ideal. Without words to tie him to a literal world (disquieting words as HOUSE OF TROUBLE or tempting words as KEEP ARMS INSIDE . . . ), Buster will rely solely on his spirit to find the perfect life.

Buster wanders to the basket and examines the sandbags as a worker, handing him a GOOD LUCK pennant, points to the top of the balloon. Unquestioningly, Buster climbs a ladder out of the frame. He illogically accepts a job that is not his; logically, however, he answers to his destiny. He also jumps at rising to an occasion that can prove his abilities—and rise he shortly will. A uniformed balloonist steps into the basket, waves goodbye, and signals takeoff, only to see the balloon pull away as he and the bottom of the basket remain on the ground. This motif of bottomless objects (Buster's trunk in *Cops*, the cat basket in *Daydreams*) now reaches its zenith; while it does not directly happen to Buster as in the other two films, it has the greatest impact on his life.

The massive balloon creates a surreal vision as it plays across the planes of the film frame. Its giant netted globe dreamily slides in and out of the frame's edges. As Keaton cuts between extreme long shots and closer shots, he toys with the proportion of the balloon relative to its backdrop. Thus, a gigantic balloon on the ground now seems no bigger than a child's balloon on a string as it drifts between the wide sky and rolling landscape. As the camera cuts in closer, its roundness slices the frame into arcs moving against the stark white sky. The dark semicircle fills the bottom half of the frame, like some alien moon on which a lone astronaut has descended. Buster is, however, unaware of his space-bound destination for he is still industriously affixing the pennant to the net. Task done, he steps forward and nearly slips off the sphere. As the truth sinks in, he crawls back to the top where he simply stands with hands on hips to survey the situation. Such a pose is comically, ironically poignant: while he momentarily looks like master of the globe with his lordly posture, his body is also uttering astonishment, helplessness, and isolation at being caught between the light-dark shapes of the frame. His tiny figure seems sandwiched between two giant slices of sky and balloon. Without words, then, Buster mobilizes himself into physical action to preserve himself against a purely physical world. He climbs down the netting (an extreme long shot cutaway shows the balloon sailing across the frame with a minute Buster plastered to the side). To allow time for Buster's progress, Keaton cuts to the real balloonist apologizing to his scoffing onlookers. Thus, when Keaton cuts back to Buster, he is now at the basket, dangling from the net with coattails flapping, legs spewing out a rich vocabulary to communicate with the basket that seems so-near-yet-so-far. He kicks, straightens, twists, and dangles, checking for terra firma. Hitching an arm over the side, he climbs into the basket and rocks in the breeze. Fade out.

In no time, we fade in to an even closer shot to see that Buster has rapidly adapted to his new lifestyle. Buster once again demonstrates his quick versatility to accommodate to the winds of change. Whether striding inside a paddle wheel or turning a necktie into a disguise, Buster runs an eagle eye over the "tools" at hand, sizes up the situation, and ekes out a novel and creative mode of operation to suit his condition. During the quick fade, Buster has determined his priorities and made himself right at home in the balloon: he is washing out his socks in a basin and hanging them on the ropes to dry, losing a soapbar over the side in the process. Keaton continues to intercut extreme long shots to ascertain Buster's ongoing flight. Whether or not Keaton actually launched his own balloon for the film or just how high he flew is not clear; the shots of Buster sprawled on the side or dangling in the air could have been created by miniatures, stock footage, or a full-sized balloon at a relatively low height. Yet the important question is not how but why these shots are so scaled: to reinforce the incredible journey Buster must undertake. His business in the basket is more comically successful *because of* the outrageous height at which he performs these actions. Thus, when Buster drops his soapbar, it falls not just the distance between bathtub and floor but rather the magnitude between heaven and earth. Likewise, when Buster hangs decoy ducks over the basket for his second priority (dinner), we cut to an irised portion of the balloon to zero in on a roosting bird. Buster's responding action in the larger shot then becomes "louder" in its intended humor: he fires a shotgun at it. With an even larger distance shot, Keaton cuts to the whole, newly punctured balloon, which now looks helpless and dwarfed against the surrounding expanse. We wonder about Buster's illogical-logic: even without many options for dinner, did he have to fire through the balloon to get the bird? The gag is unconvincing, but Buster's prize facial reaction makes up for it: his "blankness" reads chagrin, curiosity, and doom simultaneously. Adjusting his porkpie, he stares over the basket, calculating the distance he is about to plunge. The shot provides a moment of fantastic suspension, as if all laws of gravity are temporarily halted so that Buster can assimilate the "gravity" of his situation. A series of cuts connects the great downward depth Buster must travel. Cut: the deflating balloon drops straight through the bottom of the all-white sky frame. Cut: the fizzled balloon descends into a shot of mountains and turns upside down. Cut: to a balloon-draped tree and Buster perched on a top branch, surveying his new kingdom. Fade.

The remainder of *The Balloonatic* becomes *Hard Luck Revisited*, as if Keaton has created a sequel to continue his adventures in the woods with another seemingly independent woman whom Buster desires. Princess and Prince will meet again in this territory, and who will save whom is the question worth pondering. Moments after the crash-landing, we fade in to Buster, adapting and spreading himself out over the wilderness. He fuels a stove on the right via a smokestack leading into the heaving, patched balloon; utensils hang on a tree. The saga of the Prince and Princess will resume almost immediately once Buster expands his comical business over stream and woods. In keeping with the fantastic nature of the film, *The Balloonatic* sustains itself with a collection of "narrative jump-cuts" to connect such far-reaching locations. Already we have "jumped" with Buster from fun house to real world to someplace perhaps over the rainbow. *The Balloonatic* resembles a "chain bracelet," an image that Kerr used to describe *Daydreams*; every episode is a "knot in a string," all following the same linear direction, but each knot (episode) separate onto itself.[2] Robinson surmised that this linear structure may have been one reason why Keaton was dissatisfied with *The Balloonatic*, but it prompts the question of why *Hard Luck*, with a similar structure, was reportedly one of Keaton's favorites. After all, flying in a balloon is far more possible than falling through the earth via a swimming pool. Perhaps Keaton considered *The Balloonatic* an inferior *Hard Luck*, falling short of its fairy-tale expectations because such a genre was not common in his repertoire. Thus, this film becomes just a secondhand arena for Buster to work in. Keaton's dissatisfaction may also have been his impatience at this point in his career to develop an in-depth feature story. Such a dream was stifled by the limits of a two-reel film. It seems that Buster was growing faster than Keaton's ability to afford him a proper vehicle.

The "chain-bracelet" of *The Balloonatic*, then, consists of vignettes exhausting the variations of earth-sea-and-sky in Buster's hands. Both he and the girl are returning to nature, reentering a slapstick Garden of Eden; there, they are destined to know each other, survive together, and if compatible, join their lives to fulfill the childlike promise with which this story began. Unlike most Keaton films, the vignettes brimming with Buster's signature gestures and expressions are surprisingly matched to a notable degree by those of the girl. Princess is endowed with more of a role and responsibility than any Keaton heroine to date. As she has already proven, she has much to offer that even Buster desires as his own.

Each vignette becomes little more than a dimensional painting of Buster trying out survival tactics in an alien landscape. He shows none of the discernible anger of recent films but rather a patience that may come from being in Nature. Buster has no right to be angry, for although he was dropped against his will, it was also *because of* his will that he fell: although Fate provided the bird, he chose to shoot it on the balloon. A primitive instinct is emerging in Buster, one removing him from rationalization, fault-finding, and all the desperate emotions that come from overthinking. He can only see basic equations such as Bird = Dinner, without thought for the complex layers that hide curveballs and backfires. Buster is almost back to the carefree existence of *The Scarecrow*, but in the Great Outdoors; and while he is still faced with challenges, they are merely pleasant puzzles and small games. He submerges himself quickly into survival of the fittest, blessed with brawn, instinct, and memories of a "former life" where mechanical ingenuity prevailed. His balloon-god has given him all the tools he will need, and he must find the best ways to use them or perish. Buster is modern man transported back in time and place, and although he must reinvent the wheel, he is equipped with that subconscious knowledge to guide him. His isolation no longer signifies loneliness, for he answers to a company of voices: a modern man joining in song with ancient voices of the wild. He does not answer in words, for he is happily humming along.

These ideas elevate Buster's slapstick business in *The Balloonatic*. They add volume to the "unspoken" signs and symbols that he performs while searching for a new life. Now clomping off in thigh-high wading boots, Buster stands beside what seems like a very small canoe named MINNIE-TEE-HEE. He picks up a middle section of the canoe and fastens it between the front and rear sections, forming a visual equation: each piece of canoe = whole canoe, with a snap of a hinge. Our lady of Ye Old Mill meanwhile fishes in the stream, a picture of quiet efficiency that Buster emulates with disastrous results. He wades in deeper with every cast until he is up to his neck and picked up by the current before splashing back to shore. Buster flips over to balance on his porkpie in order to drain his overflowing boots. A veteran fishing gag follows, a variation of the icehole fishing in *The Frozen North*: Buster casts his line behind him over a low branch and around to the seat of his pants; he pulls his legs out from under him and dangles momentarily before falling promptly into the water. Princess notices the escapade, but her dignity never wavers. Buster = seal; his boots slide down to his knees like flippers as he waddles along a peninsula to resume fishing.

Buster's repartee with a fish in the next sequence recalls his best earlier outdoor routines. More important, it records Keaton's play with space and symmetry as Buster crawls back and forth on land to keep up with the fish in the water. As with the ball-eating fish of *Convict 13*, Buster communicates with this potential catch, hoping it will voluntarily hop into his creel. He dangles the line invitingly, shoos the fish from side to side, waves at it, even smacks it. Princess by contrast nets a big one, and although she drops it, she leaps on it with a victory cry and lopes off with her prize. She is unintentionally mocking Buster by her hands-on treatment of nature and recouping her near-loss; she facilely combines luck and daring. Buster, however, strains his luck by trying to be too nice. Though he also attempts to be hands-on, he is hesitant, approaching the wilderness as if it were a playroom of breakable toys. He is not fully aware that he must master his wooded kingdom and all creatures great and small before being worthy of his intended title.

As Keaton leisurely develops "variations on a theme" with the fishing sequence, he punctuates Buster's business with that of Princess, as verses in a song are punctuated by a refrain. Princess's refrain is an anchor in Buster's unpredictable existence, made rocky by the clash between Reality and Fantasy. In her vintage 1923 bathing suit, Princess heads off for a swim with skips and hops, an odd combination of coy femininity and rugged outdoorsmanship (coincidentally, Phyllis Haver was one of Mack Sennett's original Bathing Beauties).[3] Their separate actions will eventu-

**321**

ally merge as Buster draws closer to her swimming area during his angling escapades. As in *Convict 13*, Buster and girl are complements: her enthusiastic method of catching fish is offset by Buster's more subtle techniques. His foray into nature also equates him with the animals that surround him, and he adapts their behaviors to himself. For example, busy as a beaver, he creates his own dam of rocks to trap the elusive fish on the drained ground. Bending and turning clockwise amid his collected catch, he slips small and large fish into his creel—not at first noticing that the bottom, like the loose balloon basket, has dropped open and each fish falls out as quickly as he feeds it in. Only when one large fish strikes him as vaguely familiar does he see his defective creel and hurl it aside. Then, like an animal who stores prey in its pouches, Buster begins stuffing fish into his vest and boots—until the snapping at his legs forces him to remove the fish. A curveball of Fate pushes Buster along his destiny—literally—when the dam breaks, and he courses with the rush of water (Buster = fish) precisely to where the girl is about to dive in. As he rides along, his legs rise in an exclamatory V, much like his upside-down legs spoke so vociferously in the barrel of *Neighbors*. Whenever Buster's face and hands become incapacitated from expressing his reactions or needs, his legs do the talking—with moves that resemble either question marks or exclamation points, or a simple reaching out for help. Her fancy dive ruined, Princess scolds and pitches a rock at Buster as he waddles away with his flipper-boots and collapses on the ground. While embarrassing, the encounter is only one-half of the picture, in the tradition of Keaton's equations. It is both a disaster and a promising initiation, and in that light, Buster's leg-talk might well be predicting a V for Victory at once more "running into" his Beloved-To-Be.

Buster's fishing exercise leads to the next phase of this linear adventure, the next knot in the string. After a mishap with the canoe (still tied to the shore, only two-thirds of it sails off with him), Buster sets about to cook his fish, just as his counterpart does. Princess, however, shows a firm grasp on reality, for she broils her fish between proper metal grills. Out of his innocence in being in the wild, or perhaps unconsciously even as an "I'll show you" retort to the bold Princess, Buster opts to cook his catch right where he is—by igniting branches in the canoe and using tennis rackets as grills. His illogical approach to such risky business may be attributed to the tension between Princess and himself and the fear/exhilaration/wonder of being in the wild. He seems to have regressed to the naive mind-set of prehistoric man who has just discovered fire and does not realize exactly how much it will burn. The gap between Buster's naiveté and experience now works to his disadvantage, canceling out his sense, blocking his growth. He is not able to combine both sides of his personality, but rather one subsumes the other, taking turns, feeling lopsided. Ironically, at the same time, as one side gives way to the other, Buster is forced to grapple with the consequences of his mistakes. So, in trying to toast his catch, Buster reacts quickly to douse the leaping flames that devour branches, rackets, and (as he bails water with his porkpie) the bottom of the canoe. Cut: a smoky parallel with the serene Princess interrupts Buster's dilemma, almost as if to leave him pondering his next move. As Princess sips her fresh coffee, her eyes suddenly bulge, and she bellows a puff of smoke and dumps out the coffee. It seems that despite the collisions and aloof feelings of this star-crossed relationship, these babes in the woods at least share an equal incompetence for cooking.

Buster's frequent fluctuations between his two personalities in the long run contributes to the major weaknesses of *The Balloonatic*. As with all of Keaton's flawed films, while individual gags shine with sharply accented Buster-trademarks, they also pull the fabric of the film apart because of their spotlighted presentation and overdeliberation (or the gag-for-gag's-sake syndrome). More important, however, the film is strained by the tug-of-war between the two most powerful influences in Buster's life: Fantasy and Reality. In a way, Keaton himself also seems uncertain about his preference in this film: while beginning with a strong fairy-tale motif and indulging in fantastic situations (fun house, balloon ride, woods), Keaton inserts enough mundane activity (love rejections, cooking, fishing, and soon hunting) to tie Buster to an ordinary existence. Buster's illogic even corrodes his versatile moments in reality, starkly depicting him as absentminded and inept—far from the princely league. His behavior is in fact so removed from "prince" that we need to remind ourselves continually of Keaton's peculiar first title. "Prince" is an image that would suit Buster if only the film itself supported this identity. The two worlds that alternate before us do little more than draw out the extremes of Buster's behavior, with too few subtle dualities that usually enrich his personality. As a result, we are left with no truly real-Reality or fantastical-Fantasy against which to measure Buster's growth into the royal ranks.

We segue into the last major "Reality" sequence of *The Balloonatic* (hunting) with a transitional gag that joins water and land. Buster skims along the surface of the water in his canoe, as though never damaged by the reckless campfire, and spots a bunny on shore. The camera pans along as he steers for land, pulls in his oar, and smoothly walks out of the water—with the canoe suspended around his waist. Buster = plug, redeeming himself for his carelessness. Wearing the canoe, he aims his loaded gun at the bunny who, in the nick of time, hops aside to reveal a poignant family. Obviously moved, Buster walks back into the water until the canoe hits the surface and glides effortlessly out of the frame. By the next shot, he drifts while relaxing and reading a magazine. This lull seems more a deliberate pause than just another scene in Buster's bucolic story; it builds the tension for another "surprise" from a "ridiculous situation." Keaton is, in fact, setting up a twist that will capsize Buster right out of his lazy hour and return him to a sterner reality. An extreme long shot reveals to us the curveball that Buster does not yet see: waterfalls ahead. As in *The Boat* when he failed to spot the approaching bridges, Buster is now due to be scolded for his laid-back attitude to duty—in this case, being alert to the unexpected threats of Nature. However, while Captain Buster made up for his negligence with rapid-fire repairs, our hero responds blandly. Buster's complacency to tame the wilds has virtually lost the competition with a woman, of all people, who sought adventure while he only (literally) glided into it. The few adventures that Buster has so far entered on his own initiative have been the fun house and Ye Old Mill, neither of which challenged him. He only paid admission for cheap thrills like any other customer or to make an easy conquest. It almost seems as if Buster's choices have fallen short of his usual headlong plunge into deeply emotional connections. Up to this moment, his choices have been as shallow as his papier-mâché monsters. Buster needs help to grow—or to grow up, and for once, Fate appears to be a Supreme Teacher, with Princess as its Assistant. It regards Buster as a promising but wayward student who must be disciplined for his greatest lesson and reward. Fate has driven Buster into a metaphorical classroom—the forest—which both nurtures and nettles him to the limit. In fact, Fate provided him with the bird, the means by which Buster landed in the woods; Fate allowed him to fall in that precise location to find his princess again, after his inappropriate behavior lost her the first time. With this view, the opening title assumes a deeper significance with the words "YOUNG"—in experience, not just age, and "TROUBLE"—not just fun house, but the trouble Buster will have as long as he flounders in the waters of Life. Fate has cast a wise eye on Buster's youthful dilemma and encourages him to grow by throwing him "back-to-basics." In doing so,

Fate is stern, demanding, but surprisingly not mean. Suddenly, too, the nature of the fairy tale begins to fit this plot like a perfect glove. Given Fate's previous cruel treatment of Buster in Reality, its offer to be his Friend and Mentor can only be believed in Fantasy. Whether Fate will remain a benevolent "fairy godperson" or turn into an ogre who destroys Buster is yet to be seen; it is not unlike Fate to delude its favorite child mercilessly until the end.

Princess spots Buster's gesticulating legs as they "shout" from the bottom of the overturned canoe. We cut between her quick thinking to fetch a rope and Buster's ride down the river with his legs poised like antennae on the hapless vessel. Princess's intention, however, is grander than her ability to throw the rope, and when she pitches the whole coil into the water, she sits in momentary defeat. The canoe rams into a bank, and Buster's boots lie speechlessly on the top of the boat's bottom. Fearless Princess scrambles into the water and upturns the canoe, only to find it empty. Suddenly, she flips into the air—Buster emerges directly under her. Slamming his waterlogged hat on his head, he leads her by the hand to the embankment. For the first time since their hit-and-miss outing at the amusement park, one shot encompasses them together. Princess shakes her head, a gesture as filled with multiple meanings as any of Buster's moves. Her expression reads disbelief, disapproval, annoyance, even regret that one so bright could fumble so well. She remembers him as the masher but now willingly, perhaps sympathetically, holds his hand and sits beside him in his embarrassed hour. Typical for this film, however, Buster's reaction is far more superficial: he spits out a stream of water and sets on his cockeyed hat. His expression reads plain and simple chagrin at being deprived of his play-time. Fade out.

This film lacks direction and a clear sense of progress or change in Buster, for there is, in fact, no real story to support the action or character. Because of the title, we expect to return to the balloon at some point to define the purpose of his aimless ramblings and rehashed gags. Yet even in these closing sequences, the balloon remains hidden away until the finale, like some well-kept secret. Buster instead putters around by rigging the canoe with a striped canopy. He seems to select pastimes as one with a surplus of time on his hands. Princess meanwhile has to contend with weightier matters: she calls out for help as she is cornered against a rock wall by an unfriendly longhorn bull. Buster vaguely discerns her muffled cry, but it could as well be a birdcall for all the logic he employs to assist her. Laying his rifle down, he dives into the stream, lands on his chest in inch-deep water, and paddles furiously with desperate gasps for air. He suddenly rises, looks around, and stalks across the water instead, dragging his rifle. What did Buster hope to accomplish by leaving his rifle onshore as he swam to help Princess? Perhaps he had delusions of wrestling the bull to the ground like mighty Samson instead of shooting it. Nonetheless, he undermines his own intentions by not attending to the moves that would ensure his success. Not aware of having flooded his weapon, then, a spray of water shoots out when he fires. Cause and effect: drag a rifle through water and it will not work. Buster has not yet absorbed the nature of cause and effect, although he has had ample opportunity to learn it. And, unfortunately, he shows little promise of doing so any time soon.

A dramatic shot of Princess standing inches from being gored is juxtaposed with comic-relief shots of Buster confounded by his rifle: he drains the gun, but the ammunition drops out in a clump; he burns his hand on it; when he fires again, a firework arcs over his head and he leaps into the bushes. By the time we return to Princess, her annoyance at his delay pumps her adrenalin into taking action—or, literally, taking the bull by the horns. As Buster emerges from his fog of confusion, each of his facial expressions triggers a corresponding shot of Princess dealing with the dilemma from which she had hoped Buster would deliver her. He double-takes; she drops the bull to the ground. He blinks, stares at us, stares at her; she pins the bull down. Buster strolls out casually, bowing, waving, and tipping his hat to her as she escapes, but she beckons sternly to him. By contrast, Buster himself has fallen on the "horns of a dilemma" because of his own stubbornly stunted growth. He did identify his role as male warrior to protect his loved one from the enemy but proved incapable of the duty. To compensate, Princess, who instinctively relinquished her personal bravado to her man, was forced to reassume the warrior role, dramatically using her bare hands for the fight. Once again, with visual contrast, Princess has pinpointed Buster's weaknesses, his Milquetoast personality, his ineptitude for survival. His poor choice of what to do in the shadow of danger is as futile as his selections in the fun house. Princess is flabbergasted, angered, and ready to rebuke him for not discovering his place as warrior, hero, and Prince. Buster, however, recognizes his gaffe but chooses to leave, not because he feels diminished, but more so because he is stunned, even afraid of the woman herself. Flashing before his mental eye is the blow she launched in the dark tunnel, and he probably now counts himself lucky that she did not pulverize him when she had the chance.

The Buster persona, for the first time in its existence, has been lulled into a composure that Fate seems reluctant to change, and his slightly spoiled-brat attitude relishes the luxury of no challenges. If *The Balloonatic* were Buster's first or only portrait, we could accept but not particularly admire the character. In light of the seventeen prior shorts, however, his persona here is pale and empty; he is full of clever inventions but scatterbrained in any actions beyond those with machines. And despite its related theme and setting, this Buster is no match for the *Hard Luck* hero who earned his heroism by climbing the mountain of sheer hopelessness to achieve the apex of success. As mild challenges befall him in *The Balloonatic*, Buster parks himself in neutral, with only the barest interest in driving himself out of the garage. Although Princess asked him to do just that during her scare, Buster acts not the least perturbed about his inability to meet her expectations. The saddest facet of Buster's personality is his own lack of patent expectations as well.

With final exam time in the concluding scenes, Buster's last opportunity to graduate approaches. Still smarting from a slightly bruised ego and Princess's persistent nagging, Buster stomps off with rifle underarm and spies more big game—something akin to a squirrel—to hunt. He intently crawls along the ground to pounce upon it like a trained soldier in combat. In one of Keaton's typical plays with space, Buster's real challenge is not what lies before him but *behind* him, and in what he does not see but what *we* can see from our frontal perspective. As Buster begins his hunt, walking, then crawling into his shots, a bear uncurls itself from sleep and steps in line directly behind him. Keaton pans the two moving toward us (toward the offscreen squirrel), with the camera positioned at a slight diagonal to minimize the distance between Buster and bear while maximizing the tension of Buster's unknown.

Meanwhile, Princess unleashes her own frustration at Buster by chopping a tree and once again must rescue herself when it falls on her. She is physically unharmed, but her clumsiness has actually toppled her from her pedestal, ironically boosting Buster by contrast: now *he* is genuinely in danger. He still fails to realize that for every hunter, there is a hunted, and sometimes the two switch roles. Once Princess extricates herself, she watches in horror as the bear nibbles at the seat of Buster's pants; ironically, she does not run to his rescue as she expected him to do for her.

# The Balloonatic

Buster shoots into the left side of the frame, supposedly at the squirrel, but instead lops off the top of a cactus. As he peers into a large hole in the ground, two furry knobs suddenly lift into the ears of another large bear, now staring directly into his face. Cut: Buster backs into a long shot in which the first bear sits like a hairy pyramid. Cut to extreme long shot: both bears bookend Buster. Only seeing the bear before him, he knocks it on the head with the gun, unintentionally firing with the impact and downing the first bear. Buster sits in shock—on the first bear—and fans himself with his hat until he realizes that his "rock" is unusually furry. He leaps aside but braves the motionless bear to check for a heartbeat. His amazement has probably as much to do with where this bear came from as it does with how he finally managed to do something right.

Buster's innocent fortune in eliminating both bears immediately impresses Princess for the first time in the film. Buster recognizes her sudden change of heart and, being somewhat superficial himself, becomes arrogantly flattered by her adulation and convinced of his superiority. Princess stretches out humble arms to him, and he begins to display his musculature in a variety of Atlas poses. Princess seems to have forgotten Buster's numerous failures in the line of duty. Her cherished dream of combined adventure and romance is now filtered through eyes that only see a virile hero before her. She quickly abandons her own machisma and lets a man do what he is "meant" to do—what she has waited for him to do. Princess has certainly been the exception to the typical Keaton heroine (except perhaps Kate in *My Wife's Relations* who, however, had no redeeming qualities). Still, Princess has had to compensate for Buster's dearth of masculinity. Once he succeeds at hunting, with two carcasses to show for it, Princess accepts a more "traditional" woman's role, in accordance with Keaton's definition of heroine. Submission becomes a radically new ingredient in her chemistry, feeding into Buster's blatant domination of her as well as of the wild. Perhaps he feels he has tamed both at last. His power is seen through his flourish of muscles and how he "speaks" to her, his facial expression suggesting a harshly reprimanding tone. Princess responds by hanging her head, as if in shame to have ever doubted him. The irony of the ending, and of *The Balloonatic* as a whole, is that Buster has *still* not accomplished anything on his own (although he did hit the bear on the head), yet his sudden self-importance will no doubt turn his simple bear story into a "tall tale" ("I was surrounded by *ten* bears") for some future grandchild. The far superior character all along has been Princess, yet she is not allowed to remain so. The happy ending assures Buster's graduation with both an A for effort and a typical Keaton woman at his side, spilling over with sentimental froth. Our own disappointment in her sudden about-face (and in Buster's self-serious ego) is consoled by knowing that, if tested again, Princess's pure love of adventure and courage will surpass any of her mate's bumblings.

Buster has not had hard luck in these woods; he has had *little* luck. But it has been enough luck to ultimately bestow upon him his royal title and degree of manhood. One test remains to reinforce the hard lessons. As the shy but proud Princess listens to her Prince, the bear in the hole awakens and emerges. In a rare twist of visual perspective, Buster now sees what approaches him while Princess does not. Buster drops weakly against her; giggling, she pushes him away, thinking he is wooing her. Each time she pushes, he drops against her until she leaves and he falls. Buster quickly leads Princess to the canopied canoe—the earlier prop that seemed lost in the roster of adventures. He welcomes her into it, camouflaging his fear with gallantry. After a last look behind him, he launches the canoe down the river. Buster rests his head on her shoulder as they converse, when suddenly Princess points offscreen—the bear in long shot is heading toward the water. Bluffing, Buster rolls up his sleeves, raises a threatening fist, and prepares to swim back. Princess pleads with him not to, and too instantly, Buster shrugs and settles back, opting to sing with a ukulele. Princess does not wish to prolong her new love's test of manhood—nor does Buster. On one level, she probably recalls his inadequacies; on another level, he is now the courtier of her dreams, and she needs him intact. To us, Buster has failed again to live up to his bravado, created by luck and sustained by bluff. He also has the expectation that Princess will talk him out of going back, and he won't argue. Buster has finally found the blend of two worlds: he has settled into fantasyland, riding a serene stream with a woman in her proper place, and the only reality he may have to face is mending his canoe.

For good measure, Fate decides to hurl a curveball, although its pitching average has been uncharacteristically low in this film. The waterfalls that we thought had been abandoned in an earlier gag are now inserted between shots of romantic crooning and a magic kiss that helps Buster strum more emphatically. Neither Prince nor Princess hear the falls, no doubt deafened by the music of love. Although Buster did not go over the falls the first time, we somehow do not expect him to go over now either. The moment is too poetic and too near the end of the film to warrant such prolonged disaster. Instead of plunging, then, the canoe glides straight out into space and across the frame. Princess panics when she casually looks over the side into space; Buster, however, shakes his head and points up. An extreme long shot depicts the balloon victoriously carrying the canoe like a cradle as it floats over the woods. Together in one shot again, Buster lays his head on her shoulder and she kisses him. The two ends of the three-part canoe suddenly fall off like a punctuation, but Prince and Princess sail along, never even noticing. Fade. THE END.

For all of Buster's shortcomings in *The Balloonatic*, his one strength has been his ability to think like a machine when dealing with machines. His most genuine challenge has not been in hunting and fishing—both of which he approached rather listlessly as one approaches tedious house chores. He has been most challenged in fixing his "machines" (canoe and balloon) and in keeping the fantasy of both alive in his mind and heart as he wades through "Reality." Sustaining Buster throughout the film is an inordinate amount of optimism that even keeps Fate at bay. Perhaps his perilous journey *on* (not in) the balloon fortified his belief in fantasy—in fairy tales—and urged him to complete his chores as quickly (and reck-lessly) as possible so he can return to re-creating fantasy. Ironically, Keaton built his film around a predictable life in the woods while only hinting at Buster's main interest in repairing his balloon; such shots were random inserts, enough to remind us of his fantastic voyage, but never lasting long enough to show us his plans. Whenever his survival skills failed, his optimism instead rescued him; in his mind, he always contin-ued floating above his travails. His fortuitous balloon trip gave him a goal and a model to follow for the rest of his life. With such a dream-life ahead of him, Buster probably knew he had enough physical stamina, basic instinct, and luck to help him through dangers.

Perhaps Buster is only a half-hero in *The Balloonatic*, flunking his terrestrial duties as a woodsman, yet still staying alive to talk about it. His other half is ensconced in the fairy tale, which permits amazing things to happen to ordinary folk like him. The spirit of the fairy tale frees Buster from obligation on earth. The balloon that began his only important adventure—transcending earthly disappointments and illusions—now promises to continue his adventure happily ever after. By leaving the world on the steam of his imagination, Buster has become Master of Nature. To master it is to dispense with it when one chooses, and Buster is more than ready for this choice.

Buster's supplies are probably exhausted—his hunting did not garner food, nor does he even have the ends of his canoe. Yet somehow, he seems to have all he needs simply by leaving a world that has always fallen short of sustaining him. Fate too has controlled itself, allowing Buster to leave only with a mere threat (waterfalls), knowing that Buster will avoid them because he has ensured the perfect escape. By not showing Buster's repairs in detail, Keaton has kept his work sacred, protected from prying eyes, including those of Fate. Buster has not been jinxed and is now doubly protected by the kiss of a Princess, whose magic reputedly turns frog into princes. With all his foibles and fumbles, Buster has indeed come a long way from tadpole.

As much as *The Balloonatic* is an absurd story for Keaton, whose fantasy-world has been embedded in dreams, this short is a lucky charm for Buster. It has resuscitated his spirit, fortified his grasp on the impossible, and revived his belief in magic—albeit within the fairy tale. Yet fairy tales have been the food with which real children, like Buster, feed their dreams. If this Prince and Princess are really heading toward their castle in the sky, may they never come back to earth.

## Chapter 20

# The Love Nest

### (March 1923)

Courtesy of the Academy of Motion Picture Arts and Sciences

Shortly into the making of *The Love Nest*, Joseph M. Schenck determined that Keaton, whose talents he felt were being wasted in short films, should begin making features. The Keaton Studios suspended operations in March 1923 to prepare for the new schedule.[1] As a conclusion to his two-reel career, *The Love Nest* condenses all the best of Buster— his dream-mind; his thoughtful perceptions of Machine, Woman, Nature, and Self; his wry humor and

**332**

mesmerizing agility—and all the best of Keaton as director into a snappy visual portrait of a whole, feeling hero. The lessons learned and unlearned over eighteen short-film lives are evident in this last, nineteenth, existence. While Keaton may have made these films with little intention of linking them thematically, nonetheless his style and outlook have aligned the films in a continuum that nurtures a uniquely dimensional comic persona. *The Love Nest*, long considered "lost" and reconstructed by Raymond Rohauer from various sources in the 1970s, is a resounding cap to Keaton's independent short films. It celebrates Buster the child grown at last into an adult.

The film opens with a poignant title, one bristling with the double-edged meaning of Life—that for every bit of beauty there is a corresponding pain. EVEN THE BEST SUNSET ISN'T MUCH GOOD WHEN YOUR GIRL CHOOSES TO TELL YOU GOODBYE. We are plunged into a situation that has been vitally important for Buster in nearly every short: having a lifelong mate. An equally moving image brands the effect of Buster's silent rejection on our minds: silhouetted by a fence against the best of sunsets on the sea, Buster and his girl fade into view. She has turned her back on him, but he reaches out to her. Whether his hand wants to hold her or to shake goodbye, it is nonetheless ignored. Another title follows: BUSTER DECIDED TO SWEAR OFF WOMEN FOREVER. Keaton emphasizes Buster's sudden about-face as his way of dealing with this blow to his romantic nature. His reaction is a sign of a desperately sensitive soul—one who pretends not to care, but whose drastic move belies the depth of his sadness. We fade into a shot of a small boat roped to a pier, then cut to a close-up of Buster's handwritten letter to the girl:

> YOU TREACHEROUS VIPER,
>     SINCE YOU BROKE OFF OUR ENGAGEMENT, I HAVE DECIDED NOT TO MARRY YOU. I AM LEAVING FOR A TRIP AROUND THE WORLD TO FORGET YOU.
>         YOURS—BUT NO MORE
>         BUSTER

The shots seem like fragments of a soul, flashes of moments, more photographs in the album of time. Buster retaliates with a stinging name for his girl, YOU TREACHEROUS VIPER—melodramatic and therefore comical, but still logical to a childlike, sometimes childish creature. He resorts to name-calling to compensate for his hurt feelings. He reminds her of what could have been hers (YOURS) and almost relishes taunting her with the loss, as if *he* is doing the breaking off (—BUT NO MORE).

The world-bound vessel reveals its ironic name to us in the next shot: CUPID. Buster stands in the nose of the boat covered by a tent; he symbolically stands in and is surrounded by the symbol of romance (as critical as the air he breathes) while holding a photo of Viper. We peer at the photo from a slightly high angle, past Buster's shoulder and hat, as if we are allowed to look upon the source of his heartbreak without trespassing, without witnessing any private emotion his face might show. When Buster turns out of the frame pulling the photo with him, we are left with the backdrop of lapping water. Keaton has rarely left a shot "hanging" after his hero exits; this is another impressionistic image of the water (a significant element in this film), which visually translates Buster's feelings for us. We imagine the sound of water as his softly breaking heart, the feel of water as his tears. The shot is briefly lonely and very much Buster at this moment.

However, as early as *One Week*, Keaton usually intends for Buster's emotional arsenal to explode only so far before it is blocked by his stone face. While his rejection drives him to uproot his life, he probably senses (in another profound equation) that rejection = freedom; therefore, sailing past tears and loneliness will eventually lead to a new land of opportunity. Buster suggests this hindsight/foresight as he carefully dabs his sudden W. S. Hart-like tears with his pinky and meticulously seals the envelope with them. Whenever Buster cries actual tears, he cues us to laugh. Keaton will not allow these messengers of misery to alter his hero's expression, but they do enhance the humor of his face and, ironically, of the situation. Keaton plays again with the paradox that tears accompany both joy and sorrow, freeing us to relish the joy while Buster absorbs the sorrow and churns it into a comic learning experience. His motivation to live on now despite rejection pays homage to the spirit that was so easily crushed in *Cops* and *Daydreams*.

Buster hands the letter to a passerby with instructions to "TAKE THIS TO MY EX-GIRLFRIEND" and proceeds to untie the rope. Buster is precise in stating his feelings: TREACHEROUS VIPER; I HAVE DECIDED; FORGET YOU; YOURS—BUT NO MORE; EX-GIRLFRIEND. With such a determined voice about what he leaves behind, Buster's progress in life will become easier. Belittling someone so important to him is a self-centered coping mechanism, to be sure, but it is also a necessary one for Buster to keep from forfeiting his life for another.

# The Love Nest

Buster steps into the shelter of his boat-tent. The setting is reminiscent of the igloo in *The Frozen North*—this time with pots and pans hanging on the luminous white canvas, instead of floating guitars on the ice wall. But while *The Frozen North* is a burlesque with surreal images, the present film is realistic while also evoking the sensation of a dream. Buster has adorned his tent with survival tools rather than silly sight-gag luxuries (guitars, ice-carpet sweepers). The simple poles that brace the interior top and sides of the tent also form a series of receding rectangles framing Buster. Boats lend themselves to womblike structures and offer Keaton imaginative ways to construct a cocoonlike environment with his sets. DAMFINO in *The Boat* was webbed with planks that embraced and circled; now the sheltering translucence of the tent over little CUPID offers an almost membranous feel, as if Buster is nestled inside a heart. The optical illusion of lines crossing and interlocking with each other is also much like staring at a series of boxes drawn within boxes until it is hard to tell whether they are moving inward or outward. This layered backdrop fastens Buster into itself, fitting his condition—physical and emotional—like a glove.

As Buster revs the engine, parts of his body are abstractly cut out of the frame with each move. Given Keaton's concern to include important elements in every shot, it is curious that Buster would now appear so fragmented and off-kilter. Yet impressions of time, place, and emotion are being created, not naturalistic photographs of everyday life. Or, perhaps Keaton is lifting everyday life into a dreamlike vision. *The Love Nest* begins to read like a visual poem, a comic ode to the sea and to those, like Buster, who turn to it for solace. Buster unrolls a map that nearly blanks out the frame with its size, like *The High Sign* newspaper; its enormity suggests the vast distances Buster thinks he must travel to forget his hurt. As he lays the map on an offscreen surface, we cut to a profile shot of CUPID with its frail captain leaning out of his tent to study his route. Before the last fade of this sequence, Buster poses against his neatly ordered kitchenware, his full-face stare penetrating our gaze with determination, tinged with resigned fatigue.

Title: LATER. How much later is unknown, but when we fade into Buster in the same pose, he now sports a beard—painted on—and can scarcely hold up his exhausted head. The last of his provisions are piled helter-skelter now. Buster peers wearily through binoculars; we enter his perspective through a binocular-shaped mask and see the bisected monotony of sea meeting sky. In addition, as has been the style from the moment Buster set foot on CUPID, we rock slightly, as though we through the camera vicariously experience the voyage with Buster. Bored and lonely, he extracts Viper's photo from within his shirt. For all his vehement intention to FORGET YOU, Buster's deep-rooted passion compels him to look at her photo when the journey wears him thin. Aside from this sentimental detour, which Keaton does not mock (as in *The Scarecrow*, he honors true romance), all else about this odyssey is satirized in subtle ways.

Perhaps the most peculiar comical vision of *The Love Nest* is that of Buster with his "beard." The two shots of Buster with and without beard, which are linked by the title LATER, wryly depict time, space, and Buster's condition. The very word LATER is a signal of how Keaton plays with these three elements. Finding Buster in the exact same position "before and after" and wearing his tongue-in-cheek beard is an instant sight gag. This identical-pose gag recalls *The Paleface* with Buster and squab kissing TWO YEARS LATER, although that situation offered a different slant. The tag-ending of the couple with the same unchanged background and action derived its punch from identical repetition; by its sameness, it alluded to Buster's quest for an unchanging love. In *The Love Nest*, however, LATER introduces a tangible change in the background; and while the foreground has not altered its *action*, the *substance* has radically transformed (Buster + beard). Its punch is then derived from realizing that no matter how Buster has staggered about in heartsick desperation and depleted his victuals, he resumes the same pose LATER as though he has never budged. He sits like an anchor in time and space, the only solid force that halts the chaos around him; and by doing so, he suggests his potential for stability and perseverance. By falling into the same pose, Buster also heightens the monotony of the trip and of his adopted life, as if he has no recourse but to sit the same way after each break. His tranquility is then actually boredom, verging on comatose despair.

Enforcing this condition is the beautiful sight gag of Buster's beard. Except for furry appliques, Buster has been eternally clean-shaven and has remained so no matter how much time elapses, without even a hint of five o'clock shadow. Here, however, the expository title is purposely vague (LATER), and we probably never considered days or weeks but only minutes or hours when first reading the word. Now this one-word title twists our expectations of time as suggested by the "growth" of his beard. Keaton demonstrates this time lapse through physical change, and so Buster, having become lost at sea, wears his beard like a calendar. In addition to creating another dreamlike effect, the painted beard also suggests that Buster is so young he cannot even grow his own. Keaton did not use a scraggly Rip Van Winkle type of beard, which would have been equally rich on Buster's face; instead, he opted for a painted design, implying his inability to sprout facial hair. Thus, more than ever, Buster's youthfulness is critical to his character and his journey into maturity more intense. Not that he will suddenly grow a real beard by the end, but through his growth, he may indeed be capable of it.

When he suddenly snaps into action, Buster presses the photo to his chest, then rummages through a crate reading HARD JACK (sea-bleary eyes could read it as HARD LUCK and not be far from the truth) and extracts a biscuit. His nonverbal actions speak of great hunger, for as he devours the biscuit, he catches crumbs in a cupped hand and pours them into his mouth like fresh water. He removes his hat and lies down, the camera tilting slightly as if to commiserate; it has all along been sympathizing by rocking with Buster as if to console him that he is not really alone. As Buster drifts to sleep, his arm and porkpie sink to the floor.

We cut abruptly to a whaling ship, and our rocking perspective lets us feel as if we are on watch while our Captain naps. BUSTER MEETS A WHALING SHIP WITH THE MEANEST SKIPPER ON THE SEVEN SEAS. Buster props himself up in his bunk and steps out on deck to survey the whaler, in a shot that not only suggests its huge size against the little CUPID but also highlights its name: THE LOVE NEST. If a captain ever reflected the name of a ship in his personality, then Skipper Joe (Roberts) and THE LOVE NEST are as far apart as the north and south poles. A title confirms: THE SKIPPER IS A BIT SHORT ON TEMPER, while a medium shot of Joe glaring ferociously speaks a thousand words. As Skipper Joe watches, a mate leads Buster up a ladder into THE LOVE NEST while another shoves off the CUPID. Buster looks wonderingly about as he follows Joe to his quarters. Buster has been forcefully deprived of his tie to sweet romance; his CUPID drifts away on the waves of Life, propelled by the brutal Skipper. Ironically, Buster has entered a new place whose name implies security and comfort. The gap between the whaler's name and the Skipper is so great that Keaton really seems to ask what THE LOVE NEST means *for Buster*. Given its deliberately coincidental appearance, THE LOVE NEST will be a symbol of his persona, who is now as loveless, homeless, and lost as anyone can be.

As usual, Joe provides strong contrast with and reinforcement of Buster's fragile, subtle demeanor. The contrast here is even clearer as Buster in his painted beard stands beside Joe with real mustache and stubble. Joe is full grown (if not overgrown), and Buster nearly shrinks while standing like a dazed child flung against the wall of adulthood. Buster's pretend-beard marks a transitional stage leading from childhood into a world fiercely controlled by an adult. After *The Balloonatic*'s fairy-tale influence, Buster can now be seen as a wee hero thrown by a giant into the prison of some enchanted castle or, fittingly, as a child carried off by a giant predator and dropped into its nest. Pursuing the "Prince" image, Buster is again destined to travel far and wide in search of his heart's goal. His means of transport is a boat, and the voyage will challenge his character, as it has heroes of legend, so that he may transform his inner self, whether or not his external goal is achieved. His angry declaration to see the world will come to naught since only his broken heart is his compass. Rather, in exploring the limits of Innocence on board THE LOVE NEST, Buster will confront Reality (via Joe, face-hair and all) to discover a new world right within the pieces of his heart.

Buster is not the only one intimidated by Joe, for a scrawny, trepidant cook fails at his coffee-pouring duties in his presence. When coffee drips on Joe's big hand, the cook drops the pot, knowing his fate. Joe jerks him upstairs by the back of the neck. With the wonder of a child watching an experiment, Buster studies Joe tossing the cook overboard, then reaching for a wreath from a well-stocked pile and throwing it after him as a memorial. Buster follows Joe like a well-heeled puppy, moving through a space designed by Keaton to stress his "captivity" on the whaler. For example, Joe walks around Buster to fetch the wreath, as if drawing an invisible circle to lock him into his tradition of punishing careless crew members. Buster is not only dwarfed by Joe's bulk but by the ascending stairs from Joe's cabin as well, and by the upper deck on which a pilot steers, like a sentry keeping Buster in check. Thus, Buster is trapped in the boat by both structure and Skipper. Keaton's play with the lines of the boat recalls his treatment of depth in *Convict 13*, with which this dreamy film has much in common.

When Joe returns to his cabin, he heads to a list of names on the wall, which in close-up reads:

THE SHIP'S ROSTER

CHARLES FRAZER
MACK BULLFROG
FRANKIE ADDAMS

# The Love Nest

SIDNEY GRAHAM

Targeting Buster with a mean eye, Joe addresses him as the camera returns to the list, tilting down to the last name that he crosses out,

and after which he clearly enters the name BUSTER. When the shot widens to the whole endlessly rocking cabin again, the movement acquires greater symbolic meaning as Buster and Joe sit across from each other at a table. Buster is on a rocky balance, a seesaw teetering between freedom and imprisonment, and his side is sorely underweighted. The seesaw, loaded with Joe's mass and his ominous announcement ("WE HAPPEN TO BE FRESH OUT OF CABIN BOYS SO YOU'RE HIRED"), suspends Buster helplessly in the air, hanging on for dear life while trying to think of an escape. Cool and collected, Buster never panics; yet his amiable handshake and solemn staring recall his numb look moments before his hanging in *Convict 13*.

NEXT DAY. These two ambiguous, simple time titles (LATER, NEXT DAY) have so far created "chapters," although not as visually structured as the calendar in *One Week* or as pun-laden as the mottos in *The Boat*. Keaton will add more time titles, all of them short, plain, and purposely vague. Doing so is just one more way to trap Buster into a twilight voyage from which there is no precise escape since there is no precise time in which to plan one. Because of his heartbreak, Buster has lost sense of real time; only his "beard" has "grown" to confirm that time does pass. In despair, he has messed up CUPID and been pulled into the whaler without protest. He has been imprisoned, but he does not count days to freedom as an average prisoner would; for him, one minute of heartbreak is the same as any other. Until he finds more purpose to life than drifting between sea and sky, LATER will be as good as NEXT DAY. Now forced by the Skipper to be shipshape on a vessel whose name will remind him of lost love, Buster must decide how to revalue his life or else spend it as fish food.

Not much changes in the course of this nebulous NEXT DAY. The pilot still steers; and as Buster travels a few times through the boat, he passes a crew member whittling down a heap of potatoes, sitting blankly like a landmark. Buster himself is ordered to swab the deck and executes some predictable, stage-based gags. He does not reenact the "broom and knot-hole" routine per se, but he does "milk" a prop within the boat's space. We see Joe leave Buster to relax with a pipe in his cabin. Thus, when Buster empties the contents of the pail overboard, but his backward move redirects the slop into the cabin, the only logical target is the Skipper. We have anticipated trouble for Buster because in seeing how Joe abolishes troublemakers, we know Buster's destiny will attract this punishment like a magnet. Buster's skill at turning simple chores like swabbing into major routines innately invites trouble. Enter the invitee: a skinny mate who gets the brunt of a mop swing and shoves Buster aside; as a result, he inherits the mop and bucket just as Joe bursts in and throws *him* over the side. Buster emerges from behind a mast and meekly hands a wreath to Joe, who was just about to reach for one. Joe tosses it and summons Buster (who peers overboard, then raises his eyes to heaven). Buster's ability to create trouble is uncannily matched by a talent to look inno-cent—the "assumed innocence" that reached its height in *The Goat*. To survive, Buster must instantly become a nonchalant bystander, playing along with Joe's trial-and-punishment and passing the buck (or wreath) onto his own "victim," another less fortunate goat. The perfect timing in which misfortune finds another pawn and bypasses Buster is one rare, lucky human victory against Fate. The plunge was intended for Buster, but perhaps there is a destiny-within-a-destiny after all, maneuvered by a minor god who sympathizes with Buster's long-suffering and secretly moves the Olympian chess piece in his favor.

As Joe deletes another name from his list, Buster thoughtfully pauses on the steps leading into the cabin. He is well aware that his life hangs by a thread under Joe's command and that his survival so far has been purely happenstance (the timely passing of the skinny mate). Buster's quick "aye-aye" salute when Joe leaves him to dust the cabin tacitly acknowl-edges that he walks a wobbly gangplank. However, Buster's caution vies with his curiosity, and when he dusts the Skipper's rifles on the wall, he cannot help playing with one. Joe coincidentally reenters at the exact moment that Buster aims in his direction. To convince Joe that he is not thinking mutiny, Buster turns the ill-timed gesture into an advantage: he abruptly heads upstairs with the gun, descends the ladder over the side of the ship, and unblinkingly disappears into the water. As Joe watches wonderingly, a puff of smoke suddenly billows from the water's surface. Buster emerges with the gun in one hand and a giant fish in the other. Just as casually, Buster retraces his steps, holding up his catch as proof of innocence while Joe scratches his head. Fade. Buster has worked a miracle: although he could not fire to save his girl from the longhorn in *The Balloonatic* after dragging his rifle through the stream, now he shoots the Skipper's dinner underwater. Buster has once more suspended our disbelief because of the dreamlike texture pervading the film. In a way, after *The Balloonatic*'s magical liberation, Buster may have been endowed with superhuman abilities that overturn the boundaries of science with pure imagination.

At this point, *The Love Nest* also evokes memories of *The Playhouse* as well as *The Boat*, not only in the box of a cabin that represents Buster's stage but also in the whimsical illusions that Keaton's theatrics create. One surreal illusion takes places as Buster sighs and gazes wistfully out a porthole through which we see a tiny distant sailing boat. He may recall happier times but is still melancholy. Reality bursts in with Joe who removes the porthole—it is only a porthole-framed painting—and hands it to Buster. Like the stormy painting in *The Boat* that momentarily seemed real when it sprouted a leak, so too this realistic porthole lures Buster to believe that a better world lies beyond his grasp. While both scenes are not real (the water did not gush from the painting; there is no far-off boat), they nevertheless encapsulate the kernels of truth that *are* Buster's life: loss, frustration, and imprisonment. Buster ends up holding both pictures in his hands, as if he is the ultimate decision maker on how to regard these truths. He can cling to his frustrations or choose something better. Unlike *The Boat*, there is no real-weather storm threatening Buster in *The Love Nest*. The storm of Life, however, is always swelling, and Buster is as usual caught in its deceptively calm eye. The porthole itself resembles an eye reflecting back what Buster *thinks* he sees; when it is removed, Buster looks *through* it, so to speak, able to see its front and back as a flat painting. The painting is an odd illusion, for why would a porthole painting even be needed when a boat is full of real portholes? Just then, Buster realizes that he cannot be guided by external visions but only by what he sees in his mind's eye. Buster next looks at the nail in the wall with disgust, as if it were an accomplice to a cruel trick. He returns to the reality of "Hurricane Joe" and to the business of survival, which will grant him another chance and a better purpose for living.

The Skipper demands coffee and Buster returns Viper's photo, which he clutched during his porthole reverie, to its hiding place. Buster uses ingenuity to succeed with the unwieldy coffeepot: he pours the coffee into the cup through a large funnel. Buster's plan to ward off disaster is again marked by meticulous attention in handling the pot; he even dries the funnel fastidiously with a handkerchief. But as in *The Blacksmith*, his exaggerated care is quickly undone because it is affected behavior; just as tending the car was negated by neglecting the white horse, he now walks away, pulling handkerchief, tablecloth, *and* coffee pot into Joe's lap. The Skipper lunges, but Buster stops him with a curt hand and melodramatically staggers upstairs. No use crying over spilled coffee, so Buster abridges Joe's wrath and heads off to his punishment. He pulls a wreath with him as he approaches the rail, pauses to reconsider his selection, exchanges it for a nicer wreath that he hangs around his neck, then prepares to dive. Buster has learned that if he cannot prevent his mistakes, he will be man enough to dole out his own punishment. In a remarkable twist of behavior, Joe pulls Buster back, removes the wreath, and shakes his head almost compassionately. Buster sighs with relief.

What has made the meanest Skipper on seven seas turn kindly to Buster, when other mates have perished with one careless act? Perhaps Buster has earned the mercy of the powers-that-be (via Joe) for the innumerable episodes of misery they have inflicted on him. It seems strange that when Buster merits punishment—guaranteed by the repetitive wreath gag—he is suddenly exonerated. Perhaps Joe was impressed with Buster's creativity with the gun and funnel and finds him handy; or perhaps he is suddenly shamed to see the victim execute a punishment that does not fit the crime. Perhaps, too, for once, this bully is silenced by a silent (and paranoid) creature who moves quickly to accept a punishment assumed to be his. Buster does not cower like the others but offers innocence (feigned or otherwise) even as he walks into a dire end. At the same time, while Buster has indeed hardened himself to the deep losses of love and home, he may prefer a watery end to his lonely life.

If Buster wished to embrace this aquatic exit rather than subjugate himself to a harsh authority, then Fate's interference through a kindly Joe is actually a cruel curveball, depriving our hero of his search for peace and quiet in another world. Yet Buster has obviously touched the irascible Skipper like no one else has. While Buster's unrequited love has forced him to reach beyond that sadness, it has also been the catalyst that softens the Skipper and beats him at his own game. Buster's growing maturity begins to equal the Skipper's, but without such a callous hide; his zeal to do what is "right" (punishing himself) startles the Skipper enough to pull him from the brink of self-destruction. With this new chance for life,

Buster must continue learning more sensible survival skills that will keep him afloat.

Having made a peace of sorts with his nemesis, Buster's saga on THE LOVE NEST now leads him into a new subplot, a comical adaptation of *Moby Dick*. A watchful mate calls out, "WHALE! WHALE!" and Joe summons "ALL HANDS ON DECK!" His order is ripe for Buster's literal interpretations, and as expected, he studies his hands and drops instantly to lay them on the deck. His statuesque motionlessness contrasts with the chaotic crossings of the crew preparing the harpoon. Against the movement, Buster becomes even more obvious in his immobile crouch, fastened to the deck, only grimacing whenever Joe steps on his fingers as he directs the crew. Buster quickly learns another lesson: while still ignorant of the *figurative* meaning of ALL HANDS ON DECK, he does know to lift his hands whenever the Skipper steps his way. When Joe turns to eye him dubiously, Buster obediently replaces hands on deck, as if to ask what fault there is in following his order to the letter.

The next gags are the usual showcases for Buster's dexterity, but they also illustrate the clear direction in which Keaton's storytelling is heading. The gags are integral to the current episode (whale-sighting), which in turn is an extension of the broader sequence—that THE LOVE NEST is on a whaling expedition. Thus, the story is unified by details that fit into the whole picture, with Keaton blending gags into the narrative, not merely performing gags regardless of story. The whaler unavoidably suggests the Melville novel, with all its ramifications for the hero's growth, although the actual connection between book and film is only a whale and a testy captain. But this well-meaning tie-in helps to make *The Love Nest* more than just a spoof of a philosophical sea tale or a forum for nautical gags as *The Boat* was. Buster's character promises to change through obstacles and sure battles with every possible nemesis—Man, Machine, Nature, Self—each looming before Buster individually as well as collaboratively. *The Boat* contained spinning cabins, ironic props, and far-fetched machinery that climaxed within Keaton's beloved storm motif. There is no physical storm in *The Love Nest*, but Buster's quest will be just as tempest-tossed and typified by this challenge of conquering "the whale." It is Everyperson's dare to win the unattainable, and Buster will partake of this conquest, whether he wants it or not. *The Love Nest* immediately assumes epic proportions, however comedic, simply by its "novel" association. Not surprisingly, this film has also been considered a blueprint or sketchbook for Keaton's longer work, *The Navigator*;[2] here, he experimented with details that he would expand from a twenty-minute comic situation into a full-length narrative. Released on the threshold of Keaton's career advance, *The Love Nest* not only prepares for one of his most popular features but proves Keaton's wish to elevate Buster into richer stories that reflect life on multiple levels.

Finally concluding that hands are more useful in action and learning that literal translations are often disastrous, Buster accepts a coil of rope from a mate who tells him to tie it to the rail. Failing at knots, Buster once again willingly offers himself to the Quest; in doing so, he not only compensates for his lack of seamanship but, more important, just tries to do the best he can with what he has. He thus creates a crucial, symbolic equation: Buster = Sailor's Knot. He braces himself, tightens his arms, and turns his fists into knots on the rope. Keaton crosscuts rapidly between Moby undulating, Joe ordering, harpoon zinging, Buster waiting, rope uncoiling. Buster's stonelike stance in his shot contrasts with the bustle in shots around him. Only his eyes move side to side to survey the rope riding out the frame toward its offscreen target as he holds the still end in his steely hands. Cut to whale; cut to the rope suddenly twanging into a straight line out over the rail and yanking Buster, like a harpoon himself, horizontally overboard. His splash into the briny deep fills the screen. Keaton then cuts between shots of the amazed crew, Buster again soaring laterally after the unseen whale, and the whaler set to pursue. Within moments, however, Keaton resolves the sequence—reflecting Buster's own rapid solution to his dilemma—in one significant scene: using a high angle shot of the water, Buster suddenly reappears, towing the rope in a visual exemplar of Man leading Nature. As he exits the same shot, he leaves us with choppy water and the taut rope bisecting the frame. Keaton again offers another "hanging" shot, this time with a different reading of the water. The rope vibrates with the tension of the two giant offscreen opponents. The water suggests a battlefield, its waves agitated by a blunt confrontation between another David and Goliath. The water no longer wears a veneer of sadness. Pulled headlong into a vigorous battle, Buster has won the great white whale, and the water moves as witness and celebrant. When Buster became a knot, merging with the rope itself, he must have understood the consequences of his decision, for he braced himself as if about to hit a mountain. With the impact, the protective shell around his vulnerable core has split open to unleash the power to tow a simple line with a mighty whale at its end.

# The Love Nest

This power has moved mountains, from the giant bulk of the whale itself to the relatively smaller bulk of Skipper Joe who pats Buster on the back when he climbs aboard. Buster hands Joe the rope as if it were only a leash, with a suspiciously innocent look on his face. Buster's "magic" works again: while he was able to hold the whale at bay with a simple grasp, Joe clutching the rope is yanked overboard by Moby like a featherweight. Through the Quest, Buster has been fortified with more than brute strength to tame the creatures of the deep; he has been granted a power to dispense with human creatures by a mere look and gesture. The disappearance of the Skipper even prompts the unflinching pilot on the upper deck to turn and look offscreen. By creating depth, the pilot redirects the space to focus on Buster, now fully in charge, in center foreground. Buster tosses a wreath over the side, bringing this memorial gag full circle back to the person who initiated it. Buster administers his own branch of justice, repaying the losses of his fellow crew and rewarding their sacrifices with that of the perpetrator. As a crowning touch, Buster dons the Skipper's hat, which was conveniently dropped, and summons the crew around him. Not surprisingly, intercut with Buster's action is a close shot of Joe perching on the rail with the hungry water beneath him, like a seething sea monster emerging with a drenched wreath in hand. Unaware of this development, Buster announces: "MEN, I HAVE DECIDED TO TAKE OVER AS CAPTAIN!" Was Buster's earlier innocent playing with the rifle actually camouflaged mutiny? Is the Skipper's meanness too great for Buster to forget, even though it was the Skipper who not only spared Buster but congratulated him on the whale? Or is Buster just stepping in because *someone* has to captain the boat and he has earned the right? Joe only sees mutiny and stalks Buster, who does not see the truth looming behind him; however, he does see the horrified looks on the faces of his men. Buster turns, sheepishly hands back the hat, and doffs his porkpie like old times. He scoots into a door when Joe lunges and orders all the men to jump overboard; they do so gladly (a later cutaway shows them congregated in a lifeboat, watching Buster and Joe). Only the pilot stands firm, but as Joe leaps for him, he suddenly dives over the rail, concluding his own running gag with a circular touch.

The inevitable chase between Joe and Buster now spans many of the potential corners, cubbies, angles, and planes that the boat offers. Keaton's choreography typically stretches out over the geography at hand, creating conflict by a visual matching of objects, and symmetry by the unpredictable alignment of elements in the frame. Joe creates a "black hole" on board ship when he yanks off both the locked door and frame to his cabin, setting it aside and opening a dark gaping rectangle that he enters in search of Buster. Buster himself will eventually emerge from this hole to run through the boat, but before doing so, he performs some brief comic business that closes the major chapters of his life—those vaguely timed, tiny tales that have composed the film thus far. This business begins when Buster futilely fires an empty rifle at Joe. He backs up against a wall, resignedly kisses Viper's photograph goodbye, stuffs it back into his shirt, and crosses his own name off the slate. In rapid succession, Buster has reenacted the earlier rifle gag—but with shattering failure; he has eliminated his own name—beating Joe again and permanently removing himself from the boat, at least in name only. Most important, he has kissed a desperate farewell to his true love. Buster has never forgotten her, and faced with doom, she receives his last thoughts. He is, however, not kissing her goodbye in another bored or lonely moment but because he senses it is the end of his life—he thinks his physical life. Kissing her photo goodbye is only one more step in his journey to maturity; he begins to embrace an unwelcome yet liberating Reality that seemed unthinkable at the start. In gingerly stepping past the Skipper and out the doorway—from dark into light, from threat of death to vitality—Buster's focus will be on saving his life. He will not have time to dwell on one who so easily tossed him aside.

Keaton builds suspense during the ensuing, requisite chase by what he lets us see and not see through Buster's movements. With such visual give-and-take come more striking pictures that maneuver time and space, creating soundless visions despite obvious heavy breathing, shuffling, and clanking along decks. Buster slides toward us as Joe's head pops out of a hatch behind him; Buster heads out left as Joe exits right, suggesting the inevitable dichotomy of the chase. When Buster works solo within the frame, he tangles effortlessly with minor props, such as with the rope that suspends from the left over to the railing. The rope divides the frame into two places and creates a pivot on which Buster spins with his collision. He is once more like an atom, generating his own energy in space. Buster staggers to the door that Joe had earlier set aside when he "unlocked" it and politely knocks before opening. Once again, Keaton neatly ties up his carefully laid-out props with delayed responses: what Joe set up earlier is reused and recycled in an expanded gag and closed up with a tidy denouement—and a sardonic twist. This twist is revealed in an unexpected cut to the side of the boat, where we learn only split seconds before Buster does that the door, in fact, opens to the ladder at the side of the boat. Buster steps past the ladder and drops into the water as Joe watches happily from above. We assume Joe's subjective perspective, looking down on Buster who looks up at us (Joe). From this point of view, it seems as if the railing that frames Buster against the water fortifies his entrapment at the same time that the water laps behind, beckoning him to freedom. We cut closer so that our view now shows a "truth" that Joe cannot see: Buster is grasping a rope of THE LOVE NEST. Like a final tongue-in-cheek jab, a wreath quietly floats past him and out the top of the frame. Joe has finally flung Buster his intended wreath, yet Buster hangs on, never succumbing to the water. Unable or unwilling to swim away, Buster throws a kiss to the wreath—another farewell that signals the end of his past "lives" on board this vessel and his return to the "womb" of the water, where he waits, perhaps, for his next life. Fade out as Buster clings to his lifeline.

THAT NIGHT. A plain yet slightly more pinpointed title implies that Buster has been busy during his escape from the Skipper's control. The vagueness of the previous time titles has somewhat dissipated now that Buster has survived and is alert to the realities of his existence. One reality is catching up on sleep, and we find Buster fast asleep, perched like a peaceful bird on the ladder, leaning against THE LOVE NEST. In his dream-state, he mimics throwing a wreath to the side; Joe's impressionable habit has obviously pervaded Buster's dreams. Once again, Keaton proves the limitless possibilities of recycling his gags, even when they seem to be exhausted. Forgetting where he is when he awakens, Buster nearly slides into the water, then continues with his plan of action. The next shot is totally black, with only the white rail spanning the foreground; from this stark, dreamy void rise two small hands that clutch the rail, followed by a slowly rising porkpie, wide eyes, a head, and shoulders. Buster pulls himself up, headfirst like a newborn entering the world, at the same time casting wary glances for danger. Keaton switches our perspective so that now *we* perch, figuratively, beyond the rail, looking into the whaler as Buster creeps toward a suspended lifeboat, aptly named THE LITTLE LOVE NEST. He cannot release the boat and, with sudden inspiration, arms himself with a handy ax and heads offscreen. A title explains his intention: UNABLE TO BRING THE LIFEBOAT TO THE WATER, BUSTER DECIDES TO BRING THE WATER TO THE LIFEBOAT.

Keaton's spoof line, which suggests a twist on moving mountains or treating the impossible as if a trifle, once more points to Buster's miraculous growth and the power acquired in the process. While he cannot wave an arm to will things to happen, he can invoke his creative muses to combine the elements at hand for his advantage. Unlike *The Boat* in which Buster tried to save his sinking vessel by drilling a hole into its deck, now Buster hacks a chunk out of the wall with an inverse purpose, namely, to sink the whaler so that the water will "rise" to the lifeboat. Retracing his steps to THE LITTLE LOVE NEST, Buster takes along a fishing rod and rifle. He settles into the lifeboat, awaiting the inevitable.

Crosscutting between the sinking whaler and Buster's leisure activities, we pass the night also waiting. Below deck, barrels begin to float in the gushing water; meanwhile, Buster plays solitaire, pausing occasionally before turning a card to check progress behind him. By the next shot, water has filled more than half the stockroom, and Buster's plan—articulated in a long shot of the vanishing whaler—is succeeding beautifully. When THE LITTLE LOVE NEST floats, Buster stands to observe his handiwork and verify that he is surrounded by water. The previous failed plan to drown the Skipper has now been perfected, and he has gone down with his ship according to tradition. Also, like tradition, Buster resurrects the inimitable wreath gag, pulling this sequence full circle. Doffing his hat in mock tribute, Buster tosses another wreath on the site of THE LOVE NEST, then rows out into the darkness as the scene fades.

The last major, totally unexpected sequence begins with another, more specific time title: NEXT DAY AT DAWN. Keaton now virtually gives us a definite time—dawn, signifying new day, new life, new challenge. Asleep in his drifting lifeboat, Buster suddenly awakens and scans his location, then rows out left. As a pan follows him, we find that he moors alongside what appears to be the back of a giant floating billboard and places one foot on its platform; unfortunately, his other foot is still in the lifeboat that begins to drift. Buster becomes another human wishbone, à la *One Week*, but twists back into the boat. As the camera pan continues to divulge more of the billboard in the frame, Keaton clues us in: A FLOAT-ING TARGET FOR NAVAL ARTILLERY EXERCISES. Buster is again ignorant of the truth, while we have been enlightened by words that trigger a dire situation. Caught between the straight lines of the billboard and the monotonous water, Buster seems isolated and helpless, yet he poses with hand on hip, lost in the private reverie of a contented fisherman. He catches a feisty whopper, which he first tries to beat with an oar into submission and which he finally shoots with his rifle. The billboard now offers an ironic juxtaposition to Buster's unawareness that his lifeboat is sinking because of the gunshot hole: it pretends to offer refuge, but we know that in reality it will inflict on him a fate worse than death. Buster's oblivion to the consequences of his hasty action (shooting) once more shreds the ingenious cloak of power that he has wrapped around himself, based on his handling of whale and Skipper. Yet while his "godlike" qualities sink along with his lifeboat, his humanity—with its tendency to misjudge, overlook, and be tragically flawed—rises quickly to the surface. After all, being human, with frequent detours into heroism, is Buster's best role. Despite his "magic moments," he is only mortal; *Cops* proved this in the extreme, whereas most other films focused only on heavy blows to his ego. Keaton himself clung with tenacity to the humanness of his persona in his own life, even when his filmmaking talents turned him into a sublime genius, as Mrs. Eleanor Keaton once revealed in an interview with Don McGregor:

> MCGREGOR: I think he was one of the few geniuses of the movies and he gave a lot to all of us.

> ELEANOR KEATON: It used to make him very nervous to have people tell him that.[3]

Whenever Buster completes a Quest, Keaton automatically sets him up for another "test" to bring him home to the business of being human, being the Everyperson to whom we can relate our own helplessness. Now, as he fishes, Buster begins the next test upon realizing that water is covering his feet in the lifeboat: he steps over to the billboard.

We cut abruptly to the front of the billboard, on which is painted a huge number 3. If Buster ever questioned why this object is in the middle of the sea, his complacent return to fishing has helped him accept this oddity as a simple fact of life. Why not? is his customary answer, for he has seen far more peculiar things in his time. After a pause, Buster peers around the right side and strolls along the front, reeling out the fishing line as he stops directly before the number. Expected curveball: gunboats in the distance prepare to fire at the targets. The next sequence rapidly cuts between long shots and medium shots of Navy and Buster, suggesting the immediacy of actions/reactions. An officer with telescope and earphones, who orders the firing, is our link between the naval exercises and Buster's looming catastrophe. Because he is on Target 3, Buster has some time before he is assaulted, and the Principle of the Magic Three has never been as pertinent or magnified as it is now.

The activity on the first target is composed of quick shots, leaving Buster momentarily absorbed in his fishing; the shots concentrate the tension and momentum of the force that will befall Buster. MS, officer orders; title, "FIRE ON TARGET #1."; MS, officer; LS, gunner fires; telescope-framed MS of Target 1 blown to bits; MS, officer approves. When we return to Buster, he is nonchalantly fishing with hand on hip, never hearing the blast. "TARGET #2!" is handled in a similar sequence, with the order exclaimed by the officer for greater thrills. When we check on Buster, he interrupts his fishing to hold out a hand as if checking for rain, obviously having felt a bit of fallout. For the third dramatic firing, Keaton sets us on board the gunboat to see Buster at the side of the billboard jutting into the left third of the frame; the other two thirds are filled with sea, sky— and a sudden splash that indicates a benevolent curveball has spared Target 3. Buster turns toward the splash, ponders it, and casts his line in its direction. By maintaining this fractional, off-kilter composition, Keaton has allowed Buster to unite the two sections of the frame by the simple toss of his fishing line; he has also created an ironic twist on the "magic three" theory. Now a *fourth* effort is needed to blow the target, and Buster obliviously faces it, thinking it is another whopper, perhaps even another whale. Cut to the whole target, and Buster disappears behind it, momentarily reappearing at its top, directly above the number; he sits with his back to us and continues to fish. Buster has created another equation: positioning himself above the bull's-eye, Buster = target. He merges again with his environment and, in this case, seals his own doom, for there is no possible escape. Only we see the vital details; the Navy does not spot Buster in its focused aim, and Buster only sees a fish with his name on it.

With "TARGET #3" reannounced, this time the Navy gives its best shot: *all* the gunners, seen in a long-shot profile, empty their rounds. The billboard splinters to smithereens; a dot of a body is flung into the air. Cut to Buster, airborne, tattered, a comically heartrending perplexity etched on his smudged face. He clings to half a rod as he hangs in space like a rag doll. Superimposed clouds float past on an upward flight. After looking around in awe for a few seconds, Buster tosses the reel and succumbs to gravity. Clouds cascade in reverse and Buster begins to wind his arms and legs as he plummets to earth.

Dissolve. At this moment of sheer helplessness, of unresolved aimlessness, of unending despair, Keaton ends his film in the only logical place that can provide a fitting denouement. The dissolve clears to Buster, back in his kitchenette tent on the CUPID, fast asleep but waving his arms as he poises on the edge of his bunk to dive into the floor. The earth that he has dreamed has been his own boat; when he runs outside, the only view through his binoculars is the same monotony of sky meeting sea. Keaton has revealed another dream-ending, and this time it is not much of a surprise; the fantastic quests and ironies of this film have always felt dreamlike. Once again, Keaton confirms that the impossible is only possible in a dream, and that his persona is both vulnerable and strong in the twilight voyage of his mind.

Buster has dreamed himself in many examples of daily life: sleeping (twice, on ladder and in lifeboat), fishing, being paranoid, overcoming obstacles, surviving. The dream-frame also supports Keaton's love of "nesting" or creating layers for these seemingly simple moments. Now that we know we have been watching a dream, we recall that Buster in the CUPID was, in reality, dreaming that he was dreaming of tossing a wreath—thus, two dreamers at work. In his dream, Buster also conjures up *day*dreams to test his mettle, which he usually brings to victorious fruition. Equally, when disaster looms, he dreams the extreme—"blowing up" but remaining intact, being tattered without injury, flying into the clouds without wings. Still, in his *waking* hours, Buster has also exhibited the same extraordinary talent to surpass human limitations and reach unimaginable goals. Keaton once again confirms that life itself is much like a dream. It is only in the attitude and stamina of the dreamer's mind that is found the resolution for both dreams and life.

Buster still wears his painted beard when he wakes up; the effects of long days of deprivation rush at us through a series of increasingly desperate titles and equally frantic actions. OUT OF PROVISIONS: Buster searches through empty crates only to drop, parched and hungry, clutching his chest. He pulls out Viper's photograph but offers it no expression or emotion. He only felt it when he clutched his chest, as if he had forgotten it was there at all. OUT OF WATER: he flings aside a bone-dry canteen. REALLY LOST! Buster crawls out of the tent and collapses in the nose of the CUPID, hanging a limp arm over the side. The camera bobs relentlessly, as it has done for the duration of this saga. Because of this motion, we have been forced to physically partake of Buster's journey, whether on whaler, lifeboat, billboard, or right in home port. The camera, Keaton's eye, now provides the real conclusion to the film. The waking-up moment is not the cap, as it was in *Convict 13*, *The Haunted House*, or *The Frozen North*; nor is it the stupendous "prologue" to the rest of a story, as it was in *The Playhouse*. Rather, Keaton plants a wry twist on Buster's dilemma, created by his romantic despair. As the camera pauses, a girl in the foreground swims past the CUPID. Buster spots her, then stands in disbelief. We cut to a full long shot, revealing that CUPID has all along been tied to the pier. We too have been fooled by the care with which Keaton showed us how Buster untied the rope at the start of the film. We have also more than once seen the monotony of the distant horizon, as if we have long left behind any vestige of city life. In addition, the constant bobbing also fooled us into believing that we were constantly en route, when in fact it was only the bobbing of home port waters. Like a final jab, Keaton cuts to a close shot of the rope. Final shot, Buster runs into the tent. THE END.

Whether this dash was indeed the last shot of the original film is hard to know, given that the film was "saved" long after it was deemed lost. What was Buster thinking as he spun back into his tent after his enlightenment? Is he ashamed that he became so destitute and lost while never even leaving the pier? Is he puzzled that he could have depleted his supplies without having sailed one knot? Because of his sudden, nearly incomplete dart into the protective covering of the CUPID, *The Love Nest* becomes a perfect meter with which to gauge our emotional responses to Buster's story, based on the "evidence" Keaton provides in his film.

Our key to deciphering Buster's last action, and guessing how he might behave back on shore, lies in the dream that constitutes the greater portion of the film. The dream wafts out of Buster's heartbroken condition before he falls into the Land of Nod, and so Buster the Dreamer is initially, understandably helpless and lost. Slowly, the dream shifts to match the transformation of the dreamer's alter ego. In the pictures of his mind, Buster grows from child to adult. He has become a dream adult through his experiences, even though Buster wakes up still wearing his painted beard; after all, it was part of his makeup when he first fell asleep. Buster then is, once again, the ultimate equation: man = boy, and vice versa. One steps rapidly into the footsteps of the other; the man who conquers the whale yields to the boy who shoots a hole in the boat. As we return to the CUPID and acknowledge the dream, the one truth that blows away the dreamy haze is that Buster will always be a child within an adult body and as such will display the best of each world. Like a holograph, Buster's stone face shimmers with the expressions of both.

Keaton was unique among his comic contemporaries in capturing this dual identity. Harold Lloyd was the "all-American boy, a true disciple of Horatio Alger, a born go-getter."[4] Though dapper and charming, he seemed stuck at adolescence and lacked the mature intensity that Keaton permitted in his adult moments. Harry Langdon, on the other hand, perpetuated a very different look, as Agee suggests: "His clothes are baby-like: tiny boots on out-turned feet; a squashed round hat that sits where it has been perched atop his head, turned up all round and with a half-formed kiss-curl creeping under it; flared and baggy trousers; an out-grown jacket with six buttons, the top one done up a bit awry at the top of his chest so that it all sticks out below, over his plump little body. His arms are stiff like a baby's, and won't lie flat by his sides; and his hands are pudgy and clumsy until you see them close and realize with a slight turn that they are the hands of a middle-aged man."[5]

Of the four major comedians, perhaps Chaplin expressed the most intensely emotional adult responses to poignant situations; yet his comical outfit always tied him to a vagabond image, and his penguinlike stroll always kept him a little apart from the rest of us. Buster, however, is a figure frozen in time, resembling adult and childlike facets without excess, exaggeration, or manipulation. In his own life, Keaton swerved between both realities from an early age: as a vaudeville performer, encased in the small facsimile Irish suit and whiskers of his father, Buster was a man in a child's body. As an adult, Keaton discovered the child in a man's body and never lost this ability to cross between the two worlds. Even when he was in his sixties, his wife recalled that neighbors' kids would often visit and ask, "Can Buster come out and play?"[6] Keaton himself once admitted "that there were two of him. 'Me and my understudy, Buster II. Buster II could do anything—play and never get tired, be rich and handsome, never grow old. And write checks until the cows came home.'"[7]

Buster's chameleon spirit to mold to situations, to color himself to the environment—to become the environment, if necessary—is his defense against the world. By the time of *The Love Nest*, Buster has learned to respond more quickly to his troubles. In *The Boat*, as a contrast, Buster was up to his chin in water before he realized the DAMFINO was submerged; in this film, he recognizes his dilemma as soon as his slapshoes touch water. By moving his hero through the narrative—in fact, focusing on story as his vehicle—Keaton has grown as director and storyteller. By now, he has abandoned the gag-for-gag's-sake syndrome and made Buster the pivot on which the story spins. Still, he is aware of the value of a potent prop to tie the story together in surprising ways, hence, the wreath that infiltrates nearly half of the film. Comparing *The Boat* and *The Love Nest* again, Buster's hand-drill in the former film clashed with the story and character, whereas the rifle of the latter was introduced early as Buster's unobtrusive and logical defense against seagoing marauders like the Skipper; it was used on the fish only as a last-ditch effort. The gunshot hole in the lifeboat was not the means to an end but an accident, and Buster simply moves on to suffer his problem heroically.

Keaton's narrative flair also begins to balance both the ordinary and the artistic for specific purposes in the story. His visuals, for example, serve to record events as well as evoke visceral responses. They either document realistically or mystify and suggest multiple layers at work by fragmenting images. As for Keaton's use of words in film, the time titles seem bland yet stimulate interpretation. Their ambiguity is as much a point of the story as is the convoluted logic behind bringing the water to the lifeboat. The organization and even punctuation of the final titles create sensations that are fed by the visuals.

Illusion is at the heart of Keaton's stories, particularly in *The Love Nest*, and his philosophy of dealing with illusion as a part of Life usually lies within simple, often insignificant gags or props. Here, he uses the porthole-painted picture to illustrate the need to define one's quest for truth in a world of illusion. Keaton easily mastered the art of illusion in *One Week*, when his camera panned to reveal double train tracks. Keaton wants us to stand guard since he, as the Master Fate, will always toss illusions Buster's way; by the same token, he will eventually reveal them, even if they must hurt in the process. Thus, the house was destroyed by the train, yet Buster sighed and walked on; DAMFINO sank, yet Buster waded on; even now, at death's door, Buster spies a swimmer and an extra rope, but he bursts into life. Was his last run into the tent a jubilant cry to gather his belongings and go home? Or did he run back in to protect himself from the punch of another curveball? Or to recuperate from the last one? More often than not, Buster's pattern has been to move on, even after disasters; most likely, he will do so again. When he cast aside that painted porthole, Keaton expected him to discern Reality in both dreaming and waking hours. With the conquered whale and Skipper still swimming in his memory, Buster has probably run back in to "shave" off his beard and resume his life.

And what will Buster go on to? In real life, of course, Keaton pushed

Buster into feature films, where he usually adopted identities that were physically different from his porkpied youth but that drew from the same emotional well. Thanks to *The Love Nest*, Buster's future journeys will be tempered by this baptism of water. Whatever his future holds, his past life will never seem the same. This was clear in the last appearance of the Viper's photo. Faced with death from the elements, Buster did not seek the photo to kiss it goodbye; rather, he seemed to remember it only when he clutched his chest in hunger. The photo is now a memento of one who has filtered out of his life even though she will remain a subconscious part of it. Although timewise, Buster's past is really just a matter of dream-moments, he still recalls the finality of their relationship. He might think of retrieving his "Dear Viper" letter and make up with her, but Buster has learned through dreams that nothing is worse than living an illusion, and Viper would only be the illusion of idealized love. When he "landed" from his dream with an eye-opening thud, Buster began to see that illusions (dream, swimmer, rope) abound and he must become their watchdog. He has already let himself be so blinded by the arrows of "Cupid" that he did not see home was only a dog-paddle away.

Now through the mercy of the dream, *The Love Nest* unearths a solid new facet in our hero's dimensionality, one nurtured over eighteen film-lives. The child-man has grown in personal esteem. Leagues from the self-effacing lad of *The Goat*, *Cops*, and *Daydreams*, Buster here is not only proud but lucky, and this dream reflects it. Past dreams have had him jailed (*Convict 13*), sent to hell (*The Haunted House*), and killed (*The Frozen North*); his one glorious dream only woke him up to a disappointing eviction (*The Playhouse*). By contrast, the dream of *The Love Nest* has tenderized the Skipper's heart (however briefly), won a whale, traveled the seas, survived an explosion. It has imbued Buster with the powers of Neptune to sink boats and tame sea creatures. And it has balanced out his good and not-so-good traits: while still paranoid and angry, he achieves justice, the impossible, and peace of mind. Like *Cops*, Buster is alone again—and that is indeed a rare occurrence in Keaton's films. Unlike *Cops*, however, the reality of *The Love Nest* keeps Buster alive and self-fulfilled. If he were to remain in his tent-boat for the rest of his days, Buster might be alone but, ironically, not lonely.

In his company would be imagination, exploring illusions and conquering defeat with optimism. It has been easy for Buster to survive when he feels his goal (usually Woman) is within arm's length; it has been devastating when he has not. Here, the only cause of his "death" would have been purely practical—lack of food and water; he may have set sail because of Woman, but by the end he certainly would not have perished for her. Keaton affirms this with his concluding titles, which focus on these "natural" causes of his impending demise.

In his company will also be dreams, through which he grows and is inspired. As in *The Scarecrow*, whose title zeroed in on a relatively short sequence of the film, Keaton stresses *The Love Nest* by making it the title. We are forced to attend to the happenings on board the whaler where Buster acts cleverly and courageously. His education aboard the whaler, although couched in a dream, was crucial for every experience that followed, even that which compelled him to sink the source of his enlightenment. His tutelage continued in his lifeboat, significantly named THE LITTLE LOVE NEST (unlike the lifeboat carrying the crew, which did not highlight a name). Buster broke off a piece of the mother ship to take with him as he set sail into the bigger world. No problem that even THE LITTLE LOVE NEST sank too, for that is the cycle of life. He merely moved on to his next lucky break, the billboard. That, too, endangered him, but his newfound luck prevailed to carry him into his next station, which was the most important of all: Life, with his eyes fully open.

Buster carries the lesson of his dream into his personal love nest. He is clearly bedraggled, worn, fragile, like a delicate bird needing the security of a cozy home. Love for Buster has always promised such a place. Buster's one true love nest now is one that he essentially creates for *himself.* THE LOVE NEST was only a dream-boat, devoid of the love its name suggested. Because of THE LOVE NEST, however, Buster was able to internalize the Quest and rediscover within a love of living. Although alone at the end, his visions inform him that he can happily live with himself. Keaton carries this optimism into his features, all of which conclude with stunning victories over illusion rather than with friendless tombstones. Buster's future awakenings promise to sail him straight home to his love nest; and each time he looks through the porthole of his mind, he will find no disappointing illusions, only the potentials that make Life miraculous.

# Chapter 21

# *Conclusion*

Courtesy of the Academy of Motion Picture Arts and Sciences

From his first released short, *One Week*, Keaton endowed his films with a romantic, inventive, stalwart persona, who won out over his "original" character, the unsympathetic Buzzard-by-proxy of *The High Sign*. Buster parallels Chaplin here, whose first slapstick "tramp" character was somewhat larcenous and even cruel—traits that Chaplin also abandoned. Short by short, Keaton molded his good guy into the character that would dominate every film. Even in Keaton's burlesque *The Frozen North* or the slapstick *My Wife's Relations* and *The Blacksmith*, the distinctive porkpied persona, employed at the job of Life, is unmistakably present. When Buster sometimes disappears in a parade of mechanical gags, intriguing composition, or remarkable feats, we are unsatisfied and yearn for his essential spirit.

Each short introduces another layer of Buster's onionskin personality, dimensioning our hero with honest humanity. As Buster repeats his idiosyncracies (usually nonverbal ones) in each film, his identity becomes suffused with an assortment of mortal quirks, fantasies, and quests. Once Keaton moves into the features, his character does not abandon his "trademarks": inquisitive stares; contemplative or frenetic bursts of action; relentless athletic drive to the chase; an innocent/clever dichotomy leading Buster into and out of trouble. But Keaton's concern in full-length films is the *story*—with dimensional plot and character development, and logical complications and resolutions. The hero responds to the twists and turns of narrative circumstances with equally thought-out narrative solutions instead of spontaneous single gags. The solutions most often come about through his ingenuity rather than a deus ex machina or dream. In the features, Buster's character truly lives a saga (*The General*, *Our Hospitality*, *The Navigator*) with a central driving focus rather than a formulaic sequence of events in a mundane situation (boy meets girl, thwarts rival, wins girl). The features also evidence Keaton's keen interest in period stories and historical detail (*The General*, *Our Hospitality*), as well as Buster's transition from comic outfit (porkpie, slapshoes) to distinguished tuxedos and costumes. We have already seen Keaton's obsession for minutiae in his choice of detailed props—the beaded vest and slapshoe moccasins in *The Paleface*, the Constance Talmadge poster in *Daydreams*, and so on. His perfection in cinematography and stunts is yet another obsession that paved the way for the grand scale of the features. In nearly every film, the rich accuracy of Keaton's detail astonishes the viewer into forgetting his slapstick heritage.

With a hawk's eye on composition, Keaton's manipulation of characters and props in the features becomes crucial to the unfolding story (*Neighbors* and *The Paleface* set the precedent in containing props, locations, and camera positions integral to the gags). More than any contemporary, Keaton used the camera to enhance his scenes, not only with special optical effects (which he minimized in his "realistic" features) but with the comedy of concealment and revelation: the simple pan or tilt of the camera serving as the visual punch line. In addition, Keaton fully incorporates the comic principles of symmetry, repetition, and transformation into his frame. As these principles affect props and humans (often props themselves), they not only create comedy but invite refreshing perspectives on the clichéd and drab. Keaton quickly tosses such sight-gag "gimmicks" as the split house in *The High Sign* into the scrap heap of experimentation. Through sneak previews and, perhaps above all, through his concern for visual narration, Keaton learned to position movement, people, objects, and camera until their interaction acquired the magnitude of a sublime paradox.

As Keaton juggled with the unlimited possibilities of his camera and artistry, he also designed incredible visions of life, often stimulated by Buster's struggles with irrepressible Fate. Conflicts and confrontations (Man–Machine, Man–Woman, Man–Nature, Man–Self) persist from film to film and link the shorts thematically. For the sake of comedy, Keaton may exaggerate a situation and even tag on a happy reconciliation (boy gets girl, à la Hollywood). The sober realist, however, is never far behind to remind us that comedy can involve defeat as well as triumph. Still, the tombstone in *Cops* can never completely replace the chuckle with the chill; the two, ironically, become inseparable. The hero is mortal, vulnerable to the ravaging forces that he adeptly battles. After all, as Buster would remark with a shrug, that's Life.

Early on, Keaton presented the possibility of dreams to rescue our hero, revealing comically how his woes were only nightmares and all was safe in "reality." Keaton often used dreams to fool and entertain us by playing on our subconscious expectations of Buster's doom. We have also witnessed what happens when Keaton does not let Buster dream. Result: the comic/tragic duality. When Keaton adds minor two-purpose objects to his films (as in *The Scarecrow*, among others), he is actually preparing for the giant dualities of Life not manipulated by the pull of a cord. Unlike the little gadgets that metamorphose before us with Buster in control, the greater dualities dwarf him and consume the screen with their untouchable presence. We see countless frame-filled chases and invisible hands thwarting him on all sides. Keaton's shorts thrive on such human, mechanical, and otherworldly titans. The shorts assault our cinematic and philosophical sensibilities with the intense speed of machine-gun fire. On the other hand, the features expand these mighty forces more leisurely until they seep into our awareness like the sea's erosion.

# Conclusion

In the features, the finest elements of the shorts are expanded, amplified, and reworked for a remarkable dual purpose: to create comedy as well as a heightened sense of dramatic and narrative structure. For example, Keaton presents a nearly frightening rendition of family feud, murder, abandonment, and desolation—all graphically depicted in just the *prologue* to *Our Hospitality*! In *The General*, we see details of the Civil War in Matthew Brady-like glory and despair serving as a backdrop for Keaton's thoughtful gags. We envision the scope of dream-as-film and film-as-dream in the entirety of *Sherlock Jr.*—unlike the all-too-brief first-reel dream illusions of *The Playhouse*. While satirizing epic histories in *The Three Ages* (reminiscent of short spoofs like *The Frozen North* and *The Blacksmith*), Keaton carefully places those exaggerations within appropriate settings (prehistoric times, Roman times, modern times) and heads toward logical denouement. We experience Buster's loneliness, familiar from *The Goat* and *Cops*, as he spends the whole of *Go West* befriending Brown Eyes the Cow and choosing her loyal companionship over a girl's. After sharing the confrontations, chases, and disasters of *One Week*, *The Boat*, and other shorts, we see how they have been magnified in *Steamboat Bill Jr.*, *College*, and *Seven Chances*. We know that the Buster persona of *The Navigator*, *Battling Butler*, *College*, and *Steamboat Bill Jr.* is purely and simply the Buster from the short films: he starts out as a spoiled or inept and sheltered boy and grows through severe tests into a strong, sensitive adult. Buster by any other name is always Keaton's aspiration. The feature, *Battling Butler* (reported to be Keaton's favorite film), graphically illustrates these stages of Buster's character development in both physical and symbolic terms. In a boxing ring, Buster's untrained body is battered by an opponent with a shuddering reality, greater than any force in his most pained short. Yet by the end, Buster reverses his fate and his ineptitude and becomes champ. And so, whoever or whatever traps and assaults Buster is ultimately no match, for he will emerge miraculously preserved and victorious.

In contrast to these many continuities and parallels, there are two striking differences between the shorts and the features. Most of Keaton's feature characters possess real names (John McKay, Rollo Treadway, Alfred Butler, Johnnie Gray, Ronald, Willie). The persona of the shorts, however, has usually been unnamed or referred to as "The Little Guy" or "Our Hero." Yet, in anonymity, he is always Buster. Blesh relates a curious anecdote, in which Keaton reflected on the affectionate names he has been dubbed in foreign countries:

## Conclusion

France: Malec
Spain: Sephonio (later, Pamplinas)
Poland: Zybsko
Czechoslovakia: Prysmyleno
Liberia: Kazunk
Cochin China: Wong Wong
Siam: Kofreto
Iceland: Glo Glo

Keaton added, "No one as yet has given me an authentic translation, but I imagine that most of these terms of endearment signify null and void, and their combined meaning, if totaled up, would equal zero."[1] In their dense brevity, the shorts clearly depict, more so than the features, how such a "zero" character can ultimately sum up the totality of Life.

From this paradox arises another major difference between the shorts and features. Each full-length film concludes with a stirring victory; but as we well remember, some of the shorts (*Cops, Daydreams*) did not spare defeat for our hero. It is as if the fatality of those shorts in which Buster fails is consciously abandoned for a hopeful, uplifting outcome (Keaton's last two shorts set the mood for this optimism after a barrage of disaster films). Keaton's fatalism instead works *throughout* the feature story instead of at the *finale*. The challenges and potential disasters become the means and not the end. Each becomes a stone of experience on which Buster must step to reach his guaranteed victory.

Thus, the features hold a kind of romanticism that the shorts only on occasion celebrate. The Buster of the shorts reveals himself to be utterly human and basically nameless—or, in typical Keaton equation: Nobody = Everybody. Paradoxically, his humanity all the more stresses the "benefits" of facing Life's challenges with a resilience that borders on superhuman. Disregarding the comic exaggerations that fill every short, Keaton's themes count as the real applications to every human life. And the essence with which Buster suffers or survives these themes becomes our exemplar for living, or the "embodiment" of *Spirit*. The features easily celebrate this Spirit's ultimate and predictable victories. In a more compelling, mysterious way, the short films celebrate the Spirit as well—ironically, when they are at their darkest. At such moments, these films acknowledge the very *existence* and *necessity* of Spirit in order to survive, and the tragedy of its loss. While the features "end" happily, the shorts smack the unwary spectator between the eyes with a totally unadulterated

**361**

and very human truth. Buster may indeed expire in the process, but his Spirit will resurrect in another film-life to toss the curveball right back.

I saw Buster the other day. He was peering out through the eyes of an elderly lady on a bus. A straw porkpie with a couple of feathers sat above her craggy, unsmiling face. It was then I accepted the fact that I was obsessed with Buster Keaton and that, happily, I would always be. I recognize Buster in myself as I scan the horizon, hand to forehead, for a taxi; or double-take and stare at an unusual sight; or "pratfall"—without Keaton's athletic grace—on the ice. Much like the innocent Sherlock Jr., picking his cues from the screen hero before him, I brace for life with Buster's philosophy tucked into my subconscious, to summon it on those days when little else makes sense.

Mrs. Eleanor Keaton once commented that Buster "used to laugh at the hidden meanings critics drew from his work . . . 'So I slipped and fell in a mud puddle—what's the deep meaning in that?' he'd say. He was really a simple man."[2] As simple as hunting for buried treasure. What we ultimately unearth from his timeless legacy depends on the depth we choose to plumb. We can seek pure entertainment and laugh at physical gags and breathtaking slides and flips. But if we venture deeper, we encounter greater personal rewards. Beyond the comedy is film, lovingly and dexterously crafted in its comic visions. Within these visions are starkly familiar themes and paradoxes. We begin to realize that Buster—exaggerated or simple, funny or serious—resembles each one of us. When his playfully challenging company fills our mind, occasionally tossing a philosophical life preserver into our personal mud puddles, then Buster Keaton's treasure is ours.

Notes
Selected Bibliography
Index

# *Notes*

## Chapter 1. Introduction

1. James Agee, "Comedy's Greatest Era," *Life*, September 3, 1949, reprinted in *Agee on Film*, vol. 1 (New York: Grosset and Dunlap, 1969), p. 16.

2. Unless otherwise referenced, the biographical sketch in this book is drawn mainly from Tom Dardis's biography *Keaton: The Man Who Wouldn't Lie Down* (New York: Charles Scribner's Sons, 1979).

3. Dardis, p. 42.

4. Dardis, p. 138.

5. Dardis, p. 144.

6. Dardis, p. 144.

7. Dardis, p. 144.

8. Buster Keaton, "Why I Never Smile," *Ladies' Home Journal*, June 26, 1926, reprinted in *Hollywood Directors 1914–1940*, ed. Richard Koszarski (London: Oxford University Press, 1976), p. 144.

9. A 1930 review that first appeared in *The Judge*, reprinted in *American Film Criticism*, ed. Stanley Kauffmann (New York: Liveright, 1972), p. 234.

10. Ashton Reid, "Strictly for Laughs," *Colliers*, June 10, 1944.

11. Dardis, p. 200.

12. Agee, p. 4.

13. Agee, p. 15.

14. Agee, p. 16.

15. Agee, p. 17.

16. Raymond Rohauer, "Buster Keaton," *The Marble*, vol. 4, no. 1 (January–February 1976), p. 3.

17. Murray Schumach, "Keaton Receives Special Film Prize," *New York Times*, April 6, 1960, p. 46.

18. Rohauer, p. 3.

19. John Gillett and James Blue, "Keaton at Venice," *Sight and Sound*, vol. 35, no. 1 (Winter 1965), p. 28.

20. Kevin Brownlow, *The Parade's Gone By . . .* (Berkeley: University of California Press, 1968), p. 474.

21. Andrew Sarris, "Buster Keaton Film Festival," *Village Voice*, September 24, 1970.
22. Film Forum, "Buster Keaton 100," Film Program, February 10–March 16, 1995, New York.
23. Stanley Kauffmann, "Buster Keaton Festival," reprinted in *Living Images*, ed. Stanley Kauffmann (New York: Harper and Row, 1975), p. 22.
24. Buster Keaton, "When Comedy Is Serious," unidentified source, p. 18.
25. The discussion of the structures of comedy is derived from the following books: repetition and the use of dreams, Maurice Charney, *Comedy High and Low* (New York: Oxford University Press, 1978); transformations and equations, Gerald Mast, *The Comic Mind* (New York: Bobbs-Merrill, 1973); symmetry, Daniel Moews, *Keaton: The Silent Features Close Up* (Berkeley: University of California Press, 1977); the comedy-tragedy dichotomy, Raymond Durgnat, *The Crazy Mirror* (New York: Delta Books, 1969).

## Chapter 2. *One Week* (September 1920)

1. Rudi Blesh, *Keaton* (New York: Collier Books, 1966), p. 84.
2. Elizabeth Peltret, "Poor Child!" *Motion Picture Classic*, vol. 12, no. 1 (March 1921), pp. 64, 96–97.
3. Blesh, p. 150.
4. David Robinson, *Buster Keaton* (Bloomington: Indiana University Press, 1969), p. 37.
5. Blesh, p. 290.
6. Walter Kerr considers the camera as barrier in *The Silent Clowns* (New York: Alfred A. Knopf, 1975), p. 129.
7. Agee, p. 10.
8. Buster Keaton, with Charles Samuels, *My Wonderful World of Slapstick* (New York: Doubleday and Company, 1960; reprint, with new introduction by Dwight MacDonald, New York: DaCapo Paperback, 1982).
9. Dardis, pp. 3–4.
10. Robinson, p. 189.

## Chapter 3. *Convict 13* (October 1920)

1. Gillett and Blue, p. 28.
2. Andrew Sarris called this film "grotesque gallows humor" ("Conversations and Concerns, Buster Keaton and Samuel Beckett," *Columbia*

*Forum*, vol. 12, no. 4 [Winter 1969], p. 42). David Robinson states, "Nothing in any of [Keaton's] films is quite so bleak . . . [it] has a disturbing quality of violence never appearing again except in the brutal finish of *Battling Butler*" (p. 45). Robinson also comments that when viewed in its original amber tint, "the hard contrasts of the black and white convict stripes have a physically disturbing effect of dazzlement" (*Buster Keaton*, p. 45).

3. Robinson speculates that for Keaton, dreams liberate "fantasy images" (*Buster Keaton*, p. 185) and that he "justifies his visions by forming them in dreams" (p. 186), such as the elastic rope.

4. Keaton already is forming a definite persona that he would describe as a "little fellow [who] was a working-man and honest" (Keaton, *My Wonderful World of Slapstick*, p. 126).

## Chapter 4. *The Scarecrow* (December 1920)

1. Blesh, p. 144.

2. The discussion of melodrama is based on Frank Rahill's book, *The World of Melodrama* (University Park: Pennsylvania State University Press, 1967).

3. Blesh, p. 54.

4. Rahill (pp. 300–301) writes of the "unimpeachable melodramatic provenance" of these early genres in "a medium which had not learned to speak" (p. 297).

5. Dardis, p. 298.

6. Rahill, pp. 242–43.

7. In his book, *Buster Keaton and the Dynamics of Visual Wit* (New York: Arno Press, 1976), Wead discusses how Keaton lengthens gags by number of shots to quicken the tempo of the comedy, as in the storm sequence of *One Week* (p. 337).

8. Blesh, p. 140.

9. Buster's subtlety, in contrast to Joe Roberts's exaggerations, can also be equated to Keaton's finesse as a comedian and director contrasting with Arbuckle's style. Blesh in fact calls *The Scarecrow* "a kind of sublimation or distillation of slapstick . . . an unearthly little comedy, leagues away from Arbuckle's extrovert slapstick" (p. 144).

10. Wead calls Keaton's titles "among the cleverest of the period" and analyzes the variety of twists and turns his titles take. He notes a general uniformity to the style and humor that indicates one ruling mind, although occasional variations in title quality point to contributions from others (*Buster Keaton and the Dynamics of Visual Wit*, p. 205). Blesh quotes Keaton writer

Clyde Bruckman: Keaton "was his own best gagman. . . . Those wonderful stories were ninety percent Buster's. I was often ashamed to take the money, much less the credit" (pp. 149–50).

11.　Wead describes the coordinated delivery of punch lines as often due to the "rule of three beats" and so regards the edited beats of the minister's words, with the shot of the splash serving as the "one-two" bridge to the third beat. " 'Rule of three' . . . maintains that the best moment to deliver the punch-line of a joke is after a pause of two beats, i.e., on the third beat: 'That was no lady . . . (one) . . . (two) . . . that was my wife' " (*Buster Keaton and the Dynamics of Visual Wit*, p. 321).

## Chapter 5. *Neighbors* (January 1921)

1.　Blesh, p. 147.

2.　Wead considers how often Keaton will shoot a scene in long shot to allow the "surroundings to fit" the action (*Buster Keaton and the Dynamics of Visual Wit*, p. 196).

3.　"The Keaton Curve" is discussed at length in *The Silent Clowns* by Kerr, p. 145.

4.　Sarris, "Conversations and Concerns," p. 42.

5.　Daniel T. Leah, *From Sambo to Superspade* (Boston: Houghton Mifflin, 1976), pp. 8–9.

6.　Leah, p. 17.

7.　Keaton, *My Wonderful World of Slapstick*, p. 130.

8.　Blesh, p. 147.

9.　Penelope Gilliatt, "Penelope Gilliatt Meets a Sunset Genius of the Cinema," *Observer Weekend Review*, May 14, 1964, p. 31.

10.　"Mr. Natalie Talmadge." "Before and After Taking." Fan magazine, Summer 1921.

## Chapter 6. *The Haunted House* (February 1921)

1.　Wead notes this title as IF NEW YORK IS THE CITY OF HIGH FINANCE, OUR HERO IS ONE OF ITS GREAT FINANCIERS. Different versions of a film may indeed have variations in titles, especially as some were lost and had to be reconstructed. This would make it more difficult obviously to capture the original essence of Keaton's titles; yet the comic impact is usually salvaged in a slightly new interpretation. Wead calls the title he cites as being the "closest to genuine irony," creating one image of Buster in his initial appearance, which is immediately deflated by his "church key" entrance to resolve the joke (*Buster Keaton and the Dynamics of Visual Wit*, pp. 218–19).

2.    In his discussion of Keaton's use of space, Wead emphasizes how he includes what is essential for the gag along with what is most interesting and attractive to the eye, as in the sequence of Buster with the female customer: "by the very fact that the shot frames both face and specific environment, we 'know' that some interrelation has to be forthcoming" (*Buster Keaton and the Dynamics of Visual Wit*, p. 291).

3.    Kerr, p. 138.

4.    Kerr, p. 129.

## Chapter 7. *Hard Luck* (March 1921)

1.    The article was written by Robert De Roos and is mentioned in George Wead and George Lellis, *The Film Career of Buster Keaton* (Boston: G. K. Hall, 1977), p. 101.

2.    Marshall Deutelbaum, ed., *"Image" on the Art and Evolution of the Film* (New York: Dover, 1979), p. 196.

3.    Richard Koszarski, ed., *Hollywood Directors, 1914–1940* (London: Oxford University Press, 1976), p. 148.

4.    Robinson, *Buster Keaton*, p. 51.

5.    Dardis, pp. 49–50.

6.    Keaton, *My Wonderful World of Slapstick*, p. 174.

7.    Keaton, *My Wonderful World of Slapstick*, pp. 174–76.

## Chapter 8. *The High Sign* (April 1921)

1.    Robinson, *Buster Keaton*, p. 40.

2.    Blesh, p. 140.

3.    In *Buster Keaton and the Dynamics of Visual Wit*, Wead refers to the "brash display of alliteration" (p. 216).

4.    Wead refers to how Keaton develops a pun from the simple juxtaposition of words in the warning message (*Buster Keaton and the Dynamics of Visual Wit*, p. 215).

5.    Keaton, *My Wonderful World of Slapstick*, pp. 134–35.

6.    Blesh, pp. 141–42.

7.    Wead, *Buster Keaton and the Dynamics of Visual Wit*, pp. 311–12.

8.    Wead discusses this and Keaton's use of "internal frames" within

the dream-frame of *Sherlock Jr.* (*Buster Keaton and the Dynamics of Visual Wit*, p. 305).

## Chapter 9. *The Goat* (May 1921)

1.  Robinson, *Buster Keaton*, p. 53.
2.  Raymond Rohauer, *The Films of Buster Keaton* (booklet from the Audio Film Center, New York, 1969).
3.  Kerr states that through this gag Keaton is "reach[ing] out and rap[ping] on the glass lens to show how hard it is. . . . [The gag] exists on principle, having nothing to do with the storyline or paving the way for another gag" (p. 129).
4.  Wead, *Buster Keaton and the Dynamics of Visual Wit*, p. 307.
5.  Or as Kerr puts it, "Keaton closes in on Keaton" (p. 128).
6.  Kerr likens Man O'War to another work of art—that of Laocoön, a Hellenistic sculpture (second century B.C.), based on the myth of a priest whose work offended the gods and was punished, along with his sons, by killer sea serpents. Kerr calls the horse—perhaps Buster as well, being one with the art—a "live thing dying" (p. 140). In addition, he calls Buster "master until the half rolls over and dies" (p. 140).
7.  In particular, Sarris calls the artist a "bearded nincompoop" and asks, in favor of Keaton's "pragmatic" expression, "What good is art, if you can't mount it to your own advantage?" ("Conversations and Concerns," p. 43).
8.  Wead, *Buster Keaton and the Dynamics of Visual Wit*, p. 251.

## Chapter 10. *The Playhouse* (January 1922)

1.  Clyde Bruckman's recollection, in Blesh, p. 152.
2.  Keaton, *My Wonderful World of Slapstick*, p. 15.
3.  Douglas Gilbert, *American Vaudeville* (New York: Dover, 1963), p. 32.
4.  Dailey Paskman, *Gentlemen, Be Seated!* (New York: Clarkson N. Potter, 1976), p. 21.
5.  Paskman, pp. 13–14.
6.  Description of minstrel show drawn from Paskman, pp. 24–27.
7.  Blesh, p. 152.
8.  Blesh, p. 152.
9.  Blesh, p. 168.
10. William K. Everson, *American Silent Film* (New York: Oxford University Press, 1978), p. 246.

11. Blesh, p. 167.
12. Deutelbaum, p. 196.
13. Blesh, p. 167.
14. Gilbert, pp. 50–52.
15. Keaton, *My Wonderful World of Slapstick*, p. 18.
16. Blesh, p. 167.
17. Keaton, *My Wonderful World of Slapstick*, pp. 74–75.
18. Robinson, *Buster Keaton*, pp. 18, 20.
19. Dardis, p. 72.
20. Blesh, pp. 163–64.
21. Wead refers again to "delivery beats" within the verbal joke—that Keaton's going out to see the two girls, then returning to the room to amend his promise in the log, is the visual beat joining the two verbal beats (*Buster Keaton and the Dynamics of Visual Wit*, p. 322).
22. Gilbert, p. 322.
23. Blesh, p. 167.
24. Blesh, p. 39.
25. Blesh, p. 66.
26. Gilbert, p. 243.
27. Gilbert, p. 54.
28. Blesh, p. 20.

## Chapter 11. *The Boat* (November 1921)

1. Robinson calls this a typical Keaton surprise, a reversal of expectations using both visual and verbal gags (*Buster Keaton and the Dynamics of Visual Wit*, p. 58).
2. Wead, *Buster Keaton and the Dynamics of Visual Wit*, p. 212.
3. Harold Schecter and David Everitt, *Film Tricks* (New York: Harlin Quist, 1980), p. 62.
4. Blesh, p. 196.
5. Brownlow, *The Parade's Gone By . . .* , p. 486.
6. Wead, *Buster Keaton and the Dynamics of Visual Wit*, p. 208.
7. Kerr, p. 134.
8. Kerr, p. 145.
9. Andrew Sarris, ed., *Interviews with Film Directors* (New York: Avon, 1967), p. 285. Christopher Bishop's interview appeared originally in *Film Quarterly*, vol. 12, no. 1 (Fall 1958), pp. 274–86.
10. Blesh, p. 192.

## Chapter 12. *The Paleface* (January 1922)

1. Blesh, p. 196. Blesh also suggests that the style may have existed here for the first time in any comedy (p. 197).

2. Kerr remarks on Keaton's choice of concentrating on just the gate as a punch line, or punch-gag, to Buster's introduction. "We are certain, of course, that before very long Buster will come through it. But at the moment we do not see him. There is only a close-up of the gate. Just that. The close-up is held for a few seconds longer than would be normal. In those few seconds, somehow, we see that the gate *looks* like Keaton" (Kerr, p. 140). McCaffrey outrightly calls the gate and Buster's subsequent head poking through it the "revelation gag" (Donald W. McCaffrey, *4 Great Comedians* [New York: A. S. Barnes, 1968], p. 89).

3. Wead refers to Buster's stage-type routines reenacted with "hesitation beats" during the butterfly hunts (*Buster Keaton and the Dynamics of Visual Wit*, p. 328).

4. Wead, *Buster Keaton and the Dynamics of Visual Wit*, p. 300.

5. This sequence recalls Buster's trot-stumble-roll in *Seven Chances* in which he triggers a massive downhill parade of rocks of every size and shape, not to mention the climactic chase by a bevy of eager brides, also of every size and shape.

6. Kerr, p. 137.

7. J.-P. Lebel, *Buster Keaton*, trans. P. D. Slovin (New York: A. S. Barnes, 1967), p. 114.

8. Blesh, p. 197.

9. Blesh calls it a height of sixty feet (p. 197); Lebel calls it seventy-five feet (p. 33).

10. Dardis, p. 100.

11. Kauffmann, *American Film Criticism*, pp. 132–33.

12. Lebel, p. 93.

## Chapter 13. *Cops* (March 1922)

1. Lebel, pp. 117–18.

2. Rex Reed, "Buster Keaton—October 1965," in *Do You Sleep in the Nude?* (New York: New American Library, 1968), p. 120.

3. Keaton, *My Wonderful World of Slapstick*, pp. 141–42.

4. Blesh, p. 203.

5. Mack Sennett, *King of Comedy* (New York: Pinnacle Books, 1975), p. 12 of Illustration section.

6. McCaffrey, p. 90.

7. Wead, *Buster Keaton and the Dynamics of Visual Wit*, p. 307.

8. Blesh, p. 199. Arbuckle was arrested and charged with the murder of Hollywood starlet Virginia Rappe during a wild Labor Day weekend party in 1921. According to several of Rappe's women friends at the party, Rappe had claimed that Arbuckle attacked her; she then fell into a coma from which she never revived. The cause of death was determined to be acute peritonitis. Arbuckle's testimony—that Rappe was drunk, screamed accusingly at him, and collapsed in his bedroom—never wavered. Medical testimony also showed that Rappe was seriously ill to begin with, the consequences of loose living, and that excessive partying had aggravated her condition. The testimony of the key witnesses often changed during the three trials. Final acquittal was not enough for Arbuckle who, by that time, was regarded as a monstrous beast in the eyes of the public who not long before had regarded him as popular as Chaplin. Virtually all of Arbuckle's films were destroyed or banned from public exhibition by the Hays Office of Censorship and vigilante moral groups. Keaton never believed his friend and mentor was capable of the heinous crime and helped him to the end of his short life with jobs and support. Keaton may have also provided Arbuckle with the pseudonym he used in credits to avoid the anger of unappeased individuals: William Goodrich or, more tragically, Will B. Goode.

9. Dardis, p. 90.

10. Keaton, *My Wonderful World of Slapstick*, p. 13.

11. Blesh, pp. 258–60.

12. Sarris, "Conversations and Concerns," p. 42.

13. Wead, *Buster Keaton and the Dynamics of Visual Wit*, p. 219.

14. Wead, *Buster Keaton and the Dynamics of Visual Wit*, pp. 246–47.

15. Wead, *Buster Keaton and the Dynamics of Visual Wit*, p. 253.

16. Blesh, p. 202.

## Chapter 14. *My Wife's Relations* (May 1922)

1. Blesh, p. 205.

2. Mast describes Keaton as following the treatment of social groups "reduced to comic stereotypes" much as his predecessors, including Mack Sennett, had done in some of their films (*The Comic Mind*, p. 53).

3. Wead extensively considers Keaton's use of verbal puns in all his films: in particular, for this film, MISS ROSE ROYCE, "a verbal sign with symbolic value"; and frequent statements of convoluted logic: "SHUT YOUR EYES

AND SEE . . . " and "LET'S MURDER HIM FIRST AND THEN WE'LL BILL HIM" (*Buster Keaton and the Dynamics of Visual Wit*, pp. 209, 215).

4. Lebel, p. 135.
5. Blesh, p. 205.
6. Blesh, p. 205.
7. Dardis, p. 95.
8. Keaton, *My Wonderful World of Slapstick*, pp. 166–67.
9. Dardis, p. 74.
10. Dardis, p. 86.
11. Wead, *Buster Keaton and the Dynamics of Visual Wit*, p. 300.
12. Wead, *Buster Keaton and the Dynamics of Visual Wit*, p. 323.
13. Penelope Gilliatt, *Unholy Fools: Wits, Comics, Disturbers of the Peace: Film and Theatre* (New York: Viking Press, 1973), p. 51.
14. From Alfred, Lord Tennyson, *In Memoriam*.

## Chapter 15. *The Blacksmith* (July 1922)

1. Leonard Maltin, *The Great Movie Comedians from Charlie Chaplin to Woody Allen* (New York: Crown Publishers, 1978), p. 33.
2. Robinson, *Buster Keaton*, p. 64.
3. Robinson, *Buster Keaton*, p. 34.
4. Gilliatt, "Penelope Gilliatt Meets a Sunset Genius of the Cinema," p. 31.
5. Wead, *Buster Keaton and the Dynamics of Visual Wit*, p. 292.
6. Blesh, p. 253.
7. Robinson, *Buster Keaton*, p. 64.
8. Kerr, p. 131.
9. Leonard Maltin, lecture on Buster Keaton at Museum of Modern Art, New York, in the series, "Remembered Laughter," July 28, 1979.
10. Robinson, *Buster Keaton*, p. 65.

## Chapter 16. *The Frozen North* (August 1922)

1. Blesh, p. 205.
2. Wead and Lellis, p. 82.
3. Blesh, p. 206.
4. Blesh, p. 206.
5. Diane Kaiser Koszarski, *The Complete Films of William S. Hart* (New York: Dover, 1980), p. ix.

6. Diane Kaiser Koszarski, p. ix, quotation from Hart's autobiography, *My Life East and West.*

7. Diane Kaiser Koszarski, pp. xv–xvi.

8. Blesh, p. 206.

9. Keaton, *My Wonderful World of Slapstick*, p. 170.

10. Keaton, *My Wonderful World of Slapstick*, p. 171.

11. Keaton, *My Wonderful World of Slapstick*, p. 172.

12. Keaton, *My Wonderful World of Slapstick*, p. 171.

13. Wead, *Buster Keaton and the Dynamics of Visual Wit*, p. 230.

14. Richard Griffith and Arthur Mayer, *The Movies* (New York: Simon and Schuster, 1970), p. 66.

15. Wead, *Buster Keaton and the Dynamics of Visual Wit*, p. 241.

16. Griffith and Mayer, p. 151.

17. Robinson, *Buster Keaton*, p. 148.

18. Wead, *Buster Keaton and the Dynamics of Visual Wit*, p. 241.

19. Everson, *American Silent Film* (New York: Oxford University Press, 1978), p. 235.

20. Robinson, *Buster Keaton*, p. 66.

21. Everson, *American Silent Film*, p. 285.

22. Everson, *American Silent Film*, p. 286.

23. Wead, *Buster Keaton and the Dynamics of Visual Wit*, p. 211; Robinson, *Buster Keaton*, p. 67.

## Chapter 17. *Daydreams* (September 1922)

1. Wead, *Buster Keaton and the Dynamics of Visual Wit*, p. 310.

2. Blesh, p. 208.

3. Blesh, p. 240.

## Chapter 18. *The Electric House* (October 1922)

1. Blesh, p. 154. Also described in *Hollywood Directors*, ed. Richard Koszarski ("Why I Never Smile"), p. 144.

2. Wead and Lellis, p. 43.

3. Wead and Lellis, p. 82.

4. Lawrence Reid, *Motion Picture News*, November 4, 1922, p. 2316.

5. Blesh, p. 152.

6. Blesh, p. 210.

7. Blesh, p. 277.

## Chapter 19. *The Balloonatic* (January 1923)

1.  Henry Herz, Notes on *The Balloonatic*, prepared for the Chicago Center for Film Study, 1963.
2.  Images from Kerr, p. 128.
3.  Blesh, p. 211.

## Chapter 20. *The Love Nest* (March 1923)

1.  Robinson, *Buster Keaton*, p. 69; Lebel, p. 46.
2.  Robinson, *Buster Keaton*, p. 60.
3.  Don McGregor, "An Interview with Eleanor Keaton, On Bridge, Buster and Film Revival," in *Buster, The Early Years, The Authorized Buster Keaton Film Festival Album* (New York, 1982), p. 26.
4.  Robinson, *The Great Funnies*, p. 78.
5.  Robinson, *The Great Funnies*, p. 82.
6.  "Hollywood Mourns a Comic, Buster Keaton at 70," *New York Herald Tribune*, February 2, 1966.
7.  Stefan Kanfer, "Great Stone Face," *Time*, November 2, 1970, p. 94.

## Chapter 21. *Conclusion*

1.  Blesh, p. 251.
2.  Eileen Foley, "Mrs. Keaton Looks Back on Her Life with Buster," *Philadelphia Evening Bulletin*, October 10, 1966.

# Selected Bibliography

Agee, James. *Agee on Film*. Vol. 1. New York: Grosset and Dunlap, 1969.

Anobile, Richard J., ed. *The Best of Buster*. New York: Darien House, 1976.

———. *Buster Keaton's "The General."* New York: Darien House, 1975.

Arnold, Gary. "Buster Keaton." In *The National Society of Film Critics on the Movie Star*, edited by Elisabeth Weis. New York: Penguin Books, 1981.

Baker, Rob. "The Luster of Buster." *New York Daily News*, August 12, 1981, pp. 49, 55.

Belton, John. "New Books." Review of *The Silent Clowns* by Walter Kerr. *Filmmakers Newsletter*, May 1976, pp. 62–64.

Benayoun, Robert. *The Look of Buster Keaton*. New York: St. Martin's Press, 1983.

Bishop, Christopher. "The Great Stone Face." *Film Quarterly*, vol. 12, no. 1 (Fall 1955), pp. 10–15.

Blesh, Rudi. *Keaton*. New York: Collier Books, 1966.

Bloch, Robert. "Buster Keaton: Stone-Faced Optimist." In *Close-Ups*, edited by Danny Peary. New York: Workman Publishing, 1978.

Boggs, Joseph M. *The Art of Watching Films*. Menlo Park, Calif.: Benjamin/Cummings Publishing, 1978.

Bordwell, David, and Kristen Thompson. *Film Art, an Introduction*. Reading, Mass.: Addison-Wesley Publishing, 1979.

Bowser, Eileen. "Recent Acquisitions." Notes on *Steamboat Bill, Jr.* New York: Museum of Modern Art, 1979.

Brakhage, Stan. *Film Biographies*. Berkeley: Turtle Island, 1977.

Braudy, Leo, and Morris Dickstein, eds. *Great Film Directors*. New York: Oxford University Press, 1978.

Breger, L. "Letter to the Editor." *New York Times Magazine*, June 15, 1980, p. 78.

Brownlow, Kevin. *The Parade's Gone By* . . . Berkeley: University of California Press, 1968.

———. Reviews of *Buster Keaton* (Lebel), *My Wonderful World of Slapstick* (Keaton/Samuels), and *Keaton* (Blesh). *Film*, vol. 49 (Autumn 1967), pp. 30–31.

Bunuel, Luis. "Buster Keaton's College." *Great Film Directors*, edited by Leo Braudy and Morris Dickstein. New York: Oxford University Press, 1978.

*Buster Keaton: A Hard Act to Follow*. Three-part documentary, written and produced by Kevin Brownlow and David Gill, in association with Raymond Rohauer. London: Thames Television (Thames Video Collection), 1987.

"Buster Keaton Dies at 70 of Lung Cancer." *New York World-Telegram and Sun*, February 1, 1966.

"Buster Keaton Film Festival de Films." Program, National Film Theatre. Ottawa, Canada: September 6–12, 1968.

"Buster Keaton, Great Stone Face, Dies at 70." *New York Daily News*, February 2, 1966, p. 5.

"Buster Keaton Is Back, But Landmarks Are Gone." *New York World-Telegram*, July 5, 1941.

"Buster Keaton Revives Career in Paris Circus." *New York Herald Tribune*, October 8, 1948.

"Buster Keaton, 70, Dies on Coast; Poker-Faced Comedian of Films." *New York Times*, February 2, 1966, pp. 1, 32.

"Buster Keaton, 70, Victim of Cancer." *Variety*, February 2, 1966, pp. 3, 22.

Byron, Stuart, and Elisabeth Weis, eds. *Movie Comedy*. New York: Grossman Publishers, 1977.

Cahn, William, and Rhoda Cahn. *The Great American Comedy Scene*. New York: Monarch, 1978.

Carey, Gary. *All the Stars in Heaven, Louis B. Mayer's MGM*. New York: E. P. Dutton, 1981.

Carroll, Noel. "The Golden Age of the Silver Screen." *Soho Weekly News*, March 1, 1979, pp. 48, 58.

Charney, Maurice. *Comedy High and Low*. New York: Oxford University Press, 1978.

Coe, R. L. "Comic Buster Keaton Succumbs to Cancer." *Washington Post*, February 2, 1966, p. B4.

Cook, Jim. "Out of the Past: Buster Keaton." *New York Post*, September 11, 1956.

Cott, Jeremy. "The Limits of Silent Comedy." *Film Literature Quarterly*, vol. 3, no. 2 (Spring 1975), pp. 99–107.

Coursodon, Jean-Pierre. *Keaton et Compagnie*. Paris: Editions Seghers, 1964.

Crowther, Bosley. "Dignity in Deadpan." *New York Times*, February 2, 1966, p. 32.

Csida, Joseph, and June Bundy Csida. *American Entertainment*. New York: Watson-Guptill Publications, 1978.

Dardis, Tom. *Keaton: The Man Who Wouldn't Lie Down*. New York: Charles Scribner's Sons, 1979.

Deutelbaum, Marshall, ed. *"Image" on the Art and Evolution of the Film*. New York: Dover, 1979.

Durgnat, Raymond. *The Crazy Mirror*. New York: Delta Books, 1972.

Edelson, Edward. *Funny Men of the Movies*. New York: Doubleday, 1976.

Everson, William K. *American Silent Film*. New York: Oxford University Press, 1978.

———. Comment on *The Buster Keaton Story*. *New York Post*, April 17, 1957.

———. "Rediscovery: *Le Roi des Champs-Elysees*." *Films in Review*, vol. 27, no. 10 (December 1976), pp. 629–32.

———. "Rediscovery: *Too Hot to Handle*." *Films in Review*, vol. 26, no. 3 (March 1976), pp. 163–66, 178.

Fell, John L. *A History of Films*. New York: Holt, Rinehart and Winston, 1979.

Fields, Sidney. "Movie Miser." *New York Daily News*, September 21, 1970.

Fine, Gerald. *Fatty*. Author's publication, 1971.

Film Forum. "Buster Keaton 100." Film Program, February 10–March 16, 1995. New York.

Film Forum. "The Most of Buster Keaton." Film Program, December 15, 1991–February 20, 1992. New York.

Foley, Eileen. "Mrs. Keaton Looks Back on Her Life with Buster." *Philadelphia Evening Bulletin*, October 10, 1966.

Forsdale, Louis. *Every Film Is a Rorschach Test*. 3d ed. New York: Teachers College, Columbia University, 1977.

Franklin, Joe. *Joe Franklin's Encyclopedia of Comedians*. Secaucus, N.J.: Citadel Press, 1979.

Friedman, Arthur B. "Buster Keaton: An Interview." *Film Quarterly*, vol. 19, no. 4 (Summer 1966), pp. 2–5.

Fry, Ron, and Pamela Fourson. *The Saga of Special Effects*. Englewood Cliffs, N.J.: Prentice-Hall, 1977.

Gardella, Kay. "Portrait of Buster Keaton on Dateline 13 Tomorrow." *New York Daily News*, November 29, 1972.

Giannetti, Louis. *Masters of the American Cinema*. Englewood Cliffs, N.J.: Prentice-Hall, 1981.

Gilbert, Douglas. *American Vaudeville*. New York: Dover, 1963.

Gillett, John, and James Blue. "Keaton at Venice." *Sight and Sound*, vol. 35, no. 1 (Winter 1965), pp. 26–30.

Gilliatt, Penelope. "Buster Keaton." In *Movie Comedy*, edited by Stuart Byron and Elizabeth Weis. New York: Grossman Publishers, 1977.

**379**

———. "Buster Keaton." In *Unholy Fools: Wits, Comics, Disturbers of the Peace: Film and Theatre*. New York: Viking Press, 1973.

———. "Penelope Gilliatt Meets a Sunset Genius of the Cinema." *Observer Weekend Review*, May 24, 1964, pp. 31–32.

Goldbeck, Willis. "Only Three Weeks." *Motion Picture Magazine*, vol. 22, no. 9 (October 1921), pp. 28–29, 87.

Goldstein, Laurence, and Jay Kaufman. *Into Film*. New York: E. P. Dutton, 1976.

Gray, Paul. "Hard Knocks." Review of *Keaton: The Man Who Wouldn't Lie Down*, by Tom Dardis. *Time*, September 3, 1979, p. 72.

Griffith, Richard, and Arthur Mayer. *The Movies*. New York: Simon and Schuster, 1970.

Guerosa, Guido. "Pamplinas Vuelve a Vivir." *El Correo Catalan*, Barcelona, August 6, 1972, pp. 2–4.

"Happy Pro." *New Yorker*, April 27, 1963.

Harrison, John. "The Pre-Mythic Keaton." Unpublished manuscript, Columbia University, 1973.

Harvey, Stephen. "Buster Keaton's Comic Genius on Display." *New York Times*, August 9, 1981, pp. D15–D20.

Herz, Henry. Notes on *The Balloonatic*. Prepared for the Chicago Center for Film Study, 1963.

" 'Ho, Ho!' But Buster Won't Smile." *Cleveland Plain Dealer*, November 9, 1958.

"Hollywood Mourns a Comic, Buster Keaton at 70." *New York Herald Tribune*, February 2, 1966.

———. "The Great Blank Page." *Sight and Sound*, vol. 37, no. 2 (Spring 1968), pp. 63–67.

Hugill, Beryl. *Bring on the Clowns*. Secaucus, N.J.: Chartwell Books, 1980.

"In Search of Buster." *New York Times*, August 26, 1974, p. 38.

Isler, Scott. "Presenting Raymond Rohauer. Part I." *The Marble*, vol. 3, no. 5 (July–August 1975), pp. 1–3.

———. "Presenting Raymond Rohauer. Part II." *The Marble*, vol. 3, no. 6 (September–October 1975), p. 3.

Jacobs, Lewis. *The Rise of the American Film*. New York: Teachers College Press, Columbia University, 1967.

Johnson, Ron, and Jan Bone. *Understanding the Film*. Skokie, Ill.: National Textbook, 1977.

Kanfer, Stefan. "Great Stone Face." *Time*, November 2, 1970, p. 94.

Kauffmann, Stanley. "Buster Keaton Festival." In *Living Images*, edited by Stanley Kauffmann. New York: Harper and Row, 1975.

———, ed. *Living Images*. New York: Harper and Row, 1975.

Kauffman, Stanley, ed., with Bruce Henstell. *American Film Criticism*. New York: Liveright, 1972.

Keaton, Buster. "When Comedy Is Serious." Unidentified source, p. 18.

———. "Why I Never Smile." *Ladies Home Journal*, June 1926. In *Hollywood Directors 1914–1940*, edited by Richard Koszarski. London: Oxford University Press, 1976.

Keaton, Buster, with Charles Samuels. *My Wonderful World of Slapstick*. New York: Doubleday and Company, 1960; reprint, New York: DaCapo Paperback, 1982.

Keaton, Joe. "The Cyclone Baby." *Photoplay*, vol. 31, no. 6 (May 1927), pp. 125–126.

"Keaton's Ex-Wife Sues Over Movie, Asks $5,000,000." *New York Herald Tribune*, August 29, 1957.

"The Keaton Who Isn't Diane." Photograph and caption for the Thalia Theatre showing. *New York Post*, September 24, 1982, p. 53.

Kenner, Hugh. "Books." Review of *Keaton*, by Rudi Blesh. *Film Quarterly*, vol. 19, no. 4 (Summer 1966), pp. 60–61.

Kerr, Walter. *The Silent Clowns*. New York: Alfred A. Knopf, 1975.

Keylin, Aileen, and Suri Fleischer. *Hollywood Album. Lives and Deaths of Hollywood Stars from the Pages of the New York Times*. New York: Arno Press, 1977.

Kline, Jim. *The Complete Films of Buster Keaton*. Secaucus, N.J.: Citadel Press, 1993.

Koszarski, Diane Kaiser. *The Complete Films of William S. Hart*. New York: Dover, 1980.

Koszarski, Richard, ed. *Hollywood Directors 1914–1940*. London: Oxford University Press, 1976.

Kyrou, Ado. "Surrealism and Film." *Cultural Correspondence*, Fall 1979, pp. 45–46.

Lahue, Kalton C. *World of Laughter*. Norman: University of Oklahoma Press, 1972.

Lahue, Kalton C., and Terry Brewer. *Kops and Custard*. Norman: University of Oklahoma Press, 1968.

Lahue, Kalton C., and Sam Gill. *Clown Princes and Court Jesters*. New York: A. S. Barnes, 1970.

"Laughs and Gags by Buster Keaton." *New York Times*, August 15, 1948.

Leah, Daniel T. *From Sambo to Superspade*. Boston: Houghton Mifflin, 1976.

Lebel, J.-P. *Buster Keaton*. Translated by P. D. Stovin. New York: A. S. Barnes, 1967.

Lee, Raymond. *Not So Dumb: Animals in the Movies*. New York: Castle Books, 1970.

Loos, Anita. *The Talmadge Girls*. New York: Viking Press, 1978.

Lorca, Federico Garcia. "Buster Keaton Takes a Walk." Translated and introduction by A. L. Lloyd. *Sight and Sound*, vol. 25, no. 2 (Winter 1963), pp. 24–25.

MacCann, Richard Dyer. *The Silent Comedians*. Metuchen, N.J.: Scarecrow Press, 1993.

MacDonald, Dwight. "Vote for Keaton." *New York Review of Books*, October 9, 1980, pp. 33–38.

Maltin, Leonard. *The Butcher Boy, Cops, The Balloonatic*, and *Pest From the West*. Program notes for the American Film Comedy Series. New York: Museum of Modern Art Department of Film, May 22, 1977.

———. *The Great Movie Comedians from Charlie Chaplin to Woody Allen*. New York: Crown Publishers, 1978.

———. Program notes on Buster Keaton for comedy series "Remembered Laughter." New York: Museum of Modern Art, July 18, 1979.

Marsh, W. Ward. "How Keaton Stirred South's Indignation." *Cleveland Plain Dealer*, August 4, 1962.

Mast, Gerald. *The Comic Mind*. New York: Bobbs-Merrill, 1973.

———. *Film/Cinema/Movie*. New York: Harper and Row, 1977.

McCaffrey, Donald W. *4 Great Comedians*. New York: A. S. Barnes, 1968.

McGregor, Don. *Buster, The Early Years, The Authorized Buster Keaton Film Festival Album*. New York: 1982.

Meredith, George, and Henry Bergson. *Comedy*. Baltimore: Johns Hopkins University Press, 1956.

Miklowitz, Gloria S. *Movie Stunts and the People Who Do Them*. New York: Harcourt Brace Jovanovich, 1980.

Moews, Daniel. *Keaton: The Silent Features Close Up*. Berkeley: University of California Press, 1977.

"Mr. Natalie Talmadge." "Before and After Taking." Fan magazine, Summer 1921.

Mulligan, W. E. "The Man Who Never Smiles." *Pantomime*, vol. 1, no. 2 (October 5, 1921), pp. 5+.

"Of the Dead." Editor's Notebook. *Film Quarterly*, vol. 19, no. 4 (Summer 1966), p. 1.

O'Leary, John. "Considering Keaton: Part 6—Head of Sap." *Classic Images*, vol. 62 (March 1979), p. 57.

Parish, James Robert, and William T. Leonard. *The Funsters*. New Rochelle, N.Y.: Arlington House, 1979.

Paskman, Dailey. *Gentlemen, Be Seated!* New York: Clarkson N. Potter, 1976.

Peltret, Elizabeth. "Poor Child!" *Motion Picture Classic*, vol. 12, no. 1 (March 1921), pp. 64, 96–97.

Pratt, George C. " 'Anything Can Happen—And Generally Did': Buster Keaton on His Silent-Film Career." *"Image" on the Art and Evolution of Film*, edited by Marshall Deutelbaum. New York: Dover, 1979.

———. *Spellbound in Darkness*. Greenwich, Conn.: New York Graphic Society, 1973.

Rahill, Frank. *The World of Melodrama*. University Park, Pa.: Pennsylvania State University Press, 1967.

"Raymond Rohauer, Archivist of Classics From Silent Film Era." Obituary, *New York Times*, November 19, 1987.

Reed, Rex. "Buster Keaton." *Do You Sleep in the Nude?* New York: New American Library, 1968.

———. "Keaton: Still Making the Scene." *New York Times*, October 17, 1965.

Reid, Ashton. "Strictly for Laughs." *Colliers*, June 10, 1944.

Reid, Lawrence. Review of *The Electric House. Motion Picture News*, November 4, 1922, p. 2316.

Robinson, David. *Buster Keaton*. Bloomington: Indiana University Press, 1969.

———. *The Great Funnies*. New York: Studio Vista/Dutton, 1969.

Rogers, John G. "Hollywood Mourns a Comic." *New York Herald Tribune*, February 2, 1966.

The Rohauer Collection Catalogues, 1982–1985.

Rohauer, Raymond. "Buster Keaton." *The Marble*, vol. 4, no. 1 (January–February, 1976), p. 3.

———. *The Films of Buster Keaton*. Booklet from the Audio Film Center, New York, 1969.

Rosemont, Franklin. "Buster Keaton." *Cultural Correspondence*, Fall 1979, p. 47.

Rosenberg, Barbara, and Harry Silverstein. *The Real Tinsel*. London: Macmillan, 1970.

Rubinstein, E. *Filmguide to "The General."* Bloomington: Indiana University Press, 1973.

———. "Observations on Keaton's *Steamboat Bill, Jr.*" *Sight and Sound*, vol. 44, no. 4 (Autumn 1975), pp. 244–47.

"A Sad-Eyed Keaton Rose to Fame in Silence." *New York Journal American*, February 1, 1966.

Sanders, Judith, and Daniel Lieberfeld. "Dreaming in Pictures—The Childhood Origins of Buster Keaton's Creativity." *Film Quarterly*, vol. 47, no. 4 (Summer 1994), pp. 14–28.

"*The Saphead* at Capitol." *Motion Picture News*, March 12, 1921.

"*The Saphead*—New Feature at Capitol Theatre." *Daily Times*, February 13, 1921.

Sarris, Andrew. *The American Cinema*. New York: Dutton, 1968.

———. "Buster Keaton Film Festival." *Village Voice*, October 1, 1970, p. 22.

———. "Conversations and Concerns: Buster Keaton and Samuel Beckett." *Columbia Forum*, vol. 12, no. 4 (Winter 1969), pp. 42–43.

———. "Films in Focus." *Village Voice*, September 24, 1970.

———. "Films in Focus. Buster Keaton—The Beautiful and the Comic." *Village Voice*, August 12–18, 1981, p. 41.

———, ed. *Interviews with Film Directors*. New York: Avon, 1969.

———. "Revivals: Andrew Sarris Picks the Best of the Classic Cinema. Buster Keaton Festival." *Village Voice*, January 26, 1976.

———. "Why 'The Silent Clowns' Isn't All That Original." *Village Voice*, March 8, 1976, pp. 97–98.

Sarris, Andrew, and Tom Allen. "Revivals in Focus: A Critical Guide." *Village Voice*, August 12–18, 1981, p. 55.

Schecter, Harold, and David Everitt. *Film Tricks*. New York: Harlin Quist, 1980.

Schickel, Richard. *The Stars*. New York: Bonanza Books, 1962.

Schumach, Murray. "Keaton Receives Special Film Prize." *New York Times*, April 6, 1960, p. 46.

Sennett, Mack. *King of Comedy*. New York: Pinnacle Books, 1975.

Shelton, Frank. Review of *Three Ages*. *Motion Picture News*, July 21, 1923.

Sherwood, Robert E. Review of *The Paleface*. *Life*, June 1, 1922. In *American Film Criticism*, edited by Stanley Kauffmann. New York: Liveright, 1972.

Silverman, Stephen M. "The Great Stone Face Who Made Us Laugh." *New York Post*, August 11, 1981, p. 39.

———. "Sad Sack Show a Side-Splitter." *New York Post*, Promo for Festival, April–September 1981.

Stephens, Michael. *Still Life*. New York: Kroesen Books, 1977.

St. Johns, Adela Rogers. "Interviewing Joseph Talmadge Keaton." *Photoplay*, vol. 22, no. 5 (October 1922), pp. 51, 93.

Toronto Film Society Silent Series. Programme I. October 25, 1971.

"Tribute to Buster Keaton." Philadelphia Museum of Art Film Program Notes. October 1, 8, 15, 22, 1966.

Twyman Films Catalogue. Dayton, Ohio, 1981.

Valenty, Duane. "The Good Old, Funny Old Days." *Modern Maturity*, August–September 1979, pp. 8–10.

Van Dyke, Stella. "Oh, Buster! You Wouldn't Kid Us, Would You?" *Silver Screen*, April 1932, pp. 22, 62+.

Wead, George. *Buster Keaton and the Dynamics of Visual Wit*. New York: Arno Press, 1976.

————. "The Great Locomotive Chase." *American Film*, July–August, 1979, pp. 18–24.

Wead, George, and George Lellis. *The Film Career of Buster Keaton*. Boston: G. K. Hall, 1977.

Weis, Elisabeth, ed. *The National Society of Film Critics on The Movie Star*. New York: Penguin Books, 1981.

Wickwire, Alison. "Believing in Buster." *Comedy*, vol. 1, no. 1 (Summer 1980), pp. 36–39.

Wlaschin, Ken. *The Illustrated Encyclopedia of the World's Great Movie Stars and Their Films from 1900 to the Present Day*. New York: Harmony Books, 1979.

Wood, Michael. "Funny Fellow." Review of *Keaton: The Man Who Wouldn't Lie Down*, by Tom Dardis. *American Film* (June 1979), pp. 68–70.

Yallop, David. *The Day the Laughter Stopped*. New York: St. Martin's Press.

Zimmerman, Paul D. "Buster Keaton's Comic World." *Newsweek*, October 5, 1970, pp. 96–99.

# Index

# Index

**389**

**395**

Gabriella Oldham, whose works include *First Cut: Interviews with Film Editors* and the children's musical *Melville and the Yellow Umbrella*, is involved in numerous fiction, nonfiction, film, theater, and educational projects. She received her Ed.D degree in film/communication from Teachers College, Columbia University, and has taught English and film on the college level. She is also artistic director of New York Children's Theatre.